L TERATURE
IN ENGLISH PRE–1914

the essentials of...

LTERATURE

IN ENGLISH PRE–1914

Tony Myers

Hodder Arnold

A MEMBER OF THE HODDER HEADLINE GROUP

First published in Great Britain in 2005 by
Arnold, a member of the Hodder Headline Group,
338 Euston Road, London NW1 3BH

http://www.arnoldpublishers.com

Distributed in the United States of America by
Oxford University Press Inc.
198 Madison Avenue, New York, NY10016

The advice and information in this book are believed to be true and
accurate at the date of going to press, but neither the authors nor the publisher
can accept any legal responsibility or liability for any errors or omissions.

British Library Cataloguing in Publication Data
A catalogue record for this book is available from the British Library

Library of Congress Cataloging-in-Publication Data
A catalog record for this book is available from the Library of Congress

ISBN–10: 0 340 81631 7

ISBN–13: 978 0 340 816318

2 3 4 5 6 7 8 9 10

Typeset in 9pt New Baskerville by Dorchester Typesetting Group Ltd
Printed and bound in Spain

What do you think about this book? Or any other Arnold title?
Please send your comments to feedback.arnold@hodder.co.uk

Contents

Acknowledgements

My first thanks go to Liz Gooster for her help and encouragement in completing this project. I am also grateful to the rest of the team at Arnold, particularly Eva Martinez and Liz Wilson, as well as the following friends and colleagues who have freely offered their thoughts *ab ovo* – Rachel Donnelly, Jim Jack, Stuart Meredith, and Dominic Schad. Finally, I would like to record my fathomless debt to Ali – *sic itur ad astra*.

Introduction

The purpose of this book is to provide a reference guide to the most important works of literature written in the English language before 1914. It is aimed at the general reader or student and, as such, requires little or no previous knowledge about the subject matter. The book seeks to provide the reader with the essential details about canonical texts and key writers. Canonical texts are those that are generally recognised as classics by specialists, are most often taught, are most often read by non-specialists, and which are most influential within their field. Within this remit, the book endeavours to equip the reader with the essentials needed to understand and appreciate the key works of literature written in English pre-1914.

The book is divided into three parts. **Part 1** comprises an A–Z listing of major writers pre-1914. Each entry of this type is composed of a mini-biography, a short account of the writer's place and influence in the field, and finally a listing of the writer's principal works, including years of publication. The writers are of different nationalities – English, American, Irish, Scottish and Welsh. Their style and subject matter vary widely, from the drawing rooms of polite London society to the inhumane conditions of slavery in the American deep South. Each entry opens with a short quotation by the writer in question.

Part 2 provides the reader with a Chronology of Literature in English pre-1914. These longer essays give a brief overview of the major historical, political and cultural influences on the literature of the time. This part of the book is subdivided into two. First the focus is on *the evolution of literature in Britain* by period: Old English Literature (450–1100), Middle English Literature (1100–1485), Tudor and Stuart Literature (1485–1660), Restoration and Augustan Literature (1660–1775), Romantic Literature (1775–1837), and Victorian Literature (1837–1890). The second section shifts the focus across the Atlantic to trace *the evolution of literature in America* under the headings: Colonial and Revolutionary Literature (1500–1800), Literature of Independence (1800–1850) and American Civil War Literature (1850–1890). The two traditions are then brought together to reveal the increasing international context of Modern Literature (1890–1914). In this way the second part of the book seeks to contextualise the individual entries, setting them in a larger social and historical framework. It also shows the developing history of the English language. Each essay is completed by a Timeline chart which places the key texts of each period alongside the major political events of the age.

Part 3 of the book comprises an A–Z listing of the canonical works of the writers listed in Part 1. For most of the writers just one key text is listed, whereas for some (e.g. Shakespeare and Dickens), the selection has necessarily been broadened to include several works. Each of these entries provides a brief account of the text in question, a summary of its plot, and an analysis of its key themes and techniques, followed by suggestions for further reading. The entries span a cross-section of the four main genres of literature written in English – the novel, the play, the poem and the short story. Other entries from seminal works of prose are also included, for example, the *Bible*, and political and early feminist tracts such as *A Vindication of the Rights of Woman*.

Cross-references between the different parts of the book are indicated by the use of small capitals, such as WILLIAM SHAKESPEARE or *HAMLET*. The entries are supplemented by a Glossary of Key Terms at the end of the book and an A–Z of the individual writers covered in Part 1.

In this way, it is hoped that *The Essentials of Literature in English, pre-1914* will prove to be a handy complement for all types of reader, offering useful insights on classic works, describing the contexts in which they were written, and stimulating further interest in the rich literary heritage of the English language.

Part 1

A–Z of Major Writers

ADAMS, HENRY (1838–1918)

Practical politics consists in ignoring facts.

The Education of Henry Adams

Henry Brooks Adams was born in Boston into a powerful political dynasty. His father, Charles Francis, was a diplomat and Congressman, his grandfather, John Quincy, was sixth President of the United States, while his great-grandfather, John, was the second President. While Adams himself did not directly follow in the family tradition, his books and articles did, however, contribute greatly to the political, intellectual and social life of the American nation.

Henry Adams was a deep and original thinker whose powerful political connections gave his enquiring mind access to all areas of American life. He recorded the development of his intellect in the Pulitzer Prize-winning *The Education of Henry Adams.*

After graduating from Harvard in 1858, Adams embarked upon the Grand Tour of Europe, travelling mainly around Great Britain, Germany, France, Switzerland, Austria and Italy, while studying law in Liverpool and Dresden. Upon completing his studies, Adams worked as a correspondent for various American newspapers, sometimes reporting on the European reaction to the events of the Civil War, as well as serving as private secretary to his father both in Washington and London. Following the death of his sister in 1870, Adams returned to America where he reluctantly accepted a post at Harvard College teaching medieval European history. At the same time, Adams assumed the editorship of the prestigious journal *North American Review*. He used this platform to denounce the corruption of government and both major political parties until the late 1870s.

In 1872 Adams married Marian Hooper, the daughter of a prominent doctor, and they promptly set off on a year-long honeymoon to Europe and Egypt. Upon their return, Adams continued as before until he resigned his post at Harvard in 1877 and the couple moved to Washington. There Adams devoted himself full-time to historical research while Marian's charm and wit helped turn their house into a salon for the Washington elite. One of their most famous intimates was the novelist HENRY JAMES, of whom Marian remarked, he 'chews more than he bites off'. However, in 1885 Marian succumbed to depression after the death of her father and killed herself by drinking potassium cyanide. Adams was deeply affected by this tragic turn of events and, although he hardly ever spoke again of his wife, to the extent of skipping the years of their marriage in his autobiography *THE EDUCATION OF HENRY ADAMS*, he did erect one of the most famous cemetery monuments in the world in her honour. Designed by Augustus Saint-Gaudens, the untitled sculpture reflects the influence upon Adams of his trip to Japan in 1886, and became a tourist attraction in Washington's Rock Creek Cemetery during Adams's lifetime.

During the period of his marriage, Adams had published two volumes of historical biography. The first of these was the story of Albert Gallatin, Thomas Jefferson's Secretary of the Treasury, and the second was the biography of the colourful Congressman John Randolph. While neither book was particularly well received, the research Adams undertook to write them formed the basis of his monumental work *The History of the United States of America during the Administration of Thomas Jefferson and James Madison*, privately published in the year of his wife's death.

Suffering from a spiritual inertia after his wife's death, Adams drifted across the world for a decade before a visit to the cathedrals of northern France reinvigorated him. He wrote about the great culture that inspired these architectural achievements in *Mont Saint Michel and Chartres* which was published in 1904. Deciding that Western culture had declined since the twelfth century, he wrote about that decline in the book's sequel – *The Education of Henry Adams*. Indeed, the summary proof of Adams's pessimism came at the end of his life with the commencement of the First

World War. He did not live to see its end but died at the age of 80 and was buried next to his wife. He was posthumously awarded the Pulitzer Prize for *The Education of Henry Adams* in 1919.

Principal Works

1885	*The History of the United States of America during the Administration of Thomas Jefferson and James Madison*
1904	*Mont Saint Michel and Chartres*
1919	*THE EDUCATION OF HENRY ADAMS*

ARNOLD, MATTHEW (1822–88)

*Resolve to be thyself; and know, that he
Who finds himself, loses his misery.*
                              'Self-Dependence'

Matthew Arnold was born on Christmas Eve in 1822 in Laleham, Surrey. His father, Dr Thomas Arnold, was a clergyman who became the headmaster at Rugby School when his son was 6. Dr Arnold became a famous educational reformer, bringing an explicit moral and social purpose to teaching and connecting it with the life his pupils would lead once they left school. Arnold was no doubt influenced by the powerful personality of his father, not least in the education he received at Rugby School, although the reaction it provoked may not have been quite what his father intended.

So it was that when Arnold went to Balliol College in Oxford, he became somewhat irreverent in appearance and outlook, almost in direct opposition to his father. After meeting him, the novelist CHARLOTTE BRONTË remarked that 'his manner displeases, from its seeming foppery'. It was an accusation that would follow him for the rest of his life in one form or another, as is evident from WALT WHITMAN's assertion that Arnold was 'one of the dudes of literature'. Despite this, Arnold still managed to secure the Newdigate Prize for his poem 'Cromwell' in 1843, and in the following year he graduated with a second-class degree. While some biographers consider this close to a disaster, he was, nevertheless, elected a Fellow of Oriel College following a short spell of teaching at Rugby.

In April 1847, Arnold became private secretary to Lord Landsdowne who was then head of the Committee of the Council on Education. In 1849 Arnold published his first important selection of poems, *The Strayed Reveller*. This met with little initial interest. In 1851, Arnold was offered the post of school inspector, a position he was to hold for 35 years. Almost immediately following this appointment, he became engaged to Fanny Lucy Wightman, marrying her in the June of that year. On their honeymoon they visited Dover Beach, which was to provide the inspiration for one of Arnold's most famous poems.

For the next few years Arnold worked diligently at his job, travelling all around Britain as well as Europe, and began establishing a family with his wife. At the same time he published two collections of poems, *Empedocles on Etna* and *Poems*, the Preface of which sets out his criteria for poetry. This early foray into literary criticism was followed up more seriously when he was offered a professorship in poetry at Oxford University. For the next ten years he concentrated more on writing the criticism for which he is perhaps best known today. Like his father before him, Arnold came to imbue the purely academic with an overt social purpose. By the time he published *CULTURE AND ANARCHY* in 1869, he was advancing a critique of the society in which he lived, claiming that it was populated by Philistines (a term that he popularised but which was borrowed from the social historian Thomas Carlyle) who were spiritually ill-equipped to lead the country into the future.

> Although Arnold began his literary career as a poet, his work as a social and literary critic comprises his greatest legacy. In essays such as *Culture and Anarchy* he criticised the English society in which he lived for its Philistinism, sectarianism and utilitarian materialism. He argued the need for greater intellectual curiosity and a broader European outlook.

During the 1870s, Arnold became more preoccupied with Biblical criticism. The *BIBLE*, he considered, was important to society, not necessarily because it was Christian, but because it was a civilising influence. He published several volumes on the subject, of which the best known is probably *Literature and Dogma* (1873). In the 1880s he went on lecture tours of America but met with a mixed reception. At one point he had to concur with the Bishop of Rochester, that 'Denver was not ripe for Mr Arnold'. However, in Washington the African American leader FREDERICK DOUGLASS received him with tremendous thanks. The first tour led to the publication in 1885 of the work of which he was most proud, *Discourses in America.* Two years after his second visit, Arnold died while running for a tram on 15 April 1888.

Principal Works

1849	*The Strayed Reveller*
1852	*Empedocles on Etna*
1853	*Poems*
1869	CULTURE AND ANARCHY
1873	*Literature and Dogma*
1885	*Discourses in America*

AUSTEN, JANE (1775–1817)

I do not want people to be very agreeable, as it saves me the trouble of liking them a great deal.

The Letters of Jane Austen

Photo credit: © Bettmann/CORBIS

Jane Austen was born on 16 December 1775 at Steventon near Basingstoke in Hampshire. She was the seventh child of eight, born to the local rector, the Reverend George Austen and his wife Cassandra Leigh. Apart from being taught by the sister of one of her uncles in 1783 in Oxford and Southampton, and a short time in a Reading boarding school from 1785, Austen's education took place within the confines of her own family. Austen's father had a well-stocked library and Jane was encouraged to read, taking particular pleasure in eighteenth-century novels, many characteristics of which she copied in the novels she herself started writing when she was 14.

By the time she was 20, Austen had begun to write the novels for which she would later become famous – *Sense and Sensibility*, NORTHANGER ABBEY and PRIDE AND PREJUDICE. At this stage the novels were called *Elinor and Marianne, Susan* and *First Impressions* respectively. However, when Austen's father invited a publisher to inspect an early version of *Pride and Prejudice* in 1797, he refused even to look at it. During her early twenties, Austen's life was not dissimilar to the ones her characters led, and she spent a deal of time at social events, dances and parties. It was at this time that she was famously described by a Mrs Mitford as 'the prettiest, silliest, most affected, husband-hunting butterfly' she ever remembered. In spite of this assertion, however, there is little evidence that Austen enjoyed any serious courtships while she still lived at Steventon.

> In terms that my be applied to some of her characters, Jane Austen was once described as 'the prettiest, silliest, most affected, husband-hunting butterfly'. While this may have seemed the case, Austen also led a secretive double life known to only her intimate circle in which she composed some of the most popular novels ever written.

In 1800, Austen's father retired and the following year decided to move to Bath, much to Austen's consternation. While on holiday, Austen discovered a mutual attraction with an unnamed and unknown man who promptly died. It is thought that this might have served as the model for a similar incident in *Persuasion*. At around the same time, Austen returned to Steventon to visit her brother who was now the rector in her father's old parish. There she received a proposal of marriage from a friend of her brother, a wealthy landowner named Harris Bigg-Wither. Austen accepted the proposal but the following morning changed her mind, apparently because he was too 'big and awkward'.

In 1803 Austen finally managed to sell *Northanger Abbey* to a publisher for the sum of £10 although the publisher subsequently decided not to publish it. In 1805 Austen's father died, leaving the remaining Austen family largely dependent on Austen's brother and living in reduced circumstances. The family moved around the south of England for a number of years while Austen resumed her literary activities. In 1811 she published *Sense and Sensibility* to moderate success. This was published anonymously (beyond the designation 'by a lady') and her immediate family were under strict instructions not to reveal her identity. Indeed, Austen famously had a creaking door in the room where she worked which she asked not to be fixed so she could hear visitors approaching and could hide her manuscript. Encouraged by the success of *Sense and Sensibility*, she revised *Pride and Prejudice* and published that in 1813 (selling the rights to one of the best-selling books of all time for £110). In the following year she published *Mansfield Park*.

In 1815, Austen published *Emma* and dedicated it to the Prince Regent who was apparently a fan of her novels. While this proved successful, a second edition of *Mansfield Park* was not and ate up most of the profit from *Emma*. Towards the end of 1816, Austen had finished writing *Persuasion*, although it was only published posthumously by her brother, together with *Northanger Abbey*. By 1817 Austen was quite ill and although she started writing another novel early in the year, by March she was forced to give up the task. She made her will a month later and moved to Winchester in May for medical treatment. She died on 18 July 1817, probably from Addison's disease. She was buried in Winchester Cathedral with, notoriously, no mention of her status as a novelist on her tombstone.

Principal Works

1811   *Sense and Sensibility*
1813   *Pride and Prejudice*
1814   *Mansfield Park*
1816   *Emma*
1818   *Northanger Abbey*
1818   *Persuasion*

BEHN, APHRA (1640–89)
I value fame as much as if I had been born a hero.
                    The Lucky Chance

The precise origins of Aphra Behn are unclear, although it is thought that she was born in Wye, Kent around 1640, some 19 years after the poet ANDREW MARVELL. Her maiden name was probably Johnson, but it is uncertain whether this name was her real or her adopted father's name. There is speculation as to the nature of her father's profession; some suggest he was a barber, others that he was an innkeeper, and others still that he was appointed Lieutenant Governor of Surinam some 23 years after she was born. Although he supposedly died on the voyage, this would explain why it is thought by some, although not all biographers, that Behn travelled to Surinam around 1664.

Surinam was an English colony producing sugar during this period, but as a result of a trade war with Holland, it soon became a Dutch possession and Behn was forced to return to London. Upon returning to the capital she may well have met and married a Dutch merchant called Behn. It is thought by some that he died of the plague a few years later, although other biographers claim that she fabricated the existence of Mr Behn in order to afford herself a sense of respectability. What does seem certain, however, is that around 1665 she entered into the service of King Charles II as a spy. Codenamed 'Astrea' or 'Agent 160', her particular role involved travelling to Antwerp to spy on the Dutch with whom the English were still at war. She appears to have been very successful in her role, unearthing the plan formed by Admiral De Ruyter, in conjunction with the DeWitts, of sailing up the Thames and burning the English ships while in harbour. Unfortunately for the English, Behn's intelligence was ignored and the following year, in 1667, the Dutch did sail up the Thames, destroying four ships of the line and towing away the pride of the fleet, the *Royal Charles*.

When Behn returned to London, she was heavily in debt. As was not unusual at the time, King Charles failed to pay her for her services in Holland; consequently Behn was soon arrested and imprisoned for her debts. It is not clear how she escaped from prison, but it is thought that she petitioned the King until she was freed. Upon her release, in 1670, she found herself 'forced to write for bread'. She made her debut as a playwright with *The Forc'd Marriage* which was performed at the Duke's Theatre in Lincoln's Inn Fields. Her witty, lewd and flamboyant work was immediately popular and from then until her death 19 years later she wrote prolifically.

In 1677 she wrote her best-known play, THE ROVER. This was generally well received although, like her other plays, she was accused of plagiarism, most probably from Thomas Killigrew's *Thomaso*. This was a not uncommon practice. While she did not have the advantage of the kind of classical education that her male counterparts enjoyed, yet she was able to speak several languages and therefore could 'borrow' from foreign sources as well as them. However, as a woman in a man's world, Behn became an obvious target for those dismayed by the vulgarity of the Restoration and she was arrested and briefly imprisoned for 'abusive reflections' on the King's son in 1682. The following year, when she found that the theatre was no longer paying as well as it did, she turned her hand to prose and wrote one of the first epistolary novels in English literature, *Love Letters between a Nobleman and his Sister*.

A technical innovator responsible for developing the form of the novel, Behn was also the first full-time female author in the English language. All she asked for, she claimed, was 'the privilege for my masculine part, the poet in me.'

In 1688 Behn composed *Oroonoko*. Widely considered to be one of the formative novels in English literature, it was published nearly two decades before DANIEL DEFOE's *Robinson Crusoe*, and tells the story of a royal slave. She claimed she had written it in only a 'few hours', probably in order to rebut rumours that her creative powers were diminishing with age.

Behn died on 16 April 1689 and was buried at Westminster Abbey, London. In the space of her relatively short life she had set many precedents. Not only was she a technical innovator, creating new narrative forms with *Oroonoko* and *Love Letters between a Nobleman and his Sister*, but she also proved something of a role model. She is widely regarded to be the first full-time female author in the English language to write and publish as a woman. As the novelist Virginia Woolf later remarked, 'All women together ought to let flowers fall upon the grave of Aphra Behn, for it was she who earned them the right to speak their minds.'

Principal Works

1677   *THE ROVER*
1683   *Love Letters between a Nobleman and his Sister*
1688   *Oroonoko*

BIERCE, AMBROSE (1842–1914)

Patience. A minor form of despair disguised as a virtue.

The Devil's Dictionary

Ambrose Gwinnett Bierce was born on 24 June 1842 in Meigs County, Ohio. He was the youngest of nine children born to Marcus Aurelius Bierce and Laura Sherwood. As a child, Bierce was not given any formal education but he did enjoy the run of his father's literature collection, books to which he later acknowledged he owed 'everything'. Bierce was quite an unhappy child and books offered a means of escape from a family whom he largely disowned when he was an adult. He earned the soubriquet of 'Bitter Bierce'.

At the age of 15, Bierce began work as a printer's devil for the *Northern Indianan* in Warsaw. He held on to this job for two years until, in 1859, he was accused of stealing money and was sacked. From there he joined the Kentucky Military Institute where he learned the skills, such as map reading, that would later serve him so well. After a year in the military, Bierce worked as a bricklayer, and as a clerk in a retail store. However, when the Civil War broke out in 1861, Bierce enlisted as a private in Company C of the Ninth Regiment, Indiana Volunteers in the Union army. Bierce rose quickly through the ranks to become a captain, specialising in topographical matters. He saw action at many famous battles, including Shiloh and Chickamauga, which he later wrote about in his short stories. In June 1864 he was shot in the head, returning to his unit in September of that year only to be captured by the Confederates from whom he later escaped.

In 1865 Bierce was mustered out of the military and later that year given the honorary title of major for his distinguished service.

Bierce then began working for the Treasury, implementing the new regime in the southern states. In 1866 he resigned that post to work under his old general, mapping part of the unknown territories in the west. He also applied to be a captain in the US army during this period but was unsuccessful. After a short spell at the local mint, in 1868 Bierce started writing a column for the *News-Letter*. A few weeks later Bierce became the editor of the whole paper at the age of 26.

Noted for his acerbic wit, Bierce lived a tough and adventurous life. He brought these qualities to his writing, publishing a dictionary for misanthropes (where he defined 'learning' as 'the kind of ignorance distinguishing the studious') and helping to develop a new kind of realism in the short story genre.

Bierce continued to write for and edit the paper until 1872. During these years he met MARK TWAIN and Bret Harte, amongst many other writers who were busy establishing themselves in San Francisco at the time.

At the end of 1871 Bierce married Mary Ellen Day. As a present from her father, they spent their honeymoon in London. The next three years were spent living in various locations in England. In 1872 Bierce published his first book, a collection of his satirical writings called *The Fiend's Delight*, written under the name of Dod Grile. Other books followed, including *Nuggets and Dust* in 1873, and *Cobwebs from an Empty Skull* in 1875. Upon returning to San Francisco, Bierce commenced writing the acerbic 'Prattler' column for which he became famous. This did not please all its audience and one day in 1877 Bierce was forced to pull his pistol on an unhappy reader who attacked him in his office.

Apart from a year (1880) spent gold mining and shotgun-riding in the Black Hills of South Dakota for Wells Fargo & Co, Bierce continued to write his satirical columns and short stories. In 1887 he was hired by William Randolph Hearst to write for his newspaper. This proved to be the most professionally successful era of Bierce's career, particularly with the publication of his collection of stories, *TALES OF SOLDIERS AND CIVILIANS* in 1891, but they were also his most difficult years personally. His two sons died, one after being shot in a duel, the other through alcoholism, while his wife moved to divorce him and then died herself. It was during this time that he coined his motto, 'Nothing matters'. It was also at this stage that he published various editions of what came to be known as *The Devil's Dictionary*, a book composed of misanthropic definitions. After composing this and a collected edition of his works, Bierce moved down to Texas at the end of 1913 and crossed the border into war-torn Mexico. He was never heard from again, although it is assumed, from what he said beforehand and subsequent investigations, that he joined the revolutionary forces of Pancho Villa and was killed in the Battle of Ojinaga on 11 January 1914.

Principal Works

1894	*TALES OF SOLDIERS AND CIVILIANS*
1906–11	*The Devil's Dictionary*

BLAKE, WILLIAM (1757–1827)

And did those feet in ancient time
Walk upon England's mountains green?

Milton

William Blake was born in London on 28 November 1757. His father, James Blake, a successful hosier, and his mother, Catherine, were aware that Blake was different from a very early age. When he was just 4, Blake claimed that he saw God 'put his head to the window', and when he was 9 that he saw a tree full of angels. Partly because of these visions and partly because of the cost, Blake was mainly educated at home. However, when he was 10 years old, Blake professed a wish to become a painter so his parents sent him to Henry Pars' drawing school. It was there that Blake started to write poetry.

When he was 14, Blake was apprenticed to the engraver James Basire. One of Blake's assignments as an apprentice was to draw the tombs at Westminster Abbey. This exposed him to a variety of Gothic styles from which he would find stimulation throughout his career. After his seven-year apprenticeship had ended, Blake married Catherine Boucher, the daughter of a market gardener. She was illiterate at the time, but he taught her to read and to accomplish basic painting and engraving tasks in order that she could help him. He also taught his younger brother Robert the same skills. However, Robert fell ill during the winter of 1787 and died of consumption. As he died, Blake said he saw his brother's spirit rise up through the ceiling 'clapping its hands for joy'. He later claimed that his brother continued to visit him in dreams and even taught him the printing method he would use for his most famous works.

> A painter, engraver and poet, William Blake was a visionary artist who decided to create his own system of symbols rather than 'be enslaved by another Man's'.

In 1783, Blake published his first collection of poems, *Poetical Sketches*. He had not yet developed his own unique style, although even in these poems, many of which were political in nature, Blake reveals a wish to break with the kind of poetic models set down by ALEXANDER POPE and others. Blake finally achieved this with his most famous collections of verse, *SONGS OF INNOCENCE*, published in 1789, and its companion, *SONGS OF EXPERIENCE*, published in 1794. To publish these and later books, Blake used a method that he called 'illuminated printing'. It required him to work directly on copper plate and write the poems in reverse so that they would print the right way. As Blake illustrated most of his poems, the illustrations were done in the same way and then coloured in with water colours, often by Catherine, before the individual pages were stitched together. It was a time-consuming project and meant that Blake published less than 30 copies of the *Songs*, and even less of his later works.

Blake's work was not particularly well received by either the public or potential patrons. After a period giving drawing lessons and engraving the work of other artists, in 1800 Blake moved to Felpham on the Sussex coast. Here he earned the patronage of William Hayley. However, by 1803 it had become clear that Blake was not going to buckle under Hayley's pressure to become a more commer-

cial artist, and neither was Hayley going to leave Blake alone and so the relationship was severed. It was also at this time that Blake narrowly missed being hung. After pushing a drunken soldier called Schofield out of his garden and back to where he was quartered, Blake was accused by Schofield of uttering a seditious remark about his king and country. As England was at war with France at the time, this was a hanging offence. However, when it came to trial, Blake was acquitted, apparently to the sounds of loud cheers from the gallery. Schofield and his friends would later appear in Blake's poems as demonic figures.

After the trial, Blake moved back to London where he pursued his single-minded vision. As he had one of his characters say, 'I must Create a System or be enslaved by another Man's.' The singularity of this vision was perhaps the reason for his poorly received exhibitions at the Royal Academy in 1708 and at his brother's house in 1709. If Blake's paintings and engravings were unpopular, so too were the epic poems he composed during this period: *Milton*, *The Four Zoas* and *Jerusalem*. Blake was not completely unknown and unappreciated, however, for SAMUEL COLERIDGE called him a 'man of genius', and WILLIAM WORDSWORTH made copies of his poems. Blake himself gave up writing altogether in his sixties and, until his death in 1827, concentrated on illustrating Dante's *Divine Comedy*.

Principal Works

1789	*SONGS OF INNOCENCE*
1794	*SONGS OF EXPERIENCE*
1797–1820	*The Four Zoas*
1804–08	*Milton*
1804–20	*Jerusalem*

BOSWELL, JAMES (1740–95)

A good pun may be admitted among the smaller excellencies of lively conversation.
Life of Samuel Johnson

James Boswell was born in Edinburgh on 29 October 1740. His mother was Euphemia Erskine, daughter of Lieutenant-Colonel John Erskine, Deputy Governor of Stirling Castle, and his father was Alexander Boswell, a judge. By all accounts Boswell was a melancholy child, subject to bouts of a psychosomatic illness that affected his early schooling at James Mundell's private academy. When Boswell was 9, his father was made the eighth Laird of Auchinleck in Ayrshire and the family moved there as a consequence.

From 1752 to 1758, Boswell studied an arts course at Edinburgh University. Here he appears to have been troubled by a number of spiritual crises over religion and his own sexuality. When Boswell returned to Edinburgh University in order to study law, his father, now Lord Auchinleck after his appointment to the Court of Sessions, quickly became dismayed with the distractions attending his son and sent him to Glasgow University instead. These 'distractions' were mainly the arts and the theatre. When Boswell went to Glasgow his education improved in so far as he attended lectures by the Father of Economics, Adam Smith. However, the distractions of the theatre remained and Boswell became involved with a Roman Catholic actress. This experience seems to have precipitated another crisis of faith in Boswell and he decided to become a monk. Upon hearing this, his father asked to see him and Boswell promptly ran away to London.

> A great writer himself, Boswell's comprehensive and witty account of the life of the celebrated man of letters Samuel Johnson set the standard for all future biographies.

Boswell was immediately seduced by all that London could offer and he soon forgot his commitment to becoming a monk. When his father got him back to Edinburgh he forced his son to study law. Boswell eventually passed his Bar exam in 1762 whereupon he returned to London ostensibly to join the Guards. On 16 May 1763 Boswell met and befriended SAMUEL JOHNSON. He then abandoned his plan to join the Guards and instead took an extended tour of Europe with a view to studying law in Utrecht. On his travels he met the two greatest living French writers of the day, Jean-Jacques Rousseau and Voltaire. He also visited General Pasquale de Paoli in Corsica, who was a hero to many of Europe's intellectuals at the time. In 1768 Boswell published a report of his trip, *An Account of Corsica, The Journal of a Tour to that Island, and Memoirs of Pascal Paoli*, which proved very popular and was translated all over Europe.

The following year, Boswell married his first cousin, Margaret Montgomerie, with whom he had five children. He also continued a diligent and moderately successful career at the Scottish Bar until 1780.

In 1773, Boswell was elected to The Club, the circle of intimates surrounding Johnson. Later that year he and Johnson toured Scotland, a visit Boswell described in *The Journal of a Tour to the Hebrides* published in 1785. This volume eventually proved more popular than Johnson's own record of the trip, *Journey to the Western Isles of Scotland*. Boswell's book was a preparation for the full record of his relationship with Johnson, which he spent the next seven years writing. In the meantime, Boswell had moved to London in 1786, after being called to the English Bar, although he never practised there. His wife died in Auchinleck in 1789 but Boswell remained in London to finish his biography. When THE LIFE OF SAMUEL JOHNSON was published in 1791, the work was praised but Boswell himself was criticised for his reverence of Johnson. Nevertheless, it was very successful, ensuring that Johnson became as well known for his conversation as for his work. It also changed the way that biographies were written thereafter. Boswell died in 1795, two years after the second edition of the *Life* was published.

Principal Works

1768   *An Account of Corsica, The Journal of a Tour to that Island, and Memoirs of Pascal Paoli*

1785   *The Journal of a Tour to the Hebrides*

1791   THE LIFE OF SAMUEL JOHNSON

BRONTË, CHARLOTTE (1816–55) AND EMILY (1818–48)

Women are supposed to be very calm generally: but women feel just as men feel; they need exercise for their faculties, and a field for their efforts as much as their brothers do.

Jane Eyre

Charlotte Brontë was born on 21 April 1816, and Emily Brontë was born two years later on 30 July 1818. They were the third and fifth of six children of Ulsterman Patrick Brontë (who had changed his surname from Brunty or Prunty), a clergyman in Thornton, Yorkshire. In 1820 the whole family moved to the rectory at Haworth on the Yorkshire moors. In the following year their mother, Maria, died from cancer. Following this, Charlotte and Emily were sent to the Clergy Daughters' School at Cowan Bridge with their two eldest sisters. Here they received a subsidised education, but the conditions were cruel and harsh and within a year both their elder sisters had died. Charlotte later portrayed the school in the Lowood section of JANE EYRE so realistically that many local people recognised the establishment. Their father then withdrew the two sisters and they returned to Haworth, where their aunt Elizabeth was now looking after the family.

Back at the Haworth, the rector set about educating his three surviving daughters and his son. Apart from the poetry and history that they discussed with their father, the four children also created their own fantasy worlds. Charlotte and her brother Branwell invented the fantasy land of Angria, while Emily and her sister Anne started a separate chronicle about an imaginary island called Gondal. Emily wrote a series of poems connected with the Gondal stories she invented, some of which have since been published. It was an unusual and isolated childhood, but the sisters were not to realise quite how different their life had made them until, in 1831, Charlotte was sent to Miss Wooler's school at Roe Head. Here she found that she spoke with a strong Irish accent and when asked by the other girls if she could play, she replied that she never had and did not know how. It is perhaps unsurprising then that Charlotte, who was considered the more outgoing of the three sisters, particularly in comparison with the painfully reserved Emily, soon fell ill and returned home.

In spite of this traumatic experience, Charlotte returned to the school in 1835 in order to teach and earn some money. Unfortunately, her lack of empathy for normal children, as well as her continued shyness and her homesickness, meant that she returned home three years later. Back at Haworth, the family's finances were in a parlous condition. They were not helped by Charlotte's decision to return home, or Branwell's drink and drugs habit. The sisters

therefore resolved to set up their own school. In order to do this, Emily and Charlotte decided, in 1842, to travel to Brussels and study languages at the *Pensionnat Héger*. Unfortunately, their aunt died soon after and they were forced to return to Haworth. The following year Charlotte returned to teach at the *Pensionnat*, but it is thought that she fell in love with Constantin Héger and thereby aroused the distrust of Mme Héger. She returned home in 1844.

> Largely raised in isolated surroundings on the bleak Yorkshire moors, Charlotte and Emily Brontë created detailed fantasy worlds while still children. As they grew up they developed these fictions and went on to write two of the most popular novels of all time – *Jane Eyre* and *Wuthering Heights*.

As Charlotte later admitted to her friend and biographer, Mrs Gaskell, she felt a compulsion to write which bordered on an illness. It was fortuitous then that in 1845 Charlotte stumbled upon the poetry of her sister Emily. Anne subsequently revealed her own poetry and, despite Emily's misgivings, the three of them published a volume of their poetry at their own expense with the money they had received from their aunt's will. The book, which they published in 1846 under their pseudonyms of Currer, Ellis and Acton Bell, sold just two copies. Undaunted, the sisters set about writing and publishing their respective novels. In 1847 Anne published *Agnes Grey*, Charlotte published *Jane Eyre* and Emily published WUTHERING HEIGHTS. These were again published under pseudonyms and it was not until the publication of Charlotte's *Shirley* in 1849 that the public became aware that they were all sisters.

By then, however, tragedy had struck the Brontë family. In September 1848, Branwell had finally succumbed to his debauched lifestyle and died of tuberculosis. This proved to be a family failing. After contracting a cold at Branwell's funeral, Emily succumbed to the disease as well and she died on 19 December of the same year. She was buried in the family vault at Haworth. Anne, whose *Tenant of Wildfell Hall* appeared in 1848, also died of tuberculosis in May 1849. Left alone by these terrible events, Charlotte no longer cared much for the encouraging reception that her novel received.

Nevertheless, she followed up *Shirley* with another novel, *Villette,* in 1853. She was by this time quite well known in London literary circles, trips to which she made on a frequent basis from her Haworth base. She became a friend and correspondent to Elizabeth Gaskell, her eventual biographer, and WILLIAM THACKERAY, to whom she had dedicated *Jane Eyre.* In 1854 she married her father's curate, Arthur Bell Nichols. Her happiness, however, was only short-lived because in the following year, on 31 March, she died during pregnancy. She was buried in Haworth. Her novel *The Professor* was published posthumously in 1857.

Principal Works

1847	*JANE EYRE*	Charlotte Brontë
1847	*WUTHERING HEIGHTS*	Emily Brontë
1849	*Shirley*	Charlotte Brontë
1853	*Villette*	Charlotte Brontë
1857	*The Professor*	Charlotte Brontë

BROWNING, ROBERT (1812–89)

Ah, but a man's reach should exceed his grasp, Or what's a heaven for?
　　　　　　　　　　　　　'Andrea del Sarto'

Robert Browning was born on 7 May 1812 in Camberwell, London. He was the first child of Robert Browning and Sarah Anna Wiedemann. Browning's father had been heir to a fortune but was disinherited when he learnt of the conditions of slavery upon which that fortune was based. Instead he became a clerk in the Bank of England, earning enough to amass an enormous library from which he read voraciously and encouraged Browning to do the same. Browning's mother was a keen pianist who adored her son and encouraged his artistic pursuits. Given this harmonious background, it is perhaps little wonder that Browning enjoyed much of his early education at home, where he was tutored in Latin, Greek, French and Italian. However, he was also a weekly boarder at a school in Peckham for a time, before he began a course of study at the newly established University of London in 1828.

Browning did not appreciate the course at the University and left to return home and continue his education in his own idiosyncratic manner. He also began writing poetry at this time, mostly in imitation of PERCY BYSSHE SHELLEY's work. This confessional style led to his first published work in 1833, *Pauline: A Fragment of a Confession.* It sold very poorly, but one review of it described the author as rather self-conscious, a fact which so discomfited Browning that he decided not to write in that style again. In 1834 Browning travelled across Europe to visit Russia and in the following year he published *Paracelsus,* a work about the Swiss physician and alchemist. This received better reviews, but critics complained of Browning's use of esoteric references, references that Browning did not appreciate were so obscure because of his singular education. The matter came to a head with the publication of *Sordello* in 1840. This was a long narrative poem written in the form of a dramatic monologue. At the time critics condemned it as unintelligible and senseless, but it was later celebrated as a pioneering work by poets such as Ezra Pound.

Robert Browning married the poet Elizabeth Barrett and the two lived a happy life in Italy where Browning wrote his most popular poems. Undervalued in his own time, Browning's innovative techniques gained him great respect with subsequent generations of writers.

Having read Elizabeth Barrett's collection of poems in 1845 and written a letter to her praising them, Browning contrived to meet her. Six years older then he, invalided and guarded by an over-protective father, Barrett was a much more popular poet than Browning. They fell in love and in 1846 they secretly married and eloped to Italy. Barrett's health improved in the better emotional and physical climate and the two enjoyed their time there, producing a son, Robert Barrett Browning in 1849. From time to time they also travelled across Europe, meeting up with other famous writers of the day, including Dante Gabriel Rossetti and ALFRED TENNYSON.

It was while staying in Italy that Browning produced perhaps his best work, the collection of poems MEN AND WOMEN. Published in 1855, this included some of his most famous poems, including 'Andrea del Sarto' and 'Fra Lippo Lippi'.

In 1861, however, the Browning's Italian honeymoon finally came to an end when Elizabeth died. Browning and his son moved back to London and, after his father died, he moved in with his sister. Perhaps reflecting public sympathy for Browning following the death of his wife, Browning's poetry began to receive more popular and critical acclaim. This reached a peak with the publication of his most ambitious work, *The Ring and the Book* in 1868. Based around a murder trial set in seventeenth-century Rome, in which a husband kills his wife and is subsequently executed, the 12 volumes of the poem relate the event from the perspectives of different characters. This technique was, again, ahead of its time and would later be taken up by such writers as JOSEPH CONRAD, James Joyce and William Faulkner. He continued to publish poetry in the years that followed and was even honoured by the founding in 1880 of a society devoted to studying his works – the Browning Society. Browning died in Venice on 12 December 1889 and was buried in Poets' Corner in Westminster Abbey, London.

Principal Works

1855   MEN AND WOMEN
1868   *The Ring and the Book*

BUNYAN, JOHN (1628–88)

The name of the slough was Despond.
                    The Pilgrim's Progress

John Bunyan was born, three years before JOHN DRYDEN, on 30 November 1628 in Elstow, Bedfordshire. Bunyan's father, Thomas Bunyan, was a tinker by trade, selling and mending pots and kettles. Bunyan's mother, Margaret Bentley, came from more socially refined stock, but this did not prevent the Bunyan family from enduring a poverty-stricken life for most of Bunyan's childhood. In spite of this, his parents still managed to send him to school, a feat for which he thanked

them by becoming, in his own words, a child adept at 'cursing, swearing, lying, and blaspheming'. Having completed his schooling, Bunyan followed his father into the tinker trade. However, in 1644 his mother and sister Margaret both died suddenly. When his father remarried his third wife barely two months after this, the father and son fell out and Bunyan joined the Parliamentary army to fight in the English Civil War.

> Persecuted for his religious beliefs, Bunyan spent many years in prison. It was while serving a sentence that he wrote *The Pilgrim's Progress*, a book which subsequently became enormously popular.

Bunyan all but failed to mention his life as a soldier and we know only that he was stationed at the garrison in Newport Pagnell under Sir Samuel Luke (later the object of scorn in the Royalist satire *Hudibras* written by Samuel Butler). When Bunyan was discharged from the army in 1647, he married his first wife. We know nothing about her except that she was as poor as he was and that she encouraged him to read. Returning to his trade as a tinker in the Bedford area, the following years saw Bunyan involved in an intense spiritual struggle of the kind that later came to form his seminal work, THE PILGRIM'S PROGRESS. In particular, Bunyan was plagued by his conscience, even to the extent where he felt obliged to abandon bell-ringing because he enjoyed it so much.

Eventually, Bunyan managed to find some sort of spiritual peace after joining St John's Church in Bedford. There he discovered his calling to preach and he began to sermonise around the Bedford area even though he did not possess the necessary licence. Bunyan was indicted for this practice in 1658 but was not imprisoned. Indeed, Bunyan not only continued to preach but also developed his sermons into books, becoming over the next 30 years one of the most prolific writers of the era. In 1658 Bunyan's first wife died leaving him with four children. He remarried in the following year to a woman called Elizabeth.

Following the Restoration in 1660, Nonconformists (those not members of the

Church of England) were once again subject to persecution. As Bedfordshire had a particularly large Nonconformist tradition, the persecution was felt most strongly there and Bunyan soon found himself in prison. The original judgement handed down to him meant that he should leave the country if he refused to attend the Church of England and not return on pain of death. For some reason this was commuted to 12 years in prison. Dedicated to his calling, Bunyan continued to preach in and around the prison during this time. He also continued to write many religious tracts, chief amongst which was his spiritual autobiography, *Grace Abounding to the Chief of Sinners*, published in 1666, the year of the Great Fire of London.

In 1672 Charles II suspended all anti-Nonconformist laws and Bunyan was allowed to leave Bedford jail. He was also granted permission to preach for the first time but as St John's had been given to another sect, he took up residence in a barn, sermonising there to large crowds. Just three years later, however, the Nonconformist laws were once again enforced and shortly afterwards Bunyan was arrested and imprisoned for six months. He spent his time writing *The Pilgrim's Progress*, the first part of which he eventually published in 1678, and the second part in 1684. It was an enormously popular book almost from the start and Bunyan became famous all around England. Bunyan used this fame to spread his religious beliefs and it was while doing this that he died on 31 August 1688 at Bunhill Fields in London.

Principal Works

1666	*Grace Abounding to the Chief of Sinners*
1678–84	THE PILGRIM'S PROGRESS

BURNS, ROBERT (1759–96)

Should auld acquaintance be forgot,
And never brought to mind?
Should auld acquaintance be forgot,
And auld lang syne?

'Auld Lang Syne'

Robert Burns was born on 25 January 1759 in Alloway, Ayrshire, Scotland, two years after WILLIAM BLAKE. He was the son of Agnes Broun and William Burnes, or Burness, who was a gardener at the time of the birth, but later became a farmer. Robert was the eldest of seven children. Although he was extremely poor, his father did what he could to ensure that the children received a good education, instructing them himself whenever possible, sending Robert to a local school when funds allowed (which they did for a total of three years), and finally employing a tutor for Robert and his brother Gilbert. One tutor, John Murdoch, commented of his young charge that he 'made rapid progress in reading and was just tolerable at writing'. By the time he was reaching maturity, Burns was well versed in the BIBLE, the classics of English literature from SHAKESPEARE onwards, and some French. Burns also became steeped in the distinctly Scottish tradition of literature, particularly the golden age of Gavin Douglas, William Dunbar and Robert Henryson.

> Born into a poor family, Robert Burns unexpectedly became a society sensation with the publication of his first book of poems. Hailed as the 'Ploughman Poet', he revived literary interest in the Scots dialect and helped pave the way for the British Romantic movement.

Before Burns began composing his own poems, however, he had to undertake his share of work on his father's farm. In 1766, his father rented additional land and in helping to till this, Burns purportedly damaged his young physique, thus beginning the heart trouble that would plague him for the rest of his life. The farming venture was not successful and in 1771 the whole family moved to Lochlea, near Irvine, to try again. Burns was sent to the local town to learn flax-dressing, although he claims to have learnt more about drinking from a drunken sailor he met there. In 1784 his father died, and Robert and his brother Gilbert decided to rent a farm at Mossgiel. Like the other farms they worked, this enterprise eventually failed. In the meantime, Burns had developed his delight in poetry, as well as his lifelong interest in women, an interest which is said to have led to any number of illegitimate children. Burns was later to claim that 'Love and Poesy' were inextricably linked.

In an attempt to get away from the failures of his farming ventures, and the censure he received for his relationships with women, Burns decided to publish a volume of his poetry in order to raise funds for a trip to the West Indies where he intended to start a new life. Unexpectedly, the volume, POEMS, CHIEFLY IN THE SCOTTISH DIALECT, proved to be extremely popular. Instead of going to the West Indies, Burns decided to go to Edinburgh, where he was received with great interest. Many held that he was a kind of 'noble savage', a poor man gifted with an innate artistry. Burns himself seemed to realise that as the 'Ploughman Poet', he was merely the man of the moment and he enjoyed his time while he could, eventually publishing a second edition of his poetry. With the funds he raised, he helped Gilbert to stock the farm at Mossgiel, and did the same for his own farm in Ellisland, near Dumfries.

In 1788 Burns finally married Jean Armour, a lover with whom he had enjoyed a long relationship, intermittently broken off by her father who had disapproved of Burns until his success in Edinburgh. In the same year, Burns also took on a new job as an excise officer, a job he held full-time once the farm failed three years later. Burns did not particularly enjoy his posting in Dumfries and his outspoken support of the French Revolution meant that he was never able to advance in the service. Indeed, he came very close to losing his job and was only saved by the actions of an influential friend. Towards the end of his life, Burns concentrated less on writing poetry and more on collecting Scottish folk songs, particularly for an anthology called *The Scots Musical Museum*. This he continued to do right up until his death on 21 July 1796. He left behind him a renewed sense of pride in the Scots dialect, as well as a new form of poetry, representing the voice of the ordinary person. In so doing, Burns laid the groundwork for much of the Romantic movement that was to follow.

Principal Work

1786   POEMS, CHIEFLY IN THE SCOTTISH DIALECT

BYRON, LORD GEORGE GORDON (1788–1824)

And what is writ is writ,–
Would it were worthier!
Childe Harold's Pilgrimage

George Gordon Noel Byron was born on 22 January 1788 in London. That he was born in Britain at all was due to the insistence of his mother, Catherine Gight, as his father, Captain John Byron, was then hiding from debtors in France. Byron's family histories were almost always dramatic, and they included such personages as his grandfather, nicknamed 'Foulweather Jack' and his great uncle, the 'Wicked Lord', who killed his relation in a duel. Byron's beginnings were slightly more inauspicious. When he was three, his father died and his occasionally violent mother took him off to live in very poor conditions in Aberdeen. There he attended the local grammar school and did his best to cope with both the club foot he had been born with and the treatments devised to heal it. Like SAMUEL JOHNSON before him, this handicap spurred Byron on to greater athletic prowess, and he eventually became a keen boxer, horseman and swimmer, as well as sexually precocious, even from a very young age.

At the age of 10, Byron's life changed forever when he inherited the title which made him the sixth Lord Byron. With his title he acquired the somewhat dilapidated halls of Newstead Abbey, although, not immediately, any great funds. For the next few years, Byron lived on and off in the beautiful surroundings of Southwell, the smallest cathedral city in England. Following the intervention of his mother's attorney, Byron received further corrective treatment on his foot, and he assumed his rightful place at Harrow School. While still at school he met and attempted to woo a distant cousin, Mary Chaworth. At one point he refused to return to Harrow because of his infatuation, and when she married in 1805 Byron was deeply upset. In the same year he went to Trinity College, Cambridge, but his distraught moods and intemperate spending meant that he did very little work and incurred large debts.

When Byron returned to Southwell in 1806, he privately published his first collection of poems, *Fugitive Pieces*. He followed this up in 1807 with another collection that was so badly criticised in *The Edinburgh Review* that he felt compelled to write his first major satire, *English Bards and Scotch Reviewers*. Byron eventually managed to graduate from Cambridge and, after assuming his seat in the House of Lords, he set out on a tour of Europe with his friend John Cam Hobhouse. This tour provided many of the materials for his later work. It also occasioned one of the most famous incidents in Byron's life when he swam the Hellespont channel (now called the Dardanelles) in imitation of the young lover Leander, a classic story retold in CHRISTOPHER MARLOWE's *Hero and Leander*. Upon his return in 1811, Byron's mother died.

> Notoriously dubbed 'mad, bad and dangerous to know', Lord Byron was, during his lifetime, one of the most famous public figures in the Western world. Despite living the archetypal Romantic lifestyle, Byron's poetry followed more in the tradition of Alexander Pope than William Wordsworth.

In the following year, Byron published *Childe Harold*, the first fruits of his European adventure. The result was, as he notoriously declared, that he 'awoke one morning and found myself famous'. With this sudden celebrity, and with what SAMUEL COLERIDGE described as his 'beautiful countenance', Byron found that he was the subject of many female passions. The most famous of these was initiated by Lady Caroline Lamb, who drove Byron to such a state of agitation that he married Annabella Milbanke in 1815, apparently in order to escape her. The troubled beginning to the marriage was not aided by Byron's aristocratic refusal to accept any of the royalties from his massively successful publications. This, despite the fact that the Byrons were visited by bailiffs. During this period, Byron seemed to be going a little insane in his wife's eyes and, speaking indiscreetly, he revealed his attraction for Augusta Leigh, the half-sister he had only known as an adult.

This proved to be the last straw for Annabella, and, after giving birth to his daughter, she left Byron less than a year into their marriage. As rumours about the relationship with his sister grew, Byron was ostracised from society and left England for ever in the April of 1816. Travelling around Europe, he soon met up with PERCY and MARY SHELLEY. They became friends and went to Italy together. For the next few years Byron led a rather dissolute life, but he also continued to work on *Childe Harold*, as well as starting work on DON JUAN. In 1819, Byron met Countess Teresa Guicciolo. He immediately fell in love with her and, even though she was married, managed to conduct an open relationship with her and was even inducted into an Italian revolutionary society, the Carbonari, by her father and brother. With the sale of Newstead Abbey, Byron was able to support himself and help contribute monies to the revolutionary cause.

He also had to use the money to support his illegitimate daughter Allegra. He had sent her to be educated in a Catholic convent in Ravenna but, in 1822, the same year in which Shelley drowned, she died of a fever. During this time, Byron had continued to publish parts of *Don Juan*, although it had been condemned as immoral, as well as his satire, *The Vision of Judgement*. However, by 1823 he wished to undertake something more strenuous than mere writing. When the London Greek Committee asked him for help in their war of independence against the Turks, Byron not only sent funds, but also set about chartering a ship to come to their aid. When he arrived in Greece, he took command of the troops he had paid for and set about training them and trying to disentangle the factionalism that undermined the Greek cause. After a year of effort, however, he succumbed to a fever and died on 19 April 1824.

Mourned as a hero in Greece, his heart was removed and buried in Missolonghi, while his body was sent to be buried in Poets' Corner, Westminster Abbey. This request was refused by the Church authorities and he was buried in Newstead Abbey instead. In 1969 a plaque was finally placed in Poets' Corner. Byron left behind him a legacy that is more than just a body of work but is best understood as an attitude towards life. This essentially Romantic attitude is perhaps what he is best remembered for, even though his poems belong much more clearly to the era of ALEXANDER POPE.

Principal Works

1812–18	*Childe Harold's Pilgrimage*
1816	*Manfred*
1818–24	DON JUAN
1822	*The Vision of Judgement*

C

CARROLL, LEWIS (1832–98)

'The time has come,' the Walrus said,

'To talk of many things:

Of shoes–and ships–and sealing-wax–

Of cabbages–and kings–

And why the sea is boiling hot–

And whether pigs have wings.'

Through the Looking Glass

Lewis Carroll was born Charles Lutwidge Dodgson on 27 January 1832 in Daresbury, Cheshire. He was the eldest son and third child born to Charles Dodgson, the curate of Daresbury at the time but who would later go on to become Archdeacon of Richmond, and Frances Jane Lutwidge, who would eventually bear 11 children. Carroll was taught by his father until he was 11 years old, but when the family moved to Yorkshire, Carroll spent a year at Richmond school before, in 1846, attending public school at Rugby. Rugby school was famous for the reforming influence of MATTHEW ARNOLD's father. Carroll spent three years at Rugby and distinguished himself academically, as he did everywhere, to the point where he claimed to be bored with hearing all the praise.

Lewis Carroll was a distinguished academic at the University of Oxford when one day, on a picnic, he made up a story about a girl falling down a rabbit hole in order to entertain the 10-year-old daughter of his friend. This became the basis for *Alice's Adventures in Wonderland.*

From Rugby, Carroll earned a studentship to study for holy orders at Christ Church College at the University of Oxford. However, he did not complete his induction into the church and instead emerged with a Bachelor of Arts, First Class Honours in Mathematics and Second Class Honours in Classics. In 1855 Carroll became the sub-librarian at Christ Church, as well as a mathematics lecturer. He

would hold the latter post until 1881, although during all this time his teaching suffered from the effects of his bad stammer. Nevertheless, Carroll continued to accrue qualifications, earning his Master's degree in 1857, and becoming ordained as a deacon in 1861. During this time he became friends with Henry George Liddell, the Dean of Christ Church College.

On 4 July 1862, Carroll paid a social visit to the Liddell household and, while on a picnic, he fell into conversation with Alice Liddell, Liddell's 10-year-old daughter. Carroll told her a story about a girl called Alice who falls down a rabbit hole and of her subsequent adventures. Alice was so enchanted by this that she asked Carroll to write it down. Carroll duly did as he was asked and in 1865 he published it as ALICE'S ADVENTURES IN WONDERLAND. It proved to be enormously popular with the public generally and with children in particular, who enjoyed the fact that it did not preach at them like most children's books of the time. Inspired by this success, Carroll followed it up in 1871 with *Through the Looking-Glass and What Alice Found There*. This was equally as popular. Carroll continued to publish with the nonsense poem *The Hunting of the Snark* in 1876, and the two parts of *Sylvie and Bruno* in 1889 and 1893, although these did not match the success of the Alice books. Carroll resigned completely from Oxford in 1892 and died in Guildford on 14 January 1898.

Principal Works

1865   ALICE'S ADVENTURES IN WONDERLAND
1871   *Through the Looking-Glass and What Alice Found There*
1876   *The Hunting of the Snark*

CHAUCER, GEOFFREY (1343–1400)

Then hold it wise, for so it seems to me,

To make a virtue of necessity.

The Canterbury Tales

It is thought that Chaucer was born in London in the mercantile parish of

St-Martin's-in-the-Vintry some time around 1342–43. His father, John Chaucer, was a prosperous wine merchant, as well as deputy butler to the King at Southampton in 1348. Chaucer's mother was probably Agnes de Copton, niece to an official at the Royal Mint. For his schooling Chaucer was most likely sent to St Paul's Almonry, where he would have received instruction in Latin and French. Mixing with all the people coming off the ships at his father's place of work, Chaucer would soon have become fluent in French, which at the time was the language of the English court.

Described by John Dryden as 'the Father of English Poetry', Geoffrey Chaucer lived a relatively privileged life which afforded him the opportunity to travel across continental Europe, bringing him in contact with the Italian Renaissance. The new verse forms and subject matter he encountered encouraged him to adopt a bold new approach to English poetry and led him to write *The Canterbury Tales*.

After leaving St Paul's Almonry, Chaucer was sent to serve as a page at one of the most important aristocratic households in the land, that of the Countess of Ulster, wife of the third son of Edward III. The first recorded mention of Chaucer comes from the accounts of her house in 1357, where it is noted that he was bought a cloak, a pair of shoes and some red and black breeches. As a page in this house, Chaucer would have learnt the manners and terms of reference of the leading courtiers which would have been an enormous boon to his later career. He also made some powerful friends, none more useful than John of Gaunt, the Duke of Lancaster, who was to provide him with patronage for most of his life.

Some time around 1359 Chaucer went into military service with the Duke of Clarence. It was under Clarence that Chaucer went to Rheims during the Hundred Years War between England and France. There he was captured by the French and ransomed. It is reported that King Edward III himself made a contribution towards the ransom. The connection between Chaucer and the King was clearly a strong one because by 1367, court records refer to Chaucer as 'our beloved valet' and state that he had been awarded an annuity. It was prior to this, probably in 1366, that Chaucer married Philippa Payne de Roet, who had also served in the Duchess of Ulster's house as a lady-in-waiting. She was a form of minor nobility herself, being daughter of the Flemish knight Sir Payne de Roet, who served John of Gaunt.

It was also around this time that Chaucer embarked on a series of diplomatic missions in the King's service, most notably to Spain in 1366, to France in 1368, and to Italy in 1372. The precise nature of these missions is unclear, although they appear to have had a commercial rather than military purpose. What was key, particularly about the mission to Genoa and a subsequent one to Milan in 1378, was that Chaucer came into direct contact with the Italian Renaissance, enabling him to read at first hand the works of Dante, Boccaccio and Petrarch. These writers, the last two of whom were still alive at the time of Chaucer's visits, afforded him access to new verse forms and subject matter.

It is not known exactly when Chaucer started writing, although his first original poem (he had translated many others) was *The Book of the Duchess*, an elegy to John of Gaunt's first wife who died in 1368. Inspired by his Italian journeys, Chaucer began writing in earnest and *The House of Fame*, an affectionate parody of Dante's *Divine Comedy*, was followed by *Troilus and Criseyde*. This poem tells the story of how the Trojan prince Troilus loves Criseyde but eventually loses her to the Greek warrior Diomede. It is a version of Boccaccio's *Il Filostrato* but despite its illustrious model, it apparently caused distress to King Richard II's wife, Queen Anne of Bohemia. She thought that it implied that women were more faithless than men. Chaucer was thus instructed to write a retraction and so, in 1386, he composed a portion of *The Legend of Good Women*. This recounts a dream in which Chaucer is accused by Cupid, the god of love, of being unfair to women. To atone for this, Cupid orders Chaucer to produce a series of legends about faithful women. The project was never finished because, it was reported, Chaucer was unable to conceive of sufficient good women.

During this time Chaucer had been steadily advancing through the ranks of the government. As well as becoming the recipient of an additional annuity from John of Gaunt in 1374, Chaucer had also worked in various customs postings until, in 1385, he became a Justice of the Peace for the County of Kent and then in 1386, a Knight of the Shire. However, at the end of that year, John of Gaunt departed for Spain, leaving the new King, Richard II, under the influence of the Duke of Gloucester. Gloucester immediately set about installing his own favourites in government posts and Chaucer was removed as a result. This left Chaucer at leisure to compose THE CANTERBURY TALES.

When John of Gaunt returned to England in 1389, Chaucer was restored to favour and office. This time he was set the task of supervising the repair of walls, ditches, bridges and sewers between Woolwich and Greenwich. Various other sinecures came his way in the years that followed and he died, a reasonably wealthy man, on 25 October 1400. He was buried in Westminster Abbey in London – the first of a long line of writers to be interred there, in what would eventually evolve into Poets' Corner. This is appropriate because he is considered by many to be, as Dryden described him, 'the Father of English Poetry'. Indeed, others, like the writer G.K. Chesterton, have gone further and declared that Chaucer was partly responsible for conceiving the very identity of Englishness itself.

Principal Works

1372–82	*The House of Fame*
1380–85	*Troilus and Criseyde*
1386	*The Legend of Good Women*
1386–1400	*THE CANTERBURY TALES*

CHOPIN, KATE (1851–1904)

I trust it will not be giving away professional secrets to say that many readers would be surprised, perhaps shocked, at the questions which some newspaper editors will put to a defenceless woman under the guise of flattery.

'On Certain Brisk Days'

Katherine O'Flaherty Chopin was born in St Louis, Missouri, on 8 February 1851. She was the daughter of Irish immigrant Thomas O'Flaherty and French-American Eliza Faris. Her father was a prominent businessman in the local community, but like several others in the area, he was killed in a railroad accident when Chopin was just 4 years old. From then on her influences were mainly the strong women on her mother's side of the family, including her pious Catholic great grandmother. Chopin herself went to a convent school, the St Louis Academy of the Sacred Heart, where she proved to be a mediocre student.

Kate Chopin gained notoriety early in her life for breaking social conventions. She continued this iconoclastic streak when she became a writer and her second novel, *The Awakening*, was heavily criticised for its sexual content.

When she graduated from the St Louis Academy in 1868, she spent the next couple of years as a society belle. It was during this period that she met Oscar Chopin, a wealthy Creole cotton merchant. In 1870 they married and a year later moved to New Orleans where they had six children. At first Oscar's cotton brokerage was successful, but by the end of the decade it had failed. As a consequence, the family relocated to Cloutierville in northwest Louisiana where Oscar opened a general store and assumed responsibility for his family's cotton plantation. Three years later Oscar died of swamp fever and his wife moved back to New Orleans to live with her mother. When her mother subsequently died, Chopin was left to raise her children alone.

It was after these terrible personal tragedies that Chopin began to write. At first she composed short stories, but 1890 saw the publication of her first novel, *At Fault*. Soon her work began to appear in fashionable magazines of the time, such as *Atlantic Monthly*. In 1894 she published her first collection of short stories, *Bayou Folk*. As the title suggests, these stories provided evocative depictions of local Louisiana life. They won her a national reputation which she cemented in 1897 with her second collection of stories, *A Night in Acadie*. Her most important work, however, was her second novel, THE AWAKENING, published in 1899. This provided a frank account of what it was like to be a woman in a world defined by men. Its sexual content alone ensured that both it and Chopin won a harsh reception. Chopin was distraught at the reaction to her novel and she wrote very little afterwards. Just a few years later, on 22 August 1904, Chopin died of a brain haemorrhage.

Principal Works

1894   *Bayou Folk*
1899   *THE AWAKENING*

COLERIDGE, SAMUEL TAYLOR (1772–1834)

In Xanadu did Kubla Khan
A stately pleasure-dome decree:
Where Alph, the sacred river, ran
Through caverns measureless to man
Down to a sunless sea.

'Kubla Khan'

Samuel Taylor Coleridge was born on 21 October 1772 in Ottery St Mary, Devonshire. Coleridge was the youngest of the 10 children of John Coleridge, the vicar at Ottery St Mary, and Ann Bowden. He suffered bouts of bullying and was not always the happiest of children. At the age of 7 he went so far as to run away from home. He did not get very far though as he was found by a neighbour the next morning, but the event cropped up in his thoughts and poetry years later. In 1781 his father died and Coleridge was sent to stay with his maternal uncle in London, where he attended Christ's Hospital School, a charity school for the children of impoverished clergy.

In 1791, towards the end of his period at Christ's Hospital School, Coleridge composed his first poem inspired by the death of one of his brothers and his only sister. In the same year he went to study at Jesus College, Cambridge. He proved to be an extremely able student but he found little at Cambridge to stretch his intellect and soon fell into a dissolute way of life, incurring a number of debts. In order to solve this problem, Coleridge decided, in 1793, that he should join the Fifteenth Dragoons, based in London. Coleridge signed up under the improbable alias of Silas Tomkyn Comberbache. Coleridge was spectacularly inept as a cavalryman, not least because he could barely ride a horse, and so he was not immediately sent to fight in France. Eventually his brother facilitated his discharge, citing the pretext of insanity.

Coleridge returned to Cambridge where he continued to study, although he never actually received a degree. Before he left Cambridge in 1794, he met up with Robert Southey, the future poet laureate. Sympathetic to the revolutionary ideals espoused in France, the two of them decided to try and create their own democratic society, for which Coleridge coined the term 'Pantisocracy'. They were joined by a small group of other utopian enthusiasts and even made plans to found the society in Pennsylvania. As they were raising funds to go, Southey persuaded Coleridge that he should marry his fiancée's sister, Sara Fricker. When the Pantisocracy project fell through, Coleridge accepted that it was his duty to complete his marriage to Sara.

> One of the intellectual giants of Romanticism, Coleridge helped to revolutionise British poetry with his friend William Wordsworth. However, Coleridge became a drug addict and dissipated much of his natural talent so that by the end of his life he was, like the Ancient Mariner, 'a sadder and wiser man'.

In 1795 Coleridge met WILLIAM WORDSWORTH and the two became friends. Coleridge considered Wordsworth to be 'the best poet of the age'. In 1796 Coleridge published his own selection of poetry, *Poems on Various Subjects*. In the same year his first son, David, was born. Coleridge followed up his first volume of poetry with a second in 1797, simply called *Poems*, which was well received. When Wordsworth moved near the Coleridges in 1797, the two poets began to collaborate and produced, in the following year, one of the most influential collections of poetry ever published, *LYRICAL BALLADS*. Opening with Coleridge's *Rime of the Ancient Mariner* and ending with Wordsworth's 'Tintern Abbey', *Lyrical Ballads* attempted to use everyday language to offer a more subjective type of poetry.

After the publication of *Lyrical Ballads*, Coleridge received an annuity from the Wedgwood brothers of £150 a year. This enabled him to join Wordsworth on a tour of Germany where Coleridge began to study the work of the philosopher Immanuel Kant, who influenced the poet's work for the rest of his life. While Coleridge was in Germany, his second son died and Coleridge returned in low spirits. Following the Wordsworths to the Lake District, Coleridge met and fell in love with Wordsworth's sister-in-law. However, by this time, Coleridge was an opium addict, having originally taken the drug to ease his rheumatism. To try and rebuild his health, Coleridge removed himself to Malta for a couple of years where he occasionally worked as a spy for the British government. He returned in a worse state than he had departed, separated from his wife and almost estranged from Wordsworth, after a fierce quarrel with the poet in 1810.

In the years that followed, Coleridge supported himself through sporadic journalism and by writing a periodical and a play. By 1816 he had found a doctor, James Gillman, who was able to control his drug addiction to some degree. This enabled Coleridge to compose his thoughts on literary criticism, as well as some of his reflections, and publish them as *Biographia Literaria*. This was also the time that he published his famous poems, 'Christabel' and 'Kubla Khan'. Eventually, he moved in with Gillman and his wife and finished his life reasonably peacefully under their watchful eyes. He managed to effect a reconciliation with both his own wife and Wordsworth and even toured the Rhineland with his old friend in 1828. He had also, by this time, established a reputation for himself and was elected a Fellow of the Royal Society of Literature in 1824 and was awarded a pension as a result. His last years were spent holding court at his rooms in Highgate to a throng of admirers. He died on 25 July 1834.

Principal Works

1798–1800   *LYRICAL BALLADS*
1816   *Biographia Literaria*

CONRAD, JOSEPH (1857–1924)

Any work that aspires, however humbly, to the condition of art should carry its justification in every line.

The Nigger of the 'Narcissus'

Jósef Teodor Konrad Walecz Korzeniowski was born in Poland on 3 December 1857. Conrad's father, Apollo Korzeniowski, worked as a translator of English and French literature, but he was also a Polish nationalist, as was Conrad's mother, involved in plotting against the Russian rule of their country. In 1861, as a result of these activities, the whole family was sent into exile in the remote Russian city of Vologda. On the journey there, Conrad caught the pneumonia that was to plague his health for the rest of his life. Conditions in Vologda were very tough and Conrad's mother eventually died when he was 7. Conrad's father was devastated by this and his own health began to deteriorate until, by the time Conrad was 11, he too was dead.

Born to Polish nationalists exiled by their Russian rulers, Conrad eventually ran away to sea, sailing with both the French and British Merchant Navies. He reached the rank of captain, and became a British citizen where, in his third language, he wrote one of the richest collection of novels in English.

Conrad was then put under the guardianship of his maternal uncle, Tadeusz Bobrowski. Bobrowski did his best to complete Conrad's education, although apparently he was a poor student who showed little aptitude, even for languages. In his mid teens, Conrad decided that he wanted to be a sailor. This did not please Bobrowski and he sent Conrad on a tour of Switzerland with his tutor Adam Pulman in the hope that this might dissuade him. It did not and in 1874, at the age of 16, Conrad left Poland for Marseilles to join the French Merchant Navy. For the next four years Conrad served on various ships, travelling to the West Indies and down the South American coast, and even smuggling guns into Spain.

Conrad seemed to enjoy life in Marseilles, but he soon ran up a large debt. One evening he knew he was about to be visited by a creditor and so he shot himself. When his uncle Bobrowski received a telegram informing him of this, he hurried to Conrad's aid but when he arrived he found Conrad was fine apart from a scar on his left breast which he later claimed to have received in a duel. Following this incident, Conrad decided to leave the French Merchant Navy to avoid being drafted and joined the British Merchant Navy instead. For the next 16 years Conrad sailed all over the world, as well as being shipwrecked, and he rose through the ranks rapidly, becoming a captain in 1886. This was also the same year that he became a British subject.

Following the disaster of his only command, sailing out of Bangkok, Conrad returned to Britain, and, through contacts in Brussels, he managed to secure a posting on a steamer in the Congo Free State in 1890, later the backdrop for his short story, HEART OF DARKNESS. The inhuman treatment of the indigenous population he witnessed there, as well as the illnesses that attended him, left him ready to quit sailing and he began to write his first novel, *Almayer's Folly*. This was published in 1895 under his assumed name of Conrad. Like all the novels that followed, writing *Almayer's Folly* was very difficult for Conrad, not because English was his third language but because he was a perfectionist.

In 1896 he married an Englishwoman by the name of Jessie George with whom he would later have two children. Conrad's output until 1914 was critically well received, but it was the publication of *Chance* that started to really improve his finances. This enabled him to travel to the United States in 1923 where he was warmly appreciated. In that same year Conrad declined an honorary degree from Cambridge University, a trick repeated in the following year when he declined a knighthood. Shortly thereafter, Conrad died of a heart attack on 3 August 1924. He was buried in Canterbury and left behind him one of the richest collections of novels in the English language.

Principal Works

1895   *Almayer's Folly*
1897   *The Nigger of the 'Narcissus'*

1900   *Lord Jim*
1901   HEART OF DARKNESS
1904   *Nostromo*
1907   *The Secret Agent*
1911   *Under Western Eyes*

COOPER, JAMES FENIMORE (1789–1851)

The tendency of democracies is, in all things, to mediocrity.
'On the Disadvantages of Democracy'

James Fenimore Cooper was born on 15 September 1789 in Burlington, New Jersey. His parents were Quakers, Judge William Cooper and Elisabeth Fenimore. His father had become extremely wealthy through land speculation and in the year of Cooper's birth they moved to Cooperstown, a settlement near Otsego lake founded by his father. This location had a huge influence on Cooper and it was here that he developed his interest in and love of the local nature and history. Initially Cooper was educated in the village school, however, in 1801 he was sent to Albany in preparation for his studies at Yale which he began at age 13. After two years at Yale, Cooper was expelled after performing a series of pranks, one of which included teaching a donkey to sit in his professor's chair.

In 1806, with his father's blessing, Cooper embarked upon a career at sea as a sailor. After two years he was awarded a commission as a midshipman in the American Navy which he held until 1811. In 1809 his father died, leaving Cooper an extremely wealthy young man. After resigning his commission, Cooper married Susan Augusta De Lancey, a descendant of the early Governors of New York colony. For the next decade Cooper moved between Mamaroneck, New York and Scarsdale, New York, living as a gentleman farmer. One day, upon finishing an English novel, he remarked to his wife that he could write a better one than that and when she challenged him to do so, he produced his first book *Precaution* in 1820. Written after the style of Jane Austen, it was not a success.

Undeterred, Cooper then went on to write *The Spy* in 1821. This novel was much more obviously influenced by WALTER SCOTT's work (an influence he would later try and shrug off by writing 'realistic' novels of mediaeval Europe). It centred around a spy operating during the American Revolution. It was an enormous success and allowed Cooper to give up farming and devote the rest of his life to writing. In 1823, he wrote *The Pioneers*, the first of a series of five books about Natty Bumppo, an old hunter also called Leatherstocking or Hawkeye, and his Indian companion Chingachgook. These stories of the frontiersman are what Cooper is best remembered for today, particularly the second book in the series, *The Last of the Mohicans* (1826). In 1827 Cooper began a series of novels about the sea, starting with *The Pilot*. These are the works that help Cooper lay claim to the title of the First American Novelist.

After making a bet with his wife that he could write a better novel than the one he had just read, James Fenimore Cooper began a writing career in which he helped to create and celebrate the myth of the American frontier.

In 1826 Cooper set off for France, ostensibly as the American Consul at Lyons. This enabled him to travel all over Europe, and he made friends with leading writers of the time, including Walter Scott. While in Europe he found himself defending the American way of life against the Old World, and in 1828 he published *Notions of the Americans*, a summary of his argument. However, when he got back to America he found that his much beloved democracy had become corrupted. He therefore set about writing critiques of his native land. These attacks did not find him many friends when he began a series of libel actions against the press. These started after journalists criticised him for becoming too aristocratic in his handling of people who trespassed on his land. Although he won most of these cases, by the time of his death on 14 September 1852 Cooper was not a popular man.

Principal Works

1824   *The Pilot*
1826   *The Last of the Mohicans*
1828   *Notions of the Americans*

CRANE, STEPHEN (1871–1900)

Do not weep, maiden, for war is kind.
'War Is Kind'

Stephen Crane was born on 1 November 1871 in Newark, New Jersey. He was the youngest of 14 children born to a father who was a Methodist minister and a mother who was a member of the Woman's Christian Temperance Union. Both of Crane's parents and several of his brothers were published writers of one sort or another and so it was perhaps little surprise that Crane himself enjoyed writing from an early age. However, he did not particularly enjoy school, partly because the family moved about a lot. Crane's father died in 1880 and the family moved to Asbury Park, New Jersey a few years later. In 1890 Crane entered Lafayette College, but he failed his course and left after barely a term. In 1891, the year his mother died, Crane attended Syracuse University. There he proved his sporting prowess by playing on the varsity baseball team. However, he showed little academic aptitude and he left after just one semester.

In the same year, Crane heard a lecture by Hamlin Garland, a proponent of realistic fiction. This greatly influenced Crane and he began to write *Maggie, A Girl of the Streets*. After leaving Syracuse University, Crane decided to move to New York where he tried, unsuccessfully, to secure a full-time job with one of the newspapers. Thanks both to family support and to the occasional piece of freelance work, Crane was not completely destitute during this period, although he did spend a lot of time living with the poorer people of the Bowery slums. He used this experience to help convey a realistic portrayal of a tough urban life in *Maggie* which he was continuously writing. After the final manuscript had been rejected on several occasions by various publishing houses, Crane decided to publish it himself in 1893. It immediately earned the plaudits of both Garland and the influential literary editor William Dean Howells, but it was not a popular success.

Undeterred, Crane then began work on the follow-up, *The Red Badge of Courage*. This Civil War novel was first serialised in a newspaper in 1894. The same newspaper commissioned Crane to write pieces about the American West in the following year when *The*

Red Badge of Courage was finally published in book form. This time Crane's novel gained acclaim from a much larger audience, becoming the first popular work of modern realism. Typically, in the same year Crane also printed a volume of his spare and honest poetry, *The Black Riders and Other Lines*. Thereafter Crane used his literary celebrity to garner more reporting assignments, and at the end of 1896 he went to cover the Cuban rebellion.

> Stephen Crane helped to institute a new era of gritty realism in American fiction. Despite never having witnessed a war at first hand himself, let alone been a soldier, Crane's *The Red Badge of Courage* was hailed as one of the most realistic accounts of the experience of modern warfare.

On his way there he met Cora Howorth Taylor, the proprietor of the Hotel De Dream in Jacksonville, Florida. She became his lifetime partner and travelled under the name of 'Mrs Crane'. On the crossing from Florida to Cuba, and heavily laden with weapons, Crane's boat sank and he spent the next couple of days adrift at sea until he was rescued. Crane did not waste the experience and turned it into one of his best short stories *The Open Boat* (1897). Eager to experience more adventures, Crane travelled to Europe to cover the war between Greece and Turkey in the same year. Later that year he stayed in England where he met and became friends with other famous authors of the time, such as JOSEPH CONRAD and HENRY JAMES.

In 1898 Crane returned to the States in order to volunteer for the war against Spain. However, he was rejected on health grounds and, although he still travelled there as a reporter, he had to return home due to illness. He continued to travel as best he could, but in 1899 he suffered a massive tubercular haemorrhage. Cora and others sought treatment for him, while he made heroic efforts to continue writing. However, he grew steadily weaker and died on 5 June 1900 in Badenweiler, Germany.

Principal Works

1893   *MAGGIE, A GIRL OF THE STREETS*
1894–95   *THE RED BADGE OF COURAGE*

DEFOE, DANIEL (1660–1731)

Wherever God erects a house of prayer,
The Devil always builds a chapel there:
And 'twill be found, upon examination,
The latter has the largest congregation.

The True-Born Englishman

Daniel was born around September 1660 in London as Daniel Foe; he changed the name around 1695. His father, James Foe, was a butcher. His mother, Mary, died when he was 10. Both of his parents were Dissenters (Presbyterians in this case), which means that at the time they were Protestants who did not belong to the Anglican Church. Although Protestant Dissenters did not suffer as much persecution as Roman Catholics, they were still barred from holding public office at the time, or earning degrees. So when Defoe graduated from Morton's Academy in 1679, he was destined for the life of a trader.

By 1684 Defoe was a moderately successful merchant. At the beginning of the year he married Mary Tuffley, an heiress of some prosperity, with whom he would eventually have two sons and five daughters. In 1685 he joined the rebellion against King James II led by the Duke of Monmouth. When the rebellion was defeated, hundreds of Monmouth's supporters were hanged at the famous 'bloody assizes' while hundreds more were transported or enslaved. Defoe was lucky to escape and he went into a form of exile for the next few years until James was deposed by William of Orange in 1688. While hiding in a churchyard during this time, Defoe noticed a gravestone with the name 'Robinson Crusoe' written on it. He jotted the name down and many years later used it as the name for his own famous hero.

Although Defoe's luck seemed to be improving for a time after 1688, by 1691 what became the first of many business disasters left him bankrupt and owing thousands of pounds. In 1701 he wrote a poem called *The True-Born Englishman*, which was a defence of the foreign-born King William. It proved to be enormously popular and quickly established itself as the best-selling poem of its day. It was so popular that years later Defoe would still sign himself as 'the true-born Englishman'. Over the next couple of years this popularity came to Defoe's aid because he wrote a pamphlet entitled *The Shortest Way with Dissenters*. It satirised the bloodthirsty attacks on Dissenters and sold well by those who took it seriously until they were disabused of the notion and had Defoe arrested as a result. He was put in the stocks, but, using his cachet as 'the true-born Englishman', he managed to turn the situation to his advantage by selling copies of an *Ode to the Stocks* which he had penned while in prison.

Lucky to escape with his life after joining a rebellion against King William, Daniel Defoe began his writing career by publishing a poem in defence of the foreign-born monarch. This became a bestseller and encouraged Defoe to turn to writing, from which point he composed some of the most influential novels in the English language, including *Robinson Crusoe* and *Moll Flanders*.

Defoe was also due to serve a prison sentence, but he wrote to his friend Robert Harley, the Tory minister for assistance. Harley secured his release and procured him a job on behalf of his party as a pamphleteer and spy. It was around this time (1695) that he changed his name from 'Foe' to 'Defoe'. This was just one of many pseudonyms that he adopted for his pamphlet writing career, including 'Eye Witness', 'Andrew Morton, Merchant' and 'Heliostropolis, Secretary to the Emperor of the Moon' (which he used on his political satire *The Consolidator, or Memoirs of Sundry Transactions from the World in the Moon* in 1705). Defoe's political tracts continued to create enemies and he was briefly jailed again, as well as being convicted for libel. Not the least of his problems was that he was seen as a political opportunist because he worked for both political parties. When the Tories lost office in 1714, he served the Whigs just as happily, and when they too were ousted, he worked for the Tories again.

In 1719, however, he published the work

for which he is most famous today – *Robinson Crusoe*. Based on the real-life adventures of Alexander Selkirk, its realistic narrative was immediately popular with the middle and lower classes. Indeed, this and the novels that followed it – including *Moll Flanders* in 1722 and *Roxana* in 1724 – gave a voice to sections of the population who were not normally represented in the more refined art of the time. Defoe continued to work at a prolific rate for the rest of his life, doing everything from collecting the tales of condemned men in prison to composing guide books and penning tales of the supernatural. He died in April 1731 at his lodgings in London.

Principal Works

1700	*The True-Born Englishman*
1702	*The Shortest Way with Dissenters*
1719	*Robinson Crusoe*
1722	*Moll Flanders*
1722	*A Journal of the Plague Year*
1725	*Roxana*

DE QUINCEY, THOMAS (1785–1859)

If once a man indulges himself in murder, very soon he comes to think little of robbing; and from robbing he comes next to drinking and Sabbath-breaking, and from that to incivility and procrastination.

'Murder Considered As One of the Fine Arts'

Thomas Quincey was born on 15 August 1785 in Manchester, England. His father, also called Thomas Quincey, was a prosperous textiles importer who died in 1793, following the death of two of his daughters. Elizabeth Penson, De Quincey's mother, then moved the family to Bath where, in 1796, she added the French preposition 'De' to the surname of 'Quincey'. De Quincey then attended Bath Grammar School, Winkfield School, and, finally, Manchester Grammar School. After two years at the Grammar School, De Quincey ran away, first to North Wales and then to London, where he eventually spent five months wandering the streets and taking charity where he could get it.

In 1803 De Quincey was reconciled with his mother and his guardians and began to attend Worcester College at the University of Oxford. It was also at this time that he began to correspond with WILLIAM WORDSWORTH, having admired his work since he first read it as a boy. The following year De Quincey began the occasional use of opium that would eventually become an addiction. His years at college, like his years at school, were characterised by his precocious abilities as a scholar. He was literate in Greek and Latin from a very early age, but at the same time he was not particularly practical and did not always cope with real-life situations in the most pragmatic fashion. An example of this came at the end of his studies at Oxford, in 1808, when he abandoned his degree because he felt unable to face an oral examination.

> Notoriously impractical, De Quincey squandered his inheritance through a mixture of generosity and drug addiction. He eventually made some money by telling the story of his dissolute life in *Confessions of an English Opium Eater*, one of the seminal tracts of British Romanticism.

Having by this time come into his majority and therefore his inheritance too, De Quincey moved to Grasmere in the Lake District to be closer to his friends, the Wordsworths. De Quincey's friendship with the poet did not last though. After suffering a series of illnesses in 1812–13, De Quincey, like his friend SAMUEL TAYLOR COLERIDGE, became addicted to laudanum, an opium-based painkiller. While this strained relations with Wordsworth, the birth of De Quincey's first son in 1816 to the unmarried Margaret Simpson, a local farmer's daughter, completely destroyed the friendship. As events transpired, De Quincey married Simpson the following year and they went on to have eight children together.

Having spent his inheritance (De Quincey was always too generous and once made Coleridge an anonymous donation of £300), and having taken on ever-growing family responsibilities, De Quincey turned to writing to try and earn more money. He became editor of the *Westmoreland Gazette* in 1818, as well

as writing various articles and reviews for other magazines, before, in 1821, CONFESSIONS OF AN ENGLISH OPIUM EATER was published, first in serial form in *London Magazine* and then in book form. This work, together with several other articles written by De Quincey, established the unconscious and its various dream worlds as fertile terrain for both science and literature. It proved a big success, although De Quincey did not initially make much money from it.

Indeed, for the rest of his life, De Quincey was constantly trying to beat deadlines and evade creditors. He moved to Edinburgh in order to write articles for *Blackwood's Edinburgh Magazine*, including 'On Murder Considered as One of the Fine Arts'. But even with their assistance, De Quincey was prosecuted for debt on numerous occasions. It was only after his mother died and bequeathed him a small legacy that De Quincey finally paid off his debts. In the last years of his life he edited a collected edition of his writing, which ran to many volumes, and which included an expanded version of *Confessions of an English Opium Eater*. De Quincey died on 8 December 1859 in Edinburgh.

Principal Work

1821–56   CONFESSIONS OF AN ENGLISH OPIUM EATER

DICKENS, CHARLES (1812–70)

Dignity, and even holiness too, sometimes, are more questions of coat and waistcoat than some people imagine.

Oliver Twist

Charles Dickens was born on 7 February 1812 in the naval town of Plymouth, England. He was the second of eight children born to Elizabeth Barrow and John Dickens, a clerk in the Navy Pay Office. Neither of Dickens's parents was very proficient with the household money and in 1824 John Dickens was imprisoned in Marshalsea Prison for being unable to repay his debts. As was normal at the time, the rest of the family went to live with Dickens's father in prison, all except Dickens himself who was put to work in Warren's shoe blacking factory where he pasted labels onto jars.

This was a singular moment in Dickens's life, fuelling him with ambition at the same time as it left him quite bitter. When Dickens's father was released from prison, he decided to remove his son from the factory and put him back into school. Dickens's mother, however, wanted to keep Dickens in what he considered to be the lonely hell of the factory, for which he never quite forgave her.

From 1824–27, Dickens attended Wellington House Academy where he studied a variety of subjects, from Latin to dance. After he left the Academy he spent 18 months as a clerk in a law office before deciding that he wanted to be a reporter. Dickens then set about learning shorthand with the intensity and dedication that would characterise his entire writing career. Within a remarkably short space of time, Dickens mastered the barbaric shorthand system then in vogue and had put it to use, first as a court reporter, and then as a recorder of debates in the House of Commons. He quickly gained a reputation as being the quickest and most accurate of shorthand reporters, and he began to contribute to newspapers on a regular basis.

In 1834, having contributed a number of sketches for publication already, Dickens adopted the pseudonym 'Boz' for his fictional work. These were popular with the public and he published his first and second collection of sketches in 1836. In the same year, Dickens also started writing *The Pickwick Papers*. The commission for the instalments that made up *The Pickwick Papers* was given to Dickens by chance, but he made the most of it and by the time the serialisation finished in 1837, Dickens was one of the most popular writers in Britain. Over the course of the next 40 years Dickens would become the most popular novelist in both Britain and America, writing such classics as *Oliver Twist*, *David Copperfield*, *A Christmas Carol*, *Bleak House*, *Hard Times*, *A Tale of Two Cities* and *Great Expectations*. Perhaps the apogee of Dickens's popularity came with the death of Little Nell in *The Old Curiosity Shop* in 1841. Half of the English-speaking world, it seemed to Dickens, implored him not to kill her in the final instalment. Crowds gathered at the New York docks to greet a ship from England in order to find out if she did die. The Irish politician Daniel O'Connell burst into tears when he discovered Nell's fate and threw his copy out of the window, while the Scottish historian Thomas Carlyle all but went into mourning.

> Sent to work in a blacking factory as a child because his father was imprisoned as a bankrupt, Dickens was both bitter towards his parents and fuelled with ambition ever after. His prolific output helped him to become the most popular novelist in the English-speaking world, creating a body of work comparable in breadth only to the Shakespearean canon.

While Dickens's public life was an unqualified success, his personal life was much less happy. He married Catherine Hogarth in 1836 and went on to have ten children with her. However, records suggest that he not only preferred her sister (who died in 1837), but that he very soon found Catherine herself dull and unsympathetic. They separated in 1858 and Dickens developed a close relationship with the actress Ellen Ternan in the latter part of his life. In the meantime, Dickens also had to help tackle the financial difficulties of not only his parents and siblings, but also, in the end, his own children, several of whom he considered to be quite feckless. While dealing with all these problems and his own punishing writing schedule, Dickens also undertook a number of extensive reading tours, both in Britain and in America. These were phenomenally popular with the public as Dickens was a skilled actor, but they left him physically exhausted. He decided to finish reading in public in 1870 and died in the same year on 8 June, leaving behind him the incomplete manuscript of *The Mystery of Edwin Drood*. He was buried in Westminster Abbey.

Principal Works

1836–37	*The Pickwick Papers*
1837–39	*Oliver Twist*
1838–39	*Nicholas Nickleby*
1840–41	*The Old Curiosity Shop*
1841	*Barnaby Rudge*
1843	*A Christmas Carol*
1843–44	*Martin Chuzzlewit*
1846–48	*Dombey and Son*
1849–50	*David Copperfield*

1852–53	*BLEAK HOUSE*
1854	*HARD TIMES*
1855–57	*Little Dorrit*
1859	*A TALE OF TWO CITIES*
1860–61	*GREAT EXPECTATIONS*
1864–65	*Our Mutual Friend*

DICKINSON, EMILY (1830–86)

'Faith' is a fine invention.

No. 185

Emily Elizabeth Dickinson was born on 10 December 1830 in Amherst, Massachusetts. Her parents, Edward Dickinson and Emily Norcross, were orthodox Calvinists. Her father in particular was very active in the local community and was partly responsible for founding Amherst College as the Calvinist answer to Yale and Harvard. Emily herself was educated at Amherst College between the years 1840 and 1846. Following her graduation, she spent a year at Mount Holyoke Female Seminary, South Hadley.

Her time at the seminary was not her happiest. Even though it was only ten miles from her house, she was terribly homesick. This was to provide the template for the rest of Dickinson's life for, apart from her time in the seminary, she only ever lived in two houses. Most of her life she spent in her room and only very rarely did she leave Amherst at all, once visiting Washington with her father, who had become a senator, and occasionally going into Boston. She also started wearing all white at about this time, a habit she maintained for the rest of her life.

> Emily Dickinson spent much of her life locked in her own room, 'Soundless as dots – on a Disc of Snow'. This isolated life helped her to create a unique and startling form of poetry.

Her family seemed to have allowed Emily to develop as individually as she did. The main point of contention came between her and her father over the matter of religion. Dickinson lived in a kind of fear of the damnation threatening her Calvinist soul, but eventually, with some encouragement from her more liberal friends, she came to her own, less hostile, view on these matters. On the whole though, the great dramas of Emily's life were mainly lived out in the literature she read. She particularly enjoyed female English writers, such as the BRONTË sisters, GEORGE ELIOT and Elizabeth Barrett Browning, and she became thoroughly intimate with the characters they created.

These literary influences led her to write her own poetry. She even attempted to get her poems published, but she was dissuaded following her rejection by the then editor of *Atlantic Monthly*, Thomas Wentworth Higginson. He went on to front a collection of her poems after her death. The only encouragement Dickinson received during her lifetime came from the lover of her brother, Mabel Loomis Todd, who was then married to the director of Amherst College. Although the two never met, Dickinson's mother mediated between them before she died, and Todd came to appreciate her poetry, so much so that she began to transcribe Dickinson's poems. Without Todd, the world would probably never have known Dickinson's great work. Dickinson died of a stroke on 15 May 1886. Todd then set about getting Dickinson's poems published, which she managed in three volumes in 1890, 1891 and 1896. These formed the basis of what became the authoritative collection of Dickinson's poetry, *THE COMPLETE POEMS OF EMILY DICKINSON*, edited by Thomas H. Johnson and published in 1960.

Principal Work

1960   *THE COMPLETE POEMS OF EMILY DICKINSON*

DONNE, JOHN (1572–1631)

No man is an island.

Devotions Upon Emergent Occasions

John Donne was born in London in 1572, the same year as BEN JONSON and only eight years after WILLIAM SHAKESPEARE and CHRISTOPHER MARLOWE. His father, also called John Donne, was a leading ironmonger, who died suddenly in 1576, leaving Donne to be raised by his mother, Elizabeth Heywood. She was a relative of the Catholic martyr Sir Thomas

More and Donne too was brought up in the Catholic faith. At that time Catholics were subject to severe penalties if they failed to take the sacrament of the Established Church and Catholic priests were still hung, drawn and quartered.

More pertinently for Donne, Catholics were prohibited by law from taking degrees or practising law or holding public office. Thus although Donne went to the University of Oxford when he was just 11 years old, and then, three years later, he spent another three years at the University of Cambridge, at neither place of learning was he allowed to graduate. This is because he refused to take the Oath of Supremacy, the declaration of the monarch's supremacy over the church. This was the same oath that More had refused to swear and which had led to his execution by Henry VIII. Equally, when Donne was admitted to Thavies Inn in 1591 and to Lincoln's Inn in 1592 to study law, he was not able to pursue a career at the Bar.

The terrible dangers of being a Catholic were brought home to Donne when his brother was arrested for harbouring a priest. The priest was hung, drawn and quartered and Donne's brother died in Newgate Prison of the plague. This led Donne to question the validity of his faith and some time in the mid-1590s he abandoned Catholicism and converted to the Church of England. As Donne's process of conversion was underway, he came into his inheritance, and this allowed him to pursue his interests in travelling, women and literature. Donne's first well-known compositions, the *Satires*, were written around this period and, although not published, were passed around in Donne's social circles.

In 1596 Donne joined the service of Robert Devereux, the Earl of Essex, and sailed with him against the Spanish at Cadiz. The following year he sailed under Essex again on a expedition to the Azores. These adventures were recorded in Donne's two poems on sealife, *The Calm* and *The Storm*. When he returned to England in 1598, Donne was appointed private secretary to Sir Thomas Egerton, Keeper of the Great Seal. This position seemed to promise much, but in 1601 Donne secretly married Egerton's niece, 17-year-old Ann More, daughter of Sir George More, the Lieutenant of the Tower of London. Despite Donne's attempt to write placatory letters, when news of the marriage reached Egerton and More's influential father, Donne was sacked from his post and imprisoned for several weeks along with two of his friends who had assisted at the marriage. Donne later summarised the experience: 'John Donne, Ann Donne, Undone'.

For the following decade or so, Donne struggled to support his ever-expanding family by working as a lawyer. He had 12 children with Ann, causing him to remark that he did not know whether it was worse that a child died and he would have one less mouth to feed, or that the child's death should cause him to incur funeral expenses. With the help of several friends, in 1609 a reconciliation was effected between Donne's wife and her father, who went on to pay Ann's dowry. Donne was able to augment this money by helping to write anti-Catholic pamphlets around this time, and in 1610 he even won the support of King James I by claiming in *Pseudo-Martyr* that Catholics could and should take the Oath of Allegiance. He also won the patronage of Sir Robert Drury who supported the publication of *An Anatomy of the World* in 1611 and *Of the Progress of the Soul* in 1612, both of which marked the anniversary of the death of Drury's 15-year-old daughter.

> Having earlier converted from Roman Catholicism, John Donne was pressured by King James into joining the Anglican ministry. Here he established himself as one of the leading orators of his day, bequeathing a legacy of sermons and poetry that was only fully appreciated when his cause was championed by T.S. Eliot at the beginning of the twentieth century.

After many years of encouragement from King James, to the point where he denied him advancement by any other means, Donne entered the Anglican ministry in 1615. Later that year he was appointed Royal Chaplain, and in the following year he became Reader in Divinity at Lincoln's Inn. His sermons quickly earned him a reputation as one of the great preachers of the era. In 1617, however, Donne's material good fortune was undermined by the death of his wife. Although Donne gained further offices after this, he became obsessed with death. Before going to Germany in 1618 Donne penned the apprehensively titled *Hymn to Christ at the Author's Last Going into Germany*.

Donne was appointed Dean of Saint Paul's in 1621, a post he held until his own death. Weeks before he died, he had completed what was his own funeral sermon, *Death's Duel*. He even found the energy to pose for a statue of himself wrapped in a death shroud before finally succumbing on 31 March 1631. As well as leaving the statue behind him, Donne left a significant body of work. Much of this work fell into disrepute in the eighteenth century and it was only when the poet and critic T.S. Eliot reappraised his poetry that Donne's reputation was reinvigorated and his legacy to English letters was fully understood.

Principal Works

1595–1635	*Songs and Sonnets*
1590–1600	*Satires*
1611	*An Anatomy of the World*
1612	*Of the Progress of the Soul*
1609–18	*Holy Sonnets*
1623–24	*Devotions*

DOUGLASS, FREDERICK (1818–95)

If there is no struggle there is no progress. Those who profess to favour freedom and yet deprecate agitation, are men who want crops without ploughing up the ground, they want rain without thunder and lightning.

'West India Emancipation'

Frederick Augustus Washington Bailey was born in February 1818 at Holme Hill Farm in Talbot County, Maryland. The exact date of Douglass's birth is unknown because he was a slave and so not permitted to inquire into the specifics of his own origins. His mother was Harriet Bailey, also a slave, and his father was a white man, most likely his owner, Aaron Anthony. As was the practice of slavery, Douglass was separated from his mother at an early age and was initially raised by his grandparents. From the age of 6 to 8 Douglass worked on Anthony's plantation before being sent to work as a house servant with Anthony's daughter and son-in-law, Sophia and Hugh Auld. Sophia set about teaching Douglass to read but when Hugh Auld discovered this, he immediately put a stop to the lessons because it was illegal to teach slaves to read and write.

Born into slavery, Douglass only managed to escape when he was a young man. Following this he became a powerful orator for the abolitionist cause, fighting on the side of the Union in the American Civil War and working tirelessly to secure equality for all. He was, according to the poet Robert Earl Hayden, a man 'superb in love and logic'.

Rightly surmising that there must be a good reason for this, Douglass continued to teach himself to read and write and became inspired by speeches denouncing oppression which he read in the *Columbian Orator*. In 1833, after seven years of working for Hugh Auld, he was sent to work as a field hand for his brother, Thomas Auld. During the year that followed, Douglass experienced some of the worst conditions pertaining to slavery and he became known for his rebellious behaviour. In order to stop this, Thomas sent Douglass to Thomas Covey, a man who gloried in his reputation for 'breaking' slaves. Douglass gradually crumbled under the inhumane treatment he received at the hands of Covey until, one day, the two of them became involved in hand-to-hand combat. The fight ended in a draw but Douglass felt he had retrieved his self-respect. Following this, Douglass made an abortive escape attempt but was returned to the Aulds. Back in Baltimore, Douglass learnt the caulking trade which enabled him to raise enough money to make a feasible escape plan. On the same day as he became engaged to his future wife, Anna Murray, Douglass disguised himself as a sailor, borrowed a free black man's papers and got on the train for New York. His escape complete, Douglass changed his name, borrowing from

WALTER SCOTT's 'Lady of the Lake', and married Anna two weeks later on 15 September 1838.

Douglass and Anna moved to New Bedford where, although life was less punishing, it was by no means easy, and Douglass had a hard time making ends meet. Continuing his interest in the cause of anti-slavery, Douglass began subscribing to William Lloyd Garrison's abolitionist paper *Liberator*. Inspired by this, Douglass made his first public speech in 1841 and was soon a colleague of Garrison, writing and lecturing for the abolitionist cause. In 1845 Douglass published his first book, NARRATIVE OF THE LIFE OF FREDERICK DOUGLASS, AN AMERICAN SLAVE, which proved to be a tremendous success. Douglass followed it up with revised and expanded versions of his autobiography *My Bondage and My Freedom* (1855) and *The Life and Times of Frederick Douglass* (1881).

Following his break with Garrison and his lecture tour to England, Douglass welcomed the onset of the Civil War in 1861 as a crusade against slavery. He worked tirelessly for the Union cause, campaigning for the rights of free black men to fight for it, and then recruiting men to do so, including two of the sons he had from five children with Anna. He was not afraid either to demand of President Lincoln that his men be given equal pay and conditions. After the war Douglass campaigned for the Fifteenth Amendment, which guaranteed suffrage to the newly emancipated male slaves. In 1877 he was appointed a US marshal, and then recorder of deeds for the District of Columbia. Anna died in 1882 and in 1884 Douglass continued to break boundaries when he married his second wife, Helen Pitts, his white secretary. Following this controversial action, Douglass was appointed American Consul-General to Haiti, a post he held until he resigned in 1891. He died on 20 February 1895, leaving behind him an inspirational legacy for the generations of black leaders that followed.

Principal Works

DREISER, THEODORE (1871–1945)

The 'first law' (in so far as humanity is concerned) is self-preservation . . . only the fit, or those favoured by accident or chance, regardless of moral or inherent worth, can or do survive.

A Selection of Uncollected Prose

Theodore Herman Albert Dreiser was born on 17 August 1871 in Terre Haute, Indiana. He was one of the youngest of a large and very poor family, born to a German immigrant father whose attempts to set up his own business ended in disaster. The family drifted from one place to another and as a consequence Dreiser received very little formal education. He appears to have been an unhappy child, as indeed were many of his siblings, many of whom drifted into various dissolute lifestyles. The exception to this was Dreiser's brother Paul, who changed his name to Dresser and became a popular songwriter of some note.

Dreiser left home when he was 16, undertaking a variety of menial jobs until one of his former teachers helped him to enrol at Indiana University. Dreiser was already a voracious reader, despite his poor education, but after a year at Indiana he left. In 1892 he managed to secure employment writing for the *Chicago Globe* newspaper, then moved onto the *St Louis Globe-Democrat*, all the while honing his writing skills. In 1898 Dreiser married Sara White, a Missouri schoolteacher. However, marriage proved to be a restrictive institution for the sexually promiscuous Dreiser, and the couple separated some years later.

In 1900 Dreiser published his first and most famous novel, SISTER CARRIE. This was a groundbreaking work at the time, not only for its subject matter, which was socially transgressive, but also for its style, which was brutal, unforgiving and would influence writers for years to come. The publisher of the book, Frank Doubleday, had a change of heart following its publication and did nothing to promote it. Dreiser did what he could to distribute the book but it was not until its reissue in 1907 that *Sister Carrie* became well known.

Following the first release of the book, however, Dreiser suffered a breakdown and only recovered with the help of his brother Paul.

Dreiser then began to forge what proved to be a successful career in publishing, finally becoming the editorial director of Butterick. He resigned from this post in 1910, following an internal scandal, and turned his attention to writing what turned out to be his breakthrough novel, *Jennie Gerhardt*. This was published in 1911 and enabled Dreiser to become a full-time writer. Dreiser then completed a trilogy of novels about an unscrupulous businessman – *The Financier* (1912), *The Titan* (1914), and *The Stoic* (published posthumously in 1947). Dreiser's most commercially successful novel was *An American Tragedy* (1925), but it, like several other of Dreiser's works, was subject to censorship and even suppression in some states.

According to the critic H.L. Mencken, Dreiser had 'a sure talent for depicting the spirit in disintegration', a talent he used to overcome his lack of formal education and write his groundbreaking novel *Sister Carrie*. This controversial work set the tone for the rest of his life and Dreiser, as well as his work, was ever after subject to censorship.

As Dreiser grew older, it was not just his books but he himself who was censored by his own society. In the 1920s Dreiser visited the Soviet Union and published his thoughts on the Communist experiment in *Dreiser Looks at Russia* in 1928. This led him to becoming a security concern for the authorities, a status that only increased when he declared his sympathy for the socialist cause in the Spanish Civil War. In 1942 Dreiser married his cousin Helen Richardson, but he died in Hollywood just three years later, on 28 December 1945.

Principal Works

1900   *Sister Carrie*
1911   *Jennie Gerhardt*
1925   *An American Tragedy*

DRYDEN, JOHN (1631–1700)

How easy is it to call rogue and villain, and that wittily! But how hard to make a man appear a fool, a blockhead, or a knave without using any of those opprobrious terms!

A Discourse Concerning the Original and Progress of Satire

John Dryden was born on 9 August 1631 in Oldwinkle All Saints, Northamptonshire. Dryden's father, Erasmus Dryden, came from a wealthy family, but as a younger son he had inherited only a modest estate worth about £60 a year. John Dryden would go on to inherit the same debt-burdened estate himself, as well as many connections to powerful people held on both sides of his family, including one of the judges at the execution of Charles I. Dryden was, ironically, a King's Scholar at Westminster School when the King was beheaded. He was taught there by the strict disciplinarian Dr Busby and became well versed in the Greek and Roman classics, recalling in a footnote to one of the translations he produced as an established critic that he had undertaken the same task as a 'Thursday night exercise' when he was a schoolboy.

In 1650 Dryden joined Trinity College, Cambridge, as a Westminster Scholar. After a minor incident for which he was punished, Dryden graduated four years later. He did not go on to take an MA (although he was granted one by the Archbishop of Canterbury at the request of Charles II in 1668), but he did stay at Cambridge for another three years. Having inherited his father's estate, Dryden moved to London in 1657 or 1658 where he remained, more or less, until his death. In 1659, he published his first important work, *Heroic Stanzas*, a eulogy on the death of Oliver Cromwell. This work was typical of Dryden in that it was motivated by a public event as opposed to personal sentiment. Perhaps more than any other major poet or dramatist, Dryden is an impersonal writer, lacking the emotional venting that would make him popular in today's confessional age. In the light of this, it was not therefore particularly hypocritical of Dryden to celebrate the return of Charles II in two poems, having previously celebrated Cromwell in verse.

Dryden's celebrations of royalty, as well as his generally patriotic work, such as *Annus Mirabilis*, published in 1667, earned him the favour of the King who made him Poet Laureate in 1668. In 1670, Dryden was also appointed Historiographer Royal, and between the two posts he earned more than three times as much as his father's estate afforded him. This estate had supplemented the resources he had accrued by his marriage to the socially superior Lady Elizabeth Howard in 1663. Dryden augmented this income by writing plays for the theatres newly licensed by Charles II. Like his contemporary, APHRA BEHN, Dryden had to write for the audience of courtiers who watched the plays and so they were generally light dramas based on wit rather than tragic emotion.

John Dryden was one of the few who were masters of more than one form of literature. Equally adept in verse, prose or dialogue, Dryden set the standards for men of letters for much of the next century.

In 1681 Dryden published *Absalom and Achitophel* and in 1682 he followed it up with the previously privately circulated MAC FLECKNOE, his two masterpieces of satire. These two works saw Dryden develop the heroic couplet, the two lines of rhyming verse, which would go on to dominate the world of satiric poetry for the following century, especially in the work of ALEXANDER POPE.

Dryden and his two sons converted to Catholicism in 1686. At the time Dryden was once again accused of opportunism as the throne had just been taken by James II, a Catholic. However, when James was forced to step down following a Parliamentary revolt in 1688, Dryden stuck to his faith even though it meant the loss of all his government posts under the new Protestant regime of William and Mary. Despite his advancing age, Dryden turned with renewed vigour to writing, this time translating the classics of Juvenal, Persius and Ovid into English so that many more could enjoy them who had not had the benefit of his education. Shortly after finishing a collection of translations, *Fables Ancient and Modern*, Dryden died on 30 April 1700 and was buried in Westminster Abbey.

Principal Works

1681	*Absalom and Achitophel*
1682	MAC FLECKNOE

ELIOT, GEORGE (1819–80)

The happiest women, like the happiest nations, have no history.
The Mill on the Floss

Photo credit: © Bettmann/CORBIS

Mary Anne Evans was born in Arbury, Warwickshire on 22 November 1819, the same year as HERMAN MELVILLE and WALT WHITMAN. She was the youngest of five children born to Robert Evans, the Warwickshire estate agent for the Earl of Lonsdale, and Christiana Pearson. Eliot was first educated at home and then at a series of boarding schools. In 1828 she attended Mrs Wallington's Boarding School at Nuneaton. There she came under the influence of Maria Lewis who did what she could to foster the development of the shy but extremely clever young Eliot; their friendship lasted long after Eliot had left the school. When she next went to Miss Franklin's School in Coventry, Eliot learned to disguise her thick Midlands accent, as well as becoming accomplished at more traditional subjects, such as French.

Eliot was forced to leave school when her mother died in early 1839. She assumed the role of her mother in the house as best she could, and her grateful father tried to compensate Eliot by gifting her Italian and German lessons, as well as the many books to which she became addicted. In 1841 Eliot's father retired from his post, handing it on to Eliot's brother Isaac. The two of them moved to Coventry where Eliot grew accustomed to a larger social circle. Part of this circle included a group of intellectuals studying the BIBLE. Eliot soon came to the conclusion that she could no longer believe in the Christian religion. This created a schism between her and her father until she agreed to a compromise whereby she attended to the rituals of church-going while not saying what she actually thought. Ironically, Eliot's first publication was a religious work. Printed in 1846, it was a translation from the German of David Friedrich Strauss's *Das Leben Jesu*, an influential tract which only brought Eliot prestige later when people found out who had translated it.

> When George Eliot published her first piece of fiction under her assumed name it was, apparently, only Charles Dickens who guessed that she was a woman. Eliot wrote some of the most accomplished novels ever published in the English language, maintaining her conviction throughout that 'men know best about everything, except what women know better'.

In 1849, when Eliot was 29, her father died. After nursing her father for the last years of his life, Eliot decided to embark on a tour of Europe. She returned in 1850 and moved to London where in 1851, following an unhappy involvement with the owner of the journal, she became an editor at *Westminster Review*. This position brought her into contact with many of London's leading intellectual figures, among them the critic George Henry Lewes. Lewes was a married man, but his marriage was something of a sham as his wife had frequently borne him the children of his friend. Nevertheless, when Lewes and Eliot began to live together as man and wife in 1854, Eliot knew she would be subjected to public and private censure. This censure emanated from many of her friends and even her own brother Isaac, who never spoke to her again. Eliot herself insisted upon being called 'Mrs Lewes', a title that EMILY DICKINSON, for one, was happy to concede.

In 1856 Eliot completed her first fiction, *Scenes from Clerical Life*. Lewes was impressed with what he read and sent it to his publisher under the pretence that the author was a male friend who wished to remain anonymous. Eliot chose the name 'George Eliot' because it included Lewes's first name and because 'Eliot' was easy to pronounce. It was serialised in *Blackwood's Magazine* in 1857 and apparently only CHARLES DICKENS guessed that it had been written by a woman. The tales proved to be very

popular and in 1859 she published her first novel, *Adam Bede*. This was so successful that it even gained the approval of Queen Victoria. Over the years that followed, Eliot wrote a series of some of the greatest novels in the English language, including THE MILL ON THE FLOSS (1860), SILAS MARNER (1861) and MIDDLEMARCH (1872).

These novels made her a very wealthy woman and even went some way to reconciling her with a public that otherwise disapproved of her lifestyle. Her way of life came to an abrupt end though in late 1878 when Lewes died. Eliot was desolate and refused to leave her room for a week. Over the course of the next year she was helped by her business manager John Cross to return to a normal life. They became closer, despite the fact that she was 20 years older than he. After several proposals, Eliot agreed to marry Cross in 1880. However, the following year, she fell ill with what the doctor diagnosed as laryngitis. It turned out to be a kidney complaint and she died on 22 December 1880 and was buried next to Lewes in Highgate Cemetery.

Principal Works

1859	*Adam Bede*
1860	THE MILL ON THE FLOSS
1861	SILAS MARNER
1871–72	MIDDLEMARCH
1876	*Daniel Deronda*

EMERSON, RALPH WALDO (1803–82)

What is life but the angle of vision? A man is measured by the angle at which he looks at objects.
Natural History of Intellect

Ralph Waldo Emerson was born on 25 May 1803 in Boston, Massachusetts. He was the second of five surviving boys born to William Emerson, a Unitarian minister, and Ruth Haskins. In 1811, when Emerson was just 11, his father died, which left the family in a very poor state financially. In order to procure enough funds to send her sons to Harvard, Emerson's mother worked in a series of boarding houses. However, even then there was barely enough to go round so they were encouraged by his aunt Mary Moody Emerson, who was probably the biggest influence on the young Emerson, to consider their experience of poverty as spiritually enriching. It is perhaps this optimistic outlook which was later to emerge in Emerson's writings.

After attending the Boston Public Latin School, Emerson went to Harvard in 1817. He was not an outstanding student but he was industrious and, despite his hardships, he managed to graduate in 1821. At this point Emerson became a teacher, but because of his inability to impose any discipline upon his students he proved to be, in his own description, 'a hopeless schoolmaster'. While doing this, Emerson pursued his interest in religion and continued to study at the Harvard Divinity School. Although he developed an eye disease which forced him to drop out, he still managed to be ordained as a minister in the Second Church in Boston in 1829.

> Ralph Waldo Emerson spent much of his life trying to foster an American philosophical tradition. Establishing himself at the centre of the cultural hub of Concord, Massachusetts, Emerson became famous as the founder of the Transcendentalist movement.

In the same year, Emerson married Ellen Tucker, a young woman from New Hampshire. However, the disease that had killed two of Emerson's brothers now struck his new bride and within 16 months she was dead from tuberculosis. The following year Emerson resigned from the Second Church for doctrinal reasons. He then took himself off to Europe for a couple of years. While there he met, among others, SAMUEL COLERIDGE, WILLIAM WORDSWORTH and his lifelong friend Thomas Carlyle. Upon his return in 1834, Emerson moved to Concord, Massachusetts where he started to receive the monies from his wife's legacy that meant he would never have to work again. The following year he married Lydia Jackson from Portsmouth, whom he called 'Lidian', and with whom he would have four children.

In 1836 Emerson published his most famous book, NATURE. It was originally published anonymously but most people around Boston seemed to know who had written it for it launched the Transcendentalist movement for which Emerson became famous. Transcendentalism was basically a form of idealism which valued the creative capabilities of the mind. Unsurprisingly, many thinkers and artists were drawn to this movement and Emerson's house became a centre of creativity. Among others, HENRY THOREAU all but lived there.

Nature was not a big seller, but it eventually became very influential and this allowed Emerson to pursue a lecturing career from which he garnered more immediate plaudits. Some of his most notable speeches included his address to the Phi Beta Kappa Society at Harvard in 1837, which Oliver Wendell Holmes described as 'the American Intellectual Declaration of Independence'. In 1841 Emerson published a collection of essays, which he followed up with another collection in 1842. This established the pattern for the rest of his life in which he continued to tour America and Europe, as well as Egypt, giving lectures and writing the occasional essay. His reputation grew throughout his life, so that even though his later writings were not as original as his earlier ones, they were better received. He died of pneumonia on 27 April 1882 in his beloved Concord.

Principal Works

1836   NATURE
1841   *Essays*
1844   *Essays: Second Series*

Henry Fielding was born on 22 April 1707 in Sharpham Park, Somerset. He was the eldest of seven children born to Edmund Fielding, an army officer, and to Sarah Gould. Although of aristocratic descent, Fielding's father was profligate with money, a family tradition that Fielding would do his best to uphold throughout his life.

When Fielding was 11 his mother died and, the following year, his father remarried. Fielding was sent to Eton at this time where he proved himself to be an admirable student of both Latin and Greek, as well as fighting. When he left Eton in 1724 he moved to London. With encouragement from his cousin Lady Mary Wortley Montagu, Fielding started writing plays. After meeting with some initial success, Fielding began to study at Leiden University in Holland.

> Always poor at managing his finances ('enough is equal to a feast,' he once wrote), Henry Fielding turned to playwriting to relieve his debts. He began his career as a playwright with the hugely popular *Tom Thumb*. His success was cut short when he was effectively banned by the government from writing plays, and he turned instead to an equally popular career as a novelist.

However, after only a year of study, Fielding returned to London in 1729 burdened with more debt. He began to write plays again and quickly found fame as a successful dramatist. His most popular play was *The Tragedy of Tom Thumb*, produced in 1730. When JONATHAN SWIFT saw the play, it was claimed that this was only the second time in his life that he had laughed. Fielding's success continued, up to, and including, the productions of *Pasquin* (1736) and *The Historical Register for the Year 1736* (1737). This latter play in particular lampooned the Prime Minster Sir Robert Walpole and his government. This annoyed Walpole so much that he introduced the Licensing Act in 1737, effectively ending Fielding's dramatic career.

Unable to pursue his theatrical writing, Fielding cast around for another career. The need for money had become imperative for Fielding because in 1734 he had married Charlotte Cradock with whom he had two children. Fielding therefore decided to study the law and in 1740 he was successfully called to the Bar. Although Fielding was eventually made a Justice of the Peace for Westminster in 1748, and for Middlesex in the following year, his ill health prevented him from pursuing his legal career with any consistency. He did, however, attempt with his brother to establish one of the first police services of its kind in London – the Bow Street Runners.

None of these projects brought him any great wealth so, in the meantime, he wrote his first proper prose work, *Shamela*. Published in 1741, *Shamela* was a response to Samuel Richardson's novel *Pamela*, published in the previous year. As the title suggests, it was a satirical riposte to Richardson's rather more solemn volume. In the following year, Fielding developed the idea of Shamela into a full-length novel, *Joseph Andrews*, which was greeted with great popular acclaim. In the same year, Fielding pursued his interest in the law into print when he rewrote the life of a notorious robber in *Jonathan Wild* – the same criminal about whom DANIEL DEFOE had also written. In 1744, Fielding's wife Charlotte died. Fielding was distraught at this, and he went on to use her as the model for Sophia Western in TOM JONES, and for the heroine of *Amelia*. In 1747 Fielding caused a minor scandal when he married Charlotte's maid, Mary Daniel.

In the years that followed, Fielding went on to have five children with his new wife. He also published his most popular work in 1749, *Tom Jones*. However, his health began to fail and he decided to seek out more clement weather and he set sail for Portugal. Fielding's account of this trip, *The Journal of a Voyage to Lisbon*, details the difficulties he experienced on the journey. These difficulties did little to ameliorate his various illnesses and, two months after his arrival, Fielding died on 8 October 1754.

Principal Works

1741   *Joseph Andrews*
1743   *Jonathan Wild*
1749   TOM JONES

> ## FRANKLIN, BENJAMIN (1706–90)
> *We must all hang together, or assuredly we shall all hang separately.*
>   'The Signing of the Declaration of Independence'

Benjamin Franklin was born on 17 January 1706 in Boston, Massachusetts. He was the youngest son in a family of ten born to Abiah Folger and Josiah Franklin, a soap and candle maker originating from Northamptonshire, England. Franklin left school at the age of 10 in order to work for his father. However, Franklin's interests lay elsewhere and he apprenticed himself instead to his brother James's printing shop in Boston. At the age of 17, Franklin ran away from home, ending up in Philadelphia, Pennsylvania. From there, he travelled to London in 1724 where he continued to study printing. Upon his return to Philadelphia two years later, he found that his old homeland was about to embark on a printing revolution.

> A noted entrepreneur, leading scientist and signatory to the Declaration of Independence, Benjamin Franklin is often called the 'First American'. Setting the tone for American politics, he proposed that 'where liberty is, there is my country.'

With a steady eye for a business opportunity which has ever after made him a hero to so many, Franklin established his own printing business in 1728. In the following year Franklin became the sole owner of the *Pennsylvania Gazette*. In 1730 he married Deborah Read and they went on to have two children together. In 1731, Franklin founded the first public library. The next year he published the first of the *Poor Richard's Almanacs*, those journals that dispensed advice on becoming wealthy and staying healthy, and which would become a national institution over the next 26 years.

In 1737 Franklin's own business skills earned him the position of Postmaster of Philadelphia. Five years later, Franklin put forward a proposal for what turned into the University of Philadelphia. Franklin would continue a course of learning throughout the rest of his life, particularly in the field of the sciences where he contributed to the building of knowledge about electricity, amongst other things. Indeed, when Franklin retired from business in 1748, he set about writing up his own theories and experiments on electricity in a book that was published in London in 1751. The following year, Franklin set up America's first fire insurance company.

Franklin spent most of the rest of his life applying his entrepreneurial savvy and pioneering acumen to the world of politics. In 1757 he served as an ambassador for the Pennsylvania Assembly to Britain, a post he held for five years. When he returned home in 1762 he had become alienated from Britain and articulated a resentment against being a colony that was shared by many others. A period of further diplomacy followed over the next few years and when he returned to Philadelphia in 1775 he was duly elected as a representative to the Second Continental Congress. In this role he signed the Declaration of Independence drafted by Thomas Jefferson in 1776. In the same year he sailed to France where he negotiated a treaty of alliance and became Minister for France. He stayed in Paris until he was able to help negotiate a peace with Britain in 1782. Further negotiations with other European powers filled the next few years, as did his witnessing the Montgolfier brothers becoming the first men to fly in 1783. He returned to Philadelphia in 1785 and died five years later on 17 April 1790. Franklin's legacy to the world was immediate and practical, but he had also left behind him an autobiography which, although not fully printed until 1868, helped to create and convey something of the spirit of the country he helped to make free.

Principal Work

1791–1868   *The Autobiography of Benjamin Franklin*

GOLDSMITH, OLIVER (1730–74)

Princes and lords may flourish, or may fade;

A breath can make them, as a breath has made;

But a bold peasantry, their country's pride,

When once destroyed, can never be supplied.

The Deserted Village

Oliver Goldsmith was probably born on 10 November 1730, in the small Irish village of Pallas, County Longford. His father was a clergyman in the Church of England, as wealthy in good humour as he was poor in money, both attributes that Goldsmith would inherit. When he was still quite young, Goldsmith suffered an attack of smallpox. This left him very badly scarred and, as he freely admitted, he grew up to present an ungracious figure with an ugly face. On top of these problems, Goldsmith developed a feckless personality, doing little to augment his natural talents with any that he might earn by industry. He was educated at Edgeworthstown School, and then he went to Trinity College, Dublin. Like EDMUND SPENSER and ANDREW MARVELL before him, Goldsmith had to pay for his education by working as a 'sizar', performing jobs for wealthier undergraduates.

Oliver Goldsmith was initially shunned both for his ugliness and his poverty, claiming that 'an ugly man and a poor man is society only for himself, and such society the world lets me enjoy in great abundance.' Nevertheless he eventually found popularity with his plays, poems and novels.

Despite several mishaps along the way, Goldsmith finally graduated in 1749. He then decided to study medicine at Edinburgh University, but he failed to settle to his task and, after trying his hand at a few other things, he set off for Europe. This was not the traditional Grand Tour undertaken by the wealthy. As Goldsmith was so poor he travelled around Holland, France, and Italy frequently by foot, paying his way by playing the flute. When he returned to London, Goldsmith had somehow acquired a degree as a doctor. However dubious this qualification was, for the next few months Goldsmith practised medicine on anyone who was willing to pay him. As it turned out, very few people were willing to pay for his services as a physician and, although Goldsmith hoped that he might work in medicine in India, he only really practised on one patient again – himself. In the meantime, Goldsmith was forced to take up a position as a school master. He despised this job and eventually wound up as an assistant editor at the *Monthly Review*.

This position proved to be the making of Goldsmith for here at last was something for which he was suited and which he actually seemed to enjoy, if only fitfully. It led him, in 1759, to publish an *Inquiry into the Present State of Polite Learning in Europe*. Not only did this begin to make Goldsmith some money, but it also drew him into the sphere of influence of SAMUEL

JOHNSON, the leading literary personage of the time. Johnson was not altogether impressed by Goldsmith, but one day in 1762, when he found Goldsmith being arrested by his landlady for yet another debt, Johnson arranged to sell the manuscript of the novel THE VICAR OF WAKEFIELD on Goldsmith's behalf. He received 60 guineas for it, but it remained unpublished until 1766 and, even then, it was poorly received.

Goldsmith continued to be in debt for the rest of his life despite the tremendous wealth he earned for his literary work. His plays, in particular, were very popular, deflating the commonly espoused sentimentality of the period with a robust humour. Two of his best dramas were *The Good-Natured Man*, produced in 1768, and *She Stoops to Conquer*, produced in 1773. As well as writing a novel and plays, Goldsmith also wrote poetry, most notably *The Deserted Village* in 1770, of which Johnson is said to have written the last four lines. In between these more artistic works, Goldsmith continued with his hack work, writing on a variety of subjects of which he knew little for a quickly developing reading public. Sadly, he did not know enough about medicine, for when he fell ill in 1774 he decided to treat himself rather than consult a qualified doctor and he died on 4 April.

Principal Works

1766   *THE VICAR OF WAKEFIELD*
1768   *The Good-Natured Man*
1770   *The Deserted Village*
1773   *She Stoops to Conquer*

HARDY, THOMAS (1840–1928)

Poetry is emotion put into measure. The emotion must come by nature, but the measure can be acquired by art.

The Later Years of Thomas Hardy

Thomas Hardy was born on 2 June 1840 in Higher Bockhampton, Dorchester. His father, also called Thomas, was a master stonemason, as had been his father before him. His mother, Jemima, had been a domestic servant. He had three siblings: a brother who inherited his father's stonemasonry business, and two sisters who trained as school teachers. Hardy developed his love of reading from his mother, while his interest in music, which led to his playing the violin at the age of 9, he inherited from his father, who was leader of the local church musicians. With these influences at home, Hardy did not attend school until he was 8 years old. After a short period, Hardy outgrew the local village school and he began to attend one in Dorchester, where he studied French and Latin.

At the age of 16, Hardy was apprenticed to a local architect, John Hicks. Hardy worked with him for six years, but during this time he also continued his education in other areas, including studying the Greek dramatists with Horace Moule, a vicar's son who would later commit suicide. In 1861 Hardy went to London to continue his training and to practise architecture with Arthur Blomfield. Hardy enjoyed the social and cultural opportunities afforded him in London but after five years, and with deteriorating health, Hardy returned to Dorset. There he resumed working with Hicks, while at the same time writing his first novel, *The Poor Man and the Lady*. Although this was rejected, he was encouraged to write another novel, *Desperate Remedies*, which was published anonymously in 1871. Hardy followed that up in 1872 with *Under the Greenwood Tree*. This proved to be such a success that Hardy felt able to give up his architectural work and devote himself to writing full time.

In 1874, Hardy published one of his most famous novels, *Far from the Madding Crowd*, and in the same year he married Emma Lavinia Gifford, the sister-in-law of a vicar for whom he had previously undertaken some architectural work. Despite suffering sporadic ill-health over the next few years, Hardy moved from one location to another but continued to produce five more novels, including *The Return of the Native*. In 1883, Hardy supervised the construction of Max Gate, his own house on the outskirts of Dorchester. In between trips to London, where he was now an important literary figure, Hardy also wrote *The Mayor of Casterbridge* in 1886, and *The Woodlanders*, his personal favourite, in 1887.

After the benign reception of his earlier novels, Hardy was unprepared for the minor moral furore that greeted the publication of *Tess of the D'Urbervilles* in 1891. However, even that was incomparable with the outrage generated by what turned out to be Hardy's last novel, published in 1896, *Jude the Obscure*. The novel was read in brown paper covers by those who dared to buy it, although the Bishop of Wakefield is said to have burned his copy for what he, and others, saw as its attack on the sanctity of marriage. Hardy's own marriage suffered from its publication because Emma deemed that the novel was in some way autobiographical.

> Originally destined to become an architect, Hardy was able to dedicate himself to writing when his early novels proved successful. However, the publication of *Jude the Obscure* caused such an uproar that he abandoned novel writing altogether and turned to composing poetry instead.

After this, Hardy decided to devote his life to writing poetry, the art form that he had in any case always preferred to novels. The year 1898 saw the publication of his first volume of poetry, *Wessex Poems*, followed by *Poems of the Past and the Present* in 1902, and with his most ambitious project, *The Dynasts*, between the years 1903 to 1908. Some of his most poignant poems, however, were published in 1914 in the collection *Satires of Circumstance*. Many of the poems in this volume were written in the wake of Emma's death in 1912 and record Hardy's deep remorse at his treatment of her. In 1914, Hardy married Florence Dugdale, who had been his secretary since 1912. Throughout the following years Hardy was awarded many honours and honorary degrees and was granted the freedom of Dorchester in 1910. When he died on 11 January 1928, Hardy's ashes were buried in Poets' Corner in Westminster Abbey, while his heart was buried in the grave of his first wife.

Principal Works

1874	*Far from the Madding Crowd*
1878	*The Return of the Native*
1886	*The Mayor of Casterbridge*

1891	*TESS OF THE D'URBERVILLES*
1896	*JUDE THE OBSCURE*
1902	*POEMS OF THE PAST AND THE PRESENT*
1903–08	*The Dynasts*
1914	*Satires of Circumstance*

HAWTHORNE, NATHANIEL (1804–64)

The world owes all its onward impulses to men ill at ease. The happy man inevitably confines himself within ancient limits.

The House of the Seven Gables

Nathaniel Hawthorne was born on 4 July 1804 in Salem, Massachusetts to descendants of Puritan immigrants. One of his ancestors had been a judge at the famous Salem witchcraft trials. Hawthorne's father was a sea captain who died in Surinam in 1808 when Hawthorne was just 4 years old. His mother became very protective of Hawthorne after that and he led a rather isolated kind of life as a child, apart from three years he spent at Sebago Lake, Maine, where he was allowed a greater amount of freedom. For the rest of his life, however, Hawthorne insisted he was shy in company.

Determined to be a writer from a young age, Hawthorne was disappointed by the moderate success of his early work. It was only when he reached middle age that he achieved both the critical acclaim and the commercial success that he had long coveted.

In 1821 Hawthorne went to Bowdoin College in Maine. There he was classmates with Franklin Pierce, the future president, and Henry Wadsworth Longfellow, the future writer. After graduating from Bowdoin four years later, Hawthorne set about establishing himself as a writer. He claims that during this period he became a virtual hermit living in an upstairs room, and although this is not true, it does reveal something of the man who would have such a 'fact' known about himself. In 1828 Hawthorne published his first novel, *Fanshawe*. As this was printed at his own expense, it was not too difficult for him then to suppress it when he suddenly determined that it was a poor effort.

After the disappointment of his first novel, Hawthorne moved on to writing short stories. Many of these were published, but often anonymously and often after they had been radically altered by editors. Hawthorne's first collection of short stories to be published under his name was *Twice-Told Tales* in 1837. This collection was a moderate success both in the United States and abroad, but it also brought the realisation to Hawthorne that he was not going to earn much money out of writing and that he should look for a job. The need for employment became more pressing when, in 1838, he got engaged to Sophia Peabody, the sister of the educational reformer Elizabeth Peabody. In 1839 he began working at Boston Custom House as a salt and coal measurer. In 1842 he married Sophia and the couple went on to have three children. They moved into a new home in Concord, living near RALPH WALDO EMERSON and HENRY DAVID THOREAU.

Hawthorne continued to write, publishing a new collection of stories, *Mosses from an Old Manse*, in 1846. This was the same year that his long service to the Democratic Party was rewarded by his being given the job of surveyor at the Port of Salem. When the Democrats were thrown out of office, Hawthorne was also thrown out of his job. This caused a scandal at the time but it allowed Hawthorne the time to write his masterpiece, THE SCARLET LETTER. This was published in 1850 and proved to be an enormous success. He followed it up in the following year with another classic, THE HOUSE OF THE SEVEN GABLES. Despite his success, Hawthorne still did not have enough money so he gladly accepted his old friend President Pierce's request that he become American Consul in Liverpool in 1853. Hawthorne worked at this post for four years before travelling around Italy until his return to America in 1860. With his health depleted and his income only fitful, Hawthorne worked as best he could until his death on 19 May 1864 in New Hampshire. He was buried in the Sleepy Hollow Cemetery at Concord.

Principal Works

1846	*Mosses from an Old Manse*
1850	*THE SCARLET LETTER*
1851	*THE HOUSE OF THE SEVEN GABLES*

IRVING, WASHINGTON
(1783–1859)

There is a certain relief in change, even though it be from bad to worse; as I have found in travelling in a stage-coach, that it is often a comfort to shift one's position and be bruised in a new place.

Tales of a Traveller

Washington Irving was born on 3 April 1783 in New York City. He was named after the first American President George Washington (about whom he would later write a biography). Irving was the youngest of 11 children born to a Scottish father, who was a wealthy merchant, and an English mother, the granddaughter of a clergyman. Irving was encouraged to study law when he grew up, which he did so privately between 1798 and 1802. However, it was not long before he showed signs of the onset of tuberculosis, and in 1804 Irving's brothers sent him on a tour of Europe. This was typical of the Irving family in so far as they remained devoted to each other throughout their youngest sibling's lifetime.

For the next two years, Irving travelled around Europe, judiciously recording everything he saw in his notebooks, including a sighting of Admiral Nelson. When he returned to America in 1806, he was admitted to the New York Bar. He also began to write a satirical magazine with his brother, William, and his brother-in-law, James Kirke Paulding. The magazine was called *Salmagundi*, after the food, and it included sketches, poems, plays and essays. It proved to be popular but it only lasted a year. In 1809, Irving's life was blighted by tragedy when his fiancée, Matilda Hoffman, the daughter of one of his law instructors, died at the age of 17. Irving was devastated by this and could not contemplate marriage again. As he wrote later, 'For years I could not talk on the subject of this hopeless regret; I could not even mention her name; but her image was continually before me, and I dreamt of her incessantly.'

Ironically, 1809 was also the year in which Irving first gained mass popularity for *A History of New York*. Written under the pseudonym of Diedrich Knickerbocker, this purported to be an account of the early Dutch settlers and was a satire on a popular history book of the time, as well as on many of the leading politicians. *A History of New York* proved to be popular on both sides of the Atlantic, with the novelist WALTER SCOTT one of its most ardent admirers. During the war with Britain from 1812, Irving edited the *Analectic Magazine*, and was made a colonel in the New York State militia. Following the Treaty of Ghent, Irving then went to Europe for 17 years. At first he worked in Liverpool in the family hardware business, but when that failed, he turned once again to writing. After a meeting with Walter Scott, in which Scott had drawn his attention to German folk tales, Irving went on to write THE SKETCH BOOK, published over 1819–1820. Written under the pseudonym Geoffrey Crayon, *The Sketch Book* contained two classic tales – 'Rip Van Winkle' and 'The Legend of Sleepy Hollow'. It was an enormous success and established Irving as the first man of American letters.

After initially finding success as a satirist, Irving was encouraged by Sir Walter Scott to write *The Sketch Book*, the collection of short stories which established him as the first man of American letters.

Although Irving's next book was moderately successful, the subsequent one was a commercial failure, and so, in 1826, he became a diplomatic attaché at the American Embassy in Madrid. Irving produced a number of books during his time there, including a biography of Christopher Columbus in 1828 and *The Alhambra* in 1832, a Spanish version of *The Sketch Book*. After a brief period working in London, Irving returned to America in 1832 where he wrote three books on the American West. In 1842 he served another four years in Spain, and when he returned home he completed biographies of both OLIVER GOLDSMITH and George Washington. Shortly after finishing the fifth and final volume of his work on Washington, Irving died on 28 November 1859.

Principal Works

1809	*A History of New York*
1819–20	THE SKETCH BOOK
1832	*The Alhambra*

J

JACOBS, HARRIET (1813–97)

When separations come by the hand of death, the pious soul can bow in resignation, and say, 'Not my will, but thine be done, O Lord!' But when the ruthless hand of man strikes the blow, regardless of the misery he causes, it is hard to be submissive.

Incidents in the Life of a Slave Girl

Harriet Jacobs was probably born in 1813 in Edenton, North Carolina. Her parents were both slaves, which automatically made her a slave too. Despite having different masters, her parents were able to live together with her father hiring himself out as a highly skilled carpenter. When Jacobs was only 6 years old, her mother died and she was taken into the home of her mother's mistress, Margaret Horniblow. Horniblow taught Jacobs how to read and write and generally treated her in such a way that Jacobs did not actually feel like a slave. However, when Horniblow died in 1825, Jacobs was bequeathed to Horniblow's 5-year-old niece, Mary Matilda Norcom.

This left Jacobs under the de facto control of the girl's father, Dr James Norcom. As Jacobs grew to adulthood, Norcom continually threatened her with his unwanted sexual advances, advances which she evaded by ever more ingenious means. For his part, Norcom refused to countenance the idea of Jacobs marrying the man that she loved. On top of this, Jacobs was also subject to the spite of Norcom's wife, who was piqued with jealousy at her husband's interest in Jacobs. The fraught bondage of Jacobs to Norcom eventually came to the notice of a white, unmarried lawyer, Samuel Tredwell Sawyer. His interest in Jacobs was encouraged by her as a defence against Norcom. The two of them began a relationship and, in desperation, Jacobs bore him two children, Jacob in 1829 and Louisa Matilda in 1833.

All this time Norcom continued to threaten and abuse Jacobs and, infuriated by the birth of her children, he finally sent her to a plantation in 1835 to be 'broken in' as a field hand. Jacobs managed to escape before her children were sent to join her and she returned to Edenton where she hid at her grandmother's house in exceedingly cramped conditions. She was not able to have proper contact with her children at this time as they were constantly subject to the blandishments of Norcom, as he tried to bribe or cajole them into revealing what they knew of her whereabouts. Eventually, Sawyer purchased Jacob and Louisa, his own two children, but he did not emancipate them. They went on to join Jacobs in the North when she finally escaped there herself in 1842, disguised as a sailor, like FREDERICK DOUGLASS a few years before her.

Born into slavery, Jacobs was forced to abandon her own children to escape. She then joined the abolitionist movement and wrote of her own experiences as a slave in order to help that cause.

Life was not much easier in the North when, in 1850, the government introduced the Fugitive Slave Law, allowing bounty hunters to pursue escaped slaves even more aggressively. It was during this time that Jacobs came to work for Nathaniel Parker Willis, looking after his children. Willis's second wife, Cornelia Grinnell, was an ardent opponent of slavery and so, in order to prevent Jacobs being returned to Norcom, she bought and emancipated her in 1853. Free at last, Jacobs began to write her account of slavery and thus contribute to the growing abolitionist movement. However, she was unable to find a publisher for it until Lydia Maria Child, a well-known woman of letters, agreed to write a preface for it. With some editorial work on the part of Child, INCIDENTS IN THE LIFE OF A SLAVE GIRL was finally published in 1861, under the pseudonym of Linda Brent. It proved to be popular both in America and Britain, although the advent of the Civil War caused it to fall out of public notice until it was rediscovered in the mid-1980s.

During the Civil War, Jacobs was based in Washington, working with others to help win the war for the North. After the war, she spent much of her time raising funds for various projects, including schools, nursing homes and orphanages. She even found time to run a boarding house in Cambridge, Massachusetts. She died there in 1897 and was buried in Mount Auburn Cemetery.

Principal Work

1861   INCIDENTS IN THE LIFE OF A SLAVE GIRL

JAMES, HENRY (1843–1916)

In art economy is always beauty.
                    The Art of the Novel

Henry James was born on 15 April 1843 in New York City. His father, also called Henry James, was a noted intellectual and a very wealthy man. His elder brother, William James, would go on to become one of America's foremost philosophers and psychologists. James also had two younger brothers and a sister. After being taken to Europe while still very young, James returned to New York and lived there until he was 12 years old. The family then decamped once more to Europe where the impressionable James was exposed to all the galleries, museums, libraries and theatres they could cram in over four years. This was James's father's idea of an education and, complemented by some private tutoring, it left James well versed in the traditions of the Old World, as well as lamenting their lack in the new one.

When James returned to the United States, he attended the Harvard Law School but after a year abandoned this in favour of his interest in literature. When the Civil War began, James was excused service on the grounds of an 'obscure hurt' he had suffered on his back. Luckily, this did not prevent him from writing and he began in earnest to compose stories and reviews, becoming a regular contributor to magazines such as *Nation* and *Atlantic Monthly* in the years after the Civil War. In 1871 James published his first novel, *Watch and Ward*, in serialised form in *Atlantic Monthly*.

It was around this time that James came to conceive of his career in a single-minded fashion in the European sense of being a literary master. As this tradition did not then exist in America, James decided to move his centre of operations to Europe. He had no wife or children, and never would have, so he was free to try different countries, in the form of Italy and France, before finally settling in England. The split between his American and European identities was to dominate his work. Often Europe would be represented by him as a place of charm and cynicism, corrupting ambassadors of the innocent but cultureless America. *The American* (1877) follows this formula, as does *Daisy Miller* (1878), and even to some extent *WASHINGTON SQUARE* (1881). These novels formed the basis of James's popularity over the next few years.

> Born an American, James was educated in Europe and eventually chose to live there. The split between his American and European identities dominated his work, most notably the novels with which he eventually established himself as a great writer. He eventually became a British citizen, claiming that 'However British you may be, I am more British still.'

The year 1881 also saw the publication of his masterpiece *THE PORTRAIT OF A LADY*. The heroine of the story is Isabel Archer whom James based on his cousin Mary Temple, another nineteenth-century victim of tuberculosis. Throughout the 1880s James concentrated on writing novels. He published both *The Bostonians* and *The Princess Casmassima* in 1886, and then *The Tragic Muse* in 1889. The novels proved to be increasingly unpopular and James was forced to try his hand at writing drama. Over the next five years, James wrote seven plays, only two of which were ever produced. They both failed and in 1895 James resolved to abandon the dramatic arts and return to novel writing.

What followed was a series of powerful shorter works, including *The Aspern Papers* (1888), *What Maisie Knew* (1897), *The Spoils of Poynton* (1897), THE TURN OF THE SCREW (1898), and *The Beast in the Jungle* (1903). These novellas and stories were infinitely more popular than his plays, and prompted James to writing some of his best work in the succeeding years. Most notably he wrote the three great novels that cemented his reputation as a literary master – *The Wings of the Dove* (1902), *The Ambassadors* (1903) and *The Golden Bowl* (1904). James also went on to write three volumes of autobiography – *A Small Boy and Others* (1913), *Notes of a Son and Brother* (1914) and *The Middle Years* printed posthumously in 1917. In 1915, James became a naturalised British subject, partly as an expression of impatience at America's refusal to enter the First World War. At the end of the same year, James suffered a stroke. Expecting to die, he declared, 'So this is it at last, the distinguished thing!' Three months later it was, and he died in Rye on 28 February 1916.

Principal Works

JEWETT, SARAH ORNE
(1849–1909)

Tact is after all a kind of mind reading.
    The Country of the Pointed Firs

Sarah Orne Jewett was born on 3 September 1849 in South Berwick, Maine. She was the middle of three daughters born to Theodore Jewett and Caroline Perry. South Berwick was a bustling inland port and Jewett enjoyed exposure to its varied life through her grandfather, who had been a sea captain and ship owner. She also enjoyed accompanying her father, who was a doctor, as he did his rounds throughout the local area. Many of these early experiences would re-emerge later in her fiction, particularly her novel *A Country Doctor*, published in 1884.

Theodore Jewett also encouraged his daughter in her reading and writing. When she graduated from Berwick Academy in 1865, Jewett was already busy composing short stories and poems. Her first story, 'Jenny Garrow's Lovers', was published in 1868 and she soon caught the attention of *Atlantic Monthly*'s influential editor William Dean Howells. With his encouragement she published the story 'Mr Bruce' in the journal in 1869, and then went on to publish an entire collection of short stories based around the fictional coastal town of Deephaven in 1877, simply called *Deephaven*.

Born and raised in Maine, Sarah Orne Jewett found inspiration for her short stories and novels in the local area, once claiming that she learnt more accompanying her father on his rounds as a doctor than she ever did at school.

With the publication of *Deephaven*, she came to the attention of a wider literary circle. In particular, she became friends with Annie Fields, a literary figure from Boston, who was married to a publishing magnate. After the death of Fields's husband in 1881, Jewett and Fields spent the larger part of the rest of their lives together. Over the following years, they travelled widely around Europe and America, meeting writers like ALFRED TENNYSON, Christina Rossetti, MARK TWAIN, Rudyard Kipling, HENRY JAMES and HARRIET BEECHER STOWE. Jewett continued to publish at an even rate, including *A WHITE HERON AND OTHER STORIES* in 1886, and her finest novel *The Country of the Pointed Firs* in 1896. She became the first woman to receive an honorary doctorate from Bowdoin College in 1901. However, in 1902 her literary output was cut short when she was injured in a carriage accident on her birthday. Despite recovering physically, she lost the ability to concentrate and her last short story was published in 1904. She died on 24 June 1909 at her home in South Berwick.

Principal Works

1884   *A Country Doctor*
1886   *A WHITE HERON AND OTHER STORIES*
1896   *The Country of the Pointed Firs*

JOHNSON, SAMUEL (1709–84)

When a man is tired of London, he is tired of life; for there is in London all that life can afford.

Life of Samuel Johnson

Samuel Johnson was born in Lichfield, Staffordshire on 18 September 1709. His father, Michael Johnson, was a bookseller. Johnson himself had an unhappy start to life for he contracted scrofula from his wet nurse. Apart from scarring his face, as did a later bout of smallpox, this left him deaf in the left ear, almost blind in the left eye, and dim of vision in the right eye. The young Johnson was not bowed by these handicaps however, and he forged a determined personality, indulging in sports which did not require him to see too clearly, such as boxing. Once, as a child at nursery school, his nurse failed to arrive in time to walk him home so the infant Johnson got down on all fours, in order that he could see the gutter, and crawled back on his own, shunning the help offered by his teacher. This physical resolve remained with Johnson throughout his life and even into his seventies he was able to leap over the same railings that he had done as a youth.

Johnson was a precocious student and used the resources at his father's shop as best he could. Unfortunately, his father's work was not well paid and the Johnsons never had much money. When Johnson's mother inherited a small sum in 1728 she used it to put her son into Pembroke College, Oxford. At the time it was hoped that Johnson might be able to secure further funding from another source, but after a year this possibility faded and Johnson was forced to leave without gaining a degree. This threw Johnson into a deep depression, which was compounded by the death of his father a few years later in 1731.

It was during this depressed state that he met the Porters, a couple who enjoyed and encouraged Johnson. When Henry Porter died, Elizabeth 'Tetty' Porter and Johnson grew even closer until, a few years later, in 1735, they married. The wealth she had inherited from her husband enabled Johnson to open up his own school, Edial Hall. Unfortunately, the fact that Johnson did not have a degree, as well as the fact that he presented a forbidding appearance with his huge physique, framed by scars, convulsions and twitches, meant that within a year the school had failed. Johnson was once again close to poverty. This time he decided to seek his fortune in London, taking with him as a companion one of the pupils at his school, David Garrick, the future actor.

Forging a determined personality from his own suffering, Samuel Johnson became England's foremost man of letters. His greatest achievement was to complete the first major dictionary of the English language, although he noted in its preface that 'I am not so lost in lexicography as to forget that words are the daughters of earth, and that things are the sons of heaven.'

Johnson and Garrick arrived in London virtually penniless, but Johnson quickly set about writing commissions for Edward Cave, the founder of *The Gentleman's Magazine*. He also started to make a name for himself writing poetry, with such poems as *London* (1738) and *The Vanity of Human Wishes* (1749), both of which were imitations of satires by the Roman writer Juvenal. In 1747 he published the *Plan of a Dictionary of the English Language*, the first major attempt to codify the English lexicon. He planned to complete the project in three years, even though it had taken 40 French scholars over 40 years to complete a similar task, and the Italians 20 years to complete theirs. In the meantime, he took over the editorship of another of Cave's journals, *The Rambler*, in 1750, and when Cave died in 1754, Johnson wrote his biography. Cave's death followed that of Tetty, Johnson's wife, in 1752, after which he ceased to edit *The Rambler*. He never remarried.

In 1755 Johnson finally completed the dictionary. It contained the definitions for over 40,000 words and was illustrated with over

100,000 quotations. The definitions were certainly marked by Johnson's own personality. The definition of a patron, for example, includes the notion that a patron is 'commonly a wretch who supports with insolence, and is paid with flattery.' It was enormously well received. This did not, however, bring an immediate financial benefit. In January 1759, for example, Johnson's mother was dying in Lichfield but he was still poor and unable to make her last days as comfortable as he wished. He thus composed the philosophical fable RASSELAS in the evening of one week, for which he received £100, in order that he might settle her affairs and pay her funeral expenses. Unfortunately, the money came too late and Johnson missed seeing his mother on her death bed or attending her funeral.

Eventually Johnson's financial position was secured when he was awarded a pension by George III in 1762. He was also awarded a doctorate by the University of Dublin in 1765, thus earning him the title by which he is still remembered today – Dr Johnson. In the meantime he met and befriended his eventual biographer, JAMES BOSWELL. Boswell determined to write the biography of Johnson, which is partly responsible for our image of the man today. The two writers were rarely parted after this time. Their most notable excursion together was a tour of Scotland in 1773 which he records in *A Journey to the Western Islands of Scotland*. Johnson followed this up in 1781 with *Lives of the Poets*, his groundbreaking work of biography, detailing the good and bad sides of popular poets. However, he was able to write to a less punishing schedule now he was no longer threatened by the prospect of debtors' prison and so his literary output declined as he grew older. As he said, 'No man but a blockhead ever wrote, except for money.' Johnson died on 13 December 1784 and was buried in Westminster Abbey.

Principal Works

1749   *The Vanity of Human Wishes*
1755   *A Dictionary of the English Language*
1759   *RASSELAS*
1773   *A Journey to the Western Islands of Scotland*
1781   *Lives of the Poets*

JONSON, BEN (1572–1637)

For a good poet's made as well as born.
To the Memory of Shakespeare

Ben Jonson was probably born on 11 June 1572, just eight years after WILLIAM SHAKESPEARE and CHRISTOPHER MARLOWE. A month before the birth, Jonson's father, a clergyman, died. Little is known of the rest of Jonson's childhood beyond the fact that he attended Westminster School and was taught by the great scholar William Camden. It was under Camden's tutelage that Jonson developed the passion for the Latin and Greek classics which would influence his work for the rest of his life.

It is likely that a shortage of funds forced Jonson to cut short his education and to join his stepfather in learning the trade of bricklaying, a job he claimed that he 'could not endure'. Although he would return to the trade before he was fully established as a playwright, Jonson decided some time in the early 1590s to become a soldier. He joined the English army in the Low Countries where England was involved in the continuing war between the Dutch and the Spanish. There he claimed to have killed a man in single combat before he returned to London and married Ann Lewis in 1594.

Determined to make a living as a writer and actor, Jonson joined a touring company until, in 1597 he became a member of the troupe run by the diarist and theatre manager Philip Henslowe. In 1597 he also collaborated on writing a play, *The Isle of Dogs*, with the dramatist Thomas Nashe. Although the play is now lost, it proved to be such a scandalous satire at the time that the authorities closed all the theatres and arrested everyone involved in the play. In 1598, just a few months after being released from prison, Jonson scored a great success with his satiric play *Every Man in His Humour*. It was performed at the Globe by the Lord Chamberlain's Men with Shakespeare taking a leading role.

The success of *Every Man in His Humour* brought Jonson fame, but very shortly after its production his career almost ended. On 22 September 1598 Jonson, who was already developing a reputation for being quarrelsome, became involved in a duel with fellow actor Gabriel Spencer whom he fought and killed. At this time duels were not only illegal but punishable by death. In order to escape the gallows, Jonson decided to plead the mediaeval privilege known as the 'benefit of clergy'. This allowed defendants who could read Latin to be tried by a more lenient ecclesiastical court. As a result, Jonson kept his life but had all his property confiscated and was given a felon's brand ('T') on the base of his thumb. Jonson also left prison having been converted by an inmate priest to Roman Catholicism.

A contemporary of Shakespeare and Marlowe, Ben Jonson lived a flamboyant life in which he killed a man in a duel, fought in a war, served time in prison, worked as a spy, and courted royalty. He is best known for his comedy of humours.

Upon his release, Jonson took to the stage again, collaborating with the playwright Thomas Dekker on two plays, as well as writing a follow-up to *Every Man in His Humour*, the imaginatively titled *Every Man Out of His Humour*. Jonson also took it upon himself to satirise his fellow playwrights, forcing them to reply in kind, most notably Dekker's *Satiromastix* in which Jonson is portrayed as a vain egotist. There is no doubt that Jonson was an obstinate and intimidating person both mentally and physically (he claimed to weigh over 20 stone at one point and had what he called a 'mountain belly'). Jonson's penchant for satire landed him in trouble again when he took it upon himself in 1605 to collaborate on *Eastwood Ho!*, a play which lampooned the new king's Scottish accent and propensity for selling favours. Jonson was imprisoned and threatened with the removal of his ears and nose. He had already been questioned by the Privy Council on charges of 'popery and treason' for writing *Sejanus* in 1603, so when he was released following the *Eastward Ho!* incident just in time for the Gunpowder Plot in November, it was perhaps as well that this time he decided to help the authorities. Indeed, it is thought that, like Marlowe before him, he

agreed to act as a spy for the Privy Council, reporting on his fellow Catholics. Just five years later he returned to the Church of England.

In the meantime, Jonson was trying to develop his career at the Court of King James and he wrote *The Masque of Blackness*, the first of what turned out to be 24 masques. These masques, upon which he worked, albeit with arguments, with the famous designer Inigo Jones, were what we would now think of as multimedia events. They featured elaborate scenery, a kind of script, music, dancing and audience participation and were most often performed on Twelfth Night (like Shakespeare's TWELFTH NIGHT) or on other special occasions, such as weddings. They were limited to royalty because of the enormous expense involved in staging them. For example, *The Masque of Blackness* cost Queen Anne some £5,000, which represented more than 500 times the sum an apprentice would have earned in a whole year.

However, it is for his plays that Jonson will probably be best remembered. He continued to write these, as well as other forms of verse, until his death on 6 August 1637. During this time he established himself as a great influence upon his contemporaries, as well as the next generation, some of whom, such as the poets Robert Herrick, Thomas Carew and Sir John Suckling, came to be known as the 'Tribe of Ben'. Jonson was also the first writer to grasp the importance of publishing his work. Indeed, when he published his *Works* in 1616, he was initially mocked for his efforts. However, his example was soon followed by Shakespeare's friends when they published the First Folio in 1623, the collected works of Shakespeare for which Jonson wrote a prefatory poem.

Principal Works

1608	*Every Man in His Humour*
1603	*Sejanus*
1606	VOLPONE
1610	*The Alchemist*
1614	*Bartholomew Fair*

KEATS, JOHN (1795–1821)

Beauty is truth, truth beauty,—that is all
Ye know on earth, and all ye need to know.
                    'Ode on a Grecian Urn'

John Keats was probably born on 31 October 1795 in London. He was the first of five children born to Thomas Keats and Frances Jennings. His father worked at a livery stable, but died after falling off a horse in 1804. Frances soon remarried but the marriage did not last and she went on to die in 1810 of the same tuberculosis, or consumption as it was then called, that would later claim Keats himself. In the meantime Keats was sent to the Reverend John Clarke's School in Enfield. There he was renowned for his fighting skills, despite the fact that he was always quite small in stature. Even as an adult he barely topped five feet tall. Luckily Keats also had a passion for writing, which he developed with the help of John Clarke's son, Charles Cowden Clarke, who introduced him to the works of Homer, amongst other writers.

When Keats's mother died, most of the monies that had been left in trust for the Keats family were tied up in court and would remain so for the rest of Keats's life. He was then placed in the care of his guardian, Richard Abbey. When Keats informed Abbey that he wished to be a surgeon, he was secured an apprenticeship with Thomas Hammond, a surgeon and apothecary in Edmonton. While taking his apprenticeship, Keats began his first attempts at poetry. By 1816 he had composed his first great poem, 'On First Looking into Chapman's Homer'. This was also the year, after working as a student at Guy's Hospital, London, that he earned his Licentiate of the Society of Apothecaries.

Despite qualifying as an apothecary-surgeon, Keats had decided by the following year to abandon the profession and become a poet. He had by then made the acquaintance of a number of other professional writers and artists, including William Hazlitt, Charles Lamb and PERCY SHELLEY, as well as the influential editor of *The Examiner*, Leigh Hunt. In 1817 Keats composed *Endymion*, a poem he would very quickly condemn as a 'trial of invention'. This was followed by *Hyperion* (later revised as *The Fall of Hyperion: A Dream*), an epic poem which he eventually abandoned because of its similarity to the work of JOHN MILTON. In 1818 *Endymion* was savagely reviewed in *Quarterly Review*, a fact which later gave rise to the legend most succinctly expressed by LORD BYRON (who did not know Keats) that he was 'snuffed out by an article'.

What is more likely to have 'snuffed out' Keats was the walking tour he undertook in 1818 of the Lake District in England, as well as parts of Scotland and Ireland. When he returned he was not in the best of health, a fact exacerbated by his falling in love with Fanny Brawne. They became engaged but Keats's illness and his poverty meant that they were unable to marry. Remarkably, set against this background of sickness and thwarted passion, Keats spent the first nine months of 1819 writing a collection of masterpieces published as *LAMIA, ISABELLA, THE EVE OF ST AGNES AND OTHER POEMS*. This contained most of the poems upon which his reputation now rests.

> The archetypal Romantic poet, Keats died of consumption when he was only 25. He thought his name would soon be forgotten but he left behind him a legacy of poems of such quality that he ranks today among England's best-loved poets.

In February of the following year, Keats began to cough up blood – what he called his 'death warrant'. In the autumn of the same year he went to Rome to seek a healthier climate for his lungs, but on 23 February 1821 he died. He was buried in the Protestant cemetery there with the inscription he had asked to be placed on his tombstone: 'Here lies one whose name was writ in water'.

Principal Works

1818   *Endymion*
1819   *The Fall of Hyperion: A Dream*
1820   *LAMIA, ISABELLA, THE EVE OF ST AGNES AND OTHER POEMS*

L

LONDON, JACK (1876–1916)

I would rather be ashes than dust! I would rather that my spark should burn out in a brilliant blaze than it should be stifled by dry-rot. I would rather be a superb meteor, every atom of me in magnificent glow, than a sleepy and permanent planet. The proper function of man is to live, not to exist. I shall not waste my days in trying to prolong them. I shall use my time.

Jack London's Tales of Adventure

John Griffith London was born on 12 January 1876 in San Francisco. He was the illegitimate son of the rich but eccentric music teacher Flora Wellman, and William Henry Chaney, a key figure in the development of American astrology. As London never knew Chaney, he took the name of his stepfather, John London, a disabled Civil War veteran, whom his mother married in the same year that London was born. The family were never as poor as London later claimed, although they were by no means wealthy. When London's mother fell ill, London was looked after by Virginia Prentiss, an ex-slave who remained an influential figure in London's childhood.

London left school at the age of 14, after a very patchy education. He then went on to undertake a series of demanding physical jobs, such as pirating for oysters in San Francisco Bay, seaman and factory worker. He also joined in some of the many demonstrations and marches at the time by the unemployed and the underpaid, as the American labour movements began to take off. At the end of one such march, in 1894, he was arrested in Niagara Falls and jailed for vagrancy for 30 days. After this experience, he returned to San Francisco determined to avoid the hard life of the poor.

In order to do this, London set about educating himself as best he could by borrowing books from public libraries. At the age of 19 he gained admittance to the University of California at Berkeley. During this period London became an avowed proponent of socialism, and he even stood for mayor on several occasions as a socialist. In 1897 London spent the winter in the Yukon, unsuccessfully prospecting for gold. The experiences of this time provided him with the material for his first successful short stories, appearing in such periodicals as *Atlantic Monthly* and *Overland Monthly*. These stories proved to be incredibly popular and by the time of the publication of his first collection, *Son of the Wolf* in 1900, London had become the highest paid author of his day.

After once being jailed for vagrancy, Jack London eventually rose to become the highest paid author of his day. His most famous works, such as *The Call of the Wild*, describe the ferociously competitive instincts which he espoused all his life.

In 1900 London married Elisabeth Maddern, with whom he had two daughters. However, he left her after three years and went on to marry Charmian Kittredge. For the rest of his life, London continued to produce an astonishing quantity of work, a feat he ascribed to writing 1,000 words a day for six days of every week. Inevitably, the quality of his output decreased as he kept up this terrific pace, but for the first years he managed to produce several modern classics. The novel that brought him fame was *THE CALL OF THE WILD*, published in 1903. In the following year he published *The Sea-Wolf*, and in 1906 he wrote *White Fang*. While London continued to write until he died, he spent much of his remaining life either building his ranch or sailing on his beloved yacht, *The Snark*. He died at his ranch of renal failure, rather than suicide (as is often reported), on 22 November 1916.

Principal Works

MARLOWE, CHRISTOPHER (1564–93)

Who ever loved, that loved not at first sight?

Doctor Faustus

Christopher Marlowe was born on 6 February 1564, just two months before SHAKESPEARE, in the cathedral town of Canterbury. His father, John Marlowe, was a shoemaker and his mother, Katherine Arthur, was a yeoman's daughter. Marlowe was a very bright boy and, at the end of 1578, he had earned a scholarship to the prestigious King's School attached to the cathedral. His fees were probably paid by local philanthropist Sir Roger Manwood, for whom Marlowe wrote an elegy in 1592. In addition to learning Latin and Greek (the boys were expected to speak only Latin, even when not in the classroom), Marlowe was also required to sing as part of the choir. He was also encouraged to compose poetry and act in plays, again in Latin and Greek.

Having completed the first part of his education, in 1580 Marlowe then won another scholarship (partly by composing a poem in Latin, and singing a plainsong on sight) to Corpus Christi College at the University of Cambridge. The course he took there was intended for those embarking upon a career in the church, but when Marlowe gained his BA in 1584 he chose a different path. While still ostensibly a student at Corpus Christi studying for an MA, the records show that Marlowe disappeared from the college for lengthy periods. At the time, the college authorities assumed it was because Marlowe had gone to Rheims to become a convert to Catholicism. As England under Elizabeth maintained a habitual enmity with Catholic countries, this was considered politically suspect behaviour on Marlowe's behalf and the college refused him his MA. They did not know that Marlowe was actually working for the government, probably as some sort of agent. Following an appeal by Marlowe, the Privy Council (whose members included the

Archbishop of Canterbury, the Lord Chancellor, and the Lord Chamberlain) wrote to the college on his behalf informing Corpus Christi that 'he had done Her Majesty good service, and deserved to be rewarded for his faithful dealing'. Marlowe was then very quickly awarded his MA.

These events did not mark the end of Marlowe's involvement in dangerous activities for, in 1593, he found himself caught up in a brawl with a William Bradley. The brawl ended when Bradley was killed by the poet Thomas Watson. Watson was later acquitted on the grounds of self-defence and Marlowe was released after spending two weeks in jail. Amidst all this nefarious activity, Marlowe still found time to write and publish plays. *Tamburlaine*, the story of an all-conquering Mongol warrior, was probably written while he was still at college, and when it was published in 1590 it proved a great success. Marlowe followed this up with a sequel, a play about the St Bartholomew Eve's slaughter of the Huguenots entitled *The Massacre at Paris*. More plays appeared – *The Jew of Malta*, *Edward II*, and his most famous play, DR FAUSTUS – all written before Marlowe was 30.

> Perhaps the most notorious of the Elizabethan playwrights, Marlowe worked as a spy for many years and was killed in a mysterious tavern brawl. In his more public role as a dramatist, Marlowe's blank verse tragedies were enormously influential, setting the pattern for Shakespeare's plays among others.

About this time Marlowe found himself in trouble again. While residing at the home of Thomas Walsingham, his patron, Marlowe was arrested and charged with atheism. This was a crime punishable by death and was due to be investigated by the fearsome Court of the Star Chamber, the English equivalent of the Catholic Inquisition and the only authority permitted to use torture. These charges were not new as Marlowe had been a member of the notorious 'School of the Night' for some time. This was a group of intellectuals led by Sir Walter Ralegh and the Earl of Northumberland who were interested in the many scientific discoveries being made at the time. The reason that they were often charged with atheism is that several of the more renowned discoveries, such as the motion of the Earth around the sun, were contrary to Church teachings. Curiously, for such a terrible charge, Marlowe was granted bail until 1 June 1593. On 30 May, however, Marlowe went to a tavern owned by Dame Eleanor Bull where he supposedly fell into an argument over the bill with Ingram Frizer, a servant of Walsingham. Marlowe managed to stab Frizer a couple of times before he was himself fatally stabbed above the eye.

There have been many theories put forward regarding Marlowe's final hours, many of them focusing upon the fact that all four people present at the time, including Marlowe himself, were involved in the business of spying and were connected with Walsingham, who was himself an illustrious agent. Some historians have even contended that Marlowe did not die in the brawl but used this as a cover to either escape his enemies or go undercover as a spy. What is not in dispute, however, is the contribution of Marlowe to English theatre. ALFRED TENNYSON called him the 'Morning Star' for the way in which he popularised the blank verse which came to dominate Shakespearean drama in particular and Elizabethan drama generally.

Principal Works

1587–90	*Tamburlaine*
1590–93	*The Jew of Malta*
1590–93	*Edward II*
1590–93	DOCTOR FAUSTUS

MARVELL, ANDREW (1621–78)

But at my back I always hear
Time's winged chariot hurrying near;
And yonder all before us lie
Deserts of vast eternity.

'To His Coy Mistress'

Andrew Marvell was born in Winestead-in-Holderness, Yorkshire, on 31 March 1621, some five years after the death of WILLIAM SHAKESPEARE. His father, also called Andrew Marvell, was a clergyman in the Church of England. When Marvell was just 3 years old,

the Reverend Marvell was offered a post as lecturer in the Holy Trinity Church and the whole family moved to Hull. Marvell was educated at Hull Grammar School until, at age 12 he became a 'sizar' at Trinity College, Cambridge. A sizar was an extremely poor student who had to work for his meals and accommodation. By taking this route through college, Marvell was following in the footsteps of his illustrious forbear EDMUND SPENSER.

At some point during his studies, Marvell ran away to London and converted to Roman Catholicism. However, he returned to college after the intervention of his father and he completed his BA in 1639. At around the same time, two of his poems, one in Greek and the other in Latin, were included in an anthology of Cambridge poets. It was also during this period that Marvell's mother, Anne, died. Marvell stayed on at Cambridge, presumably to complete an MA, but he abandoned his studies when his father drowned in the Hull estuary in 1640/41.

In 1642, the English Civil War broke out between the Parliamentarians and the Royalists. Marvell seems to have spent most of the duration of the war abroad, travelling in France, Holland, Switzerland, Italy and Spain. While his sympathies as a youth may well have been with the Royalists, by the end of the war, the execution of Charles I in 1649 and Oliver Cromwell's assumption of power, Marvell was very much a declared Parliamentarian. Indeed, in 1650 he took up a post as tutor to the 12-year-old Mary Fairfax, daughter of Sir Thomas Fairfax, retired general of the Parliamentary army. This marked the beginning of a relatively peaceful time in Marvell's life during which he wrote many of his best known works, including 'To His Coy Mistress', 'The Definition of Love' and a poem about his surroundings, 'Upon Appleton House'.

In 1653 Marvell met and befriended the blind poet JOHN MILTON. Milton was much taken with Marvell and exerted all his influence to secure him the post of Assistant Latin Secretary to the Council of State, a position Marvell finally won in 1657. There he worked with Milton for £200 a year. He augmented this income by tutoring Cromwell's ward and nephew, William Dutton, both at Eton and travelling in Europe. Two years later, in 1659, Marvell changed jobs and became the Member of Parliament for Hull, his home town.

The following year Marvell outwardly accepted the Restoration, the return of the King, the Stuart monarch Charles II. Milton, on the other hand, was less forgiving and was duly imprisoned for his views and would undoubtedly have stayed there longer had it not been for the intervention of Marvell. Perhaps learning his lesson from this incident, Marvell published his anti-Royalist polemics and satires, such as *The Rehearsal Transposed*, anonymously. He also published a poem on Milton's PARADISE LOST in the preface to the second edition of the poem in 1674. In addition to his writing, Marvell spent most of the rest of his life engaged in political activity. Early in his parliamentary career, for example, Marvell embarked on two lengthy diplomatic missions – to Holland (1662–63), and to Russia, Sweden and Denmark (1663–65). This earned him a reputation as a fierce patriot. Marvell died on 16 August 1678, apparently of a fever and the incompetence of his doctor, although there was a rumour at the time that he had been poisoned by political opponents. He was buried in the church of St Giles-in-the-Fields in London.

Known more as a satirist and as the Member of Parliament for Hull in his own day, Marvell is now best known as a leading member of the group of poets referred to as the Metaphysicals.

That we care anything at all about Andrew Marvell these days is in large measure due to the efforts of the poet and critic T.S. Eliot, who reintroduced the world to 'the former Member for Hull' in 1921. Marvell was primarily known as a satirist during his own lifetime and his poems were only collected and published after his death in 1681. Even then this collection was put together by what is assumed to have been his landlady, Mary Palmer, who passed herself off as Mary Marvell in order to claim Marvell's pension. We have no reason to believe that the collection was widely read. Nowadays Marvell is widely regarded for his witty changes of subject and register and his ability to argue both sides of the case, a crucial skill given the times in which he lived.

Principal Works

1650–51	'An Horatian Ode Upon Cromwell's Return from Ireland'
1651–53	'Upon Appleton House'
1651–81	*MISCELLANEOUS POEMS*
1672–73	*The Rehearsal Transposed*

MELVILLE, HERMAN (1819–91)

We die of too much life.

Mardi

Herman Melvill (the 'e' was tacked on the end in the 1830s) was born on 1 August 1819 in New York City, the third of eight children born to Alan Melvill, a merchant trader, and Maria Gansevoort. Melville's father took pride in tracing his family back to the Queen of Hungary, while his mother came from one of the great Dutch settler families. The early years of Melville's life were lived in relative luxury. This good life was only spoilt by a bout of scarlet fever in 1826 which left the young Melville with poor eyesight. However, in 1832, following a period when he had borrowed exceedingly heavily, Melville's father went bankrupt. A short period of insanity ensued and then he died. This left Melville's mother dependent upon the kindness of her relatives, particularly her brother, Peter Gansevoort.

Following his father's death, Melville was taken out of school and worked for two years as a clerk in a bank. He spent the next two and a half years working in his brother's fur cap shop. He followed that up with a short stint running his uncle's farm, and then he taught in a school near Pittsfield, Massachusetts. During this run of different jobs, Melville continued to educate himself, reading all the world's great literature that was available to him. He also completed a course in engineering at Lansingburgh Academy, near Albany, but still found it difficult to secure a job. In 1839 he signed on for voyage to Liverpool, but when he returned there was still no work available. In 1842, at the age of 21, he signed on to a whaling ship, the *Achushnet*, that was setting sail for the South Seas. In the years that followed, Melville had many adventures, including living for a few weeks with a tribe untouched by western civilisation, getting embroiled in a mutiny, being imprisoned in Tahiti, and joining the American Navy.

Unable to find any other work, Melville fell into working on board a whaling ship, an experience which taught him that 'If not against us, nature is not for us'. Writing about the adventures he had in the South Seas formed the basis of his popular success as well as providing the basic materials for his masterpiece, *Moby Dick*.

When Melville returned from sea he was 25. He stayed with his brothers in New York City while he wrote his first novel, *Typee*. Published in 1846, it centred around adventures in the South Seas, and was an enormous success. Melville followed it up in 1847 with another similar kind of novel, *Omoo*. This was even more popular than *Typee* and Melville felt able to marry Elizabeth Knapp Shaw, the daughter of the Chief Justice of Massachusetts, a friend of Melville's father. In 1849, Melville published his third, and far more philosophical novel, *Mardi*. This did not receive such favourable reviews and so, needing more money to support his growing family, Melville returned to the adventure stories that had made him famous in the first place and produced the two novels *Redburn* (1849) and *White-Jacket* (1850). Confident that he had secured an audience, Melville then set about writing another of his philosophical novels and the one that would eventually turn out to be his masterpiece, MOBY DICK (or *The Whale* as it was called in Britain, which was published in 1851.

Unfortunately, *Moby Dick* was poorly received at the time and so Melville next attempted a novel that combined both adventure and philosophical elements. The result was *Pierre* (1853), a book that was roundly condemned as immoral. After this, Melville's writing career became sporadic and he was generally thought to be at least occasionally insane, even by his own wife.

Financial pressures continued for Melville until, in 1866, he finally obtained a government job as a customs inspector, which his family had been trying to secure for him for years. During this period he published some poetry, *Battle-Pieces* (1866) and *Clarel* (1876). Although neither of these received much acclaim at the time, they have since been esteemed as some of the best poetry of the period. This has been the story of Melville's career, for at his death on 28 September 1891, he was little appreciated, particularly in America. By his centennial in 1919, however, he had become revered as one of America's greatest writers. This revival was capped in 1924 by the publication of a story found among his papers at his death – BILLY BUDD, SAILOR.

Principal Works

1846	*Typee*
1847	*Omoo*
1851	MOBY DICK
1853	BARTLEBY, THE SCRIVENER
1853	*Pierre*
1924	BILLY BUDD, SAILOR

MILTON, JOHN (1608–74)

Truth is as impossible to be soiled by any outward touch as the sunbeam.
Doctrine and Discipline of Divorce

According to the family Bible, John Milton was born at half past six on the morning of Friday, 9 December 1608. His birthplace and childhood home was a house in Bread Street, London (the same street where Mary Godwin and PERCY BYSSHE SHELLEY were later married). His father, also called John Milton, was a scrivener by profession, a job which meant he not only performed the work of a scribe but also that of notary, investment broker and money-lender. His father was also a Protestant, a fact which had caused Milton's grandfather to throw him out of the house when he caught him reading the BIBLE in his room.

Milton's father was passionate about his son's education and paid for him to be taught by private tutors until he was about 13 when he sent him to St Paul's, the school adjoining the famous cathedral. It is likely that Milton heard the poet JOHN

DONNE preach at the cathedral while he was there as Donne was Dean of St Paul's at the time. Milton was as passionate about his education as his father was and he records in *Defensio Secunda* how, even though he started at 7 o'clock in the morning, he rarely left off reading until midnight. Milton also thanked his father in *Ad Patrem* for the gift of five languages – Hebrew, Latin, Greek, French and Italian – which he learnt at this time.

> Milton was obsessed with his own education and became the most erudite poet of his time. He was also a man of deep convictions who was imprisoned for his beliefs and was only saved by the intervention of his fellow poet Andrew Marvell. Despite going completely blind, Milton went on to write the English language's greatest epic, *Paradise Lost*.

In 1625, Milton was admitted to Christ's College, Cambridge, probably with the intention of becoming a clergyman. Almost immediately, however, Milton clashed with his tutor William Chappell and, it is said, was whipped by him and expelled from the college. He was readmitted a short time afterwards under the guidance of an alternative tutor and he continued his studies until he gained his BA in 1629. This was also the year in which he wrote his first work of note, 'On the Morning of Christ's Nativity'. Milton then pursued a further course of study and graduated with an MA in 1632. As part of the MA ceremony it was customary to swear an oath confirming one's intention to continue studying for a further five years. This was generally considered a formality left over from a bygone age, but Milton took it seriously and for the next half a decade he locked himself away with his books and a good portion of his father's money with the result that he became widely regarded as the most learned poet in the English language.

In 1638 Milton was asked to write a poem in memory of Edward King, a former Cambridge classmate, poet and priest who had drowned in the Irish Sea. Milton promptly wrote *Lycidas*, one of his most famous poems, and then embarked on a tour of Europe. He spent most of his time in Italy where he enjoyed a warm reception from many of the intellectuals of the day, including the scientist Galileo Galilei. Emboldened by this, Milton decided to return to London earlier than planned in 1639 in order, like Spenser before him, to become a great poet. However, when he returned, this ambition was temporarily put to one side as he became embroiled in the controversies surrounding the English Civil War, where Milton supported the Parliamentarian cause, and the reform of the Church of England, which he felt was long overdue.

During this period Milton wrote a series of pamphlets on these subjects, as well as finding time to teach his two nephews (he taught them Latin in a year) and, in 1642, to marry Mary Powell. Powell was only 17 at the time of their marriage and Milton, it seems, was rather idealistic about the state of matrimony. Consequently, within a few months, Powell had returned to her own family. Typically, Milton responded to this personal difficulty by penning a tract advocating divorce on the grounds of incompatibility. At the time this was roundly condemned and Milton failed to find a publisher. This then spurred him to compose another tract, *Areopagitica*, in which he argued for the freedom of the press and the free exchange of views. This was published in 1644, the same year in which he also published *Of Education*, a treatise on pedagogy born from his own practical experience of teaching.

Milton continued his pamphleteering throughout the 1640s until, in 1649, he published *The Tenure of Kings and Magistrates* which advocated the right to execute unworthy kings. This was far from being an academic matter at the time given that Charles I had been beheaded at the beginning of the year. Consequently, Milton was drafted into Cromwell's government as Latin Secretary. This position entailed drafting letters, mostly in Latin, to foreign governments and heads of state. It was an employment not helped by Milton's deteriorating eyesight. Milton had been losing his sight since 1648, when his left eye had ceased to work, but early in 1652, his right one went the same way and Milton was left completely blind at the age of 43. In that same year, having been reconciled in 1645, Milton's wife died giving birth to their fourth child. Six weeks later, Milton's only son, John, died too.

In 1656 Milton married again, to Katherine Woodcock. The following year they had a daughter, but within four months Katherine was dead and, a month later, so was their daughter. She probably became the subject of one of his most famous sonnets, 'Methought I saw My Late Espousèd Saint'. As if these agonising personal tragedies were not enough for Milton to cope with, in 1660, following Charles II's restoration, Milton was obliged to go into hiding. Milton was eventually arrested and imprisoned, but as a result of help from his friend, the poet ANDREW MARVELL, he was pardoned and released. Many thought Milton had already been punished enough by being struck blind.

As it was, Milton was left in much reduced circumstances. However, he determined to commence with his long-held project to write a great English epic, and although it did not turn out to be the Arthurian drama he had imagined in his youth, it is still considered one of the greatest poems written in any language – *PARADISE LOST*. Milton published this in 1667, having married his third wife Elizabeth Minshull in 1663, survived the Great Plague in 1665, and the Fire of London in 1666. In 1671, having published a history of Britain in the meantime, Milton followed it up with *Paradise Regain'd*, the story of the temptation of Christ, and *Samson Agonistes*, a classical tragedy focusing on the fortunes of the blind and pain-wracked Samson. Milton's own suffering from severe gout continued until his death on 8 November 1674. He was buried in St Giles', Cripplegate in London.

Principal Works

PAINE, THOMAS (1737–1809)

These are the times that try men's souls. The summer soldier and the sunshine patriot will, in this crisis, shrink from the service of their country; but he that stands it now, deserves the love and thanks of man and woman.

Crisis

Photo credit: © CORBIS

Thomas Paine was born on 29 January 1737 in Thetford, Norfolk. Following a cursory education, Paine attempted, at the age of 12, to follow in the footsteps of his Quaker father and become a corset maker. However, at the age of 19, Paine abandoned the apprenticeship and ran away to sea. Paine did not last long as a sailor either and he returned home to work as an exciseman, taxing various goods for the government. In an unprecedented move, Paine began to organise his fellow excisemen and eventually petitioned Parliament for an increase in their wages. Paine's efforts in this regard were undermined when he was sacked from his post for the second time after failing to do his job properly.

Paine's first wife died a year into their marriage and although he remarried, Paine left his second wife after three years. So when he met BENJAMIN FRANKLIN in London in 1774, Paine was at a low ebb. Franklin advised Paine to seek a better life in America and even gave him letters of introduction. Paine took Franklin up on his offer and sailed for Philadelphia at the age of 37. Paine soon found work as a journalist, and also found time to write an anti-slavery tract. When the war broke out against the British in 1775, Paine sided with the American rebels as they attempted to throw off their colonial masters, a view articulated in his *COMMON SENSE* of 1776. It was enormously popular and sold hundreds of thousands of copies.

Joining the revolutionary army, Paine then went on to compose 16 tracts entitled *Crisis*. These were widely distributed and did much to raise the morale of the American army. As a reward for his services, Paine was made Secretary of the Committee of Foreign Affairs in Congress, but he proved to be too indiscreet to hold the post and so he returned to England in 1787. There he tried to procure the finances for building a bridge and although that did not happen, he went on to compose *Rights of Man* (1791–92). This book argued against the role of a hereditary monarchy and Paine had to flee to France to avoid a charge of treason.

Born in England, Thomas Paine became a champion for the cause of American independence when he wrote *Common Sense*, optimistically proclaiming that 'We have it in our power to begin the world over again'. Reviled in his own country, he was initially greeted as a revolutionary hero when he travelled to France, but was soon imprisoned before returning to an ignominious end in America.

In France Paine was greeted as a revolutionary hero and made a citizen. However, when Paine protested against the execution of Louis XVI, he was imprisoned by Robespierre in 1793. Paine was never brought to trial because the American Ambassador James Monroe intervened on his behalf. Paine then stayed in France for the next few years while he completed his next book, *The Age of Reason*. This earned Paine a reputation as an atheist and when he returned to America in 1802 he found he was reviled by most of society. He died a pauper in New York City on 8 June 1809.

Principal Works

1776	COMMON SENSE
1776–1883	Crisis
1791–92	Rights of Man
1794	The Age of Reason

POE, EDGAR ALLAN (1809–49)

All that we see or seem

Is but a dream within a dream.

'A Dream within a Dream'

Edgar Poe was born in Boston, Massachusetts, on 19 January 1809, six months before the death of THOMAS PAINE. His parents, David Poe and Elizabeth Hopkins, were itinerant actors and Poe was the second of three children. Poe's father chose to desert the family and probably died just a year after Poe was born. Poe's mother, who had been a teenage widow already, died just before Poe's third birthday. Poe was taken in by John Allan, a merchant in Richmond. Although never legally adopted by Allan, Poe did take his name. The family's bad luck would continue: Poe's brother would go on to die young, while his sister would go insane.

Poe went with Allan to England in 1815. They stayed there for five years and Poe attended Manor School in Stoke Newington. Upon their return to America, Poe continued his studies, and attended the University of Virginia in 1826. However, he left after only a year, supposedly because he had not paid his gambling debts. It is claimed that Poe only gambled in the first place because Allan refused to fund Poe's education properly, although this, like many of the details of Poe's life (such as the claim that he led an expedition to Greece after the fashion of LORD BYRON) is difficult to verify. Whatever the truth of its origin, Poe's gambling debt led him to quarrel with Allan who all but disowned him.

Poe did somehow manage to find the money to pay for an edition of his poetry, *Tamerlane and Other Poems*, published anonymously in 1827. It sold very poorly at the time, although its worth is now extraordinary. He then decided to join the army under the name of 'Edgar A. Perry'. Poe was apparently quite successful as a soldier and when he left the army two years later, it was with the rank of sergeant major. Poe's army career and the death of Allan's wife led to a partial reconciliation between Poe and Allan. After revising *Tamerlane*, Poe released a second volume of poetry, *Al Aaraaf, Tamerlane, and Minor Poems* at the end of 1829. In the following June, he entered West Point. Possibly after discovering that this would not actually benefit him financially in the eyes of Allan, Poe got himself dishonourably discharged in 1831 by deliberately neglecting his duties. In the same year he published his third volume of poetry, simply titled *Poems*.

In 1833 Poe lived with his aunt, Maria Clemm, and her daughter Virginia, whom Poe would go on to marry twice – once secretly in 1835 when she was 13 years old, and once publicly in 1836. In the meantime Poe won a prize of $50 for his short story 'MS Found in a Bottle'. This helped him gain an entrée into the world of publishing and over the next few years Poe lived a hand-to-mouth existence, working as a staff member for various magazines, as well as publishing some of his best short stories, poems and literary criticism in periodicals such as *Burton's Gentleman's Magazine* and *Graham's*. In 1840 Poe published TALES OF THE GROTESQUE AND ARABESQUE, a collection of short stories which included his most famous work 'The Fall of the House of Usher'.

Edgar Allan Poe lived a troubled life, battling his addiction to alcohol, although he once claimed that 'Man's real life is happy, chiefly because he is ever expecting that it soon will be so.' While waiting on this promise, Poe managed to pioneer several literary genres, including science fiction and the detective story, as well as becoming a moderately successful poet.

This volume sold poorly and Poe's financial worries continued, particularly as he was fired in the same year from his editorial job for excessive drinking. In 1842 his wife burst a blood vessel in her throat which left her incapacitated for the next five years, at the end of which she died from tuberculosis. Poe himself grew increasingly despondent and drank more and more, making it difficult to make the most of his talents. In 1845 he at last achieved some fame and fortune when his poem 'The Raven' was published in *American Review*. This led to another collection of poetry, *The Raven and Other Poems*, being printed later in the same year. Poe also hoped his new fame would help launch his own magazine to great acclaim, but that failed early in the following year. After that and Virginia's death, the rest of Poe's life was an alcohol-fuelled blur that ended with him dying in a Baltimore gutter on 7 October 1849. Although largely unappreciated in his own lifetime, Poe is now recognised as a pioneer of literary genres, all but inventing science fiction and the detective story.

Principal Works

1831	*Poems*
1840	*Tales of the Grotesque and Arabesque*
1844	THE PURLOINED LETTER
1845	*The Raven and Other Poems*

POPE, ALEXANDER (1688–1744)

To err is human, to forgive divine.
An Essay on Criticism

Alexander Pope was born in London on 21 May 1688. His father, also called Alexander Pope, was a prosperous linen merchant. His mother, Edith Turner, came from a large family divided on religious grounds. Edith and her husband were Roman Catholics and brought their son up in the same tradition. The year Pope was born also saw the Glorious Revolution, in which a bloodless coup allowed the Protestant William of Orange to depose the Catholic James II. Life became very difficult shortly thereafter for many Roman Catholics, particularly with the implementation of the Test Act in 1673. This required all holders of civil and military posts to take the sacrament in the Anglican Church, thereby largely excluding Roman Catholics from public life. Catholics were also banned from owning a house within ten miles of London, so the Popes were forced to move to Windsor Forest, west of the capital.

Pope's education also suffered because he was a Catholic. He was able to attend some schools, but he also had to rely on home tuition from his aunt and various priests. Nevertheless, in spite of or because of this, Pope was actually very accomplished at a young age, being fluent in Latin, Greek, French and Italian, as well as writing sophisticated verse. Unfortunately, upon moving to Windsor, Pope contracted tuberculosis of the spine. This left him permanently prone to other illnesses, as well as stunted in growth (he never grew above four and a half feet) and with a hunchback.

Undaunted by his physical ailments and encouraged by his father, Pope continued to write verse and, in 1711, he published his first masterpiece, *An Essay on Criticism*. Despite the title, this was actually a poem after the manner of the Roman author Horace. This brought him to the attention of many of the leading intellectuals and wits of the time, such as Joseph Addison and William Congreve. However, he was soon to fall out with most of these early associates, partly because they were Whigs. The Whigs were one of the two political parties formed out of the political turmoil of the seventeenth century. Broadly speaking, they were the progressive party, supporting the emergent merchant class and opposing any augmentation of the powers of the king. The Tories, on the other hand, were conservatives who wished to maintain traditions and support the landed gentry and clergy. Pope soon fell in with the influential group of Tory writers, such as JONATHAN SWIFT and Dr Arbuthnot, and with them formed the *Scriblerus Club*.

> Stunted and humpbacked, Pope fought all his life against the prejudices he encountered, a fact which perhaps afforded him the insight that 'Hope springs eternal in the human breast'. An accomplished poet, Pope allied this skill to his gifts as a linguist in establishing translation as a viable form of literature.

Life over the years that followed was turbulent but successful for Pope. As he described it himself, 'the life of a wit is a warfare on earth.' When Pope announced his intention to compose a translation of Homer's *Iliad*, Pope's Whig enemies (Addison's 'little senate' as Pope referred to them) did all they could to deter potential subscribers. Even though the translation was a success, Pope never forgot and exacted his revenge in print, ridiculing Addison in the *Epistle to Dr Arbuthnot* in 1735. He had already similarly ridiculed the Shakespearean scholar Lewis Theobald, making him the king of the dunces in *The Dunciad* in 1728.

Pope was already a popular author when he published his translation of the *Iliad*. He had previously published the first volume of his collected works in 1717, following the commercial success of poems such as THE RAPE OF THE LOCK in 1712 and *Windsor Forest* in 1713. This popularity enabled Pope to become one of the first authors to live off the income

generated from his own writing, as opposed to subsidising it with patronage or performing. He was then able to retire from the increasingly volatile London and move back to Twickenham, where he leased a villa with his widowed mother, his father having died in 1717.

Pope lived out his days in Twickenham, enjoying the country and taking an increasing interest in horticulture. He followed up the success of his translation of the *Iliad* in 1720 with a translation of the *Odyssey* in 1726 and, in 1733 published *Essay on Man*, an account of the human condition. Although the *Essay* was initially published anonymously, when the identity of the author was disclosed, Pope was once again attacked for the religious views which he espoused. Pope, for his part, felt he was championing traditional values, a cause he held fast to until he died at Twickenham on 30 May 1744.

Principal Works

1711	An Essay on Criticism
1712–14	THE RAPE OF THE LOCK
1728	The Dunciad
1733	Essay on Man
1735	Epistle to Dr Arbuthnot

S

SCOTT, SIR WALTER (1771–1832)

Oh what a tangled web we weave,
When first we practise to deceive!

Marmion

Walter Scott was born on 15 August 1771 in Edinburgh, Scotland. His father, also called Walter Scott, was a lawyer, and his mother, Anne Rutherford, was the daughter of a professor of medicine. He had 11 siblings, although six died in infancy. Scott himself suffered from an attack of polio when he was 2 years old which left him lame in his right leg, although it did not prevent him from being otherwise of an athletic build when he grew up. In order to aid the healing process, Scott's parents sent him to stay with his paternal grandfather at Sandyknowe in the Borders. In 1775 Scott's grandfather died and he was sent to Bath, Somerset, to attempt a cure using the famous waters there. Scott finally returned to Edinburgh in 1778 and in the following year began to attend the High School of Edinburgh.

In 1783 Scott enrolled at Edinburgh University where he studied for three years, although one of those years was spent with his aunt in the Borders recovering his health. In 1786 he was apprenticed to his father's law firm and, while on business, he not only met a man who had duelled with Rob Roy MacGregor (about whom Scott would later write a novel), but also ROBERT BURNS, the great Scottish poet. In 1789 Scott resumed his law studies at Edinburgh University. He qualified in 1792 and was duly admitted to the Faculty of Advocates and began practising law. In 1797 he married Charlotte Carpenier on Christmas Eve in Carlisle Cathedral. Together they had five children.

> Scott originally dedicated himself to writing narrative poems but he stopped when he read the far superior work of Lord Byron. From then on he turned to writing historical novels, a genre he all but invented and made his own.

In 1799, following the death of his father and the birth of his first daughter, Scott was made Sheriff-Deputy of Selkirkshire, a post he held until his death in 1832. Six years later, Scott also became Principal Clerk to the Court of Session in Edinburgh which made him financially comfortable. By this time Scott had already begun to publish as a poet, at first documenting his translations of German poems and his collection of ballads, most notably *Minstrelsy of the Scottish Border* (1802–03). He went on to publish two enormously popular narrative poems – *Marmion* (1808), and *The Lady of the Lake* (1810). With the proceeds from these and other poems, Scott began to build his great home at Abbotsford in the Borders. However, Scott all but stopped writing poetry when he read the work of, and met, LORD BYRON in 1813. The same year he turned

down the position of Poet Laureate.

Following the collapse of a business enterprise he had undertaken with a friend in 1813, Scott set about writing the first of his novels, *Waverley*. Published in 1814 and dealing with the Jacobite rebellion of 1745, this proved an enormous success and inaugurated the new genre of the historical novel. In the ensuing years, Scott wrote over 25 novels including *Old Mortality* (1816), *Rob Roy* (1817), *The Heart of Midlothian* (1818), and IVANHOE (1819). In 1818 he accepted a baronetcy, and in 1822 he played a leading role in the visit of King George IV to Edinburgh. However, these prosperous times came to an end in 1826 when his business partner once again went bankrupt owing vast sums of money which Scott took it upon himself to repay. In order to do this, Scott set himself a punishing schedule of work for his printers, writing two projects at once. Scott's wife died in 1826 and thereafter his own health began to suffer. Scott suffered gallstones, haemorrhages, a stroke, paralysis and then, finally, in 1832, after returning from Italy, he died on 21 September. He was buried beside his wife in Dryburgh Abbey, Scotland.

Principal Works

1814   *Waverley*
1816   *Old Mortality*
1817   *Rob Roy*
1818   *Heart of Midlothian*
1819   IVANHOE

SHAKESPEARE, WILLIAM (1564–1616)

Some are born great, some achieve greatness, and some have greatness thrust upon 'em.

Twelfth Night

William Shakespeare was born in the town of Stratford-Upon-Avon, probably on 23 April, the same day on which he would die 52 years later. His father, John Shakespeare, was a prominent local businessman, and his mother, Mary Arden, was a respected landowner. Despite the fact that his parents were illiterate, his father's distinguished position in Stratford entitled William to an education at the King's

New School. As with all Elizabethan grammar schools, Shakespeare would have taken the majority of his lessons in Latin, the language of much official life all across Europe. In particular, Shakespeare would have studied Latin authors like Seneca, Cicero, Ovid, Virgil and Horace from whom he borrowed many of the plots of his plays.

At the age of about 13, it is likely that Shakespeare was forced to leave school because of his father's worsening financial situation. Indeed, his father's fortunes declined for most of the rest of his life, resulting in a fine for not attending church in 1592. Following Shakespeare's success as a playwright, however, his father was finally granted a coat of arms in 1596 and so, when he died in 1601, he died a gentleman.

> William Shakespeare is widely regarded as the greatest writer in the English language, one for whom 'All the world's a stage, and all the men and women merely players'. His plays, written in some of the most beautiful poetry ever conceived, contain a depth and variety of theme and characterisation unmatched by any other writer in any other medium.

What happened to Shakespeare himself after leaving school is less well documented and despite tales of poaching and working in a butcher's, the next recorded incident of his life was his marriage to the 26-year-old Anne Hathaway at the age of 18. There is some confusion surrounding the marriage as there are two entries in the Episcopal register at Worcester on the dates of November 27 and 28, 1582. The first entry suggests that William was issued a marriage licence for an Anne Whately, and the second that he was issued one for Anne Hathaway, the woman whom we know he did marry. It has been argued that either this reveals nothing more than a clerical error, or that Shakespeare really loved Anne Whately but felt obliged to marry Anne Hathaway because she was already a few months' pregnant with his child. That first child, Susanna, was born in 1583 and was followed in 1585 by the twins Judith and Hamnet. Hamnet died in 1596 from an unknown cause.

Very little is known about Shakespeare's life in the seven years after 1585, but it is clear that by 1592 he had established himself as a successful actor and playwright in London. This success was enough to provoke the playwright Robert Greene into making the first printed reference to Shakespeare, calling him an 'upstart crow'. Indeed, Shakespeare was obviously important enough to warrant an apology from Greene's editor for this remark. While the theatres were shut down in 1593 during an outbreak of plague, Shakespeare made his first published appearance in his own right with the poem *Venus and Adonis*.

In 1594 the theatres were re-opened and Shakespeare helped to found the Lord Chamberlain's Men, the leading theatre company of the day. For the next five years, Shakespeare wrote and performed at various theatres, including the Curtain and the Theatre, as well as performing at Court in front of Queen Elizabeth I on several occasions. When the Lord Chamberlain's Men lost the lease on the Theatre in 1599, they used some of the timbers from that building to build the Globe, the theatre most associated with Shakespeare, on the banks of the river Thames. Shakespeare enjoyed his most successful years at the Globe, writing such plays as *HAMLET, KING LEAR, OTHELLO* and *MACBETH*. His company was so successful that when James I came to the throne in 1603 they were re-designated the King's Men. Unfortunately, the Globe burnt down in 1613 when a canon fired for a production of *Henry VIII* set fire to the roof. Although Shakespeare invested in the rebuilding of the theatre the following year, he retired from acting at this point and returned to live in Stratford in one of the properties he had bought using the wealth from his success – New Place, the largest house in the town. There he remained until his death in 1616. Infamously, in his will, Shakespeare left most of his fortune to his daughter Susanna whereas his wife Anne received not much more than the second-best bed (this being the marriage bed, the best bed being that for guests).

During Shakespeare's lifetime, only half of his plays had been published in what are called Quartos (the name refers to the fact that printers made eight pages out of each sheet of paper). These were often pirated versions of the plays and not ones authorised by

Shakespeare himself. After his death, in 1623, Shakespeare's friends brought out a collected edition of 36 of his plays in what is now known as the Folio (the name refers to the fact that publishers made four pages out of each sheet of paper). In the first edition of the Folio, known as the First Folio, the playwright BEN JONSON famously declared of Shakespeare that 'He was not of an age, but for all time!'

Principal Works

1589–91	*The Two Gentlemen of Verona*
1589–94	*The Comedy of Errors*
1590–93	*The Taming of the Shrew*
1590–96	*King John*
1590–92	*Henry VI, Part One*
1591–92	*Titus Andronicus*
1591–92	*Henry VI, Part Two*
1592–93	*Henry VI, Part Three*
1592–93	*Venus and Adonis*
1593–94	*The Rape of Lucrece*
1593–95	*RICHARD III*
1593–1603	*The Sonnets*
1594–95	*Love's Labour's Lost*
1594 –95	*ROMEO AND JULIET*
1595	*A MIDSUMMER NIGHT'S DREAM*
1595	*Richard II*
1596–97	*THE MERCHANT OF VENICE*
1596–97	*Henry IV, Part One*
1597–98	*The Merry Wives of Windsor*
1597–98	*Henry IV, Part Two*
1598	*Much Ado About Nothing*
1598–99	*Henry V*
1599	*Julius Caesar*
1599–1600	*As You Like It*
1600–01	*HAMLET*
1600–02	*Troilus and Cressida*
1601	*TWELFTH NIGHT, OR WHAT YOU WILL*
1602–05	*All's Well That Ends Well*
1603	*Measure for Measure*
1603–04	*OTHELLO*
1604–05	*Timon of Athens*
1605–06	*KING LEAR*
1606	*MACBETH*
1606	*ANTONY AND CLEOPATRA*
1607	*Pericles*
1608	*Coriolanus*
1609–10	*Cymbeline*
1609	*The Winter's Tale*
1610–11	*The Tempest*
1611–14	*The Two Noble Kinsmen*
1613	*Henry VIII*

SHAW, GEORGE BERNARD (1856–1950)

A drama critic is a man who leaves no turn unstoned.

New York Times

George Bernard Shaw was born on 26 July 1856 in Dublin. Shaw was the youngest of three children born to George Carr Shaw, who was in the grain trade, and Lucinda Elizabeth Gurly, daughter of a landowner. Shaw's father was a perpetual drunkard, a fact which led Shaw himself to become a teetaller. He also maintained ambivalent feelings towards his mother about whom he stated that, 'she went her own way with so complete a disregard and even unconsciousness of convention and scandal and prejudice that it was impossible to doubt her good faith and innocence'. The scandal to which he refers is the fact that she brought her singing teacher, George John Vandeleur Lee, to live in the house with them. Meanwhile, Shaw was educated at a variety of schools including the Wesleyan Connexional School and the Central Model School, although he claims that he was largely self-taught and ever after maintained a dislike for organised education.

When he was 15, Shaw left school and, unable to afford a university education, became an office clerk, all the time improving his knowledge of the arts. He kept this job for five years but in 1876 he decided to follow his mother to London. She had followed Lee there some years earlier in order to try and make her fortune teaching Lee's own singing technique. Shaw later considered him to have been a fraud. In London, Shaw continued his process of self-education by joining the Reading Room of the British Library. He became an admirer of the work of Karl Marx at this stage and even became friends with one of his daughters. Unlike Marx, however, Shaw believed in evolutionary rather than revolutionary socialism and to this end he joined the Fabian Society, a collection of like-minded intellectuals. Shaw quickly became a leading member of the Fabians and, although he was naturally retiring in company, he became a good public speaker. Through the Fabian Society he met the wealthy Irish woman Charlotte Payne Townshend. Never particularly obsessed with women (Shaw's first sexual experience occurred when he was 29), Shaw offered to marry her only because he thought he was dying. She accepted and they remained married until her death in 1943.

After championing the work of Henrik Ibsen, George Bernard Shaw decided to become a playwright himself. Like Ibsen, he used his plays to advance his ideas on social reform. Dedicated to his craft (he once argued that 'A perpetual holiday is a working definition of hell'), Shaw eventually penned over 50 plays.

When he first arrived in London, Shaw also tried to develop his career as a writer, and, after completing five unpublished novels, he eventually met with some small measure of success. Shaw's real income, however, came from his work as a critic. Despite knowing very little about it, he began as an art critic and then became a music critic under the pseudonym of Corno di Bassetto. Shaw brought a fearless wit to his criticism, once remarking of Schubert's 'Death and the Maiden' that it made him 'reconciled to Death and indifferent to the Maiden'. He later brought the same verve and insight to his drama criticism, where he championed the work of the Norwegian playwright Henrik Ibsen. In 1891, the year after publishing his book on Ibsen, Shaw wrote his first play. It was not a great success but it set him on the course which would see him write over 50 plays and would make him the most famous man of letters in the English-speaking world. He used this platform to advocate a number of ideas, including vegetarianism, feminism and the reform of English grammar. Despite the waxing and waning of his popularity, particularly during the First World War, he won the Nobel Prize for Literature in 1925. Shaw died in Hertfordshire on 2 November 1950 while pruning an apple tree. His remains were cremated with his wife's.

Principal Works

1891   *The Quintessence of Ibsenism*
1894   *Arms and the Man*
1902   *Mrs Warren's Profession*
1905   *Man and Superman*
1905   *MAJOR BARBARA*
1913   *Pygmalion*
1923   *Saint Joan*

SHELLEY, MARY WOLLSTONECRAFT (1797–1851)

Life is obstinate and clings closest where it is most hated.

Frankenstein

Mary Wollstonecraft Shelley was born on 30 August 1797 in London. Her father was William Godwin, the political reformer and philosopher, and her mother was MARY WOLLSTONECRAFT, the author of *A VINDICATION OF THE RIGHTS OF WOMAN*. Shelley's mother fell ill immediately after giving birth to her daughter and died within ten days from puerperal fever. Four years later Godwin married Mary Jane Clairmont, a widow who brought with her two children from her previous marriage, one of whom would later change her name to Claire Clairmont. After several years in which frictions grew between Mary Shelley and the stepmother she hated, at the age of 14 Mary was sent to live in Dundee with a friend of Godwin, William Baxter.

On one of several return visits to Godwin's house, Mary met PERCY BYSSHE SHELLEY in 1812. Percy Shelley was still with his wife Harriet at the time, but when Mary met Percy again in 1814 the couple had separated. Mary and Percy fell in love with each other over the course of the following two months, and Mary became pregnant at the age of 16. The couple decided to elope to Europe with Claire Clairmont. Mary described their trip through France, Switzerland, Germany and Holland in *History of a Six Weeks' Tour*, published in 1817. When they returned to England, Mary gave birth to a premature daughter who subsequently died. In 1816 she gave birth to a son, William.

A few months later Mary, Percy and their son travelled with Clairmont, who by this time was pregnant with LORD BYRON's daughter, to meet up with Byron in Switzerland. Here Mary began to write her novel *FRANKENSTEIN* which was finally published anonymously to great acclaim in 1818. When Mary and Percy returned from Switzerland later in 1816, they were informed that Percy's wife Harriet, pregnant by an unknown man, had drowned herself in the Serpentine, a small lake in Hyde Park, London. Fifteen days later, Mary and Percy finally married, with the blessing of Godwin who had not spoken to his daughter since the elopement.

This small moment of happiness did not last, however, for in 1818 the Shelleys' third child died in Venice, while the following year saw the death of their second child in Rome. A miscarriage followed in 1820, and in the wake of that came the death of Clairmont's child with Byron in an infamous Italian convent. The only glimmer of hope in all this tragedy was the birth of Percy Florence, Mary's second and, in the end, only surviving son. However, even this could not save her from depression when her husband drowned in the Gulf of Spezia in 1822.

Daughter of social reformers William Godwin and Mary Wollstonecraft, Mary Shelley became pregnant and ran away to Europe with Percy Shelley when she was just 16. While staying with Lord Byron, she wrote *Frankenstein*. Following Percy's death, she devoted herself to restoring his poetic reputation.

When Mary Shelley returned to England at the age of 24, she received some financial support worth £100 per year rising to £400 from Percy's father, Sir Timothy Shelley, although only on the condition that she did not write a biography of his son's scandalous life or publish any more of his work. Shelley agreed to this but it was not an onerous condition in so far as she wanted to escape from the scandalous legacy of Percy anyway, as well as that bequeathed her by her mother and father. Shelley did, however, want to re-establish her husband's poetic reputation and she eventually persuaded Sir Timothy to allow her to publish Percy's collected poetry in 1838. Meanwhile, Shelley augmented the money given her by Sir Timothy by writing. She composed five more novels, including *Valperga* in 1823 and *The Last Man* in 1826, as well writing articles and contributing to books. When Sir Timothy died in

1844, her devoted son Percy inherited the baronetcy and she was able to live the last years of her life in comfort. She died on 1 February 1851 and was buried between her parents.

Principal Works

SHELLEY, PERCY BYSSHE (1792–1822)

The great instrument of moral good is the imagination.

A Defence of Poetry

Percy Bysshe Shelley was born on 4 August 1792 in Horsham, West Sussex. His father was Sir Timothy Shelley, a Member of Parliament, and his mother was Elizabeth Pilford. In 1802, as befitted this wealthy and conservative background, Shelley was sent to Syon House Academy, and from there he went to Eton in 1804. Six years later he went to University College, Oxford. Here he met Thomas Jefferson Hogg, a young man who shared Shelley's growing radicalism. At the beginning of 1811 the two of them composed a pamphlet called *The Necessity of Atheism*. As the title suggests, this was an attack on the empirical existence of God, and for good measure they posted it to the bishops and heads of colleges of Oxford. When they refused to answer questions regarding the authorship of the pamphlet, the two of them were immediately expelled.

Understandably, Sir Timothy was not pleased at his son's endeavours, a displeasure that deepened when Shelley eloped with Harriet Westbrook, a 16-year-old inn-owner's daughter. The two of them ran away to Edinburgh and were married in 1811 (a fact that did not prevent Hogg from trying to seduce Harriet). Living on a small allowance from his father, Shelley spent the next couple of years moving around Britain and travelling to Ireland where he wrote pamphlets in the cause of Catholic emancipation. In 1813 he also printed his first major work, the poem *Queen Mab*.

It was at this time that Shelley had grown

to be part of the circle surrounding the radical philosopher William Godwin. Shelley subsidised Godwin and continued to do so until his death. Here he also met Godwin's daughter, MARY SHELLEY, and in 1814, with Harriet already pregnant with his second child and Mary carrying their first child, Shelley eloped again. This time he fled to the Continent where he stayed for six weeks. When he returned he found that he was a social outcast. When Harriet drowned herself in the Serpentine in Hyde Park in 1818, Shelley was then free to marry Mary.

> Born into the aristocracy, Shelley eloped with his first wife when he was 18, and his second when he was 21 – both brides were just 16. Finding himself a social outcast, he turned increasingly to poetry. He drowned while sailing his boat, the *Don Juan*.

Mary had already published her masterpiece, FRANKENSTEIN, by this time, but it was not until the Shelleys returned to Italy at the end of 1818 that Shelley began to compose his greatest works. Over the next few years, Shelley wrote PROMETHEUS UNBOUND, *The Mask of Anarchy, A Defence of Poetry, Adonais* and *Hellas*. What is remarkable is that all this work was written against a background of intense personal tragedy as he and Mary lost their second and third children, events which threw them both into a deep depression. He was also hounded by creditors, despite helping to defray the expenses of others, and he was writing for an audience that did not exist.

On 8 July 1822, Shelley drowned while out sailing in his boat the *Don Juan* with his friend, Edward Williams, in the Gulf of Spezia. LORD BYRON cremated the body and Shelley's ashes were buried in the Protestant cemetery in Rome, near the grave of his son and that of JOHN KEATS.

Principal Works

1813   *Queen Mab*
1819   *The Mask of Anarchy*
1820   PROMETHEUS UNBOUND
1821   *A Defence of Poetry*
1821   *Adonais*
1822   *Hellas*

SPENSER, EDMUND (1552–99)

Ill can he rule the great that cannot reach the small.

The Faerie Queene

Edmund Spenser was probably born in 1552, some 12 years before WILLIAM SHAKESPEARE and CHRISTOPHER MARLOWE. His father was possibly John Spenser, a journeyman cloth maker from Smithfield in London, although it is thought that the Spenser family originated from Lancashire. Despite his modest background, in 1561 Spenser managed to gain entry to the newly opened Merchant Taylors' School. This was the school attended by the dramatist Thomas Kyd and the poet Thomas Lodge shortly afterwards. It was run by the renowned pedagogue Richard Mulcaster who oversaw the teaching of Latin and Greek and the skills of rhetoric.

In May 1569, Spenser left school and matriculated as a 'sizar' at Pembroke College, Cambridge. A sizar was an extremely poor student who had to work for his meals and accommodation. With this in mind, as well as the fact that Spenser was determined to become a great English poet, he made considerable efforts while at Pembroke to make the acquaintance of possible patrons, particularly Robert Dudley, the Earl of Leicester, and John Young, the Bishop of Rochester. After gaining his BA in 1573 and his MA in 1576, Spenser moved to Kent in the employment of Young. While there, he was suitably inspired by the Kent landscape and he wrote his much derided poem *The Shepheardes Calendar*. Spenser wrote the poem in a deliberately archaic language in order to produce an imitation of his rustic surroundings, but his contemporaries, such as the critic Sir Philip Sidney and the dramatist BEN JONSON, complained that it did not pay due homage to the Greek and Latin classics.

Spenser published *The Shepheardes Calendar* in 1579, although by this time he was probably already working for Dudley as his private secretary. With Dudley's influence, Spenser was able to secure a posting in Dublin with Lord Grey of Wilton who had himself just been appointed Lord Deputy of Ireland. Shortly after arriving, Spenser accompanied Grey to Smerwick where he witnessed the destruction of a much larger force of papal and Spanish troops by the English. This was not the last such event that Spenser was to witness in the years that followed, for, as he undertook a succession of, government posts over the next few years, he was involved in or an observer of many acts of military oppression. Spenser probably wrote about his unhappiness with this state of affairs in the anonymously published *A View of the Present State of Ireland.*

> Forever frustrated in his political career because of a lack of useful contacts, Spenser was able to exert far more influence with his poetry. *The Faerie Queene* in particular elicited the admiration of many of his contemporaries and several subsequent generations have learnt the art of verse from his work.

As a reward for his services in Ireland, Spenser was given 3,028 acres of land near Doneraile, including the old castle at Kilcolman – both of them confiscated from the disgraced Earl of Desmond. Some time prior to 1589, Spenser made the acquaintance of the influential courtier, explorer and writer Sir Walter Ralegh. Ralegh was living on his estate in Munster at the time and after he had read Spenser's draft of the first three books of THE FAERIE QUEENE, he invited Spenser to accompany him to London in 1590 where Ralegh presented him to Queen Elizabeth. Elizabeth, who was a poet herself, was impressed by Spenser's work and promised a generous pension which would have enabled him to live in England. However, Lord Burghley, Counsellor to the Queen, intervened and argued that the pension should be reduced, and it duly was. Incensed by Burghley's intervention, Spenser wrote a lampoon of him in a volume of poems called *Complaints*, published in 1591. This caused such offence that the publication was immediately withdrawn and Spenser was forced to return to Ireland. There, he met and fell in love with Elizabeth Boyle, a relation of the first Earl of Cork. They were married on 11 June 1594, an event Spenser celebrated in *Amoretti and Epithalamion*, published in London in the following year.

During this time Spenser continued to

work on *The Faerie Queene*, and in 1596 he published the revised six-book version. He also tried to secure further court patronage to enable him to remain in London but once again he failed and by 1598 he was back in Ireland. This time, by order of the Privy Council, he was appointed Sheriff for County Cork, a position that promised future advancement. However, in August 1598 the Earl of Tyrone defeated the Queen's army and thus begun the uprising in Munster. Spenser's home was sacked and he and his family fled to Cork. From there he was dispatched to London with messages for the Privy Council. Residing in King Street in Westminster, Spenser died suddenly on 13 January 1599. According to a letter written by JONSON, Spenser was impoverished and 'died for lake of bread'.

It is said that the Earl of Essex paid for his funeral, and that, as befits the poets' poet, a number of writers carried Spenser's coffin, throwing their verses and pens into his grave. He was buried in Poets' Corner in Westminster Abbey, appropriately next to GEOFFREY CHAUCER, the poet he had always admired. Like Chaucer, Spenser's influence has been most keenly felt in the tradition of English letters. He was a prolific experimenter with verse forms and a host of other poets, including JOHN MILTON, PERCY SHELLEY, LORD BYRON and JOHN KEATS, learned the art of versification from him.

Principal Works

1579	*The Shepheardes Calendar*
1590–96	THE FAERIE QUEENE
1595	*Amoretti and Epithalamion*

> ## STERNE, LAURENCE (1713–68)
> *Certainly it was ordained as a scourge upon the pride of human wisdom, that the wisest of us all, should thus outwit ourselves, and eternally forego our purposes in the intemperate act of pursuing them.*
> The Life and Opinions of Tristram Shandy

Laurence Sterne was born on 24 November 1713 in Clonmel, Ireland. His father, Roger

Sterne, was a British army officer who happened to be posted in Ireland at the time of Sterne's birth. His great-grandfather was the Archbishop of York. Sterne's father died in 1731 and his mother stayed on in Ireland. Although Sterne spent much of his childhood in Ireland, at the age of 10 he was sent to live with a relation in Yorkshire. From there he went to a school in Halifax and then, with a little help, to Jesus College, Cambridge. Sterne was not a particularly distinguished student, although he did seize the opportunity to make some rich and, eventually, powerful friends. While there, Sterne also suffered from a haemorrhage in his lungs – the first attack of a poor health that would come to plague him sporadically for the rest of his life.

Ostensibly a clergyman, Sterne was always drawn to writing. When he published the first two volumes of *Tristram Shandy* they proved to be such a success that he was commissioned to write many more and he became famous around the world.

After he left university, Sterne studied for the priesthood and in 1738 became a priest in the Anglican Church, with the help of his family. He was given the living of Sutton-in-the-Forest, in Yorkshire, in the same year, where he remained until 1759. Over the next few years, Sterne gradually improved his income to the point where he was able to marry the woman he had been courting for the previous 18 months, a Miss Elizabeth Lumley. She brought with her additional financial benefits to Sterne's life, but she did not bring a great deal of happiness other than the birth of a daughter, Lydia. Indeed, at one point in the marriage his wife was regarded as insane. Matters were probably not helped by Sterne's own intemperate nature, which often found him associating with other women.

In 1758 Sterne made his first attempt at writing something other than a sermon when he penned a satire ultimately entitled *The Good Warm Watch Coat*. This was not well received by his superiors in the church who were the targets of its attack and so it was suppressed. Undaunted by this, Sterne set about writing his great work, THE LIFE AND OPINIONS OF TRISTRAM SHANDY, GENTLEMAN. The first two vol-

umes were printed in 1759 and proved to be an enormous and perhaps surprising success. He soon became famous and was feted wherever he went, even to the point of having his portrait painted by Sir Joshua Reynolds. In the following year Sterne produced two more volumes of *Tristram Shandy*, as well as a book of sermons, *The Sermons of Mr. Yorick*.

In 1761 Sterne completed another two volumes of *Tristram Shandy*. However, his health was suffering and he went to France in search of a cure. Although Sterne was famous in France too, he tired of travelling about and in 1764 he returned to England, leaving his family there. He then published another two volumes of *Tristram Shandy* in 1765 and fell ill once more. He travelled to France and Italy, before returning to London in 1766 where he published the final volume. This was also the year he met Eliza Draper, a woman with whom he had an affair and about whom he wrote *Journal to Eliza*, which was not published for 150 years. In 1768 he completed *A Sentimental Journey*, recounting his travels in France and Italy. However, a month later Sterne died on 18 March 1768, leaving behind him a large debt. It was reported that his grave was subsequently re-opened and his body was used for the study of anatomy.

Principal Works

1759–66	THE LIFE AND OPINIONS OF TRISTRAM SHANDY, GENTLEMAN
1768	*A Sentimental Journey*

STEVENSON, ROBERT LOUIS (1850–94)

Politics is perhaps the only profession for which no preparation is thought necessary.
   Familiar Studies of Men and Books

Robert Lewis Balfour Stevenson was born on 13 November 1850 in Edinburgh. His father, Thomas Stevenson, was an engineer who helped to build Scotland's lighthouses. Stevenson's mother was Margaret Isabella Balfour, and she came from a family of lawyers and churchmen. As a child Stevenson was dogged by ill health. He continually suffered from bouts of tuberculosis which left him unable to leave his bed. Nevertheless, he managed to turn his enforced convalescences to some account by inventing stories, even before he could actually read. By the time he was 16, Stevenson had composed his first historical tale. The following year he entered Edinburgh University where he intended to study engineering and follow in his father's footsteps by joining the family lighthouse business.

> Born into a family of lighthouse engineers, Stevenson took the view that 'there is no duty we so much underrate as the duty of being happy' and so, much preferring to travel, he did this instead and wrote about his journeys as a way of paying for them. Eventually he turned his talents to writing stories and novels, including *Dr Jekyll and Mr Hyde* and *Treasure Island*.

However, Stevenson was not long into his studies before he realised the impracticality of his plan, given his poor health and switched to studying the more sedentary subject of law. In 1875 he was called to the Scottish Bar, although by now he had decided that he wanted to be a writer so he did not pursue a career in law. Instead Stevenson set off to travel around various parts of Europe. It was during this period that he met Fanny Vandegrift Osbourne, an American woman, with whom he fell in love despite the fact that she was married already with two children. When she returned to the United States to get a divorce, Stevenson followed her to California where they were married in 1880. They honeymooned at an abandoned silver mine, an account of which Stevenson wrote in *The Silverado Squatters* in 1883.

By this stage Stevenson had established himself as a travel writer of some repute. However, it was when he composed his collection of short stories in *New Arabian Nights* in 1882 that he began to earn a reputation as an intelligent writer of fiction. He also wrote *Treasure Island* at this time, having returned to Scotland for a holiday and been forced inside because of the rain. Stevenson was seized by the idea when he helped his stepson create a treasure map. In 1885, Stevenson and his fam-

ily moved to Bournemouth where he made the acquaintance of HENRY JAMES and other literary figures of the time. In 1886 Stevenson published, *THE STRANGE CASE OF DR JEKYLL AND MR HYDE*. Well received by critics, Stevenson was encouraged to write *The Master of Ballantrae* (1889), which many writers consider to be his best work.

By the time this was published, Stevenson had set off on a voyage around the South Pacific, taking with him his whole family. In 1889 they arrived in the Samoan islands and decided to settle there. This proved to be a beneficial move for his health and, removed from the distractions of literary life in Britain, his written output increased, despite problems with Fanny who suffered from a mental breakdown. Stevenson also became enchanted by Polynesian culture and began, but never finished, a lengthy volume of his observations of island life. He even composed correspondence on behalf of the islanders, condemning French colonial exploitation. Eventually, however, a lifetime of bad health caught up with Stevenson and he died on 3 December 1894. He was buried, in accordance with his wishes, at the top of Mount Vaea in Samoa.

Principal Works

1882	*New Arabian Nights*
1883	*Treasure Island*
1886	*Kidnapped*
1886	*THE STRANGE CASE OF DR JEKYLL AND MR HYDE*
1889	*The Master of Ballantrae*

> ## STOKER, BRAM (1847–1912)
> *I have not yet seen the Count in daylight. Can it be that he sleeps when others wake, that he may be awake whilst they sleep!*
> Dracula

Bram Stoker was born Abraham Stoker on 8 November 1847 in Clontarf, a coastal village near Dublin. He was the third of seven children whose father was a civil servant working at Dublin Castle. Stoker spent much of his childhood laid up in bed, suffering from a mysterious disorder which left him unable to stand up on his own. Stoker only overcame this illness when he was about 8 years old.

Thereafter, Stoker seemed determined, like SAMUEL JOHNSON before him, to overcome his physical frailty by becoming an outstanding athlete. When he eventually went to study at Trinity College, Dublin, he became the star of the football team and the university athletics champion.

While at university, Stoker studied, and ultimately graduated in, pure mathematics. He also became the president of the Philosophical Society, as well as indulging his love for the theatre. It was during one of his visits to the theatre that Stoker first saw the great actor Henry Irving, for whom he would later go on to work. Following his graduation from university, Stoker joined the Civil Service in 1870. Stoker did not find this the most fulfilling of jobs and so, while there, he took up an unpaid post as theatre critic for the *Evening Mail* and the *Irish Echo*. It was after reviewing Irving's performance in *HAMLET* that Stoker and the actor became good friends.

> Bram Stoker spent most of his adult life working for the actor Henry Irving. His first attempt at writing was a Civil Service manual, followed by a collection of children's stories, and it was only relatively late in his life that he wrote the novel that made him famous, *Dracula*.

In 1878, this friendship led to Irving offering Stoker the job of manager at the Lyceum Theatre in London, which Stoker accepted and moved to London. In the same year, he also married the former girlfriend of OSCAR WILDE, the 20-year-old Florence Balcombe. Stoker and Florence went on to have one son together, a boy called Noel, but after that they are thought to have become covertly estranged. Working for Irving afforded Stoker a number of opportunities, such as travelling to the United States and Canada, and meeting famous authors like Sir Arthur Conan Doyle, the creator of Sherlock Holmes, and the poet WALT WHITMAN.

During this time, Stoker continued to write. Ironically, his first book had been about the Civil Service, but in 1882 he, like Wilde a few years later, published a collection of children's short stories, *Under the Sunset*. In 1890 Stoker published his first novel – *The Snake's Pass*. At around the same time he met a Hungarian professor who recounted to Stoker the story of Vlad Tepes, the Romanian aristocrat who became the model for Dracula. In 1897 Stoker published *DRACULA* and it was a massive success. Although Stoker continued to write after this, including two more novels, *The Jewel of Seven Stars* in 1903 and *The Lair of the White Worm* in 1911, it is for *Dracula* that he is now remembered. Stoker also continued to work for Irving until the actor died in 1905, and he went on to publish *Personal Reminiscences of Henry Irving* in the following year. However, after the death of Irving, Stoker's health began to suffer and he died on 20 April 1912 in London and was buried in Golders Green Crematorium.

Principal Work

1897   *DRACULA*

STOWE, HARRIET BEECHER (1811–96)

No one is so thoroughly superstitious as the godless man.

Uncle Tom's Cabin

Photo credit: © Bettmann/CORBIS

Harriet Beecher Stowe was born Harriet Elizabeth Beecher on 14 June 1811 in Litchfield, Connecticut. Her father was Lyman Beecher, a controversial Calvinist theologian, and her mother was Roxana Ward Foote. Stowe was the fourth daughter and seventh child born to her parents, but, after two more children, Stowe's mother died in 1816. Her father then remarried but Stowe did not entirely get on with her stepmother. Nevertheless, her father continued to exert a powerful influence over his children and, in the end, all of his sons ended up joining the ministry, while many of the daughters became renowned educators. Within this atmosphere, Stowe went to study at Litchfield Academy, one of the first schools to offer academic courses to women.

In 1824 Stowe moved to Hartford, Connecticut to join the Hartford Female Seminary founded by her sisters. When Stowe graduated she went on to teach at the school herself. In 1832 Stowe's father decided to accept the presidency of Lane Theological Seminary in Cincinnati, Ohio and so the whole family moved from the comforts of New England to what was then the largest city in the West. Stowe's sister founded another school, the Western Female Institute, and Stowe began to teach there too. In 1836 Stowe married Calvin Ellis Stowe, from whom she took the name. Calvin was the widow of Stowe's best friend, Eliza Tyler, who had just died. Calvin was devoted to her memory and the two of them named one of their twins after her, as well as hanging a painting of her over the fireplace. In addition, Calvin was a good friend of Stowe's father, and he taught Biblical literature. The couple went on to have seven children, although only Stowe's first three outlived her.

> When her husband struggled to make enough money, Harriet Beecher Stowe decided to try and augment his income by writing stories. This proved to be moderately successful until, outraged by the Fugitive Slave Act, Stowe wrote the anti-slavery novel *Uncle Tom's Cabin* which became the bestselling book of its day.

As Calvin did not make much money from his job, Stowe decided to try and augment their income by writing stories. She had, in fact, been submitting stories for publication since 1834, but in 1843 she completed her first collection of stories in a book – *The Mayflower: Sketches of Scenes and Characters among the Descendants of the Puritans.* Although this went some way towards improving their situation, her family continued to live in poor circumstances until 1850, when Calvin was offered a professorship at Bowdoin College, Maine. In the same year, the Fugitive Slave Act was passed. This made it a criminal offence for anyone anywhere in the United States to help a fugitive slave. Stowe was outraged by this, as were many other New Englanders who lived in the North precisely because slavery was illegal there. Stowe decided upon writing a book which she hoped would demonstrate to people in the South quite how unconscionable slavery was. The result of her efforts was *Uncle Tom's Cabin.*

It was initially published in serial form in an anti-slavery journal, *The National Era*, in 1851. Although well received, this format did not lend itself to persuading anyone but the converted. However, in 1852 *Uncle Tom's Cabin* was reprinted as a book. This time its impact was enormous and by the end of the year it had gone on to sell 350,000 copies. By the end of the century it was the best-selling book in America, apart from the *BIBLE*. The novel helped to bring the abolition of slavery to the top of the political agenda, where it remained until the issue was resolved by the Civil War.

Stowe went on to write another anti-slavery novel, *Dred: A Tale of the Great Dismal Swamp* (1856), but this proved nowhere near as popular. Indeed, Stowe continued to write for much of the rest of her life. She was one of the first contributors in 1857 to *Atlantic Monthly*, and also produced a host of other books and novels. These other works pioneered and belonged to the so-called Regionalist School of writing, as practised too by KATE CHOPIN. Perhaps the best of these were *The Pearl of Orr's Island* (1862), *Oldtown Folks* (1869) and *Poganuc People* (1878). After the death of her husband in 1886, Stowe's own health began to fail and she died on 1 July 1896.

Principal Work

1851–52   *UNCLE TOM'S CABIN*

SWIFT, JONATHAN (1667–1745)

Satire is a sort of glass, wherein beholders do generally discover everybody's face but their own.

The Battle of the Books

Jonathan Swift was born to English parents in Dublin on 30 November 1667, seven years before the death of the poet JOHN MILTON. His father, also called Jonathan Swift, was a lawyer and an English civil servant who died seven months before his second child and only son was born. Abigail Erick, Swift's mother, was left unable to support her family and so Swift was taken to relatives in England by his nurse. Four years later, Swift was sent back to Ireland, even though Swift's mother returned to England, leaving her son to the guardianship of her wealthy brother-in-law, Uncle Godwin.

From 1674–82, Swift was educated at Kilkenny Grammar School, alongside the dramatist William Congreve, and from there he went to Trinity College in Dublin. Swift was apparently a rather headstrong student but despite this he managed to earn a BA in 1686 and an MA in 1689. For the next few years Swift found employment as secretary in the house of his kinsman, Sir William Temple. Temple was a retired diplomat, friend of King William (for whom he helped to arrange his marriage with Mary) and ardent advocate of naturalness in garden design. Swift lived with him in his house at Moor Park in England. It was during this time that Swift met Esther Johnson, whom he later referred to as 'Stella', and became her tutor.

Although Swift only lived in Ireland reluctantly, he became a national hero when he exposed a plot to flood the country with corrupt coinage. He became even more popular when he penned 'A Modest Proposal', exposing the famine crisis there. All his works, including *Gulliver's Travels*, were marked by a fierce scepticism for, as he remarked, 'The most positive men are the most credulous'.

Unhappy with his life as a *de facto* servant, Swift then decided, albeit reluctantly, to embark upon a career in the Church. Unable to find a church in England, Swift returned to Ireland where he was ordained an Anglican priest and, in 1695, was given a modest prebend at Kilroot. Very quickly, however, the prebend proved to be too modest for Swift and so, in the following year, he returned to Moor Park where he remained until the death of Temple in 1699. During this period he composed two of his most famous works, *The Battle of the Books*, a satire on the supremacy of ancient and modern authors, and *A Tale of a Tub*, a satire on the excesses of religion. Both of these were not printed until 1704. Sadly, much of the rest of Swift's work from this era was burned by the author himself.

Forced to return to Ireland when Temple died, Swift once again found gainful employment hard to come by and ended up as the vicar at Laracor. Esther moved over to Ireland with Swift and lived near him, although the two never lived together or, as far as we know, ever spent any time alone with each other. She also returned with him on Swift's many trips to London. On these trips Swift made the acquaintance of many of the leading writers of the day, such as Joseph Addison and Richard Steele, with whom he contributed to popular political magazines of the day, such as *The Spectator* and *The Tatler*.

Through them he was introduced to the Whig party with whom he briefly considered forming a political career. However, he was perturbed by the Whigs' indifference to the state of the Anglican Church in Ireland and so he left them in 1710 for the other major party in England at the time, the Tories. By this time, Swift was already known for his spirited satires and polemics and so the Tories were happy for him to take over the editorship of their party journal, *The Examiner*. As a reward for his services, if not quite the one he might have hoped for, Swift was given the deanship of St Patrick's Cathedral in Dublin in 1713. This was also about the time that he cemented his position as a leading member of the English *literati* when he helped to found the *Scriblerus Club* with other eminent writers such as ALEXANDER POPE, John Gay and John Arbuthnot.

This unusually blessed period of advancement in Swift's life soon came to an end when the Tories fell from power the following year. Returning to Ireland, Swift became involved with another woman, Esther Vanhomrigh, the 'Vanessa' of his poem *Cadenus and Vanessa*. However, she, like everyone else, was never certain of Stella's role in Swift's life, and, having probed too far, he broke off the relationship and she promptly died. In the following year, 1724, Swift became a national hero of the Irish when he wrote a series of letters under the pseudonym 'M.B. Drapier'. These letters were instrumental in revealing the corruption behind a scam to debase the Irish currency through favours gained corruptly at the English court. In 1729, Swift confirmed his status as a defender of liberty when he wrote an essay on the problem of famine in Ireland, *A Modest Proposal*. This masterpiece of satire advocates eating surplus children as the most efficient way to solve the food crisis.

In between these two works, in 1726, Swift wrote the book for which he is now most famous, *GULLIVER'S TRAVELS*. This too is a satire, following Captain Gulliver on his travels around the world and describing the different peoples he meets on his way. It is generally considered to express a dim view of humanity, and one shared by the writer himself. Swift, however, declared that he was only a misanthrope in general, whereas he quite liked individuals. As proof of that, Swift donated a large portion of his income to good causes throughout the later part of his life, and even set aside an amount each year for the building of St Patrick's Hospital for Imbeciles (no nation needed it as much, he argued), which was built in 1757. Swift's perceived misanthropy may well not have been helped by his suffering from what is now generally considered to be Ménière's disease. This caused him nausea, deafness and dizziness. After 1739 he was no longer able to fulfil his duties at the cathedral and he retired, living out his years in some misery until he died on 19 October 1745. He was buried in St Patrick's next to Stella.

Principal Works

1704   *The Battle of the Books*
1704   *A Tale of a Tub*
1717   'A Proposal for Correcting the English Language'
1726   *Gulliver's Travels*
1728   'A Short View of the State of Ireland'
1729   'A Modest Proposal'

TENNYSON, ALFRED, LORD (1809–92)

Theirs not to reason why,
Theirs but to do and die.
        'The Charge of the Light Brigade'

Alfred Tennyson was born on 6 August 1809 in Somersby, Lincolnshire. He was the fourth of 12 children born to Elizabeth Fychte and George Clayton Tennyson. Tennyson's grandfather had defied the tradition which generally saw the eldest child inherit the father's wealth and title, and instead bequeathed his wealth to the brother of Tennyson's father.

While Tennyson's uncle got to live in a castle, Tennyson's father entered into the Church, much against his will. Tennyson's father was then an unhappy and sometimes abusive man by the time that Tennyson was born. In addition to this, in 1833, one of Tennyson's brothers was detained in a mental institution and stayed there all his life. Tennyson's father was a heavy drinker, as was another of his brothers, who also happened to be an opium addict. Rows were frequent in the small rectory in Somersby and there was little form of escape as Tennyson's father taught his own children after Tennyson had spent only five years at his local school.

> Critically, as well as commercially successful, Tennyson was the most popular poet of the Victorian era in both Britain and America. Tennyson succeeded Wordsworth as Poet Laureate in 1850.

As some form of escape from this domestic turmoil, Tennyson turned to poetry from an early age. This stood him in good stead when he attended Trinity College at the University of Cambridge where his poems caught the attention of a club known as 'The Apostles'. The Apostles were a group of young scholars interested in debating the arts and sciences. Chief among them was Arthur Hallam, a man who later became engaged to Tennyson's sister. The two of them became firm friends and Hallam did much to develop Tennyson's confidence, which was generally hidden somewhere inside his massive ambling frame. Unfortunately, Tennyson was unable to finish his studies because of the parlous state of his family's finances. Returning home, Tennyson published two volumes of poetry, *Poems, Chiefly Lyrical* in 1830 and *Poems* in 1832. He had won a prize for his poetry while at Cambridge so was perhaps surprised by the savage reviews he received at the hands of some of the more prominent publications of the day. Following these attacks, Tennyson did not publish another poem for ten years.

In 1833 Tennyson suffered one of the greatest blows of his life when his friend Hallam died unexpectedly. To make matters worse, Tennyson's life in the 1830s was dogged by financial insecurity which affected his engagement to Emily Sellwood. Feeling unable to marry her because of his lack of money, Tennyson broke off with her in 1840 and did not resume contact with his future bride until the golden year of 1850 when he was at last able to marry her. In 1842 Tennyson published a revised version of *Poems*, which showed a huge leap forward in terms of his technique. It proved to be hugely popular this time around and it eventually established his reputation. Although Tennyson had a breakdown in 1843 following the loss of his entire fortune the previous year, by 1844 he had been awarded a small pension by the government which would ease his money worries forever.

In 1850 Tennyson published his masterpiece, IN MEMORIAM. Born out of the grief he felt for the loss of Hallam, it struck a chord with both critics and public alike and established him as the most popular poet in both Britain and America (to the extent that even WALT WHITMAN called him 'the Boss'). On top of his success with *In Memoriam* and his marriage to Emily, with whom he would go on to have two sons, Tennyson was also made Poet Laureate in the same year, taking over the post from WILLIAM WORDSWORTH. In the years that followed Tennyson continued to write poetry that was extremely popular (including 'The Charge of the Light Brigade' in 1854), although not all of it is as well received by critics today. Most of his poetic energies in the last half of his career were spent on writing *Idylls of the King*, first published in 1859. In 1884 he was made Lord Tennyson at Queen Victoria's insistence. He died on 6 October 1892 and was buried in Poets' Corner at Westminster Abbey in London.

Principal Works

1850 IN MEMORIAM
1855 *Maud*
1859 *Idylls of the King*

THACKERAY, WILLIAM MAKEPEACE (1811–63)

How hard it is to make an Englishman acknowledge that he is happy!

Pendennis

William Makepeace Thackeray was born on 18 July 1811 in Calcutta, India. He was the only son of Anne Becher and Richmond Thackeray, an administrator in the East India Company. In 1815 Thackeray's father died of a fever and, shortly afterwards, his mother sent him to England. On his way to England, Thackeray is supposed to have stopped at the island of St Helena where a servant pointed out Napoleon who was being kept prisoner there. In England, Thackeray initially attended schools in Southampton, but he was unhappy there and it was only when his newly re-married mother returned to England that his spirits lifted. He then attended Charterhouse School where he studied, albeit poorly, for six years.

In 1829 Thackeray went to Trinity College at the University of Cambridge. There he made a few important friends, but he did precious little work and left after just over a year without gaining his degree. Thackeray next went to the Continent, staying in Weimar over the winter of 1830–1831. There he met the ageing German writer Johann Wolfgang von Goethe, and learnt about the German tradition of Romanticism represented in Britain by poets such as SAMUEL TAYLOR COLERIDGE and WILLIAM WORDSWORTH. When Thackeray returned to England, he had spent much of his fortune and so he decided to study law at the Middle Temple. This, like much of Thackeray's life at the time, was more of a token effort and much of his time was taken up following the pursuits of the leisurely gentleman.

In 1833 he decided to become a newspaper proprietor and bought the *National Standard*. When this failed and an Indian bank in which he held investments also folded, Thackeray's fortune was almost completely gone and after a brief experiment trying to support himself as an artist in Paris, he returned to London with the serious intention of making some money. This he did by writing sketches and articles for various periodicals, most notably *Punch*, using various ridiculous names, such as George Savage Fitz-Boodle, Michael Angelo Titmarsh. It was also at this time that Thackeray met his wife Isabella Shaw, whom he married in 1836. At the beginning of the marriage the two of them were very happy. However, as time wore on, and as Thackeray struggled under an ever-increasing burden to write in order to support his family, his wife suffered a nervous breakdown. This led him to try several cures but nothing seemed to work. He therefore decided upon letting his mother bring up his two children, while he put Isabella into the care of an institution.

After losing his fortune in India, the country of his birth, Thackeray turned to writing to support himself and his mentally unstable wife. With the publication of *Vanity Fair*, Thackeray found the kind of success as a novelist that was only surpassed in his own time by his great rival Charles Dickens. This rivalry did not always suit Thackeray for, as he remarked, 'The true pleasure of life is to live with your inferiors.'

Ironically, just as his personal life was reaching its nadir, Thackeray's professional life hit its zenith with the publication of his most famous novel *VANITY FAIR*. It was originally serialised in *Punch* in 1847–48 and, after an inauspicious start, it became incredibly popular. Thackeray was at last able to free himself from the burden of writing anything that would sell. He followed it up with *Pendennis* in 1849–50, and in 1852 with *The History of Henry Esmond*, the novel which he considered to be his finest, and for which he wrote a sequel, *The Virginians*, in 1857–59. During this time Thackeray was competing with CHARLES DICKENS, although Dickens always proved more popular, and the two even quarrelled on occasion. However, Thackeray followed in Dickens's footsteps and went on lucrative lecture tours, both in Britain and America. He also edited the *Cornhill* magazine for a few years and this made him sufficient money that when he died, on 24 December 1863, he was able to leave his daughters the inheritance that he had lost during his lifetime.

Principal Works

1847–48	*VANITY FAIR*
1849–50	*Pendennis*
1852	*The History of Henry Esmond*
1857–59	*The Virginians*

THOREAU, HENRY DAVID (1817–62)

The mass of men lead lives of quiet desperation.

Walden

Christened David Henry Thoreau, although his parents always called him Henry, Thoreau was born on 12 July 1817 in Concord, Massachusetts to John Thoreau and Cynthia Dunbar. He was the third of four children. Apart from a brief move to Boston, four years at college and six months at Staten Island, Thoreau spent his whole life in and around Concord. He spent much time as a child exploring the natural environment of the area, and by the age of 4 he had already fallen in love with Walden Pond, which through his poetry he would go on to make famous around the English-speaking world. He was also a highly capable student and after performing well at Concord Academy in the years from 1828 to 1833, Thoreau's parents raised the necessary funds for him to attend Harvard. Before he graduated in 1837, nineteenth out of a class of 44, he undertook some teaching so that after attaining his degree it seemed natural for him to continue in that profession. However, after just two weeks at Center School, he was forced to resign because he refused to inflict corporal punishment upon the students.

In the same year, he met the local writer and thinker RALPH WALDO EMERSON. The two men became friends and Thoreau accepted a reference from him in his attempt to find employment. At that time Thoreau worked in his father's pencil-making factory but in the following year, 1838, Thoreau re-opened Concord Academy with his brother, John. The rubric of the school was practically based and encouraged field trips and nature walks. It proved to be a success but it had to close a few years later when John fell ill. John eventually died of tetanus in 1842. During this era, Thoreau enjoyed a series of romances and even went so far as proposing to one woman by letter, but was refused. Thoreau would remain single for the rest of his life. After the Academy closed in 1841, Thoreau went to work for Emerson as a handyman, performing odd jobs in return for board and lodgings.

This arrangement continued for a couple of years, during which time Thoreau also met the writer NATHANIEL HAWTHORNE. Hawthorne was impressed with the unruly-looking Thoreau's knowledge of and sympathy with the natural environment. Thoreau put this knowledge and sympathy to good use in 1845 when he moved into a log cabin he had built on Walden Pond. Finding that he had become an object of much local curiosity, as most Harvard men did not live in wooden huts, Thoreau kept a journal, recording each day his thoughts and philosophy on his way of life and, when he returned he gave a series of lectures. Thoreau used these lectures as the basis for his books *A Week on the Concord and Merrimack Rivers* in 1849 and *WALDEN* in 1854. While still living at Walden Pond, Thoreau spent a night in jail for refusing to pay a poll tax. His objection was based on his dislike of the government's slavery laws, which he refused to support. From this experience he wrote his most famous essay 'Resistance to

One of the earliest exponents of an alternative lifestyle, Thoreau famously abandoned the conventional life of a Harvard graduate in order to live in a log cabin by Walden Pond. During this time, he refused to pay a tax because it went to a slavery-supporting government and he became notorious for his pamphlet 'Resistance to Civil Government'.

Civil Government' or, as it is better known, 'Civil Disobedience'. This work later went on to inspire such civil rights leaders as Mahatma Gandhi and Martin Luther King. Thoreau himself dedicated the greater part of his remaining life to anti-slavery protests, as well as recording the lives of the indigenous population and the natural environment. He contracted a heavy cold while counting tree rings in late 1860 which aggravated his natural tendency to tuberculosis and he died on 6 May 1862.

Principal Works

1849   'Resistance to Civil Government'
1849   *A Week on the Concord and Merrimack Rivers*
1854   *WALDEN*

TWAIN, MARK (1835–1910)

What are the proper proportions of a maxim? A minimum of sound to a maximum of sense.

Holograph

Mark Twain was born Samuel Langhorne Clemens on 30 November 1835 in the village of Florida, Missouri. He was the third of five children and he grew up in Hannibal, Missouri, where his father opened a general store. In 1847 Twain's father died and, in the following year, Twain was apprenticed to a printer, Joseph Ament of the *Courier* newspaper. When his brother Orion returned to Hannibal in 1850, he bought the *Western Union* newspaper and Twain went to work for him. Over the course of the next few years, Twain began to publish the first of his short stories, including 'The Dandy Frightening the Squatter' in 1852.

In 1853 Twain left Hannibal to become a journeyman printer, travelling through St Louis, New York, and Philadelphia, amongst other places, and hiring himself out on a day-by-day basis. By 1857, however, he had decided to give that up and become a steamboat pilot. To this end he apprenticed himself to Captain Horace Bixby of the *Paul Jones*, and two years later he was a fully qualified pilot. Twain practised his lucrative trade for another two years before the start of the Civil War put paid to traffic on the river. After a brief stint as a Confederate soldier, Twain joined his brother in Nevada in the hope of becoming a miner. When this did not work out, he became a reporter for the *Territorial Enterprise*, the newspaper where he first used the pseudonym 'Mark Twain', named after a riverboat call indicating two fathoms of water.

Over the next few years, Twain worked for a variety of newspapers on a variety of jobs, including the onerous task of covering the new route from San Francisco to Honolulu. He also went on the first of many lecture tours across America, and took a trip to the Holy Land which he later recorded in his first book, *Innocents Abroad* (1869). The following year Twain married Olivia Langdon, the daughter of a wealthy industrialist and the complete opposite of the cigar-toting, wild-drinking Twain. Their first son was born and died in the same year. They would go on to have three daughters together.

In 1875 Twain published seven instalments of *Old Times on the Mississippi* in the influential journal *Atlantic Monthly*. This was an account of his life as a steamboat pilot and it became the basis of his book, *Life on the Mississippi*, eventually published in 1883. In 1876 Twain drew on the same material to publish *The Adventures of Tom Sawyer*. This proved to be successful and so Twain set to work on his, and what many critics think to be America's, masterpiece – THE ADVENTURES OF HUCKLEBERRY FINN, published in 1885. This too was very successful and he followed it up in 1889 with *A Connecticut Yankee at King Arthur's Court* and in 1894 with *The Tragedy of Pudd'nhead Wilson*.

> After working for many years as a printer, Twain fulfilled his ambition to become a riverboat pilot. He drew on this experience to compose his masterpiece, *Adventures of Huckleberry Finn*. Suspicious of such accolades, he once declared that a 'classic' is merely 'a book which people praise and don't read'.

It was here that things started to go wrong for Twain. His investments, which included a number of patents (his most successful being one for the self-pasting scrapbook) began to fail and he was left bankrupt. In order to pay off his debts, Twain embarked on a world lecture tour and while he was away his oldest daughter died of meningitis. After clearing his debts, Twain's wife fell ill and although Twain moved to Italy for the third time in his life in order to help her recuperate, she died in Florence in 1904. Five years later, his youngest daughter, who had become a severe epileptic, also died. Twain, who was showered with honorary degrees and other plaudits in his later years, died just four months later on 21 April 1910.

Principal Works

1869   *Innocents Abroad*
1876   *The Adventures of Tom Sawyer*
1883   *Life on the Mississippi*
1885   THE ADVENTURES OF HUCKLEBERRY FINN
1889   *A Connecticut Yankee at King Arthur's Court*
1894   *The Tragedy of Pudd'nhead Wilson*

WALPOLE, HORACE (1717–97)

The world is a comedy to those that think, a tragedy to those who feel.
Letter to Sir Horace Mann

Horace Walpole was born on 24 September 1717 in London. He was the fourth son born to Sir Robert Walpole, effectively British Prime Minister between 1721 and 1742. Sir Robert famously went to war with Spain over a severed ear and was notoriously corrupt, making him the subject of many satires by HENRY FIELDING, JONATHAN SWIFT and ALEXANDER POPE amongst others. Born into this atmosphere, Horace Walpole proved to be quite different from his domineering father to the extent that some people suspected he was not actually his father's son. This rumour was not helped by the fact that Horace lived mainly with his mother who had become all but separated from Sir Robert.

As a privilege of his class, Walpole attended Eton school between 1727 and 1734, and then King's College at the University of Cambridge from 1735 to 1738. Walpole was not an outstanding scholar but he left Cambridge without taking a degree mainly because he did not need one. In 1739 Walpole commenced the Grand Tour of Europe with the poet Thomas Gray (who would go on to pen 'Elegy Written in a Country Churchyard'). Gray and Walpole had been friends since Eton, and Gray once even agreed to compose an ode in memory of Walpole's drowned cat. However the two of them quarrelled and Walpole returned alone in 1741; the two were only reconciled several years later.

Upon Walpole's return, Sir Robert secured a seat for his son as a Member of Parliament. Although Horace was not ambitious after the manner of his father, he did continue to sit as an MP following the death of Sir Robert in 1745. Sir Robert had already provided several lucrative posts for Walpole, but Sir Robert's death meant that Walpole would remain a wealthy man for the rest of his life. In 1747

Walpole used some of his wealth to buy Strawberry Hill, a small estate in Twickenham, near where POPE had lived just a few years before. He quickly set about remodelling the main house in a miscellaneous fashion that came to be considered a precursor to the new Gothic tradition and which was very much the opposite of the prevailing trend for neo-classical features.

The son of effectively Britain's first Prime Minister, Horace Walpole led a privileged life. He used his wealth to establish a new architectural style and accompanied that with the first Gothic novel, *The Castle of Otranto*.

The newly refashioned house or castle (Walpole himself originally and endearingly called it 'the prettiest bauble you ever saw') proved to be very popular with visitors. In 1757 Walpole established a private press there and went on to print some of Gray's poems. In 1764 Walpole published the literary accompaniment to Strawberry Hill in the form of his novel – THE CASTLE OF OTRANTO. This was wildly popular and set in motion the new genre of Gothic fiction which would dominate the British literary world for many years to come. Walpole continued to write other novels and plays, as well as books on art and gardening. Many of these were moderately successful, but over time it has been his voluminous correspondence (some 3,000 letters) which has proved to be the most rewarding part of his output, detailing, as it does, a long period in British history. Walpole died on 2 March 1797 in London.

Principal Work

1764   THE CASTLE OF OTRANTO

WHARTON, EDITH (1862–1937)

One knows one's weak points so well, that it's rather bewildering to have the critics overlook them and invent others.

The Letters of Edith Wharton

Edith Wharton was born Edith Newbold Jones on 24 January 1862 in New York City. She was the youngest and only female child of three in the wealthy family of Lucretia Rhinelander and George Frederic Jones. In 1866 the family set off for Europe where they spent the next six years, travelling and living in Italy, Spain and Germany. After suffering from typhoid fever, Wharton returned with her family to New York in 1872. There, her education continued under private tuition.

In 1876 Wharton began writing, beginning with a novella, before she moved on to composing poetry that her mother privately printed for her in 1878. These poems were eventually seen by William Dean Howells, the editor of the influential journal *Atlantic Monthly*. He printed five of them in the magazine in 1880. In the same year, Wharton, who had been presented to society only in 1879, became engaged to Harry Stevens. His mother opposed the engagement and two years later it was broken off. Three years after that Stevens died. In the meantime Wharton had met the great love of her life, Walter Berry, as well as Edward Robbins Wharton.

Edward Wharton was a banker from Boston, 12 years older than Wharton, and she apparently felt no great enthusiasm for him. Nevertheless, in 1885 the couple were married. Thereafter they lived in Newport and New York, while holidaying extensively in Europe. Meanwhile, Wharton continued to write poetry and short stories, both of which were published in *Atlantic Monthly*, as well as in the newly influential *Scribner's Magazine*. However, from 1890 onwards, Wharton began to suffer from a series of mysterious nervous complaints. These developed throughout the 1890s into nausea and respiratory illnesses. Her problems were not helped by her husband's own mental instability which also began to exhibit itself at this time.

By the beginning of the twentieth century, Wharton was publishing books, as well as maintaining her intensive schedule of magazine work. Unlike her contemporary, JACK LONDON, her prolific output was not for the want of money because when her mother died her income from various trusts topped $22,000 per year. In 1904, after meeting HENRY JAMES (of whom she became an ardent admirer and secret benefactor), Wharton began to write *The House of Mirth*. Set in New York, like many of the books that followed, it described the travails of a young woman in a pitiless city. This turned out to be her first major novel and when it was published in 1905 it proved a big success.

Wharton married her husband with no great enthusiasm and the two of them spent their lives together suffering from various mental illnesses. During this period Wharton produced her best novels and it was only after she finally divorced her husband (remarking that 'a New York divorce is in itself a diploma of virtue') that her work began to lose its edge.

Wharton followed up *The House of Mirth* with her most popular story, ETHAN FROME. This was published in 1911, two years after she had moved to Paris, and in 1913 she produced her next great work, *The Custom of the Country*. In the same year, Wharton finally divorced her husband who, some few years previously, had embezzled $50,000 from her accounts. After her divorce, Wharton's work was never quite as strident again, even though she still managed to produce popular work, such as *The Age of Innocence* in 1920, for which she won the Pulitzer Prize when Sinclair Lewis's book *Main Street* was rejected. She spent the rest of her life in comparative happiness, travelling round Europe and North Africa and fundraising for the American Hostels for Refugees. She died on 11 August 1937 in St.-Brice-sous-Forêt, France.

Principal Works

1905   *The House of Mirth*
1911   ETHAN FROME
1913   *The Custom of the Country*
1920   *The Age of Innocence*

WHITMAN, WALT (1819–92)

O Captain! my Captain! rise up and hear the bells;

Rise up – for you the flag is flung – for you the bugle trills.

Memories of President Lincoln

Walter Whitman was born on 31 May 1819 in New York. Whitman's father was a former farmer who became a carpenter, moving the family to Brooklyn. Whitman was taught in local schools, but he left formal education behind him when he joined a law firm as an office boy at the age of 11. Just a year later, and already enthralled by the novels of WALTER SCOTT (which MARK TWAIN would later accuse of ruining American literature), Whitman began his apprenticeship working as a printer while contributing mawkish items to the local newspaper. By the age of 16 he had become a journeyman printer, working largely in Manhattan. In fact, Whitman rarely left the New York area for the rest of his life, taking just one important trip to New Orleans and another trip to the West.

When he was 17, Whitman found himself out of a job and so he returned home to Long Island where he worked as a teacher. However, he did not make himself particularly popular at home, or among the parents whose children he taught, largely because he appeared to them to be lazy and would do little outside of normal classroom hours. This charge of laziness followed Whitman about for the rest of his life and caused a considerable rift in his own family. For his part, Whitman considered that he was becoming a great writer and all the purposeless walking he did (which was a habit also enjoyed by his contemporary CHARLES DICKENS), as well as the late-night reading and general day-dreaming were all contributing to his uncompromising cause as a poet.

Walt Whitman was America's first great national poet. He dedicated most of his life to revising and adding to his collection of poems – *Leaves of Grass*.

At the age of 21 Whitman returned to Manhattan where, after publishing stories in the *Democratic Review* and becoming something of a minor politician, Whitman secured the editorship of a local newspaper, *Aurora*. Whitman managed to lose this posting when, once again, he was publicly charged with laziness. Over the next few years, Whitman continued as a journalist and hack writer for various magazines and papers. He was sacked from the Brooklyn *Eagle* in 1848 for his political views and, a couple of years later, all but gave up journalism in favour of working as a carpenter. In

1854, Whitman also gave up being a carpenter and settled down to finish the collection of poems he had been working on for several years, LEAVES OF GRASS. In 1855 the first edition of Whitman's book was finally published.

The book was not an immediate success and because Whitman was having to devote more time to his family following the death of his father, he had little time initially to publicise it. Whitman did, however, manage to secure the backing of RALPH WALDO EMERSON who famously wrote to Whitman saying: 'I greet you at the beginning of a great career.' Whitman then printed out Emerson's letter and inserted it into copies of his book and sent it out to other influential literary people. Whitman's life and career thereafter largely consisted of revising and adding to *Leaves of Grass*. This he did assiduously, despite the fact that some of the more frank erotica in the collection once caused him to lose his job with the post-war government.

The same problem meant that Whitman's work was often rejected by some of the more prestigious literary magazines of the day. Indeed, on another occasion he was even unable to print the book at all following threatened legal action on the grounds of obscenity by the Boston district attorney. Whitman's British reception, on the other hand, did much to bolster good opinion in the United States. When he died at Camden on 26 March 1892, Whitman knew that he would not be forgotten. Now many critics think that Whitman's groundbreaking poetic sequence is one of the greatest pieces of literature ever written, and certainly America's greatest epic.

Principal Work

1855–81   *LEAVES OF GRASS*

WILDE, OSCAR (1854–1900)

I can resist everything except temptation.
Lady Windermere's Fan

Credit: Illustrated London News

Oscar Fingal O'Flahertie Wills Wilde was born on 15 October 1854 in Dublin. He was the second son of Sir William Wilde, a renowned ear and eye surgeon, and Lady Jane Francesca Elgee, a writer whose pen name was Sperenza. Wilde's sister died at an early age and it has been conjectured that Wilde's mother consequently enjoyed dressing him as a girl, a fact that later led to Wilde's own outrageous clothing. Wilde attended Portora Royal School at Enniskillen in 1864, then he went to Trinity College, Dublin in 1871, and finally, in 1874 he went up to Magdalen College, University of Oxford.

A brilliant wit and conversationalist, when W.B. Yeats met Oscar Wilde he reported that he spoke in 'perfect sentences'. Wilde put this wit to good use in such plays as *The Importance of Being Earnest*, although his literary career was cut short when he was imprisoned for being a homosexual. On his deathbed he is supposed to have uttered, 'Either that wallpaper goes or I do.'

At Oxford Wilde proved himself to be a brilliant student. Like MATTHEW ARNOLD before him, Wilde won the Newdigate Prize in 1878 for his poem 'Ravenna'. It was here also that he came under the influence of the aesthetic philosophers Walter Pater and John Ruskin. When Wilde graduated from college he went to live in London where he quickly became the leading spokesperson for the philosophy of 'art for art's sake'. Like T.S. Eliot 40 years later, Wilde developed his own literary lineage, tracing back his poetic ancestors to writers such as Dante Rossetti and JOHN KEATS. In espousing these views, Wilde made a lecture tour of the United States in 1882 where, upon arriving at customs, he purportedly said, 'I have nothing to declare but my genius.'

The lecture tour was a great success, as was the one he made afterwards in Great Britain. However, the early plays he wrote proved to be failures. In 1884 Wilde married Constance Lloyd, the wealthy daughter of a Dublin barrister, with whom he went on to have two sons. They lived in the fashionable district of Chelsea in London. In order to support his new family, Wilde became editor of *Woman's World* in 1887. In 1888 he published *The Happy Prince and Other Tales*, a collection of children's stories. These were enormously popular and in the following year he was able to give up his editing work and concentrate on writing *The Picture of Dorian Gray*.

First published in serialised form in 1890, *The Picture of Dorian Gray* was published as a novel in 1891. Telling the story of a man who stayed young while his picture grew old, it was both a great scandal and a success and launched Wilde on the most productive part of his writing career. In 1892 he wrote his first great play, *Lady Windermere's Fan*, following that up with *A Woman of No Importance* in 1893, and *An Ideal Husband* and THE IMPORTANCE OF BEING EARNEST in 1895. However, in the same year as his greatest triumph, Wilde also met his nemesis. Since 1891 he had been courting Lord Alfred Douglas. Wilde's marriage had effectively ended in 1893 and Wilde had, since then, been more open about his homosexual relationship with Douglas. When Douglas's father accused Wilde of being a homosexual, Wilde sued him for libel and during the course of the trial Wilde's sexual activities were exposed. As homosexuality was then a crime in England, Wilde was sentenced to two years in jail with hard labour.

While in prison Wilde wrote his best poem, *The Ballad of Reading Gaol*, as well as a prose work, *De Profundis*. When he was released, Wilde went to live in Paris under the assumed name of Sebastian Melmoth. He died there of cerebral meningitis on 30 November 1900. He said before he died that he had put his genius into his life but only his talent into his work.

Principal Works

1891	*The Picture of Dorian Gray*
1892	*Lady Windermere's Fan*
1893	*A Woman of No Importance*
1895	*An Ideal Husband*
1895	THE IMPORTANCE OF BEING EARNEST
1898	*'The Ballad of Reading Gaol'*

WOLLSTONECRAFT, MARY (1759–97)

A slavish bondage to parents cramps every faculty of the mind.
A Vindicaton of the Rights of Woman

Mary Wollstonecraft was born on 27 April 1759 in London to John Wollstonecraft and Elizabeth Dickson, as the second of six children. Wollstonecraft's father had inherited a large fortune which he set about spending on farming. He was not particularly skilled at this occupation, however, and the family moved about continuously when one farm after another failed. This led her father to drink quite heavily and beat his wife whom Wollstonecraft used to try and protect as best she could. During this time, in 1775, Wollstonecraft became friends with Fanny Blood.

In 1778 Wollstonecraft left home to become a companion to a rich widow in Bath, but she returned in 1780 to look after her mother through a long illness that eventually led to the mother's death in 1782. In 1784 Wollstonecraft's sister Eliza had a difficult birth and was, according to Wollstonecraft, abused by her husband. Wollstonecraft persuaded her to flee from her husband and after lying low for a while, they set up a girls' school at Newington Green, London, with Fanny Blood and one of Wollstonecraft's other sisters. This project soon collapsed, however, when Blood went to Lisbon and married. She became pregnant in the same year, 1785, and died in Wollstonecraft's arms of a difficult birth.

> Inspired by the French Revolution, Wollstonecraft composed one of the founding texts of feminism – *A Vindication of the Rights of Woman*. After marrying the social reformer William Godwin, she died giving birth to their daughter, the future Mary Shelley and author of *Frankenstein*.

After this terrible tragedy, Wollstonecraft went to work as a governess for Viscount Kingsborough in Ireland. However, Wollstonecraft soon came into conflict with Lady Kingsborough for the affections of the children and was dismissed. Wollstonecraft then published her first novel, *Mary, A Fiction* in 1788, as well as a children's book, *Original Stories from Real Life*. This proved to be very popular and a second edition was illustrated by WILLIAM BLAKE. In 1790, angered by Edmund Burke's *Reflections on the Revolution in France*, Wollstonecraft published a sympathetic account of the French Revolution, *A Vindication of the Rights of Men*. This powerful polemic was followed in 1792 by her ground-breaking work *A VINDICATION OF THE RIGHTS OF WOMAN*. In the same year, Wollstonecraft went to France to observe first-hand the Revolution in action.

While in Paris she met Gilbert Imlay, an American businessman, explorer and author. The two became lovers and in 1794 Wollstonecraft had their first child, Fanny Imlay. In 1795 she published *An Historical and Moral View of the Origin and Progress of the French Revolution*. She then returned to London where she was persuaded that Imlay no longer loved her. After a brief flirtation with suicide, Wollstonecraft set off on a business trip to Scandinavia, which inspired her *Letters Written During a Short Residence in Sweden, Norway, and Denmark* (1796). Back in London, Wollstonecraft discovered Imlay with his mistress and promptly threw herself off Putney Bridge in desperation. Luckily she was rescued by a passer-by.

Firmly convinced that Imlay's passion for her was over, Wollstonecraft renewed her acquaintance with William Godwin, the radical author of *Inquiry Concerning Political Justice* and *Caleb Williams*. The two quickly became lovers, Wollstonecraft fell pregnant, and, in 1797, they married in a private ceremony. Their joy, however, was short-lived. On 30 August Wollstonecraft gave birth to Mary Wollstonecraft Godwin, the future MARY SHELLEY, author of *FRANKENSTEIN*, but in doing so she suffered a massive haemorrhage. Wollstonecraft then contracted puerperal fever and on 10 September 1797 she died.

Principal Works

1790   *A Vindication of the Rights of Men*
1792   *A VINDICATION OF THE RIGHTS OF WOMAN*

WORDSWORTH, WILLIAM (1770–1850)

All good poetry is the spontaneous overflow of powerful feelings.

Lyrical Ballads

William Wordsworth was born on 7 April 1770 in Cockermouth, Cumberland, on the edge of the Lake District which he would eventually make famous through his poetry. His father,

John Wordsworth, was a lawyer to Sir James Lowther, a local and much detested aristocrat. His mother, Anne Cookson, died when Wordsworth was just 8. Wordsworth was one of five childen. Wordsworth was then sent to lodge with Ann Tyson while he attended Hawkshead Grammar School, near Esthwaite Lake. During that time Wordsworth became a little unruly, but also deeply influenced by the surrounding countryside. In 1783 Wordsworth's father also died, bequeathing him and his four siblings only the money he was owed by Lowther.

Inspired by the revolutionary fervour of France, Wordsworth helped to orchestrate the Romantic revolution in British poetry when he published *Lyrical Ballads* with Samuel Taylor Coleridge. As he grew older, Wordsworth became more conservative and he finally became part of the establishment when he accepted the post of Poet Laureate.

With the help of two uncles, Wordsworth was able to complete his schooling and then attend St John's College at Cambridge University. Wordsworth was not particularly stimulated by university and he graduated without distinction in 1791. While at university, Wordsworth had taken a walking tour to the French Alps and had been impressed by the excitement of the Revolution. After graduating, Wordsworth decided to return to France. During his time there, from November 1791 to December 1792, Wordsworth met and fell in love with Annette Vallon, the daughter of a barber-surgeon. They planned to marry and soon had a child, Caroline. However, Wordsworth was forced to return to England because of his diminishing funds and then war broke out between England and France and he was unable to go back to Annette.

This experience brought Wordsworth to the edge of a nervous breakdown, but in 1794 he was reunited with the sister upon whom he doted for the rest of his life – Dorothy Wordsworth. She became his confidante and secretary, keeping a journal valuable in its own right. Following the death of a friend, Wordsworth came into an inheritance which enabled him to live off the proceeds of his poetry. At the same time Wordsworth met his great collaborator, SAMUEL TAYLOR COLERIDGE and two years later he moved to Alfoxden House, Somersetshire in order to be nearer to Coleridge. The two poets spoke to each other every day, inspiring and debating with each other, until in 1798 they published the groundbreaking LYRICAL BALLADS. Though not immediately popular, Wordsworth was able to produce a second edition by 1800 with his legendary 'Preface', advising his readers that poetry was the 'spontaneous overflow of powerful feelings'. At the same time, Wordsworth began to write his greatest work, THE PRELUDE, a project he continually revised during his lifetime, but which was not published until after his death.

In 1802 Wordsworth finally received the inheritance due to him from his father. This enabled him to make a settlement with Annette Vallon, whom he met at Calais, and then to marry Mary Hutchinson, a woman he had known since childhood. During the succeeding years, Wordsworth's life was both blessed and blighted. He had five children with Mary by 1810, but two of them died in 1812. One of his brothers died at sea in 1805, and in 1810 he fell out with Coleridge, who was by then a drug addict. On top of these tragedies, his sister Dorothy suffered a mental breakdown in the 1830s from which she never recovered, despite Wordsworth's best nursing. Wordsworth himself grew ever more materially prosperous as the years advanced, earning money from various government sinecures, including his post as Poet Laureate from 1843. While Wordsworth continued to write during these latter years, his poetry rarely approached the quality of his early work. He died on 23 April 1850.

Principal Works

1798–1802	LYRICAL BALLADS
1799–1850	THE PRELUDE

Part 2

A Chronology of Literature in English (450–1914)

(A) LITERATURE IN BRITAIN

Old English literature (450–1100)

Origin of the English language

English is now the most widely spoken language in the world. Part of the reason for its wide circulation comes from its diffusion as a language of conquest. It is therefore appropriate that English itself began as the language of the conquest of what we now call Britain. After the Romans abandoned the southern part of Britain (or Britannia as it was known) at the beginning of the fifth century AD, the Celts who lived there were displaced by invaders from northern Continental Europe. These invaders, the Angles, the Saxons and the Jutes, established themselves over large parts of the country, pushing the indigenous Celts westwards into Wales and Cornwall. Meanwhile, the Scots, a tribe from Ireland, invaded what is now western Scotland pushing the Picts into the north and east of the country.

The country of Britain, if so it can be called at this time, was a mess of small kingdoms each speaking a variety of Germanic dialects that we now call Old English. Old English probably has a more distant relationship to Modern English than Latin has to French. Although we now understand it, it is virtually impossible for a Modern English speaker to read it. One reason for this is that it tended to be written according to local dialects. The people of Northumbria, for instance, wrote it differently from the people of Wessex. Another compelling reason why Old English is hard to read is that there is very little of it remaining.

Bede, Alfred and Aelfric

This is partly because Old English was not the language of official culture. The earliest known English poet, Adhelm (c. 640–709), wrote in English but only his Latin works survive because only they were considered important. Similarly, the work of Saint Bede, or the Venerable Bede (c. 673–735), both a poet and Britain's first great historian, survives almost entirely in Latin, with barely a few lines of his Old English poetry still in existence. Indeed, most of English poetry at the time was passed on orally and was never written down in the first place. One of the reasons this changed was the threat of invasion which was an ever present danger during this period, forcing the small kingdoms to consolidate. With the consolidation of power came the consolidation of the language.

The man chiefly responsible for the consolidation of the English language was King Alfred of Wessex (849–899). When he came to power in 871 he complained of the poor state of education in his kingdom and pledged himself to make English a great language. Before he could fulfil this grand ambition, Alfred first had to defeat the Danes, who had hitherto conquered all other parts of England except the kingdom of Wessex. Having done this, Alfred then set about his task with increasingly personal devotion, translating many books into Old English himself from the Latin he only learnt as an adult. He expressed the hope that 'all young men in England born of free men, and who are rich enough to dedicate themselves to it, be sent to study as long as they are not required for any other purpose, until they are proficient in reading English'.

One of the books that Alfred had translated was Bede's *Historia Ecclesiastica Gentis Anglorum* which became the *Ecclesiastical History of the English People*. One of the reasons for doing this was that Alfred saw in the work the first history of the English-speaking peoples which he thought would give a unity to the history of the English which they had hitherto lacked. By translating it from the Latin into colloquial English, Alfred provided for its dissemination throughout the country. Using it as a foundation and a benchmark, Alfred then initiated *The Anglo-Saxon Chronicles*, a series of annual diaries recording the key events of the year and distributed this around the country. Only the Irish have an older vernacular history than the *Chronicles* and they continued to be kept until 1154, some 250 years after Alfred's death.

Alfred had been inspired to transmit and foster learning by the example of Bede before him. In turn, Alfred then set his own cultural example which finally bore fruit some two generations later in the revival of the culture of Benedictine monks under the reign of Archbishop Dunstan. One of the chief exponents of Old English at this time was Aelfric (*c.* 955–1020), a monk at Cerne Abbas in Dorset. He composed a series of texts that made up *Lives of the Saints*, as well as *Catholic Homilies* – 'Catholic' here used in the sense of being broad-based because they were written in English and therefore available to the laity as well as the Latin-speaking clergy. Aelfric was also known as *Grammaticus* because he produced a book about grammar – one of the first attempts to standardise and codify the English language. Wulfstan, one of Aelfric's contemporaries, also produced a number of Old English works, chief among them his *Sermon of the Wolf to the English*. This was a powerful address intended to steady those, including King Ethelred II, who were uncertain in the face of the Danish invasion, commanding them instead to hold fast to the unity of English culture.

Christianity and Old English literature

The fact that Bede, Aelfric and Wulfstan were all leading figures both in the Church and Old English literature is no coincidence, for the Church was the repository and disseminator of everything literate. As part of the Roman Empire, Britannia had been a Christian country but when the Romans withdrew at the beginning of the fifth century, Christianity became a secondary faith to local forms of paganism. Determined to counteract this trend, the evangelising Pope Gregory sent Augustine of Hippo to head up a group of missionaries and convert the Anglo-Saxons to Christianity. Within three years of arriving in 1597, Augustine managed to convert King Aethelbert in Kent, establishing a see at Canterbury. This began the spread of Christianity across the southern part of Britain, while, in the north, Columba set up a series of monastic communities throughout western Scotland and northern Ireland. The two sets of missionaries, Roman and Irish, though ostensibly teaching the same message, disagreed on a number of points, including the date of Easter. The Council of Whitby in 664 finally decided the Anglo-Saxon church in favour of Roman Catholicism.

The missionaries brought with them the skill of literacy. Prior to their arrival, the various kingdoms of Britannia had been oral cultures, but the Roman emissaries offered up their clerical skills and became the administrators of the Anglo-Saxon world. Indeed, one of the oldest pieces of surviving text in Old English is a manuscript of laws which Aethelbert had committed to writing on the advice of his new monk friends. Centred upon an increasingly powerful series of monasteries, such as the ones at Iona, Lindisfarne and Monkwearmouth, these imported literary skills opened up fresh avenues of cultural commerce with the rest of Europe. The kingdoms of Britain shared in the learning of the rest of the Christian world, contributing their own practical-minded forms of wisdom to the common good. One of the most famous of these contributions is the treatise written in 725 by Bede, *De ratione temporum* [*On the reckoning of time*], which advanced the AD method of calculating the time in years, which the Christian world still uses today.

Given this context, then, it is hardly surprising that most of the surviving literature written in Old English is Christian in orientation. One of the most famous examples of the surviving literature is Caedmon's *Hymn*, a prayer of devotion to God. Written sometime in the second half of the seventh century, the hymn was composed by Caedmon, an uneducated farmhand who, working for the abbey at Whitby, was visited by a vision calling him to sing verse in honour of God. This he promptly did with great skill, and his legend was recorded by Bede in his *Ecclesiastical History*. Very little remains of Caedmon's verse in the vernacular, although in the margins of several copies of Bede's *History*, clerics have scribbled down a version of his *Hymn*.

If a work such as Caedmon's *Hymn* seems obviously and clearly Christian, then the Christian influence can also be seen in the other surviving Old English manuscripts recording poetry of the time. In *The Dream of the Rood*, for example, the vision of the rood or cross tells of an inspiring devotion to Jesus. This work mixes the story of Christ's crucifixion with the traditional warrior code, explaining the Passion in the idiom of traditional heroic verse. The code of loyalty to one's lord, conventionally the subject of oral Old English verse, was adapted to celebrate loyalty to the Lord God. In this idiom, the *Gospels* became war-like stories with mighty heroes performing honourable deeds. Indeed, the most famous work written in Old English, BEOWULF, shows how the template of a Christian religion accommodated the everyday heroic culture of Britain at the time. Beowulf is both a warrior of uncompromising fierceness who honours his lord, but also a Christian hero, considerate to the weak and charitable to the needy.

The Norman Conquest

That Old English literature concentrated more on martial exploits than, for example, the subject of love, is perhaps not surprising given the continual battles that were fought not only between the small kingdoms of Britain, but also between them and various Viking invaders, both from the east and the west. Alfred's defeat of the Danes at the end of the ninth century was something of a compromise as it still left them with a vast swathe of the eastern side of England, called the Danelaw. Following Alfred's death, the work of consolidation was continued by his son, and then, under his grandson King Athelstan, an invasion force of Irish Vikings, Scots and Britons was defeated, enabling him to claim most of what we now call Britain. Internal divisions and further sporadic invasions put paid to this temporary unity and, after a particular piece of political treachery led to the St Brice's Day massacre of all Danes in 1002, the Danes gained revenge by invading England in 1013 and destroying much of the south of the country. The whole of England, Denmark and Norway was then temporarily united under the rule of King Canute, but his successors once again divided the kingdoms.

Britain was not the only country to suffer from Viking invasions. France too was continually subject to attack along its northern coasts but, in 911, a treaty was brought into effect ceding the Duchy of the Northmen, or Normandy, to the Vikings. A marriage between the Norman widow of King Ethelred and King Canute sealed the connection between Normandy and England that led, in 1066, to the last effective invasion of England by Duke William II, or William the Conqueror as he defeated King Harold at the Battle of Hastings to claim the English throne. Although, as a Norman, William had a Viking heritage, he belonged to a people that had thoroughly assimilated themselves into French life. Therefore when he took charge of England he brought with him both a French language and a French culture. While Latin was still the language of the church, the official language quickly became French and it remained so for the next 300 years. Under these conditions Old English literature all but disappeared in its written form.

Figure 1: Texts and contexts of Old English literature (450–1100)

Text			Context	
		400–600	Romans withdraw from Britain; invasion of Angles, Saxons and Jutes
		597	Augustine's mission to Canterbury; conversion of Britain to Christianity
658–80	Caedmon – *Hymn*	664	Council of Whitby
700–1000	*Beowulf**		
731	Bede – *Ecclesiastical History of the English People*		
800–1000	*The Dream of the Rood*	871	Accession of King Alfred
878–1154	*The Anglo-Saxon Chronicles*	954	England united under Wessex
993–998	Aelfric – *Lives of the Saints*		
1014	Wulfstan – *Sermon of the Wolf to the English*	1066	Invasion of England by William the Conqueror

Note: *Work featured in Part 3

Middle English literature (1100–1485)

The story of Middle English

The victory of William the Conqueror at the Battle of Hastings in 1066 inaugurated a period of massive change for the English language. William made some attempt to learn his new country's native tongue, but he failed. Almost overnight, Old English was displaced as the language of the ruling class in favour of a form of Germanic French known as Norman French. Latin continued as the primary language of religious institutions, but Old English, apart from a few exceptions, such as in *The Anglo Saxon Chronicles* written at Peterborough monastery, disappeared as a written idiom. Nevertheless, Old English continued as a verbal language spoken by most of the indigenous population. This strange situation in which the ruling elite conducted their daily lives in one language, while the masses conducted theirs in another, inevitably produced not only a large number of bilingual households, but also a compromise language.

This compromise language, which was only produced over a period of several hundred years, is what we now refer to as Middle English – the language of CHAUCER. Middle English was the product of both centripetal and centrifugal forces. On the one hand, lacking either a core of written texts or daily use by the organs of state, Old English became highly localised, fragmenting into ever greater dialectical varieties. Whereas in Modern English, dialect is largely a matter of pronunciation, in the eleventh and twelfth centuries it was also a matter of grammar and vocabulary. On the other hand, in attempts to make sense of the language they heard about them, the Norman scribes wrote down the sounds of English words using the principles hitherto reserved for the French language. For example, the Old English *cwen* became the Middle English *queen*. The standardisation of the written language, as approximate as it was, also led to the simplification of English. Among the changes, perhaps surprisingly, was the loss of inflections (in the sense of endings indicating case and number, such as are still used in Spanish and Italian) and the gender of nouns (such as exist in French and Portuguese).

The commingling of Norman French and Old English also led to the introduction of thousands of French words into the language, many of which are still with us today. Very often these words would refer to the same thing, co-existing for a while before coming to indicate slightly diverse meanings. An example of this might be the Old English word *house*, alongside of which was the Norman French word *mansion*. Over time these two words began to refer to different things. In this way, Middle English, and eventually Modern English too, became an extremely subtle language which, although simple in grammar, was correspondingly complex in meaning. Old English had been a concrete language with many words for specific things but, as King Alfred found when translating Boethius's *Consolation of Philosophy* from the Latin, it did not have such abstract dexterity. Norman French brought with it a large number of conceptual words which enriched the available vocabulary of English speakers.

New forms of literature: The Romance

The Normans not only brought new words to the English language, they also brought new literary forms to English literature. In fact, it is difficult to talk of an 'English literature' during the century or so after the Norman invasion because not only were the new genres French but they were, initially, written in French too. The dominant new genre, replacing epics of the likes of BEOWULF, was the romance. *Romance* can still be used, as it originally was, to refer to any language deriving from Latin, such as French. However, following the Norman invasion it came to designate anything written in French, and then anything associated with French literature, and, finally, more specifically, a form of narrative, usually in verse, which depicts the loves, trials and adventures of knights. Such stories are usually episodic in form in which a knight will go from one battle to another with often only the slenderest of threads holding the battles together, such as the love of a virtuous woman.

Ironically, many of the French romances were based on the stories of the British legend of King Arthur and his knights of the Round Table. The origin of many of these stories is Geoffrey of Monmouth's *Historia Regum Britanniae*, or *History of the Kings of Britain*. Composed in Latin by a man who has been described as either Welsh, Cornish or Breton and who happened to be canon of St George's in Oxford, the *Historia* was, Geoffrey claimed, based on an 'ancient book in the British language'. No such book has ever been found. Completed in 1138, many believed even then that the stories of Arthur were fake but, nevertheless, they were hugely popular, forming one of the staple stories of the romance.

The route they took is suggestive of the complex interactions between the various languages and cultures in north west Europe at the time. For having been based on a Celtic legend, then written up in Latin in England, the stories of Arthur were translated into French some 60 years later by Robert Wace, a monk residing in Jersey. His *Roman de Brut* soon after provided the basis for Chrétien de Troyes' *Erec et Enide*, sometimes put forward as the first Arthurian romance. Troyes' book was thereafter converted into *lais*, short verses by one of the first female poets, Marie de France, who lived in England but wrote for a Norman audience. The popularity of these *lais* led a Worcestershire priest named Layamon to translate Wace's *Brut* into Middle English. Layamon's translation is actually an adaptation of Wace's work and is much longer but it remains recognisably cognate with Wace's *Brut* and it also remains the oldest surviving work of any length in Middle English.

The rise of Middle English literature

The stories of Arthur's adventures took on an enormous potency in English politics, despite the fact that Arthur, had he ever existed, would have been a Briton ranged against the invading Angles who became the English. Part of the reason for this, ironically enough, stemmed from the death of Arthur of Brittany, the heir to the English throne and supposedly killed by King John in 1203. The divisions caused by this fight for the throne led to Normandy being seized by the French and the beginnings of a conflict that would set the French and the English at war with each other on and off for centuries to come. The eventual result of this never-ending conflict was that England began to assert a sense of its own identity. Part of that process involved developing a literature of its own, written in its own language. This process was not immediate, as is evident from the fact that Parliament conducted its business in French until 1362, but over time French gave way to English as the language of choice for the whole population.

The literature that accompanied this resurgence in the English language largely came to fruition during the difficult reign of Richard II (1377–99). In particular there was a great flowering of English poetry. This took two forms – a revival of the alliterative verse of Old English and an adoption of the French and Italian decasyllabic verse forms. In terms of the first of these, the most important poems of the period were William Langland's *Piers Plowman*, and the anonymously written *Sir Gawain and the Green Knight*. *Piers Plowman* is a highly complex work which recounts a dream of spiritual salvation. Like *Beowulf*, each line of the verse is self-contained and uses the internal rhymes of alliteration, such as in the opening, 'In a somer seson, whan soft was the sonne,' where the words play off the 's' sound. *Sir Gawain and the Green Knight* espouses a kind of earthly spirituality in the form of chivalry. It recounts the tale of the Green Knight's challenge to the Round Table which is taken up by Sir Gawain. Written some 250 years after Geoffrey of Monmouth first invoked the Arthurian legend, it shows quite how compelling the romance genre had become.

If *Sir Gawain and the Green Knight* and *Piers Plowman* were in one way revivals of old stories and forms, albeit they were written in the comparatively new literary language of Middle English, then the work of Geoffrey Chaucer seemed to offer a new direction for English literature. Chaucer took this direction largely from the great Italian writers of the fourteenth century: Dante, who wrote *The Divine Comedy*, Petrarch, whose *Canzoniere* inspired generations of love poetry, and Boccaccio, who composed the tales of the *Decameron* as a distraction from the ravages of the plague.

In particular, Chaucer wanted to attempt to match in Middle English Dante's achievement of creating an Italian vernacular poetry for the first time. To this end, in *The Canterbury Tales* and other works, Chaucer imitated the rhythms of natural speech in order to construct the verse form of what basically became the heroic couplet – two lines of ten syllables each. In imitation of Dante and Boccaccio, Chaucer placed his work self-consciously at the beginning of a vernacular tradition of English literature and ever since then, other writers have not only accepted Chaucer's position but have attempted to situate themselves in regard to him.

The word on the page and the word on the street

In 1399, a year before Chaucer died, Henry IV became the first English king since the invasion of William the Conqueror to assume the throne speaking English as his primary language. This was an affirmation of the upsurge in the English tongue, symbolically setting the seal on the destiny of the language over the following century. Of less symbolic import but far more practical effect was the introduction of the printing press into England by William Caxton in the 1470s. Like Chaucer, Caxton had learnt his trade on the Continent and had then decided to put it to a specifically

English use. The move towards regularised modes of writing was already under way, but Caxton, with his powerful new machine, decided early on to give that move a helping hand. He thought that only when English had developed a uniform standard of grammar and spelling could it compete with the national literatures of other countries. To this end he both refused to publish the old irregular forms of standard verse and heavily doctored new works.

One of the new works which Caxton had a big hand in editing was Sir Thomas Malory's *Le Morte D'Arthur*. Like JOHN BUNYAN's *THE PILGRIM'S PROGRESS*, *Le Morte D'Arthur* was written while its author was in prison. Although the title belonged to Caxton, the story itself of the Arthurian legend was undoubtedly Malory's. Its tale of chivalry and good knightly conduct may have been a form of penance for Malory who, although a knight, spent much of his life engaged in less than chivalrous behaviour. It is perhaps appropriate that this, one of the most popular refashionings of the Arthurian legend, should also be one of the first works to be printed in English. For although Caxton, to some extent, created the English reading public, he also published for pre-existing tastes.

There was only one other topic of English literature that matched the subject of romance for popularity, and that was anything that dealt with religious or spiritual matters. Particularly popular in this regard were the liturgical dramas that formed the mystery or miracle plays performed by various guilds of workers on the midsummer feast day (as it then was) of Corpus Christi. These plays, such as *The Second Shepherds' Play* attributed to the Wakefield Master, retold in vernacular form stories from the *BIBLE*. Of the surviving manuscripts, a particularly English practicality infects these spiritual dramas (in much the same way as it does Malory's *Morte D'Arthur*). For example, *The Second Shepherds' Play* is ostensibly concerned with the birth of the saviour of the world, but the majority of the drama is taken up with the search for a stolen sheep disguised as a baby. Such dramas remained popular until the youth of SHAKESPEARE in the second half of the following century, when a newly privatised form of drama would become one of the high points of English literature.

Figure 2: Texts and contexts of Middle English literature (1100–1485)

Text		Context	
1138	Geoffrey of Monmouth – *Historia Regum Britanniae*		
		1149	Foundation of University of Oxford
1154	End of *The Anglo-Saxon Chronicles*		
		1170	Murder of Thomas à Becket, after dispute with Henry II
1185–1225	Layamon – *Brut*	1189	Richard the Lionheart becomes King
		1204	French seize Normandy.
1375–1400	*Sir Gawain and the Green Knight**	1337–1453	Hundred Years' War
		1362	English becomes the language of Parliament
1377–79	William Langland – *Piers Plowman*		
		1381	Peasants' Revolt ends with death of Wat Tyler
1385–87	Chaucer – *Troilus and Criseyde*		
1386–1400	Chaucer – *The Canterbury Tales**	1399	Richard II deposed by Henry IV*
		1415	Henry V wins Battle of Agincourt
1450–75	Wakefield Mystery Cycle – *The Second Shepherds' Play*	1453	Charles VII wins Battle of Castillon, ending English occupation of France
1470	Sir Thomas Malory – *Le Morte D'Arthur*		
		1476	William Caxton sets up first printing press in England
		1485	Henry VII wins War of the Roses

Note: *Work featured in Part 3

Tudor and Stuart literature (1485–1660)

The emergence of Modern English

The most influential book written by an Englishman in the first half of the sixteenth century was composed and published in Latin. The book in question, Thomas More's *Utopia*, continued the long line of important works penned in Latin which stretched from Bede's *Historia Ecclesiastica Gentis Anglorum* in 731 through to Geoffrey of Monmouth's *Historia Regum Britanniae* in 1138. More's *Utopia* would also be the last of that line of major works because, by the end of the sixteenth century, English would have proved itself to be capable of expressing the kind of diverse and elastic modes of address that many writers once thought was only possible in either Latin or a Latinate language. The English that would prove itself in this way is what is now referred to as Modern English. As with the transition from Old English to Middle English, the change from Middle English to Modern English was a gradual one but still one that was accelerated by a key event. If the event that helped to turn Old English into Middle English was the invasion of England by William the Conqueror in 1066, then the introduction of the printing press by William Caxton in 1476 expedited the transition from Middle English to Modern English.

Very quickly, the commercial possibilities of printing for a mass audience called for a standardised form of English that could be understood by everyone. This, the printers decided, should be more closely related to the way words sounded. In standardising the English language, the printers also had to contend with two disharmonious forces. The first of these was what is now called the Great Vowel Shift. The Great Vowel Shift involved an alteration in the pronunciation of long and short vowel sounds in a way that enabled a differentiation, for example, between *room* and *Rome*. The other factor that precluded stabilising the English language was its seemingly infinite capacity to absorb new words. These new words largely came from two sources. The first of these sources was the physical aggrandisement of England as, over the next few hundred years, it expanded its borders, amalgamating its nearest neighbours, Wales, Scotland and Ireland. This was by no means a peaceful task and the speaking of English was brutally enforced, particularly in Ireland, all but destroying the old Celtic languages. What English gained from being forcibly exported into neighbouring lands was the import of a whole host of new words, such as *slug* and *smithereens*. As England developed an empire over the following years, the remit of the English language expanded correspondingly, leading to a constant stream of neologisms from almost every part of the world.

The other source of new words at the time was an almost frenzied period of linguistic invention broadly occurring during the course of the sixteenth century. Partly this was an attempt to address the concerns of anyone who might wish to emulate More in writing a social or philosophical tract like *Utopia*. The new words were designed to supplant the Latin and, to a lesser extent Greek, idioms traditionally associated with the learned discourses, such as philosophy, law and medicine. The seemingly unrestricted licence to make words up, which perhaps reached its apogee in the work of WILLIAM SHAKESPEARE who was always happy, for example, to turn a noun into a verb, invoked consternation in many observers. Critics accused those who flaunted the practice of creating new words of being 'inkhorns'. They also expressed the concern that if English were to become a suitable medium for the serious arts, its very openness to change made it unsuitable to record the supposedly immutable truths of philosophy. This proved to be an unfounded worry, and later attempts to regulate the English language by a Continental-style Academy failed wherever they were suggested.

The three 'R's: Renaissance, Reformation and Restoration

There were other external influences on English literature during this period besides the development of the language. One of these influences was what we now term the Renaissance. The Renaissance (meaning 'rebirth') refers to a revived interest in learning based upon the classical principles of ancient Rome and Greece. While this may sound a backward step, it was actually a way of creating distance from the medieval past and initiating something new. Indeed, the Renaissance not only marks the dawn of Modern English, but also the dawn of modernity itself and the kind of scientific, human-centred individualistic society which we recognise as our own. Part of the reason we still refer to the 'Dark Ages' as such is because we have inherited the attitudes of the Renaissance which preferred, in the stereotype, the expansive, sun-drenched pagan philosophies of the Romans and Greeks to the narrow theological discussions of cloistered monks under feudal law.

The Renaissance came late to England. Italy, in particular, enjoyed the fruits of an interest in new areas of knowledge, such as astronomy and painting (paid for on the back of an expanding mercantile empire) some 200 years before England. The problem with England was that it was largely bankrupt and unstable following a series of wars both externally with France and inside its own territories. The advent of the Tudor reign in 1485 brought the kind of peaceful and centralised regime that encouraged prosperity and, with it, England's own Renaissance. This began as a scholarly endeavour on behalf of the likes of Thomas More, the Chancellor of England under Henry VIII, which advanced a general concern for cultural education along classical lines. This, in turn, led to an increased interest in translating Greek and Roman works, a process which also fostered the production of many of Modern English's new words. In their turn, these translations provided material for the chief gain of England's new culture – Elizabethan drama. The best-known example in this regard is the work of SHAKESPEARE who, lacking a classical education himself, had to rely on the translations of Terence and Plautus to furnish him with the stories and plots of his plays. Indeed, not only did Shakespeare and others employ classical plots, they also used the classical five-act structure of the Romans. This classically inspired culture in sixteenth-century England, combined with its emergent capitalist economy, also gave birth to the first professional theatres in England during this period and thereby offered a platform for the work of Shakespeare and his contemporaries, including CHRISTOPHER MARLOWE and BEN JONSON.

If the Renaissance created the conditions for a burgeoning English literature, the Reformation almost simultaneously destroyed it. Begun in northern Europe by Martin Luther, a professor of theology at the University of Wittenberg, the

Mr. WILLIAM
SHAKESPEARES
COMEDIES,
HISTORIES, &
TRAGEDIES.

Publifhed according to the True Originall Copies.

This engraving by Martin Droeshout appeared in the first Folio edition of Shakespeare's plays (1623).
© Bettman/CORBIS

Reformation describes a group of people, often conflicting, who were opposed to the corruption they thought lay at the heart of the Roman Catholic church. Broadly speaking, reformers felt that Roman Catholicism had drifted too far from the text of the *Bible* in pursuit of earthly wealth and power. In order to counteract this problem, they worked to initiate a Protestant religion in which the *Bible*, rather than the Church or priests, was the mainstay of a form of personal devotion not mediated by the institution of Catholicism. The key to this new Protestant religion, itself a kind of Renaissance project involving a return to roots, was individual access to the *Bible*, hitherto denied people who could not read Latin. In order to answer this need, a series of vernacular translations of the *Bible* soon appeared, aided in its dissemination by the flourishing publishing business.

In Roman Catholic England the Protestant religion had long been suppressed to the point where a law had been passed at the beginning of the fifteenth century exacting the death penalty for such heretics. However, when Henry VIII demanded that Pope Clement VII grant him a divorce from Catherine of Aragon in order that he might marry someone else who could provide him with a male heir, the Pope, under pressure from Emperor Charles V, Catherine's nephew, refused. Henry quickly took matters into his own hands, forced the Church in England to grant him a divorce and then declared himself Supreme Head of the Church of England. A series of acts was quickly passed forcing people to swear allegiance to Henry rather than to the Pope. One who refused was the King's old friend, Thomas More. As a token of their friendship, More was spared being hung, drawn and quartered and was merely beheaded instead.

Initially, the Church of England remained a Catholic rather than Roman Catholic church. However, after Henry had dissolved all the monasteries, claiming their wealth for himself and in the process burning most of the literature written in Old and early Middle English, the country edged ever closer to a form of Protestantism. By the time Henry died and his sickly son Edward became King, England had firmly rejected Catholicism as witnessed by one of the most enduring pieces of English literature – the *Book of Common Prayer*, published as the mainstay of church services in 1549. However, the situation was never stable for very long. As Henry's various heirs took turns at claiming the throne over the following years, the country lurched from staunch Roman Catholicism to extreme Protestantism. Although Protestantism finally established itself as the country's religion under Elizabeth I, it remained an issue that dominated English and British life for the next few centuries. Catholics, in particular, suffered greatly. Among other restrictions, they were unable to join any part of the Civil Service or to take a degree. Many writers, from JOHN DONNE to JOHN DRYDEN, had their careers blighted by such prejudice.

A religious matter precipitated the next major crisis when Charles I attempted to force Scotland to use the Book of Common Prayer. The Presbyterian Scots refused and Charles I attempted to organise an invasion. This failed and in order to raise funds, he was forced to recall Parliament, which he had earlier dismissed as an affront to his divine right to rule as king. Once Parliament was recalled, old divisions arose over the extent of the monarch's powers. When Irish Catholics massacred thousands of English and Scottish Protestants in 1641, Parliament again refused the funding for

Charles to create an army. Charles tried to arrest several Parliamentarians and in consequence the country fell into civil war. The war only ended when Charles was executed in 1649 and a republic was then declared. Once again, in Renaissance fashion, it was more an imitation of classical republics in which the elite ruled, rather than anything truly democratic. Although initially popular, under the rule of Oliver Cromwell the new style of government became increasingly autocratic and, because it was largely Puritan in orientation, its strict laws were felt to be repressive. By 1660 the populace, if not JOHN MILTON, was ready to welcome back Charles II and the restoration of the monarchy. This time, however, the power of the monarchy was tempered by that of Parliament.

The Theatre

The dramatic events of the period from 1485 to 1660 were matched, when political conditions allowed, by an equally dramatic literature, largely and not coincidentally dominated by the theatre. The few theatres licensed to put on plays were all in London. From their inception in the latter quarter of the sixteenth century, they offered the only viable way for a professional writer to make a living. Poets were often sponsored by rich patrons, but it was a precarious source of income, whereas being a playwright made economic sense in a country obsessed with spectacle and the theatricality of royalty and the clergy. MARLOWE, SHAKESPEARE and JONSON are the best known of a close-knit group of writers, actors and theatre managers who dominated the culture of the relatively stable Elizabethan and Jacobean era. Shakespeare's work in particular offers a range and quality unsurpassed by any writer in any medium writing in English. Less educated, and therefore less self-conscious about his place in the canon of English literature than CHAUCER, Shakespeare has, since his death, become the writer most admired by other writers.

Marlowe, with tragedies such as *DOCTOR FAUSTUS* and *Tamburlaine*, may well be said to have provided the template for the kind of drama that Shakespeare went on to perfect. Jonson, on the other hand, invented his own kind of drama – the comedy of humours based on stock types. Such comedy had to jostle for space with the revenge tragedy, brought to its apotheosis by John Webster in such plays as *The White Devil* (1612) and *The Duchess of Malfi* (1613). Shorn of heroes, these plays mimic the intrigues of court politics and, with their bloody endings, they anticipate the Civil War in the years ahead. They also signalled the death knell of the English Renaissance because, with the commencement of hostilities in 1642, the theatres were shut down and not reopened again until the Restoration in 1660. It was at this point that the effects of the Reformation upon English culture really began to tell. Dominated by a Puritan sensibility which shunned everything from the most obvious religious idols through to the small spectacle of the theatre, the English elevated the written word to pre-eminence over the image and the picturesque. Aided and abetted by a language more than twice the size of some European tongues, the cultures of the English-speaking world embraced Protestantism and became decidedly bookish.

Figure 3: Texts and contexts of Tudor and Stuart literature (1485–1660)

Text		Context	
		1485	Reign of Tudors begins with Henry VII
		1509	Henry VIII becomes King
1516	Thomas More – *Utopia*		
		1534–35	Henry VIII declares himself head of Church of England. Thomas More beheaded
1549	*Book of Common Prayer*		
		1558	Elizabeth I becomes Queen
		1587–88	Mary, Queen of Scots executed; failure of Spanish Armada
1590–93	Christopher Marlowe – *Doctor Faustus**		
1590–96	Edmund Spenser – *The Faerie Queene**		
1595–1635	John Donne – *Songs and Sonnets**		
1600	William Shakespeare – *Hamlet**		
1603–05	William Shakespeare – *Othello**, King Lear**	1603	Reign of Stuarts begins with James I (James VI of Scotland)
		1605	Gunpowder Plot attempt by Catholics to blow up Parliament
1606	Ben Jonson – *Volpone**, William Shakespeare – *Macbeth**		
1611	*Authorised King James Version of the Bible**		
		1620	*Mayflower* pilgrims land in New England
1637	John Milton – *Lycidas*		
		1642–49	Civil War. Ends with execution of Charles I and declaration of Republic
		1660	Restoration of Charles II

Note: *Work featured in Part 3

Restoration and Augustan literature (1660–1775)

Restoration literature

By the time of the restoration to the throne of Charles II in 1660, England had suffered 18 years of bitter civil war and government by the Puritan-inspired Oliver Cromwell and his son. The people wanted a change of mood and they welcomed the flamboyant Charles back from the Continent with open arms. The literature that accompanied the King's return is marked by two different approaches. On the one hand, the minority of writers looked to deal with the political and religious issues raised by the preceding 20 years. Amongst the literature written by these writers are two of England's most revered works – JOHN MILTON's *PARADISE LOST* in 1667 and JOHN BUNYAN's *THE PILGRIM'S PROGRESS* in 1678. Milton was the great apologist for Cromwell's government and he railed against the return of Charles. He was briefly imprisoned for this but freed thanks to the influence of ANDREW MARVELL. Milton continued to press his case by writing what is widely acknowledged as the greatest epic in the English language, *Paradise Lost*. However, the poem's allegorical references to the Civil War were subtle enough to keep him out of prison.

Although less avowedly political than Milton's work, John Bunyan's *The Pilgrim's Progress* was nevertheless religious and therefore, given the divisions in society at the time, necessarily an intervention into politics. Indeed, the topic of religion continued to dominate English and British history all through this period. Most notably, in 1688 England suffered its second, albeit relatively bloodless, revolution in 50 years when the Protestant William and Mary were invited to depose the Catholic James II. James II fled and two years later he and representatives of several Catholic nations from across Europe were defeated at the Battle of the Boyne. A decade later, the Act of Settlement was passed outlawing any Catholic accession to the throne. Then in 1746, the last serious attempt to overturn the Act was defeated when Bonnie Prince Charlie was beaten at Culloden in Scotland. Paranoia about Catholic plots continued until the end of the eighteenth century, most notably in the Gordon riots in 1780 which cost the lives of hundreds of Londoners and which provided CHARLES DICKENS with the historical backdrop for *Barnaby Rudge* in 1841.

If the works of Milton and Bunyan represented the political and spiritual reaction to the homecoming of Charles II, others were less keen to go to prison than these two and more eager to join the festive mood occasioned by the King's return. In particular, as Charles II was a keen patron of the arts, one of his first acts upon resumption of the throne was to reopen the theatres. These were not the theatres of Shakespeare's day, however, in which the masses and the higher classes mixed within the same audience, if not quite the same space. Rather, the new theatres were firmly directed at an elite audience centred around Charles and his courtiers. As such, the Restoration occasioned a new kind of play which catered to the new kind of audience. As the mood was less conducive to tragedies, these plays were, more often than not, comedies. Chief among these were William Wycherley's *The Country Wife* (1675), APHRA BEHN's *THE ROVER* (1677), and William Congreve's *The Way of the World* (1700). Until quite recently, later generations found many of these plays to be indecent as they revelled in the sexual attitudes of the day and the hypocritical manners with which strategies of love were negotiated.

Augustan literature

Contemporary audiences too soon became sated by glorying in immoral excesses and turned increasingly to the more controlled exuberance of satire and wit. This more refined sensibility became known as *Augustan*. It referred to the reign of the Roman Emperor Augustus who, after the murder of Caesar, instituted a period of stability when the arts flourished. The parallel was made between Caesar and Charles I, and Augustus and Charles II. While the relative merits of the two leaders is a moot point, what is certain is that following the Restoration, classical values such as harmony and elegance began to dominate literature. The forerunner in this regard was JOHN DRYDEN, a writer who excelled in just about every form of creative writing. He continued the English language tradition of translation by writing popular versions of several classical works, including Virgil's *Aeneid*. ALEXANDER POPE, perhaps the leading exponent of the Augustan mentality, would follow in Dryden's wake and make his fortune with a translation of Homer's *Iliad*.

Dryden not only translated classical authors, he also 'translated' the relatively recent work of WILLIAM SHAKESPEARE into a classical mould. The work of Shakespeare still dominated the landscape of English literature, but it was not bound to the conventions of the classical world even as it borrowed classical plots. To some people's minds, Dryden included, it was therefore a bit untidy in the sense that it did not obey the specious laws of unity supposedly advanced by the Greek philosopher Aristotle. Dryden therefore rewrote Shakespeare's ANTONY AND CLEOPATRA as *All for Love* in 1677 and had the plot obey the unity of time, place and action, in the stead of the disparate scene and time changes of the original work. While not many writers chose to rewrite Shakespeare, Dryden's effort was typical in the regard it paid to the classical values of unity, reason, clarity and restraint. These values helped to engender a polished sensibility to literature which, in terms of verse, lasted well into the work of LORD BYRON. Indeed, one of the great legacies of Augustan literature is the mock-heroic epic. First mastered by Dryden in *Absalom and Achitophel* in 1681 and in MAC FLECKNOE in 1682, the mock-epic (a verse narrative which uses the form of an epic to satirise its victim), was later practised by POPE in THE RAPE OF THE LOCK and by Byron in DON JUAN.

Development of English prose

The wit evident in such works as MAC FLECKNOE and *The Rape of the Lock* was part of a broader culture of satire which saw its most pervasive form in prose. Indeed, the Augustan age saw a hitherto unprecedented development of English language prose. For while there had always been works of prose, imaginative literature tended to have been poetry or drama, or, as with Shakespeare, a combination of the two. However, as vernacular English took a hold of the literary imagination (a feat aided in 1755 by the publication of SAMUEL JOHNSON's *Dictionary*) and became more or less the only language of expression, so the informality of using the native tongue paved the way for the looser forms of prose. The new prose took a variety of modes, from the humble essay, through to the biography and the innovative world of the novel.

Once again, Dryden was at the vanguard of Augustan prose, writing a series of pioneering works on literary criticism such as *Essay of Dramatic Poesie*. He was followed at the beginning of the eighteenth century by a collection of brilliant satirists, including JONATHAN SWIFT, Joseph Addison and Sir Richard Steele. Addison and Steele were responsible for devising the periodicals that would dominate during this time – the *Tatler* (from 1709) and the *Spectator* (from 1711). Consciously moralising but nevertheless witty, the essays contained in these periodicals were lapped up by the new metropolitan audience of coffee-house frequenters and artists. Their massive success bred dozens of imitators, including Johnson's *Rambler* and OLIVER GOLDSMITH's *Bee*, as well as establishing the gold standard for essay writing that remained influential for the following century. Their most striking characteristic is the typically Augustan claim to being guided by the light of reason.

Indeed, reason became the battleground on which the competing essayists tried to outdo each other, particularly over support for the two main political parties – the Whigs and the Tories. While the Tories were, broadly speaking, a conservative party bound to the upkeep of traditional ways of life, the Whigs embraced the new mobile world of international trade and science. Swift, briefly intoxicated by the thrill of the new, flirted with the Whigs before settling down to edit the *Examiner*, the Tory magazine. His career as an essayist was topped in 1729 by probably the most famous essay ever written – *A Modest Proposal*. Pushing reason to the extreme, this essay left reasonableness far behind in advocating that babies be eaten as a way to solve the famine in Ireland.

The novel

Before he wrote *A Modest Proposal* in 1729, Swift had already completed his most famous work, GULLIVER'S TRAVELS in 1726. *Gulliver's Travels* belonged to a new species of prose that came to be called, for its very freshness, the novel. As with *Gulliver's Travels* (1726), or BEHN's *Oroonoko* (1688), the novel was initially not unlike the old form of the romance written in prose rather than verse. That is to say, the early novels were largely episodic involving a central figure engaged in a series of unrelated adventures. The model for such narratives was Cervantes' *Don Quixote*, published in 1604 and popular in English as well as Spanish. However, during the early part of the eighteenth century, such episodic narratives were given more shape by the simple device of arranging the story around the life of the protagonist. One of the most famous examples of this is DANIEL DEFOE's *MOLL FLANDERS*, published in 1722. Defoe was used to employing a life as a narrative template from his work composing the biographies of famous criminals, such as that of Jonathan Wild, which were best-sellers at the time.

It was a relatively small leap therefore from writing about a real person's life to writing about a fictional one, not least because biography was then, as it often is now, a forum for scandal and half-truths. Many readers assumed that *Moll Flanders* was the story of a real woman as it bore all the same hallmarks of reality as the supposedly 'real' biographies did. The value and appeal of the biography, and thus also the fictions based upon the same pattern, were the insights it afforded into the minutiae of people's lives. In particular, it delved into people's inner and private lives. Privacy, while not a new concept, was still developing at the time, partly from the recent stress laid upon the individual's inner life in the Protestant religion, and partly from the new morality of the late 1690s. The art of reading silently also made it a highly personal activity and allowed the literate public to feel more intimate with those about whom they read. Finally, the democratic impulses of post-revolutionary Britain, with its burgeoning capitalist economy which emphasised individualism and fostered the growth of the middle class, had given rise to a new public that demanded a form of literature addressed to them.

The novel answered this call and from the 1740s it attained the status of an art form in its own right, developing techniques and levels of sophistication that took it beyond mere fictional biography. Perhaps unsurprisingly, these techniques initially found inspiration in classical models. HENRY FIELDING in TOM JONES (1749), for example, deployed an intricate plot line in which, in accordance with Augustan principles, each part balances the other to such a level of detail that SAMUEL COLERIDGE was later moved to declare it one of the 'three most perfect plots ever planned' (the other two being Sophocles' *Oedipus Rex* and JONSON's *The Alchemist*). If *Tom Jones* revolved around the orbit of Augustan harmony, then LAURENCE STERNE's *THE LIFE AND OPINIONS OF TRISTRAM SHANDY* left the galaxy altogether. Pushing the concept of personal minutiae to the extreme, this massive work explores the subjective world by a myriad number of digressions that make a joke out of the idea of any plot. In one go, it suggested dozens of possibilities for the novel and is probably still one of the most influential works of the genre ever written.

Figure 4: Texts and contexts of Restoration and Augustan literature (1660–1775)

Text			Context	
		1660	Restoration of Charles II	
		1666	Great Fire of London	
1667	John Milton – *Paradise Lost**			
1677	Aphra Behn – *The Rover**			
1678	John Bunyan – *The Pilgrim's Progress**			
1682	John Dryden – *Mac Flecknoe**			
		1688	Protestant William and Mary succeed Catholic James II in a 'Bloodless Revolution'	
1700	William Congreve – *The Way of the World*	1701	Act of Settlement bans Catholics from the throne	
		1707	England and Scotland joined in Act of Union	
1717	Alexander Pope – *The Rape of the Lock**			
		1720	South Sea Bubble bursts	
1726	Jonathan Swift – *Gulliver's Travels**	1721–42	Robert Walpole effectively Britain's first Prime Minister	
		1746	Defeat of Jacobite rebellion under Bonnie Prince Charlie	
1749	Henry Fielding – *Tom Jones**	1752	Gregorian calendar introduced	
1755	Samuel Johnson – *Dictionary*	1753	Rioters destroy home of John Kay, inventor of the flying shuttle	
1759	Samuel Johnson – *Rasselas**			
1759–66	Laurence Sterne – *Tristram Shandy**	1763	Treaty of Paris; France cedes Canada to Britain	
1764	Horace Walpole – *Castle of Otranto**			
1766	Oliver Goldsmith – *The Vicar of Wakefield**			
		1770	Captain Cook returns from voyage to Australia	
		1775	Start of American War of Independence	

Note: *Work featured in Part 3

Romantic literature (1775–1837)

Revolutionary literature

The beginning of the Augustan period of English literature was defined by the two English revolutions in 1642 and 1688, which eventually procured a period of domestic peace. Similarly, the end of the Augustan period was defined by two more revolutions, in America in 1775 and in France in 1789. The revolutionary sentiments unleashed by these two great events found literary expression in the new cultural ethos of Romanticism. Romanticism announced its revolutionary credentials by claiming to be everything that the old guard of Augustan literature was not. On the one hand, the Augustans aspired to an impersonal, urban, carefully calibrated and classically sourced form of verse, whereas the Romantics valued personal, rural, spontaneous and vernacular expression. In short, the Augustans were cooked and the Romantics were raw.

These contrasting outlooks, however, are perhaps best revealed by the differences in the points of interest they share with each other. For example, both Augustan and Romantic literature took nature for their subject, but while the Augustans saw in nature the embodiment of universal truths, the Romantics saw it as the embodiment of their subjective realities. Similarly, if both styles of literature were predicated upon a form of nostalgia, the Augustans looked back to a period of classical antiquity while the Romantics turned to an imaginary organic society that pre-dated the industrial revolution. These strands of continuity with Augustan literature mixed with revolutionary fervour, particularly that generated by the French Revolution, and other cultural influences from the Continent (such as Goethe's *The Sorrows of Young Werther* and Rousseau's *Julie*) to produce SAMUEL TAYLOR COLERIDGE and WILLIAM WORDSWORTH's LYRICAL BALLADS (1798). Often considered to be the defining text of the new Romanticism, *Lyrical Ballads* announced itself as a revolutionary text, ushering in a new era of Romantic literature understood as 'the spontaneous overflow of powerful feelings'. While hopes for the French Revolution soon died with the advent of the Terror and Napoleon, this new understanding of literature as a form of subjective, emotional expression proved to be more durable, for it is a conception with which many writers are still struggling today.

The return of poetry

Romantic literature was dominated by poetry. In some ways this was a reaction to the recent dominance of prose. After the death of POPE, the new poets failed to match the success of previous poets as the public instead gorged itself on different types of prose. Part of the reason for this is that poetry under the classically inspired Augustan influence of DRYDEN and Pope was generally rather impersonal. Although often articulating a personal opinion, even if only indirectly, such expressions were about public matters and did not convey the deepest fears and wishes of particular individuals. This was in stark contrast to the novel, which had fed the public's appetite for insights into the private lives of people and had made the individual the centre of its focus. Romantic poetry, with its emphasis on the subjective experience of individuals, challenged the hegemony of the novel in this area by bringing new levels of expressiveness to bear on its subject matter.

Indeed, if Romantic poetry was paradoxically influenced by the development of the novel, this was only part of a broader set of influences that date back at least to the Reformation. The Reformation itself fostered an emphasis upon personal adherence to the word of God, as opposed to the public displays of worship encouraged by the Roman Catholic church. In turn, this helped to foster a culture of individualism, in which morality and conscience became private matters forged by inner convictions. Such individualism, was compounded by the growth of competitive capitalism and a meritocratic culture accompanied by the concomitant disintegration of a rural, organic society. This rapidly atomising world was also the one in which the new poets had to make a living, if, like KEATS, they had to rely on their writing for their income. Alienated from the commercialism of the industrial world, marginal to the concerns of politics and power, the new writers were solitary people, isolated and distant.

With all this in mind, then, it is little wonder that Romantic poetry valued the individual, wrote about the subjective, and romanticised the loner. The archetypal image of the Romantic poets is very telling in this regard. Think of Wordsworth wandering 'lonely as a cloud' across the Lake District, or Coleridge steeped in abjection and drug addiction succumbing to the dark night of the soul, or even BYRON, exiled from his home and dying in a foreign land: each one of these discloses an obsession with solitary and subjective experience. The poems they wrote, perhaps with the exception of Byron, are explorations of inner worlds and private crises. The best of all these, Wordsworth's *THE PRELUDE*, is often referred to as the great Romantic epic, fit to stand with MILTON's *PARADISE LOST*. However, while *Paradise Lost* takes for its subject the creation of the world and the Fall of Man, *The Prelude* takes for its world the creation of a subject and the fall of a man. The difference is telling and shows how, in just 150 years, the obsessions of literature had changed.

Although the Romantic poets shared some concerns, they were also, in other ways, quite individualistic. For example, WILLIAM BLAKE, who is often not even considered to be a Romantic poet, nevertheless developed his own personal system of symbolism so as not to be enslaved by the system of anyone else. This highly developed individualism is typically Romantic, but his poems, particularly his more famous *SONGS OF INNOCENCE AND EXPERIENCE* (1789–94), are written in a deceptively plain prose style and bear little relation to the more descriptive verse of Wordsworth or Keats. Similarly, while Wordsworth and, to a lesser extent, Coleridge, claimed to be writing a new type of poetry in the vernacular, their verse style has less of the common tongue about it than the work of ROBERT BURNS. Equally, while Burns shares with Byron an admiration for the poetry of Alexander Pope, the provincial subject matter of Burns's best work is utterly different to the exotic locations of Byron's verse.

Romantic prose

The art of the polemic continued in the Romantic era, albeit in a slightly less prolific fashion than in the early part of the eighteenth century. Unsurprisingly, the revolutions of France and America threw up some of the best prose of the period.

Edmund Burke's *Reflections on the Revolution in France* (1790) represented the conservative response to the situation, while MARY WOLLSTONECRAFT's *A Vindication of the Rights of Men*, published in the same year, articulated the liberal, optimistic view. Imbued with the revolutionary spirit, Wollstonecraft went on to advance the claims of women in A VINDICATION OF THE RIGHTS OF WOMAN (1792). More radical than the French revolutionaries, who while happy to accept their initial support later denied women the vote, Wollstonecraft outlined the case for women to receive equal rights with men. In so doing, she composed one of the founding texts of modern feminism.

Later in the Romantic period, when the early enthusiasm for the French revolution had given way to disillusion, some of the most outstanding essayists of the period turned from politics to art for their subjects. Among their number were William Hazlitt, Charles Lamb and THOMAS DE QUINCEY. Lamb was a close friend of both Coleridge and Wordsworth. He developed the closest equivalent of Romantic poetry in the essay form, in so far as his work was largely personal. He explained his subjective view using a highly subjective prose style in essays such as 'Old China', which work almost to charm rather than persuade the reader. Hazlitt also offered his experiences for the edification of the reader, but he did so using an energetic, modern type of prose shorn of the ornamentation of Lamb's work. His best essay, 'My First Acquaintance with Poets' (1823), describes a most intimate portrait of Wordsworth and Coleridge. Meanwhile, another prolific essayist, De Quincey, is perhaps best known for CONFESSIONS OF AN ENGLISH OPIUM-EATER, in which he recounts the personal torment of his drug addiction and the nightmares that accompanied it.

The novel

As befits such an individualistic period of history, there was very little drama performed during this time, although this was mainly because only two theatres held licences. However, the more solitary form of the novel continued to develop both in its form and its audience. One of the most striking additions to the novelistic genres was the Gothic novel. Conceived as a reaction to the purity and refinement of Augustan literature, the Gothic novel was a dark repository for the excesses which classically inspired prose could not accommodate. The first major work in this field was HORACE WALPOLE's THE CASTLE OF OTRANTO (1764). Hugely popular, this set in motion a trend for Gothic literature that still exists today. In such works as Ann Radcliffe's *The Mysteries of Udolpho* and M.G. Lewis's *The Monk*, the basic characteristics of Gothic fiction were worked out. These included mysterious settings, usually in exotic locations, crumbling buildings shrouded in fog and bedevilled by lost passageways, supernatural phenomena, bloody secrets and characters with irrational obsessions.

With its overt sensuality and focus on the extremities of the mind, the Gothic novel foreshadowed some of the elements of Romantic poetry. It also helped to create the atmosphere for other less formulaic fictions which were nonetheless Gothic. The most outstanding of these works was MARY SHELLEY's FRANKENSTEIN (1818).

Imbued with neither the Victorians' faith in progress, nor the Augustans' belief in reason, *Frankenstein* was a profoundly pessimistic response to the modern world. It demonstrated a prescient anxiety at the ability of human beings to control the natural forces they were unleashing in the new machine age. It thus proved to be an overdue corrective to the Romantic vision of the world, which held humankind at its egotistical centre. Another conservative response to the modern world, and one that also drew upon the medieval atmosphere of the Gothic novel, was SIR WALTER SCOTT's *IVANHOE*, published in 1819. This, and many of Scott's other works, returned the novel to its roots by reviving the chivalrous subject matter of the older romances. His work was highly influential and pushed popular novels towards more dynamic plotting.

While Shelley and Scott employed elements of the Gothic to furnish their novels with depth and atmosphere, JANE AUSTEN, the other main novelist of this period, used the Gothic only in order to make fun of it. Austen was an example of the persistence of the Augustan sensibility well into the Romantic era. She managed to ignore its pervasive influence as readily as she managed to avoid any reference to the revolutions and wars of the period. In *NORTHANGER ABBEY* she brought her Augustan wit to bear on the clichés of Gothic fiction and hammered a refined stake through its heart. In her other novels, such as *PRIDE AND PREJUDICE*, Austen focused on the plight of middle-class women, the largest constituency of the novel's audience at the time, and described courtship rituals with an irony so deft as to exceed anything penned by her illustrious predecessors in the art, ALEXANDER POPE and SAMUEL JOHNSON. What the works of Austen, Scott and Shelley, the three pre-eminent novelists of the era, show is quite how heterogeneous the form already was. The Gothic novel of Walpole, the historical novel of Scott, the thesis novel of Shelley and the novel of manners by Austen were the forerunners of different genres that would develop over the next 100 years, and become part of the burgeoning diversity characteristic of the novel form.

Figure 5: Texts and contexts of Romantic literature (1775–1837)

Text		Context	
		1775	Start of American War of Independence
		1780	Gordon riots
1786	Robert Burns – *Poems, Chiefly in the Scottish Dialect**		
		1789	Start of French Revolution
1791	James Boswell – *The Life of Samuel Johnson**		
1792	Mary Wollstonecraft – *A Vindication of the Rights of Woman**		
		1793	France and England at war
1794	William Blake – *Songs of Innocence and Experience**	1794	French abolish slavery
1796	M.G. Lewis – *The Monk*		
1798	William Wordsworth and Samuel Taylor Coleridge – *Lyrical Ballads**		
		1799	George Washington becomes first American President
		1807	British abolish slavery
1813	Jane Austen – *Pride and Prejudice**		
		1815	Battle of Waterloo
1818	Mary Shelley – *Frankenstein**		
1819	Sir Walter Scott – *Ivanhoe**, Lord Byron – *Don Juan**	1819	Peterloo Massacre
1820	John Keats – *Lamia, Isabella, the Eve of St Agnes, and Other Poems**, Percy Shelley – *Prometheus Unbound**		
1821	Thomas De Quincey – *Confessions of an English Opium-Eater**		
		1823	Monroe Doctrine

Note: *Work featured in Part 3

Victorian literature (1837–90)

The spirit of the age

Like Elizabethan literature, Victorian literature takes its name from its ruling queen. In the intervening 250 years, however, the status of the monarch had changed. Where Elizabeth was the real ruler of an emerging nation, Victoria could only claim to be the symbolic figurehead of an established empire. Nevertheless, like Elizabeth, Victoria was an iconic figure (albeit that her image was the first monarch's to be captured on a photograph). In the spirit of the times, she was a strangely middle-class queen, upholding the values of sobriety, propriety and duty to others. These steady virtues were the indispensable foundations of a country that was undergoing the fastest and most momentous period of change hitherto known in any nation on earth.

Large-scale industrialisation, at first unregulated by any laws, contributed to a massive upheaval in the distribution of the population as Britain made the transition from a largely rural economy to an urban one in the space of a few generations. London trebled in size during Victoria's reign, becoming for a while the capital of the world. The rest of the world was also the destination of millions of Britons as they emigrated to various parts of the empire, taking up administrative posts that secured for their country huge markets and raw materials. Indeed, by 1890 a quarter of the world's population were Victoria's subjects. This enormous empire did not come without a cost, however, and towards the end of her life the colonies increasingly came under attack, both internally and from other European powers and the newly confident United States of America.

The confidence of the Victorians, stemming from their enormous industrial economy, innovations in science, huge navy and overseas acquisitions, led to a belief in the inevitability of progress, a myth most artfully advanced by Thomas Babington Macaulay in *History of England from the Accession of James the Second* (1848). The same year also saw most of Continental Europe succumb to the spectre of revolution, a spectre theorised in Karl Marx's *Communist Manifesto*, also published in 1848. The fear of revolution had haunted Europe ever since the bloody aftermath of the French Revolution in 1789, causing most governments to adopt reactionary policies. Britain had already undertaken a series of piecemeal reforms, freeing up trade and beginning to enfranchise the powerful new middle class, and so it escaped without a revolution. The middle classes were starting to appreciate their power but they lacked, according to MATTHEW ARNOLD, a concomitant sense of their cultural responsibilities. In a series of works, beginning with the influential CULTURE AND ANARCHY, Arnold accused them of being Philistines and argued that they should submerge their love of profit with more noble ideals.

The age of the novel

In terms of literature, the Philistine middle classes most often found their noble ideals in the novel. The Victorian era saw the novel dominate the literary scene and become a form of enlightening entertainment of such importance that on two occasions the British electorate even voted a novelist, Benjamin Disraeli, into the office of Prime Minister. Nor were the delights of novelists such as CHARLES DICKENS and WILLIAM MAKEPEACE THACKERAY restricted to the higher echelons of society because, for the first time, written literature was becoming a democratic pursuit. When Victoria assumed the throne in 1837, nearly half of the population could claim some level of literacy. By the time she died, compulsory education to the age of 10 meant that, theoretically, the whole population would soon be literate. This meant that novels were able to appeal to an even wider constituency than they had previously. To this end Victorian novels became huge inclusive affairs, in which, in the most prominent of them, such as *DAVID COPPERFIELD* and *VANITY FAIR*, the whole of society from the road sweeper to the aristocrat were represented.

This inclusive character of the Victorian novel was not just a matter of content either, for novel reading became, for a while, the kind of social affair that the theatre had been in SHAKESPEARE's day. Novels were read out loud to the whole family or became the focus of theatrical events, such as Dickens's lucrative tours of Britain and America in which he read his own books in character. The communal aspect of novels was heightened by their form of publication. The early part of the Victorian era witnessed a huge proliferation of periodicals and journals in which almost all new novels were serialised before being published as novels. This impinged upon the structure of novels, leading authors to adopt cliff-hanger endings to encourage readers to buy the next instalment of the periodical. The most famous example of this was Dickens's *The Old Curiosity Shop*, which left the life or death fate of little Nell uncertain. When the copies of the next instalment were shipped over to America, they were met at the dockside by huge crowds wanting to find out if she had survived.

The taste for novels was also abetted by the most common theme with which they dealt – the question of social mobility. In an extremely class-conscious society, one which was stratified by subtle but always perceptible divisions, heart-warming stories of characters who managed to meet their dreams and exceed their lot were lapped up by an aspirational public. Once again, Dickens's work is supreme in this matter as hero after hero, from Oliver Twist and Nicholas Nickleby to David Copperfield and Esther Summerson, prove that by hard work, a dutiful bearing and a belief in the goodness of the general sum of humanity, anyone can climb the social ladder in a meritocratic society. The pertinence of this message was not least of all appreciated by the many women novelists who had begun to dominate the popular market since the beginning of the century. For while Dickens's characters, and Dickens himself, had to overcome the prejudice of class, female writers described heroines who had to surmount the equally ingrained male chauvinism of the times. In disparate ways, CHARLOTTE BRONTË's Jane Eyre and GEORGE ELIOT's Dorothea Brooke are archetypes of a gender mobility who, like their counterparts in novels of class, opt to clamber over and around the obstacles to equality rather than destroying them.

This social conservatism was typical of the most popular Victorian novels. It is also true, to some degree, in regard to experimentation in the novel, for the Victorian public expected and were offered (with notable exceptions such as LEWIS CARROLL's *ALICE'S ADVENTURES IN WONDERLAND*) only realist novels, ones that seemed to represent the world about them in the most natural way. However, within the parameters of the realist novel, the Victorians enjoyed an unprecedented diversity of form and content. The technical innovations and caricatures of the comedic Dickens in *The Pickwick Papers* bear little relation to the sober, psychological probing of Eliot's MIDDLEMARCH. Equally, the Gothic terrors of EMILY BRONTË's WUTHERING HEIGHTS finds only a distant kinship in the society comedy of THACKERAY's VANITY FAIR or the bucolic love triangle of THOMAS HARDY's FAR FROM THE MADDING CROWD.

Victorian poetry

The Victorian novel cast a long shadow over its less popular counterparts – poetry and drama. Nevertheless, while the dramatic canon had little of note added to it during this period, poetry did not suffer the same fate. This was perhaps surprising given that, to some extent, poetry was still dealing with the legacy of Romanticism. As most of the Romantic poets died at a comparatively young age, they left something of a gap in the available pool of talent. Equally, one of the great motivating forces of Romanticism, the French Revolution, had failed to live up to its utopian promise and instead, with the advent of Napoleon, had embroiled Europe in its most savage war to date. This and the moral flexibility of Romanticism's most flamboyant poets, LORD BYRON and PERCY BYSSHE SHELLEY, led to something of a reaction against the tenor of Romantic poetry. The sense of this reaction was shared by the ever more conservative WILLIAM WORDSWORTH and so, by the time he died in 1850, an era had died with him, enabling a new one to begin.

The most prominent figure of the new Victorian poetry, and the one who succeeded Wordsworth as Poet Laureate, was LORD ALFRED TENNYSON. Tennyson was very much the poet of the age. Not only did he take to the post of Laureate with a sense of public duty not seen before or since, but he tackled the kind of themes that even the novelists seemed, at first, unable to handle. Among these themes was the question of humankind's place in the universe. Confronting the issues raised by the new geological theories, which showed the Earth to be millions of years old and humanity's place in it very recent and insecure, Tennyson, particularly in his masterpiece IN MEMORIAM, managed to negotiate a form of truce with his religious beliefs which, of course, proposed quite the opposite view.

Tennyson's adroit handling of the diminished status of humankind appeared to offer a genuine form of solace for his anxious reading public, who would very soon have to deal with the troubling news of Darwinism too. Tennyson would also tackle this and the other great issues of the day, such as industrialisation, and, in so doing, he established himself on the bookshelf of almost every poetry reading house in both Britain and America. In terms of popularity, his contemporaries, such as Elizabeth Barrett Browning, Christina Rossetti and ROBERT BROWNING, suffer by comparison. However, in terms of legacy, certainly Browning is able to match Tennyson with his development of the dramatic monologue. Probably the single greatest innovation of Victorian poetry, the dramatic monologue borrowed from the novel the technique of an individual voice telling a story. In his best work, MEN AND WOMEN, published in 1855, Browning uses the dramatic monologue to give immediacy to the poem and draw readers into the world of the poem's speaker, enabling them to infer the situation and become, effectively, the other half of the poem's conversation. Browning was sometimes ignored in his own time, but his seductive technique became one of the mainstays of popular poetry in the next century.

Figure 6: Texts and contexts of Victorian literature (1837–90)

	Text		Context
1837	Charles Dickens – *Oliver Twist**	1837	Accession of Queen Victoria
		1845	Famine in Ireland leads to mass emigration to America
1847	Charlotte Brontë – *Jane Eyre** Emily Brontë – *Wuthering Heights**		
1848	William Makepeace Thackeray – *Vanity Fair**	1848	Revolutions in France, Germany, Italy, Hungary and Austria
1850	Charles Dickens – *David Copperfield** Alfred Tennyson – *In Memoriam**	1850	Public libraries established in Britain
1852	Charles Dickens – *Bleak House**	1851	Great Exhibition in London
1855	Robert Browning – *Men and Women**	1854–56	Crimean War
1860	Charles Dickens – *Great Expectations**	1861–65	American Civil War
1865	Lewis Carroll – *Alice's Adventures in Wonderland**		
		1866	Telegraph cable links Britain and America
		1867	Second Reform Bill substantially improves franchise
1869	Matthew Arnold – *Culture and Anarchy**		
1872	George Eliot – *Middlemarch**	1872	Secret ballots legalised
1874	Thomas Hardy – *Far From the Madding Crowd**		
		1877	Queen Victoria becomes Empress of India
		1885	Invention of petrol-driven engine for 'horseless carriage' by Karl Benz
1886	Robert Louis Stevenson – *Dr Jekyll and Mr Hyde** Thomas Hardy – *The Mayor of Casterbridge*		

Note: *Work featured in Part 3

(B) LITERATURE IN AMERICA

Colonial and revolutionary literature (1500–1800)

Literature of discovery

For the first 1,000 years of its life, literature written in the English language was almost exclusively published in England. However, after the period roughly coinciding with the emergence of Modern English in 1500, English language literature also began to be produced not only in Wales, Scotland and Ireland, but also, and eventually more consequentially, in the New World of America. English, of course, was not the first tongue of what we now call North America. The indigenous population spoke any one of hundreds of different languages when the first European explorers landed there. The culture of these peoples was, like the culture of the Angles before the arrival of the Catholic missionaries at the end of the sixth century, a largely oral one and was only written down subsequent to their encounter with and eventual conquest by the Old World. The first European explorers were from the same Nordic stock as the Angles and attempted to settle in what they called *Vineland* some time around the year 1000.

A few inscriptions, rather than any substantial texts, are all that remain of those early settlements which were eventually destroyed by local Native Americans. When the Europeans returned in 1492, led by Columbus, it was the Spanish language that initially came to predominate as a result of the more aggressive expansionism of King Ferdinand V and Queen Isabella I. A century later, interest began to be generated in England by a series of texts that described the glories of the New World. These texts were largely collected in the influential book by Richard Hakluyt, *The Principall Navigations, Voyages, Traffiques and Discoveries of the English Nation*, published around 1598–1600. The early efforts to settle America at the time, particularly following the initial expedition of Walter Ralegh in 1584 which named Virginia after virgin Queen Elizabeth I, met with one set of difficulties after another. Although the first child born in the New World to English-speaking parents, Virginia Dare, proved that some form of settlement was possible, the experiences of the first major colonies at Roanoke Island and Jamestown eventually ended in death and failure. Success only came as a belated effect of the Reformation.

Religious literature

A group of Puritans from the East Midlands, who later came to call themselves the Pilgrims, remained disappointed by the laxity of the Church of England and, in 1608, moved to Holland where they could practise their Nonconformist religion without persecution. However, as the next generation began to lose itself in Dutch customs, the leaders of the Pilgrims decided to take the opportunity to sail to the New World. Crossing the Atlantic in the now famous *Mayflower*, the Pilgrims landed in a place they named New England. As one of their leaders, William Bradford, recorded in his book *Of Plymouth Plantation*, the Pilgrims were a different type of settler to the ones at Jamestown. Disciplined, hard-working, grateful and well-organised, the God-fearing Pilgrims managed to survive their first winter with the help of the local Wampanoag Indians and continued to thrive thereafter.

With the arrival of more Puritans in the ensuing years, it is perhaps unsurprising that the best of the early American-English literature was largely theological in content. The first published poet of the New World was Anne Bradstreet with her volume of poems, *The Tenth Muse*, printed in England in 1650. Famous for her doubts occasioned by her understanding of Puritan theology, she was the first in a long line of American writers, including RALPH WALDO EMERSON and HENRY DAVID THOREAU, who were inspired to affirm their belief in a divine glory by the overwhelming majesty of the American landscape. Towards the end of the first century of English settlement, the most prolific author of the period, Cotton Mather, was already regretting the dilution of the early Puritan ideals in New England. Such dilution led to one of the most famous incidents of the turn of the century when 19 people were accused of witchcraft in the Salem trial of 1692. Reporting on the event in *The Wonders of the Invisible World* in 1693, Mather inadvertently tendered an image of zealous Puritanism that would remain for generations to come.

As in post-civil war England, people eventually tired of the strictures of the kind of Puritan religion represented by Mather, particularly as the doctrine of predestination, which maintained that God had already chosen those who would be saved and those who would be damned, seemed to some eyes to invalidate any individual effort towards self-improvement. Instead, much of the populace drifted into a form of religious apathy, one which paid lip-service to the worship of God but only as a kind of mechanical habit that had little to do with conviction. However, from the late 1720s, religion was subject to a massive upheaval that has since become known as the 'Great Awakening'. At the forefront of this revolution in religious worship was a man called Jonathan Edwards.

Edwards, who belonged to a minor clerical dynasty in Connecticut, began from the realisation that people understood themselves to be Christians only at an abstract level and that, in order to reinvigorate their belief, he had to make them feel it too. The key to this feeling was to imbue people with a sense of joy and delight in the work of God. Edwards managed to do this partly by disavowing the scenario of damnation associated with the theory of predestination advanced by the early Puritans. On the whole, Edwards' God was one who made your heart exalt in delight rather than tremble with fear. At his revivalist meetings, Edwards would employ reasoned arguments in his sermons, but he would deliver them in a thrilling manner that was every bit as persuasive as what he was actually saying. Playing to packed crowds, he and his followers managed to rejuvenate religious worship all along the east coast of America and in parts of England too. However, while people did not tire of exultation, they did begin to resent Edwards when he returned to some of the practices of the early Puritans which amounted to forms of public humiliation. Eventually, in 1750, they voted him out of office and the revivalist movement ground to a halt.

Revolutionary literature

The Treaty of Paris in 1763 marked the end of years of fighting between the British and the French, and to a lesser extent the Spanish, over the ownership of the North American continent. The treaty saw Britain consolidate its control of both Canada and the 13 colonies that went on to form the first states of the United States of America. However, Britain's victory was short-lived. In 1764 Parliament passed the Sugar Act, the first law specifically aimed at raising money from the colonies. A couple of weeks later, Parliament followed that up with the Currency Act, which banned any of the colonies from printing their own paper money. Somewhat annoyed at the impositions of the British Government, merchants in Boston began to organise a boycott of British goods.

Seemingly undaunted by this mild protest, the British decided in the following year to pass both the Stamp Act and the Quartering Act. While the first of these taxed stamps used on certain types of printed matter, such as the thriving trade in journals, the second required the colonies to provide food and lodgings to British troops stationed in America. By the time word of these new taxes had travelled across the Atlantic and round the colonies, riots had broken out. The home of the Massachusetts Governor, who had supported the taxes, was burnt down by an angry mob. It took another six months for Parliament to learn of American disquiet and repeal the Stamp Act, but the British authorities still insisted on shutting down the New York Assembly because it refused to ratify the Quartering Act. In retaliation, the following year, Parliament passed the Townshend Acts, heaping more taxes on the 13 colonies. Before these were appealed, the boycott of British goods had spread to most of the colonies.

A campaign of civil disobedience soon set in with customs boats being attacked and Committees of Correspondence being set up. In 1773, three British ships loaded with tea were boarded by Americans and their cargo was thrown into Boston harbour. Known as the Boston Tea Party, this act of defiance soon led to further punitive measures by Britain and an increase in tension that by 1775 had become the first battle of a possible war. Many colonists still felt uneasy about going to war with Britain, but in 1776 THOMAS PAINE, an Englishman living in America, produced a pamphlet called COMMON SENSE, which called for independence for the colonies. It was enormously influential, and proved to be one of the turning points of the war, persuading many colonists to join the fight.

Although having a greater effect than any other pamphlet of the day, Paine's *Common Sense* was typical of the many political texts in circulation during the second half of the century. With no laws restricting printing, unlike in England, America enjoyed a high degree of press freedom and the first American newspaper had been set up in 1704. By the time of the War of Independence, there were dozens of news-papers and periodicals in circulation. These discussed all manner of topics but the first half of the century had been dominated by debates about religion, and the sec-ond half had given itself over to politics. Inspired by the success of *Common Sense*, but surprisingly in debt despite the fact that it had been a best-seller, Paine produced a series of papers for the duration of the war called *Crisis*. The first issue in particular proved to be a major morale boost for the new army and helped to lead to a victory for the colonists.

The First American

The War of Independence ended for all intents and purposes in 1781 with George Washington's victory at Yorktown. However, the peace was not ratified until the Treaty of Paris in 1783, in which Britain formally recognised the newly formed United States of America. One of the chief negotiators responsible for prosecuting the peace was BENJAMIN FRANKLIN. Scientist, author, businessman, philanthropist and politician, Franklin has been called the First American. Certainly as a signatory to the Paris Treaty, the Declaration of Independence and the Constitution, Franklin can lay more claim than most to being one of the founding fathers of America. Beyond these accomplishments, however, Franklin laid out in his AUTOBIOGRAPHY, which was only published posthumously, the principles of this new energetic, entrepreneurial and democratic country. What is more, Franklin abided by those principles during his life-time, becoming the very model of the self-made man. His *Autobiography* established itself as one of the blueprints for the American Dream, a dream which to sought to match effort to opportunity in order to produce the happiness the new Constitution promised to its citizens.

Figure 7: Texts and contexts of Colonial and Revolutionary literature (1500–1800)

Text		Context	
		1492	Columbus lands in America
		1584	Walter Ralegh names Virginia after Queen Elizabeth I
		1587	First child of English descent born in America
1598–1600	Richard Hakluyt – *The Principall Navigations, Voyages, Traffiques and Discoveries of the English Nation*		
		1620	*Mayflower* lands in New England
1630–50	William Bradford – *Of Plymouth Plantation*		
1650	Anne Bradstreet – *The Tenth Muse*	1664	Dutch Governor Peter Stuyvesant surrenders New York to the English
1693	Cotton Mather – *The Wonders of the Invisible World*	1692	Salem witch trial
1741	Jonathan Edwards – *Sinners in the Hands of an Angry God*	1739	First slave rebellion
		1773	Boston Tea Party
		1775	Start of American War of Independence
1776	Thomas Paine – *Common Sense**	1776	Declaration of Independence
		1783	Treaty of Paris ends War of Independence
		1787	Northwest Ordinance annuls Native American land rights Constitution grants inalienable right to happiness
1789	Olaudah Equiano – *The Interesting Narrative of the Life of Olaudah Equiano*	1789	George Washington elected first American President
1791	Benjamin Franklin – *The Autobiography of Benjamin Franklin**		

Note: *Work featured in Part 3

Literature of independence (1800–50)

Expansionism

Having just won its independence from Britain, then the mightiest power in the world, the new nation of the United States of America was supremely confident as it began the nineteenth century. Beating Britain again in the war between 1812–14, partially fought over who ruled the seas, America was confident enough in 1823 to issue the Monroe Doctrine, which threatened war against any European power who presumed to interfere in any part of the Americas. This was just part of the process which saw the United States consolidate its borders at the beginning of the century, as well as – like the other great European powers – expanding beyond them. Its first, and in some ways most impressive, action in this regard was the negotiation of the Louisiana Purchase from the French at the end of 1803. Taken from the Spanish by Napoleon, the area in question included the whole of the Mississippi valley and amounted to some 828,000 square miles (nearly ten times the size of Britain). The purchase effectively doubled the size of the United States overnight for just $15 million.

Having gained ownership of the land, at least in European terms, America then set about exploring and populating it. This was part of the push westwards which has dominated the American popular psyche ever since, as the frontier advanced slowly towards the Pacific Ocean. Expeditions were organised to navigate the overland route, including the pioneering Corps of Discovery led by Captains Lewis and Clark who took 18 months to cross the Continental Divide and reach the sea. Wagon trains followed, establishing the southern route to California in 1830. These early feats of exploration were soon followed by mass settlements; soon state after state was joining the original number of 13. Among those states that swelled the union during the first half of the century were Indiana (1816), Mississippi (1817), Illinois (1818), Alabama (1819), Michigan (1837), Texas (1845) and Iowa (1846). With the acceptance of California in 1850, America was composed of 31 states as it was poised to enter the second half of the century.

The cost of expansionism

This rapid expansion was, however, bought at an enormous cost. The original European settlers who had gone on to form the United States of America had brought with them from Europe any number of diseases to which the indigenous populations had previously not been exposed. These diseases, which although harmful were not deadly to Europeans, resulted in the decimation of the Native Americans. On top of this, the settlers also insisted on living on lands that were held dear by the Native Americans as part of their spiritual heritage. Conflicts inevitably ensued and the indigenous population, decimated by disease and hopelessly outgunned technologically, began a series of retreats westwards themselves. During the first half of the eighteenth century, this resulted in more and more local battles, of which the Creek War of 1814 was one of the most famous episodes.

Many European Americans felt even then that what they were doing was barbarous and so politicians were forced to concede to the claims of humanity when establishing policies. One of the most zealous exponents of westwards expansion, President Andrew Jackson, veteran of any number of skirmishes with the indigenous population, passed the Indian Removal Act of 1830 which allowed for Native Americans to be moved into western territories where they were promised they would not be forced to move again. This, of course, proved to be untrue. Partly this was because of another war that America fought during the first half of the eighteenth century, this time against Mexico in 1846. Having been inspired by the myth of the battle of the Alamo in 1836, the Americans eventually managed to capture Mexico City itself. Mexico was then forced to cede the lands that became New Mexico, California and Texas.

These concessions increased the land mass of America by nearly a third. While the total area of the country was increasing, so was the population. In 1800 the census showed that the population stood at around 5.3 million, comparable to Britain's 10.4 million. In 1810 that figure had reached 7.2 million, in 1820 10 million, in 1830 13 million and in 1840 17 million. This tripling of the population in 40 years stemmed, at least initially, from immigration out of Europe. While the original settlers had been English, and many more still streamed in, America's reputation as a land of opportunity proved seductive to natives of other countries too. Not the least of these countries was Ireland where the famines of the 1840s led to mass emigration. Such a mixed population also brought with it a series of ethnic tensions which occasionally erupted into violence, such as the anti-British riots in New York in 1849, or the anti-Irish protests started by Protestants fearful of Catholicism.

Few issues produced more tensions during this period though than that of slavery. It permeated everything. A simple surveying task carried out by Charles Mason and Jeremiah Dixon in the second half of the previous century, established the line of demarcation, known as the Mason–Dixon line, which split the country between the southern slavery states and the northern anti-slavery states. It was an issue that Congress did its best to tiptoe around, for example, banning the import of slaves in 1807 but ensuring the law was not enforced too rigorously, or only accepting one state joining the union if another one of the polar persuasion joined to keep the balance of slave and non-slave states even. The slaves themselves often revolted against their slavery. However, localised rebellions, such as the one in New Orleans in 1811 or in Florida in 1816, were met with brutal reprisals that left scores of people dead. Part of the effort to persuade people of the evils of slavery came from narratives written by former slaves who had escaped to the north. One of the first of these was FREDERICK DOUGLASS's NARRATIVE OF THE LIFE OF FREDERICK DOUGLASS, published in 1845. Written for a white audience, it recounted Douglass's life as a slave where he was deprived of education, beaten and humiliated until he fought back and eventually escaped. It proved to be an inspiration for a whole generation of anti-slavery writers that would eventually help turn the country towards civil war some 20 years later.

A language of its own

The twin forces of expansion and immigration brought Americans into contact with a variety of cultures. With these contacts came an influx of new words. From the

Native Americans came words such as *canoe* and *pecan*, from the Dutch came *cookie* and *coleslaw*, and from the French *chowder* and *bureau*. These and other new words vastly enriched the vernacular although the language itself remained recognisably English. For while they were no longer beholden to their former colonial masters in Britain, Americans were still left using English as their language after the War of Independence. This inheritance was not widely admired and there were deliberate efforts to fashion an American as opposed to an English language.

At the forefront of these efforts was America's first great lexicographer, Noah Webster. His original plan at the turn of century was to try and institute radical changes that would clearly differentiate American from its mother tongue. In particular, he advanced a series of phonetic spellings that, had they been carried through, would have made American all but unrecognisable to someone schooled solely in English. As it was, when Webster published his landmark work, *An American Dictionary of the English Language* in 1828, the changes were minimal. Indeed, a century later, when H.L. Mencken produced his famous list of differences between the two varieties of English in *The American Language*, the majority of the alternative spellings were those mild reforms first devised by Webster, such as *honor, color* and *humor* for *honour, colour* and *humour*. The changes were enough to let people know they were reading a different language, but not enough to stop people reading it at all.

A literature of its own

The fact that Webster did not try and initiate huge changes to the English written and spoken by Americans was perhaps just as well. For in the early part of the republic's new life, the literary heritage of most Americans was still largely British. Works by American writers were relatively difficult to get hold of. Indeed, someone in London was more likely to have read the poems of Anne Bradstreet, for example, than someone in Virginia. The best-selling American work of recent years was written by THOMAS PAINE, an Englishman later reviled by Americans for being an atheist. Another aspect of the dominance of British literature was the fact that there was no copyright on imported texts. This was an issue that just about drove CHARLES DICKENS to despair, but it meant that books written in Britain could be printed more cheaply than books written in America where the author would have to be paid. Consequently, as people preferred to pay less for their books, there was no incentive to publish American writers and therefore there were initially very few American authors because nobody could afford to become a writer.

Those writers that did exist often worked for newspapers in order to earn a living, and wrote books only as a sideline, such as EDGAR ALLAN POE, Caroline Kirkland and William Bryant. One of the few exceptions to this rule was WASHINGTON IRVING. His *SKETCH BOOK*, which contained 'Rip Van Winkle' and 'The Legend of Sleepy Hollow', made him internationally famous. It also answered the call for a national literature that had been dogging American letters since soon after the Revolution. Earlier writers had attempted to employ the epic as the appropriate form for this new literature, but with his short stories Irving popularised a form that American literature would develop and dominate for the next century and a half. *The Sketch Book* was also something of a travelogue and this too appealed to expansionist America. Indeed, many American writers formed careers from travel writing, such as HERMAN MELVILLE in *Typee* and *Omoo*, or Kirkland in *A New Home – Who'll Follow?*, or they supplemented their fictional output with travel journalism, such as AMBROSE BIERCE and MARK TWAIN would later do.

If Irving was popular in his day, the one other writer who could rival him in this was JAMES FENIMORE COOPER. Taking his cue from the immensely popular historical novels of SIR WALTER SCOTT, Cooper devised his own American legends in the series of pioneer novels featuring frontiersman Natty Bumppo or Hawkeye. Probably the best known of these now is *THE LAST OF THE MOHICANS*, a tale set amidst the carnage of the Anglo French wars. Displaying a sensitivity to the Native Americans that would later turn into a contempt for his fellow European Americans, Cooper's accounts of life in the previous century helped to create a myth about the republic's ancestry which fuelled demand in the American public for stories about its own world.

While not writing stories, RALPH WALDO EMERSON certainly found inspiration in the American country for his writings. These, including the philosophical work *NATURE*, exalted in the glories of the New World. However, Emerson's popularity was limited in his own lifetime and his claim to be one of the founding fathers of American literature lies with his influence upon the small group of Concord writers who included HENRY DAVID THOREAU and WALT WHITMAN. Equally as circumscribed in the influence he effected upon his native land at the time was EDGAR ALLAN POE. All but inventing the detective story in adventures such as 'The Purloined Letter', or the horror story in 'The Fall of the House of Usher', as well as modern science fiction in 'MS. Found in a Bottle', Poe failed to find an audience for anything other than his poetry. His influence strangely by-passed America at first, but he found recognition in France and thus joined the process begun by Irving which would eventually see America become a net exporter of culture.

Figure 8: Texts and contexts of the literature of independence (1800–50)

Text			Context	
		1800	Founding of Washington as nation's capital	
		1818	White House rebuilt after being burnt down during second war with Britain, 1812–14	
1820	Washington Irving – *The Sketch Book**	1823	Monroe Doctrine	
1826	James Fenimore Cooper – *The Last of the Mohicans**			
1836	Ralph Waldo Emerson – *Nature**	1836	Battle of the Alamo	
		1837	Victoria accedes to throne	
1839	Caroline Kirkland – *A New Home – Who'll Follow?*			
1840	Edgar Allan Poe – *Tales of the Grotesque and Arabesque*			
		1842	Canadian border established with Britain	
1844	Edgar Allan Poe – *The Purloined Letter**			
1845	Frederick Douglass – *Narrative of the Life of Frederick Douglass** Edgar Allan Poe – *The Raven and Other Poems*			
1846	Herman Melville – *Typee*	1846	US war with Mexico	
1847	Henry Wadsworth Longfellow – *Evangeline* Herman Melville – *Omoo*	1847	War ends with capture of Mexico City	
		1849	Californian Gold Rush	
1850	Nathaniel Hawthorne – *The Scarlet Letter**			

Note: *Work featured in Part 3

American Civil War literature (1850–90)

The American Civil War and the slave narrative

The period between 1850 and 1890 was dominated by the Civil War that tore America apart. The root cause of the Civil War was slavery. When Abraham Lincoln was elected to the office of President in 1860, he did so on an anti-slavery ticket. This came on the back of years of compromise between the northern and southern states which had effectively aimed at keeping a balance of slave and non-slave states in the Union. One of the most pernicious pieces of legislation designed to bolster this compromise was the Fugitive Slave Act passed in 1850. Designed to answer the requirements of slave owners who wished to pursue and capture escaped slaves who had crossed over into non-slave states, many northerners berated the law for effectively instituting slavery in their part of the country.

Examples soon abounded of the terrible effects of the Fugitive Slave Act on runaway slaves. One of the most notorious cases was that of Margaret Garner, who was so desperate for her children not to be returned to a state of slavery when she was recaptured in Ohio, in 1856, that she killed her daughter and attempted to kill all her sons. The incident later became the basis for Toni Morrison's novel *Beloved*. At the time it was just one of a growing number of stories that helped to persuade people in the northern states that they could no longer tolerate slavery in their nation. Many of these stories were written down by ex-slaves or runaways to form the body of literature known as slave narratives.

The first major slave narrative, *The Interesting Narrative of the Life of Olaudah Equiano*, was written by Olaudah Equiano as far back as 1789. As the abolitionist campaign became more organised and widespread, more and more of these narratives were written recounting the stories of people's lives under slavery and very often their escape from it too. Consciously using the most shocking aspects of the brutality of slavery to entice a sensationalist readership, these narratives negotiated a difficult balancing act between the need to keep an audience interested and the need to engage their sympathies for the slaves' cause by appearing to be thoroughly Christian at the same time. This was particularly difficult for women who also had to maintain a sense of their virtue while depicting the sexual violence done to them.

The success of the slave narratives also drew on the history of the popular captivity narratives which thrilled readers with stories of capture by Native Americans. Like these stories, the slave narratives typically focused on someone being brought from a state of innocence into a confrontation of the truth of their slavery, such as in INCIDENTS IN THE LIFE OF A SLAVE GIRL, published in 1861, when HARRIET JACOBS learns on the death of her mother that she was born and raised a slave. Describing a life that is a living death, slave narratives usually involved a form of resurrection when the slaves escape or rebel, such as in FREDERICK DOUGLASS's NARRATIVE OF THE LIFE OF FREDERICK DOUGLASS (1845).

Nowhere is such a Christian paradigm more evident than in the biggest selling novel of the period, HARRIET BEECHER STOWE's UNCLE TOM'S CABIN. Although not strictly a slave narrative because it was not told by a slave, it nevertheless had an enormous impact when it was published in 1852. By the end of the year, the story of Uncle Tom's martyrdom had been read by hundreds of thousands of people. In the end, these narratives helped to persuade people to vote for Abraham Lincoln on the promise of abolishing slavery. Just one month after the election, South Carolina seceded from the Union and went on to form the confederacy of slave states. The Civil War then began in 1861, ostensibly to prevent the division of the Union, but effectively to end slavery. After four years of the most vicious fighting, the north defeated the south and slavery was abolished. In the same year, 1865, President Lincoln was assassinated. The years that followed were spent sorting out the after-effects of abolition, a task that in the south eventually led to the segregation and impoverishment of the African American community.

Concord: America's literary hub

Commentators often note that the literary establishment of nineteenth-century America was a small and tight-knit group. Nowhere is this fact more clearly exemplified than in the group of writers who gathered around the town of Concord, Massachusetts. Central among these writers was RALPH WALDO EMERSON. His book NATURE, published in 1836, became one of the key texts of the religious movement known as Transcendentalism. Transcendentalism was never laid out as a system of thought. Partly this was because it valued intuitive contemplation of the natural world above abstract reasoning. Abstract reasoning, it was argued, along with the gaudy aberrations of modern culture, had worked to diminish humanity's spirit and its connection to a transcendental spirit.

As derided as these notions were in the popular press, they were remarkably influential upon the next generation of American writers. HENRY DAVID THOREAU, who was born and raised in Concord, eventually went to live on Emerson's property and, while there, composed his masterpiece on the spiritual salvation of America, WALDEN, which was published in 1854. Another writer who owed much to Emerson was WALT WHITMAN. Emerson wrote a letter congratulating him on the publication in 1855 of the first edition of LEAVES OF GRASS, the original epic of American poetry. Whitman then used the letter to promote the book. Whitman would later visit Emerson and walk the Walden woods with him. Another writer who already knew the area intimately was Louisa May Alcott, the author of *Little Women* (1868). As a child, Alcott took lessons in Emerson's house and later found herself rowing across Walden pond with Thoreau. She absorbed the Transcendentalism of her neighbours and grew to idolise Emerson. The future philosopher William James and his younger brother, the future novelist HENRY JAMES, also stayed with Emerson as part of their schooling.

The making of the American novel

One writer who did not necessarily idolise Emerson, partly because of a disagreement over slavery, which Emerson vehemently opposed, was NATHANIEL HAWTHORNE. Hawthorne lived in Concord, including in Emerson's grandfather's old house, on and off for many years. However, he wrote his most famous works, the novels *THE*

SCARLET LETTER and THE HOUSE OF THE SEVEN GABLES elsewhere. Although there had previously been attempts to write about America's Puritan heritage, *The Scarlet Letter* was by far and away the most successful novel on the subject. Selling more than 4,000 copies within the first ten days of its release, *The Scarlet Letter* became hugely popular, and, in the process, helped to sway a morally conservative public towards reading more novels.

Until the middle of the nineteenth century and the publication of works such as *The Scarlet Letter*, the novel had been considered an inappropriate and even immoral form of literature. Thomas Jefferson, for example, the third President of the United States and the man largely responsible for drafting the Declaration of Independence, once remarked that reading novels led to 'a bloated imagination, sickly judgment, and disgust towards all the real businesses of life'. Novels, he urged, were a 'mass of trash'. Jefferson's generation was never won over by the novel form but succeeding generations were raised on British imports and early American works, such as JAMES FENIMORE COOPER's Natty Bumppo stories, and they cultivated a readership for Hawthorne and his contemporaries. As many of the objections to the novel form were Puritan in origin, it was perhaps not accidental that a writer with a strong Puritan heritage like Hawthorne should compose *The Scarlet Letter*, a novel questioning Puritan hypocrisy that would kick-start the era of the great American novel.

Indeed, although not as commercially popular, the next year, 1851, saw the publication of HERMAN MELVILLE's masterpiece, *Moby Dick*. Melville, who had become friends with Hawthorne while writing his novel, self-consciously set *Moby Dick* at the beginning of an American tradition of literature which he hoped would one day match that of its European, and particularly, British predecessors. The encyclopaedic tendencies of *Moby Dick* (by which everything ever written about whales in whatever form, from SHAKESPEARE to scientific treatises, is included in the novel) are intended to show it has absorbed all previous cultures in its quest for a new one. In the short term, Melville's novel proved to be a glorious failure and he was remembered more fondly for the travel books, *Typee* and *Omoo*, that he had written in the first half of the century.

Someone who did find an audience for his works during the period in which he wrote was MARK TWAIN. Writing about American issues in an American idiom, Twain perfected the confident vernacular style of writing that would go on to characterise much of the best literature produced by the republic in the ensuing years. In fact, many critics have argued that Twain's THE ADVENTURES OF HUCKLEBERRY FINN is the greatest American novel ever written. Ernest Hemingway even went so far as to declare that 'all modern American literature comes from' it. Dealing with the legacy of the slavery era, the book examines the nature of freedom in America and questions whether the spiritual inheritance of the New World has been properly cared for. In its day *The Adventures of Huckleberry Finn* was only outsold by *Uncle Tom's Cabin*.

Other forms of American literature

American theatre produced nothing of any note during this period. Indeed, it is better known for providing the *mise en scène* of President Lincoln's assassination when he was shot by John Wilkes Booth while watching *Our American Cousin*. American poetry, however, fared much better. Most notably, WALT WHITMAN established himself as the self-styled 'American bard' with *LEAVES OF GRASS*, the epic collection of poems that spanned his entire life. Like Melville, Whitman situated himself at the beginning of a specifically American tradition of poetry. Ironically, it was only when he received massive praise from ALFRED LORD TENNYSON, the ever popular Poet Laureate of Britain, that poetry readers in America began to appreciate the genius in their own midst.

Among the works that eventually made up *Leaves of Grass* was *Drum-Taps*, published in 1865, a collection of poems formed from the experience of the Civil War. Together with Melville's work *Battle-Pieces* (1866), *Drum-Taps* was the best of innumerable volumes of poetry to record the terrible conflicts of the war. Melville was also responsible for continuing to develop the form of the short story, following in the wake of EDGAR ALLAN POE. His masterpiece in this regard was *BARTLEBY*, published in 1853. This is one of the first stories to deal with the burgeoning new world of the office and white-collar work. Continually averring that he would rather not do anything, Bartleby rivals Captain Ahab for the status of most arresting character in American literature. Less alarming but still as gripping, Mark Twain also wrote short stories but more in the tradition established by WASHINGTON IRVING. His best works, such as those collected with *The Celebrated Jumping Frog of Calaveras County* are humorous tales, the stings of which are delivered in a deceptively relaxed prose style.

Figure 9: Texts and contexts of American Civil War literature (1850–90)

Text		Context	
1850	Nathaniel Hawthorne – *The Scarlet Letter**	1850	Fugitive Slave Act
1851	Herman Melville – *Moby Dick**	1851	Shadrach Minkins, a waiter, is first victim of slave-catchers
1852	Harriet Beecher Stowe – *Uncle Tom's Cabin**		
1853	Herman Melville – *Bartleby, The Scrivener**		
1854	Henry David Thoreau – *Walden**	1854	Abolitionists attack Boston court where fugitive slave being held
1855	Walt Whitman – *Leaves of Grass**	1856	Margaret Garner, a fugitive slave, kills her daughter rather than give her up to slavery
		1860	Abraham Lincoln becomes President on anti-slavery ticket. South Carolina leads the southern states in seceding from the Union just one month after the election.
1861	Harriet Jacobs – *Incidents in the Life of a Slave Girl**	1861	Civil War commences
		1863	Gettysburg Address Lincoln proclaims government of the people, by the people and for the people
1865	Walt Whitman – *Drum-Taps*	1865	Civil War won by Union. Slavery abolished and Lincoln assassinated
1867	Mark Twain – *The Celebrated Jumping Frog of Calaveras County and Other Sketches*		
		1867	America buys Alaska from Russia
1868	Louisa May Alcott – *Little Women** Horatio Alger – *Ragged Dick*	1868	Citizenship granted to all born in America apart from Native Americans
		1870	Universal male suffrage in America for those over-21
1876	Mark Twain – *The Adventures of Tom Sawyer*	1876	Battle of the Little Big Horn
1881	Henry James – *Washington Square**	1881	Chinese immigration is suspended
1884	Mark Twain – *The Adventures of Huckleberry Finn**		
		1887	Dawes Severalty Act latest piece of legislation to reduce Native American lands

Note: *Work featured in Part 3

MODERN INTERNATIONAL LITERARY CONTEXTS

Modern literature (1890–1914)

Transatlantic influences

Almost from the time when English settlers first landed in the New World at the beginning of the seventeenth century, there has always been a form of literary commerce between Britain and America. To begin with, this commerce was based upon a shared inheritance of literature written in English. As America developed its own distinctive literature in the nineteenth century, the two cultures began to exchange literary ideas, each taken with the unique identity and particularities of the other's works. However, towards the end of the nineteenth century, the forces acting upon the writer, and the culture within which literature was produced, began to take on similar qualities on both sides of the Atlantic. The most important aspect of this homogenisation was the rapid and accelerated industrialisation of the United States following the end of the Civil War in 1865.

Before the Civil War, America was still largely a rural economy, with most of its inhabitants living in villages and small towns. However, the development of transcontinental railroads, of which there were four by 1890, led to the development of great industrial centres, such as Pittsburgh and Chicago. There, huge monopolistic businesses developed, based around such commodities as steel, oil and meat-packing. These businesses sucked in great tides of labour and the dozen or so big cities of the time increased their size many times over. By so doing, America followed in the footsteps of Britain's earlier industrial revolution, but it did so at a much faster pace and with much greater resources, both human and non-human. Consequently, by the end of the century, America had already overtaken Britain in key areas of production and output, foreshadowing its rise in the twentieth century as the most powerful country in the world.

The shared experiences of industrialisation, and its concomitant urbanisation of the population, led to shared cultural responses across the international scene. The generalised condition of rootlessness, as whole populations went on the move, transferring from the country to the city, was recorded in such disparate works as THEODORE DREISER's SISTER CARRIE and THOMAS HARDY's JUDE THE OBSCURE. Of course, many of the people on the move, as in these novels, were working class and in recording this fact, the new fictions brought a fictional democracy into being. In this new fictional democracy, all kinds of people became the protagonists, rather than just the middle classes and aristocrats who had dominated earlier works. Maggie, in STEPHEN CRANE's *MAGGIE: A GIRL OF THE STREETS*, for example, ends up as a prostitute, as, to her way of thinking, does Tess, in HARDY's *TESS OF THE D'URBERVILLES*. Indeed, the Bowery, New York's legendary street of vagrants and drunks, became one of the most written about locations in fiction, portrayals of which can be found in *Maggie, Sister Carrie* and William Dean Howell's *Hazards of New Fortune*, amongst others.

These new protagonists also belonged to a new form of realism that came to dominate fiction in various ways for the next few decades. The term 'realism' stems from this particular type of literature's accurate portrayal of reality. This is rather a broad remit, but for nations with populations brutalised by different wars and industrialisation, in part this meant telling the truth about the modern world and its often barbarous progress. In this regard, CRANE's *THE RED BADGE OF COURAGE*, which purports to convey the truth of the battlefield, resonates with JOSEPH CONRAD's *HEART OF DARKNESS*, which purports to convey the truth of imperialism. However, the works of HENRY JAMES, which usually centre upon the circumscribed worlds of the leisured middle classes, are equally realist in the sense of being psychologically accurate. That is, they offer a detailed insight into the minds of the central characters, as opposed to offering detailed accounts of their environments. Other writers, such as Dreiser, opted to go the other way and wrote fiction in a spare documentary style that diminished the role of the narrator in favour of a form of reportage.

The Regionalists

Another of the most popular, but at first sight paradoxical, responses to the industrial homogenisation of the world was regional writing. Regional writing was writing (usually fictional, and in parts of America dominated by the short story format) that described local tales about local customs in local settings, often using a local vernacular. In Britain, the most famous regional writer is THOMAS HARDY, who composed all of his major novels and short stories in and about Wessex, his self-conscious revival of the Anglo-Saxon name for south west England. In America, New England was represented by the tales of SARAH ORNE JEWETT, amongst others, the south by Joel Chandler Harris and KATE CHOPIN, and the west by Bret Harte.

The creative impulse behind these, and the many other writers who can be called regionalist, was the need to record the distinctiveness of the areas in which they lived before that distinctiveness disappeared in the wake of the homogenising forces of international capitalism. The history of literature shows how the forces of unity are always met by a creative reaction designed to recall difference, a feature as evident in King Alfred's translation of Boethius into Old English as it is in MARK TWAIN's representation of the local dialects of the Mississippi. Very often though, rather than resisting the homogeneity of the new urban landscape completely, many of the regionalist writers helped to draw their readers together, pooling their knowledge of local peoples. This is most evident in the tactic of using a narrator who explains local customs and behaviours, rather than showing them in the expectation that readers will understand them. Such explanations presupposed a readership constituted from places above and beyond the local area about which the story is told. In this sense, these works helped to unify communities, particularly in America after the Civil War where misunderstandings between the north and south persisted as a result of the conflict and its propaganda.

Literature in the wake of Darwin

If urbanisation was one of the influences that shaped fiction right across the world towards the beginning of this period and beyond, then another was the work of Charles Darwin. His *On the Origin of Species*, published in 1859, and *The Descent of Man*, published in 1871, proved to have profound implications for the whole of nineteenth-century society. These books demonstrated the evolutionary origin of animals and humans and, for many, effectively undermined the creation story of the BIBLE, showing that humans were just another form of animal rather than chosen by God. Indeed, despite the protestations of Darwin himself, a lot of people felt that his revelations challenged the very concept of God and left human beings to the mercy of their environment, where they were subject to the law of the survival of the fittest.

These themes cropped up again and again in the fiction of the period. Hardy's novels, in particular, showed people to be at the mercy of environmental forces much greater than any individual. Many of his characters, such as Jude and Tess, succumb to pitiless fates in a world that fails to protect the good from the bad. The absence of God or any other benign force lies at the heart of darkness in Conrad's novel of the same name. While in JACK LONDON's *THE CALL OF THE WILD*, published in 1903, the survival of the fittest comes to indicate not only the Darwinian message that those animals that adapt best to their environment survive, but also the more bellicose theory that the more aggressive an animal is, including humans, the better able they will be to dominate their surroundings. This proved to be a popular message and London was one of the best-selling authors at the beginning of the twentieth century.

Art for Art's Sake

Apart from being godless, literature was also touched by the increasingly commercial culture in which it functioned. Indeed, with a mass literate audience, it was now easier to live and work as a full-time author. The popular forms of literature, such as Sir Arthur Conan Doyle's Sherlock Holmes stories, had helped to make writing an increasingly lucrative profession. Whereas literature had once been used as an instrument of moral correction, as MATTHEW ARNOLD had urged in the middle of the nineteenth century, it now had no such pretensions and essentially existed in its own right, pleasing with its beauty but not allying that beauty to any message. Rather than despair about the rootless situation of art, it actually became a cause for celebration in the 'Art for Art's Sake' movement in the 1890s.

The leading exponent of this approach to literature was OSCAR WILDE. Delighting in the tautological form of the epigram, Wilde's works, he insisted, were about nothing but themselves. Indeed, the greatest of his works was actually himself. Many critics have since seen in this approach to literature and art a message of its own, which was a reaction against the utilitarianism of the industrial world in which everyone's value was measured in the wealth they could lay claim to or the work they contributed to the economy. In a godless world, Wilde argued that a person was a means to nothing but his or her self. His works, such as THE IMPORTANCE OF BEING EARNEST, were, by virtue of their very pointlessness, examples of his philosophy in action. Wilde's plays also did much to reinvigorate the dying art of the theatre in the English language.

Another playwright, and one who took his inspiration from the Norwegian work of Henrik Ibsen, was GEORGE BERNARD SHAW. While Wilde revelled in the isolated status of literature in modern society, Shaw, in the spirit of Ibsen, did his best to a re-engage the two. In particular, he used plays as a way of seducing people into considering his political messages, which were essentially reformist rather than revolutionary. One of these political messages was pacifism. It was a message that the English-speaking countries failed to heed as they approached 1914 and rushed headlong into a war that would change the whole world forever.

Figure 10: Texts and contexts of Modern literature (1890–1914)

Text		Context	
		1890	Massacre at Wounded Knee
1891	Thomas Hardy – *Tess of the D'Urbervilles**		
1893	Stephen Crane – *Maggie: A Girl of the Streets**	1893	Formation of the Labour Party in Britain
1894	Ambrose Bierce – *Tales of Soldiers and Civilians** Stephen Crane – *The Red Badge of Courage**		
1895	Oscar Wilde – *The Importance of Being Earnest**	1895	Oscar Wilde jailed for being homosexual
1896	Thomas Hardy – *Jude the Obscure**	1896	Utah becomes 45th state of America
1897	Bram Stoker – *Dracula**	1897	First moving picture
1898	Henry James – *The Turn of the Screw**	1898	America acquires Cuba, Puerto Rico, Guan and the Philippines from Spain. Hawaii annexed
1899	Kate Chopin – *The Awakening**	1899	Boer War
1900	Joseph Conrad – *Lord Jim* Theodore Dreiser – *Sister Carrie**	1900	Freud advances theory of dreams
1901	Joseph Conrad – *Heart of Darkness**	1901	Death of Queen Victoria
1902	Thomas Hardy – *Poems of the Past and the Present** Henry James – *The Wings of a Dove*		
1903	Jack London – *The Call of the Wild**	1903	Wright brothers fly first plane
1905	George Bernard Shaw – *Major Barbara**, *Man and Superman*	1905	Einstein's Theory of Relativity
1907	Joseph Conrad – *The Secret Agent*		
1911	Edith Wharton – *Ethan Frome**	1911	Senate becomes a directly elected body
		1912	*Titanic* sinks
1913	George Bernard Shaw – *Pygmalion*		
1914	James Joyce – *Dubliners* Thomas Hardy – *Satires of Circumstance*	1914	Commencement of First World War

Note: *Work featured in Part 3

Part 3

A–Z of 100 Key Works

THE ADVENTURES OF HUCKLEBERRY FINN (1885)
by Mark Twain

Persons attempting to find a motive in this narrative will be prosecuted; persons attempting to find a moral in it will be banished; persons attempting to find a plot in it will be shot.

Phot credit: © Bettmann/CORBIS

The Adventures of Huckleberry Finn follows the adventures of Huck, a runaway boy, and Jim, an escaped slave, as they travel down the Mississippi river in the 1840s. Critics have vied with each other to tender the greatest homage to this novel, but Ernest Hemingway offered one its most telling tributes with his declaration that, 'all modern American literature comes from one book by Mark Twain called *Huckleberry Finn*. There was nothing before. There has been nothing as good since.'

Summary

The novel opens with a reminder by Huckleberry Finn of what happened to him previously in *The Adventures of Tom Sawyer*. After splitting the money he found with Tom, Huck now lives in the care of Widow Douglas and Miss Watson, while his money has been invested by Judge Thatcher. However, Huck is not keen on this state of affairs and particularly not the 'sivilizin' process he is subject to by the two sisters. He wants to leave but Tom persuades him to stay so he can be an effective part of his gang. One day, Huck discovers footprints in the snow bearing the tell-tale sign of his father, Pap. Huck knows that Pap is merely after his money and he signs it all over to Judge Thatcher just in case. Eventually, Pap takes Huck out to live with him in an isolated cabin. There Pap continues to drink and beat Huck, locking him in for days at a time while he goes to town. After a period of this, Huck seizes his chance and escapes, slaughtering a

pig to make it look like he has been murdered. Huck then steals a canoe and sails down to Jackson's Island. While camping there, Huck meets Jim, one of Miss Watson's slaves.

The two runaways decide to make their journey to the Free States together and clamber aboard a raft, borne along on the tide of the rising Mississippi. They also loot a house floating past where Jim discovers the body of Pap, but doesn't tell Huck for fear of upsetting him. After narrowly escaping from three villains, Huck and Jim's raft is run over by a steam boat and the two are separated as they swim to safety. Huck finds himself adopted by the Grangerfords, a seemingly kindly family. However, it soon transpires that the Grangerfords are locked in an ancient feud with the Shepherdsons and this leads to a gun battle in which many family members are killed. During the confusion, Huck locates Jim's hiding place and the two of them set off down the river again.

> The Adventures of Huckleberry Finn explores the personal and public freedoms of the American nation, championing the ideals of equality and liberty against the kind of prejudices which had recently engulfed the country in a civil war.

Shortly afterwards, they save two white con men – the king and the duke. The two men commandeer the raft and make their way down the river, conning people as they go. Their crimes get worse and worse until, eventually, they sell Jim to a local farmer, informing him that he is a runaway. When Huck finds out, he resolves to liberate Jim and he goes up to the house where Jim is being held only to be addressed as 'Tom'. It transpires that the people holding Jim are Tom Sawyer's aunt and uncle and they have mistakenly assumed that Huck is Tom because he is due to visit. When Tom does turn up, he pretends to be his own younger brother and hatches an unnecessarily complex plan to free Jim. When they finally execute the plan, Tom is shot while escaping. Jim looks after Tom as best he can, but then Huck has to get a doctor who hands Jim back over to the Tom's aunt and uncle. However, when Tom's other aunt arrives, she confirms Tom's claim that Jim has in fact been a free man for two months since Miss Watson died and freed him in her will.

THEMES AND TECHNIQUES

The Adventures of Huckleberry Finn centres around a critique of different types of freedom and captivity. The most obvious manifestation of this is Jim who is an actual slave, legally bound to whoever buys him. Although slavery had been abolished for some 20 years by the time the novel was published, it does address some of the issues of equality left over from the days of slavery. In particular, Huck learns to appreciate that Jim not only has the sympathies and feelings he expects to find in white people, he also often has them to a greater degree than his would-be captors.

Huck also yearns for his own type of freedom. Primarily, he wants to be free from the hands of his drunken father, but he also yearns to be free from the constraints of civilisation. In this, Huck represents a brand of American sentiment typical of the time, one that romanticised the pioneering spirit of the American West. The freedom of Huck and Jim upon the river is symbolic of the fluid state of American life on the frontier, where the ideals of equality and liberty could be championed against the congealed prejudices of the established states, particularly the Biblical hypocrisy of the south.

Further Reading

Johnson, Claudia Durst, *Understanding 'The Adventures of Huckleberry Finn'*. Westport: Greenwood Publishing Group, 1996. This is a casebook, providing both analysis of the text and source materials from the time, including slave and river gambler memoirs, as well as the controversial Fugitive Slave Law.

Budd, Louise J. and Elliot, Emory (eds), *New Essays on 'The Adventures of Huckleberry Finn'*. Cambridge: Cambridge University Press, 1985. This is a collection of essays which looks at a number of issues, including the novel's use of the vernacular, its humour and its realism.

De Koster, Katie *Readings on 'The Adventures of Huckleberry Finn'*. San Diego: Greenhaven Press, 1998. This book contextualises Twain's novel, as well as providing a biography of the author.

ALICE'S ADVENTURES IN WONDERLAND (1865)
by Lewis Carroll

'Curiouser and curiouser!' cried Alice.

The first of two novels set by Lewis Carroll in Wonderland (the other being *Through the Looking-Glass*), *Alice's Adventures in Wonderland* occupies a unique place in English literature. The comic-absurd tale describes what happens to Alice when she follows the White Rabbit down the rabbit hole and into Wonderland.

Summary

When the novel opens, Alice, a young girl, is sitting by the river, becoming increasingly bored. Suddenly she sees a rabbit rush by her consulting a watch and worrying that it is late. Intrigued by this irregular occurrence, Alice follows the White Rabbit down a large rabbit hole and from there she falls into a long tunnel. It takes so long to fall down, Alice is on the verge of sleep when she hits a patch of dry leaves and finds herself unhurt. She spies the White Rabbit further down a hallway full of locked doors and chases after him but he soon disappears and she is left alone. She finds a key on a glass table which fits a tiny doorway leading onto a beautiful garden but it is too small for her to get through. Back on the glass table is a bottle marked 'DRINK ME'. After due consideration, Alice drinks it and shrinks small enough to fit through the door. Unfortunately, she is now too small to get the key off the table.

She then eats a cake underneath the table which causes her to grow to twice her normal size. Upset that she will not be able to see her feet anymore, Alice starts crying. When the White Rabbit rushes by her again he is so startled by her appearance that he drops his fan. Alice picks it up and in the act of wafting her face, she shrinks again and falls into the salty lake created by her own large tears. She meets a number of creatures in the lake and swims to the shore where she is mistaken by the White Rabbit for his housekeeper. Inside his house, Alice drinks from another bottle and grows enormous again. In an effort to get rid of her, the White Rabbit and his friends pelt her with pebbles that turn into cakes. Alice eats one, shrinks once more, and then runs away into the forest. There she meets a smoking caterpillar who advises her that if she eats one side of a mushroom, she will grow tall and if she eats the other side, she will become small.

Using the strange but comforting imagery of dreams, *Alice's Adventures in Wonderland* depicts the process of growing up and the difficult task of adapting to the world of adults whom she eventually decides are 'nothing but a pack of cards!'

Having finally mastered her size, Alice next encounters the Duchess and her Cheshire Cat whose smile lingers in the air even after it is gone. Next she joins the March Hare, the Mad Hatter and the Dormouse for a Mad Hatter's Tea Party, but finding them too rude and sleepy, she leaves them and once more finds herself in the hallway where she started her adventure. Learning from experience, this time she manages to get through the small door and into the garden she had seen earlier. There she meets the execution-loving Queen of Hearts who introduces her to the Gryphon and the Mock Turtle who tell Alice about their school under the sea. At the end of their story, the Gryphon takes Alice to see the trial of the Knave of Hearts who is charged with stealing tarts from the Queen of Hearts. The trial is a farce and Alice becomes angrier by the minute until she is called to the witness stand herself. As the proceedings continue, Alice grows larger and larger and when the Queen orders her head to be cut off, Alice denounces the lot of them as a pack of cards and they all attack her. Alice then wakes up on the riverbank while her sister brushes leaves from her face and sends her to tea.

THEMES AND TECHNIQUES

Carroll's novel is primarily a children's story. It contains a number of elements that draw on the tradition first set down by the Grimm brothers, such as talking animals and being eaten, which define children's literature. However, *Alice's Adventures in Wonderland* is also about children and, specifically, about the process of growing up. Much of the novel is given over to the problems Alice has with her

size. One minute she is too tall and the next she is too small. This exaggerated sense of her own body alludes to teenage difficulties with 'fitting in', both physically and mentally. Alice has to adapt herself to the inconsistent and often illogical world of Wonderland, a world in which many adult behaviours are apparent, at least from a child's point of view, such as the Queen's insistence on punishing someone before the trial itself even gets underway. Consequently, Alice spends a lot of time in the book learning the rules of different games. Once Alice has learnt these rules and adapted herself to the vagaries of Wonderland, she is able to assert her own identity more forcibly, as she does on the witness stand, and from there she is able to leave it all behind her.

Further Reading

Carroll, Lewis, *The Annotated Alice: Definitive Edition*. Edited by Martin Gardner. London: Penguin, 2001. This edition of the text includes John Tenniel's seminal illustrations, as well as Gardner's excellent annotations.

ANTONY AND CLEOPATRA (1606)
by William Shakespeare

Age cannot wither her, nor custom stale Her infinite variety.

Antony and Cleopatra is a tragic drama which follows the fortunes of Antony, one of the triumvirate (or government of three) ruling the Roman Empire, and Cleopatra, the Queen of Egypt. The play charts their tempestuous relationship and eventual downfall at the hands of Octavius Caesar.

Summary

Antony and Cleopatra opens with Antony tending to Cleopatra in her Alexandrian palace. He is already deeply infatuated with Cleopatra and because of this he is neglecting his duties as a triumvir – a member of the three-person council ruling the Roman Empire. The other two members of the triumvirate are Octavius Caesar (adopted son of Julius Caesar, after whom SHAKESPEARE has written another play) and Lepidus, the least powerful of the three. Caesar and Lepidus are furious that Antony will not return to Rome even though Antony's wife is in open rebellion against Caesar.

When Antony learns that his wife has died and that Pompey is threatening Rome, he finally decides to return from Egypt, but not before promising his undying love to Cleopatra. Arriving in Rome, Antony soon begins a quarrel with Caesar, and Lepidus does his best to mediate between them. Eventually, it is agreed that Antony should marry Caesar's sister, Octavia, as a way of establishing an alliance between them. Facing a united triumvirate once again, Pompey abandons his plans to invade Rome and the four men sign a truce. Meanwhile, Cleopatra is furious when she hears that Antony has broken his pledge to her and married Octavia instead. She is only comforted when she hears that Octavia is not a beauty in the same mould as herself.

> Set in a world where the personal and the political are in constant friction with each other, Shakespeare's *Antony and Cleopatra* contrasts the excesses of Egypt with the balance of Rome, and the passion of Antony and Cleopatra with the cold calculations of Caesar.

Convinced that matters are now settled, Antony decides to leave Rome for Athens with Octavia. Once there, he learns that Caesar has reneged on their pact and attacked Pompey. Matters worsen when reports reach Antony that Caesar has defeated Pompey, killed him, imprisoned Lepidus, and slandered Antony in public. Octavia begs Antony not to start a civil war with Caesar and so he sends her back to Rome as a peace envoy. Antony then repairs to Egypt where he hands over part of the Roman Empire to Cleopatra and their children. Caesar is incensed both by this and by Antony's poor treatment of his sister, Octavia. He decides to make war against Antony and takes his army to Egypt.

Despite the obvious disadvantages, Antony resolves to fight Caesar at sea. However, when Cleopatra sees Antony losing, she withdraws the Egyptian fleet. Antony follows her, leaving his men to defeat at the hands of Caesar. Despite this setback, Antony tries one last time to defeat Caesar. He scores an initial victory but ultimately finds himself undone by the desertion of his Egyptian troops. Livid with this betrayal, he threatens to kill Cleopatra but she has word sent to him that she has committed suicide. Distraught, Antony inflicts a fatal wound upon himself, giving him just enough time for one last reunion with Cleopatra before he dies. Cleopatra then learns of Caesar's intent to parade her in Rome and so, to avoid this ignominy, she kills herself by having two asps bite her.

THEMES AND TECHNIQUES

Antony and Cleopatra presents its audience with a conflict between balance and excess. Curiously, perhaps, the conflict is not embodied between Antony and Cleopatra, after whom the play is named, but between them and Caesar. On the one hand, Antony and Cleopatra share a love so passionate and so unique that it is beyond measure, and on the other hand Caesar is able to calculate quite accurately how to beat Antony and precisely what he wants from Cleopatra. In this regard, Egypt is not just another place in the play, rather it represents extravagance and wonder, causing 'a gap in nature'. Compared to this, Rome is a place of niggardly calculation where even Caesar's sister is prudently bartered for concord, as if she were a piece on a chessboard. These differences are dramatised in the play by the difference between the masculine values of Caesar in contrast to the feminine values of Cleopatra. While the other characters attribute Caesar's actions to his sense of duty and his honour as a warrior, Cleopatra's actions are condemned as whorish and manipulative. In the end, however, the play itself shows that Cleopatra refuses to cede her honour by becoming Caesar's trophy, while Caesar betrays the plaudits heaped on him by proving inconstant in his dealings with all the main characters.

Further Reading

Shakespeare, William, *The Arden Shakespeare: 'Antony and Cleopatra'*. Edited by John Wilders. London: Arden, 1995. In addition to a forensically edited text, this book also looks at the context of the play, the sources Shakespeare used to write it, and the uneven history of its performance.

Shakespeare, William, '*Antony and Cleopatra':
New Casebook Study*. Edited by John Drakakis.
London: Palgrave Macmillan,1994. This book
provides a series of fastidiously edited essays
offering different interpretations of *Antony
and Cleopatra* by many of the leading experts
in the field.

AUTOBIOGRAPHY OF BENJAMIN FRANKLIN, THE (1791–1868)
by Benjamin Franklin

*Were it offer'd to my choice, I should have
no objection to a repetition of the same life
from its beginning, only asking the
advantage authors have of a second
edition to correct some faults of the first.*

As the title suggests, *The Autobiography of
Benjamin Franklin* tells the story of BENJAMIN
FRANKLIN, one of America's founding fathers
and a signatory to the Declaration of
Independence.

Summary

The *Autobiography* is split into four parts. The
first part begins with an address to Franklin's
son, William Franklin, the Governor of New
Jersey. Admitting that he would happily repeat
his life, but knowing that he cannot, Franklin
tenders the hope that at least he will be
allowed to recollect it and that others might
find it worth imitating. He commences his
story with an account of his ancestors in
England, bringing it up to date with his own
father's move to America in 1682 in order to
pursue religious freedom.

Franklin then describes how he is the
youngest son in a family of ten born to his
father's second wife, Franklin's father already
having seven children from his first marriage.
At the age of 10 Franklin is removed from
school in order to become an apprentice to
his father's candle and soap business.
Unhappy at this, Franklin notes that his father
makes every effort to find him an apprenticeship useful to his nature. Concluding that
Franklin is 'bookish', he records that his
father then sends him to be a printer in his
brother's print shop.

There Franklin notes how he advances
himself by writing verse, studying how to
argue, learning a wider vocabulary, teaching
himself arithmetic and geometry and reading
philosophy. He also becomes a vegetarian at
this time and changes his lodgings in order to
save money which he then spends on more
books so as to improve himself.

After a fallout with his brother, which
Franklin advises us is one of his 'errata', he
leaves his brother's shop and moves to
Philadelphia. While there, Franklin's writing
skills earn him the attention of the Governor,
who wants him to set up a printing shop of his
own. In order to learn more of the trade,
Franklin travels to England. Upon his return,
he finds the Governor is no longer in office
but he still determines to succeed and eventually, after enormous diligence, he sets up his
own successful business. It is at this time that
he also gets married.

> One of the first popular biographies of a
> secular man, Franklin's extraordinary
> account of his dedication to public and
> private enterprise helped to establish him
> as the 'First American'.

The second part of the *Autobiography* was
written in Paris and it begins with letters com-
mending Franklin on what he has written so
far. Picking up the story where he left off,
Franklin notes that the library he set up
proves to be very popular. He also continues
to try and improve himself by attending to a
list of 13 virtues, one a day, although he feels
he is too proud of his humility to overcome
his pride.

The third part of the *Autobiography*, written
in Philadelphia, follows this improvement
up and suggests that the 13 virtues might
provide the foundations for forming an international sect or 'Party of Virtue'. Franklin also
continues to improve himself by learning languages, making advancements in his career,
such as becoming the Postmaster General,
producing *Poor Richard's Almanac* and
organising the first professional fire-fighting
company.

Franklin goes on to help found the
University of Pennsylvania with the help of the
debating society he started called the 'Junto'.

He also organises funding for the defence of the colonies. Franklin then invents the stove, for which he refuses to take out a patent in order that its use may become widespread. When he is elected to the Pennsylvania Assembly, Franklin negotiates better relations with the Native Americans and improves street lighting and sweeping. After war breaks out with France, Franklin organises troop provisions and is made a colonel. Concurrently, Franklin undertakes a series of experiments which prove the relationship of lightning to electricity. This provides him with enormous international prestige, a prestige which is then put to use as he negotiates for more legislative powers with England. The fourth part of the *Autobiography* notes that the negotiations go badly but Franklin is thanked in Pennsylvania anyway.

THEMES AND TECHNIQUES

The Autobiography of Benjamin Franklin is a remarkable account of an extraordinary man, deceptively simply written (it is not, as HERMAN MELVILLE noted, a book of poetry), with a healthy dose of self-deprecating humour. Apart from the historical interest of Franklin's life, the *Autobiography* was the first popular biography of a secular man, as opposed to a saint or other religious person. It also, and more importantly, embodied the vision which came to be known as the American Dream. Franklin came from a large family of ordinary working people, but through hard work and self-improvement he became one of the most important men, not only of his age, but ultimately of all time. Combining great wealth with moral purpose, business acumen with public works, Franklin and his book became the model for the self-made man which went on to inform the books of such writers as Horatio Alger and F. Scott Fitzgerald.

Further Reading

Franklin, Benjamin, *Benjamin Franklin's Autobiography*. Edited by J. A. Leo Lemay and Paul Zall. London and New York: W.W. Norton, 1986. This was the first edition of the autobiography to be taken directly from the manuscript itself and it remains the standard edition. This book also provides an insight into the history of its publication.

Isaacson, Walter, *Benjamin Franklin: An American Life*. London: Simon & Schuster, 2003. As well as providing one of the most detailed accounts of Franklin's life, this book also looks at how Franklin turned himself into the archetypal American at the precise moment in history that he was needed.

AWAKENING, THE (1899)
by Kate Chopin

But the beginning of things, of a world especially, is necessarily vague, tangled, chaotic, and exceedingly disturbing. How few of us ever emerge from such beginning! How many souls perish in its tumult!

The Awakening follows the gradual dawning of Edna Pontellier's spiritual, sexual and material independence in New Orleans. When this novel was first published at the end of the nineteenth century it caused a scandal from which the author never recovered.

Summary

When the novel opens, Edna is on holiday with her husband, Léonce, and their two boys on Grand Isle, an exclusive summer resort used by residents of the French Quarter in New Orleans. While Léonce feels that Edna is inattentive to both him and the children in some inexpressible way, Edna also begins to find her husband's presence oppressive. When Léonce returns to work, Edna stays on the island and starts a friendship with Robert, the resort owner's son. Although this starts innocently enough, the relationship soon inspires in Edna passions and thoughts which she had not previously had. It marks the dawn of her awakening as she begins 'to realise her position in the universe as a human being, and to recognise her relations as an individual to the world within and about her'.

Following the advice of a mutual friend and his own realisation at the intensity of their relationship, Robert eventually leaves Grand Isle. The resort then seems duller for Edna and she takes solace in speaking about him with others and in the barbed company of Mademoiselle Reisz, a talented pianist. When she returns to New Orleans at the end of the summer, she finds that she is still under the spell of Robert. Furthermore, she is no longer satisfied with her life. Instead of receiving callers, as is normally expected of her, she goes out, leaving no excuse. She also continues her interest in painting that she started while on Grand Isle, and is encouraged in this by the passionate philosophy of Mademoiselle Reisz, whom she takes to visiting. However, Léonce is disturbed by this change in his wife and, thinking that she might have become mentally unstable, he goes to consult the family doctor, Mandelet. Mandelet advises Léonce not to contradict his wife for a few months and that the issue should eventually resolve itself. Privately, however, Mandelet concedes the possibility that a man may be involved in Edna's behaviour.

> The frank portrayal of a woman's dawning material, sexual, and spiritual independence from her husband caused *The Awakening* to be extremely controversial when it was first published in 1899.

When Léonce departs for New York on an extended business trip and the children are sent away to their grandparents, Edna effectively finds herself a free agent. She continues to see Mademoiselle Reisz who becomes a type of role model to her and who also receives letters from Robert. While still carrying her passion for Robert, Edna becomes involved with another man, Alcée Arobin. At the same time, and having won money through gambling, as well as having made it by selling her painting, Edna leaves the house she shared with Léonce and moves into her own home.

Following the establishment of her independence from Léonce, Edna learns one day that Robert has returned. After an initial awkwardness, it becomes clear that the two are still in love with each other. Unfortunately, however, their reunion is interrupted when Edna is called to assist her friend in a difficult childbirth. When Edna returns from this traumatic event Robert has already gone, leaving a note which says only: 'I love you. Goodbye – because I love you.' The next day she travels to Grand Isle and goes down to the beach. There, throwing off all her clothes, she swims out into the sea until she is too exhausted to return.

THEMES AND TECHNIQUES

When *The Awakening* was published in 1899, it proved to be an extremely controversial book because of its frank portrayal of Edna's spiritual and sensual desires. While this caused Chopin to be ostracised at the time, now it is these elements of the novel that are celebrated. *The Awakening* is seen as part of the beginning of a feminist movement in which women have achieved equality and independence. This is expressed most vividly in the novel by Edna's relationship to the sea. The sea is where Edna learns to swim on her own and for the first time comes to an appreciation of her own strength. In doing so, Edna also learns to value her own feelings of sensuality, feelings which balk against the constraints of married life with Léonce. In this sense, Edna does not so much commit suicide at the end of the novel, as she refuses to cede her desires to a conventional and dependent life and in the act of this refusal, she dies. Aside from the content of the story, *The Awakening* is also interesting for the way in which it is told. For the shock of the novel at the time would, in some measure, have issued from the natural and realistic manner in which Edna and the other characters are portrayed. This sense of realism is enhanced by the detailed portrait CHOPIN provides of southern Louisiana life at the turn of the last century. It was such portrayals of local and regional life that had initially brought fame to Chopin at a time when ways of life were much more place-specific than they are today in the United States.

Further Reading

Chopin, Kate, *The Awakening: An Authoritative Text, Biographical and Historical Contexts Criticism*. Edited by Margo Culley. London and New York: W.W. Norton, 1994. This is the second edition of the most authoritative version of *The Awakening* and it also contains a biography and valuable historical documents, such as reviews from the time of its publication.

Elliot, Emory and Martin, Wendy (eds), *New Essays on 'The Awakening'*. Cambridge: Cambridge University Press, 1988. Following an introduction which offers a detailed look at the publication history of *The Awakening*, this book also provides a series of essays on different aspects of the novel, including its status as a feminist classic.

BARTLEBY, THE SCRIVENER (1853)
by Herman Melville

I would prefer not to.

Written during a difficult period in Melville's life, *Bartleby* is now widely considered to be one of the greatest ever short stories. It tells the story of the eponymous clerk and his seemingly self-willed descent into doing nothing until he dies.

Summary

The story is told by an elderly and unambitious property lawyer. He describes his staff of two copyists, nicknamed Turkey and Nippers, and one office boy, Ginger Nut. Having recently taken on more business, he hires another scrivener or copyist to assist Turkey and Nippers. Bartleby applies for the position and the narrator hopes his sedate countenance might quell tempers in the office. After initially proving to be an assiduous worker, one day Bartleby is asked by the narrator to proofread one of his own documents, to which the scrivener replies, 'I would prefer not to.' After completing some more work over the following days, when he is asked again to perform some proofreading, Bartleby again states that he would prefer not to, a reply he makes to every further request for an explanation. Over the ensuing weeks Bartleby declines to take part in fewer and fewer activities in the office, all the while refusing to give any explanation beyond the refrain, 'I prefer not to.'

One day, the narrator discovers that Bartleby is actually living in the office. Feeling strangely unable or unwilling to do anything about Bartleby's behaviour, it eventually reaches the point where Bartleby is doing nothing. The narrator then gives Bartleby his notice, but after the six days' notice has expired, Bartleby is still there. He then gives Bartleby some money on the understanding that he will leave, but Bartleby remains. The narrator accepts this arrangement initially, but it soon transpires that it is giving him a bad reputation amongst his peers and so, not being willing to throw Bartleby out, the narrator moves offices instead. However, the new tenants of the office complain to the narrator that Bartleby is still there. The narrator returns and pleads with Bartleby to leave, even offering him a room in his own house, but Bartleby remains. The next time the narrator hears of Bartleby, the scrivener is in prison on a vagrancy charge. The narrator visits him and finds him facing a wall. He bribes the guard to feed Bartleby, but within a short time he hears that Bartleby is dead after preferring not to eat.

> Foreshadowing the type of anti-heroes common in modern fiction, Bartleby is a lone and isolated figure who slowly but fatally disengages from life.

THEMES AND TECHNIQUES

Bartleby is one of the most iconic figures in modern literature. Completely and utterly alienated from his job of work, seemingly exiled from his family, and friendless in an unforgiving city, Bartleby is a lone and isolated figure who foreshadows the type of anti-hero common in works of the twentieth century. Forced to look through his window at a wall, Bartleby is hemmed in by a form of modern life that is, in fact, little more than a living death. The constant references to him as some sort of ghost or phantom underwrite his precarious hold on life and illustrate how he is effectively numbed to death by the mindlessness of his existence. Indeed, the slow process by which Bartleby disengages from life is essentially a matter of Bartleby giving up on established routines, the habits that constitute the basis of monotonous employment. When he finally gives up on one of the most basic habits of them all, eating, his physical body joins his spirit in death. That MELVILLE considers Bartleby to be representative rather than unique is indicated by the famous closing words of the story: 'Ah Bartleby! Ah humanity!'

Further Reading

Bloom, Harold (ed.), *Herman Melville's 'Billy Budd', 'Benito Cereno', 'Bartleby the Scrivener' and Other Tales*. Millstone: Roundhouse Publishing, 1987. A collection of modern critical interpretations of Melville's shorter work, including *Bartleby*.

BEOWULF (*c.* 1000)
by Anonymous

They said that of all the kings of the world Of men he was the gentlest, the most gracious,
The kindest to his kin, and the keenest for glory.

Written by an anonymous poet, *Beowulf* is the founding work of English literature. It is the longest, richest epic poem surviving in a manuscript written in Old English in about 1000, although it was originally composed some 200 years earlier and records historically verifiable events of the year 521. It recounts a world of heroes and mythical creatures in which the warrior Beowulf engages in three great battles.

Summary

Beowulf begins by recounting the genealogy of the Danish kings leading up to the much-loved and respected Hrothgar. Hrothgar decides to build a great hall, in fact the greatest hall of them all, a place where his soldiers can feast and he can pass out shares of his treasure (it is worth noting here that because Beowulf is translated from a dialect of Old English into modern English, the spelling of proper names is not standardised, so that, for example, the name of the hall can be variously 'Herot', 'Heorot' and 'Heoret' among others). All goes well until Grendel, a demon outcast from the clan of Cain, is enraged by the noise of the festivities at the hall and emerges from the swamp to kill 30 of Hrothgar's men in the night.

For the next 12 years Grendel continues to attack the Danes. He eventually takes over the great hall built by Hrothgar, while the king himself is unable to stop him. After this time, a great warrior from Geatland hears of Hrothgar's plight and resolves to help him. His name is Beowulf. Gathering a small army about him, Beowulf sets off for Hrothgar's kingdom. When he arrives he is greeted fairly by Hrothgar who had previously aided Beowulf's father in a time of need. That night, after a feast in the hall, Grendel attacks again, quickly killing one of Beowulf's men. However, Beowulf picks his moment and grabs Grendel's arm in the most powerful grip in the world. Beowulf's men try to stab Grendel but he is charmed against metal and it is left to Beowulf to rip Grendel's arm off with his bare hands. There is a celebration of Beowulf's victory but Grendel's mother seeks revenge for the death of Grendel and kills one of Hrothgar's advisors.

Hrothgar again calls on Beowulf to rid Denmark of the monster and so they track Grendel's mother to a deep lake. After dispensing with one of the sea-dragons that haunt the water, Beowulf dons his armour and jumps in after Grendel's mother. After descending for nearly a day, Beowulf finally

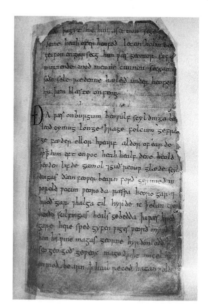

Credit: Cotton ms Vitellius A xv f. 133, 9140751, British Library

reaches the bottom of the lake where he is attacked by Grendel's mother, amongst several other monsters. After throwing away his own sword in disgust, Beowulf spies a giant's blade in the vault of Grendel's mother. Only he has the strength to wield it and he chops her head off.

Recounting the story of the hero's three epic battles with monsters, *Beowulf* is the richest epic poem surviving in manuscript form and is widely considered to be the founding work of English literature.

When he returns to the surface with the head of Grendel, Beowulf is once again rewarded by Hrothgar for his deeds. Beowulf then takes his treasure and returns to Geatland where, eventually, he becomes king. Beowulf rules for 50 years, bringing great prosperity and peace to Geatland. However, a thief stupidly arouses the ire of a dragon who has been sleeping for 300 years and the dragon unleashes a wave of destruction across Geatland. Sensing that he may be about to die, Beowulf gathers a dozen warriors around him and confronts the dragon. In the battle that follows Beowulf is bitten in the neck and fatally poisoned. All but one of his warriors runs away when they see this, but one remains and with his help Beowulf manages to slay the dragon before dying himself. According to Beowulf's wishes, his corpse is then burnt on a huge funeral pyre and then buried with the dragon's treasure.

THEMES AND TECHNIQUES

As *Beowulf* is the first major poem written in vernacular English (all previous poetry is written in Latin) and therefore stands at the beginning of the history of English literature, it is appropriate that the poem itself is about origins. It begins with a list of the ancestors of Hrothgar and continues by establishing the kinship bonds and lineage of every character that follows. Where a relation is not accorded by family, fellowship forged upon a code of honour unites the warriors in the poem. The warrior code itself is part of a Pagan tradition that is set against the poem's Christianity. While these might seem inimical, the two belief systems are bound together in their detestation of the monstrous and unnatural evil of Grendel and his mother. Paganism and Christianity are also bound together by the oral tradition which lies at the heart of *Beowulf*. Passed down through the ages orally before it was ever written down, the poem's alliterative verse celebrates the role of the *scop* or bard in establishing the identity of a community and maintaining it through storytelling.

Further Reading

Baker, Peter S. (ed.), *The 'Beowulf' Reader: Basic Readings*. New York: Garland, 1995. This is one of the best guides to recent scholarship on *Beowulf* in the past 30 years.

Heaney, Seamus (trans.), *Beowulf: A New Verse Translation*. London and New York: W.W. Norton, 2001. This is one of the most recent, and certainly one of the most vaunted, translations of Beowulf, here undertaken by the Irish Nobel Prize-winning poet. Apart from a discussion led by Heaney on translating the poem, his creation is a wonderful read, sticking as faithfully as possible to the strictures of the epic while investing it with a mythic potency.

Irving, Edward B. Jr., *Rereading 'Beowulf'*. Philadelphia: University of Pennsylvania Press, 1989. The rereading of the title refers to an earlier study of the poem by the same author. It provides a detailed examination of the oral character of Beowulf and the tradition from which it sprang.

BIBLE, AUTHORISED KING JAMES VERSION (1611)

In the beginning was the Word, and the Word was with God, and the Word was God.

The most influential and popular work ever written in English, the *Authorised Version* was the official translation of the *Bible*, bringing God to the masses in a language they could understand for the first time. In doing so, it changed the cultural landscape of English-speaking literature forever.

Summary

The *Authorised King James Version of the Bible* consists of the Old and New Testaments, two collections of books that constitute the basis for the Christian faith. The Old Testament relates the story of the Creation of the world by God through to the Fall of humanity and from there to the history of the Hebrews with whom, it is recorded, God established a covenant or testament, declaring them to be the chosen people destined for the Promised Land. The Old Testament understood in this way, and split into three parts, is basically the same as the Hebrew scriptures which form the *Tanak* – the basis of Judaism. However, Judaism would not refer to these books as the Old Testament. This is a term derived from the Christian religion, which splits the Old Testament into four parts and contends that God's pact or covenant with the Hebrews was forfeited by the way the Jews treated Jesus. While the Jews are held accountable for his execution, those who believe in him as the Messiah, or 'anointed one', inherit the old Hebraic covenant or testament with God. This is the New Testament, and it is mainly concerned with detailing the teachings of Jesus.

> Since its publication in 1611, the King James translation of the *Bible* has become the most influential text ever written in the English language.

The *Bible* is a work of translation, in whatever language it is now read. The type of Hebrew and Greek that it was originally written in are known now only to scholars. By the fourth century the Catholic church was united in using a Latin translation of the *Bible* and in the English-speaking world this remained the predominant translation until the advent of the Reformation in the early 1600s. The new Protestantism demanded that each person be able to read the *Bible* for themselves and so, as only the educated could read Latin, it had to be translated into English. The early translations into English, such as William Tyndale's version of the New Testament, were popular but illegal. When Protestantism became the established religion of England, the church ordered its own version of the *Bible* in English, but it was not until King James succeeded Elizabeth in 1603 that there was an authorised version for the whole populace. Indeed, such was its dominance over not just other versions, but in English-speaking life generally, that the King James *Bible* remained unaltered until the end of the nineteenth century.

THEMES AND TECHNIQUES

The *Bible* has influenced our culture in many ways, from the literal manner in which its stories are re-told by MILTON through to the way we understand that culture in the first place. For, fundamental to the *Bible*, is the idea that life has a meaning above and beyond pure existence. If this forms the literal theme for some texts, such as THOMAS HARDY's *JUDE THE OBSCURE*, for example, it also provides us with a model for reading itself. In particular, the Christian tradition is based on re-reading the Old Testament in the light of the New Testament. Whereas the tripartite arrangement of the *Tanaka* conveys a sense of open-endedness to the reader, one in which God's purpose remains inscrutable, the four-part structure of the Old Testament in the *Bible* is structured toward the events of the New Testament in which God's purpose is revealed with the coming of the Messiah. Consequently, the Christian tradition of reading and writing tends to be teleological – that is, it is end-oriented. We are concerned with discerning the grand design of the plot and the ultimate meaning of the story.

The particular value of the *Authorised King James Version of the Bible* lies in its unifying power. At the level of reference, it became the standard text of education, one which bound the English-speaking cultures together with a repertoire of wisdom and phrases, such as 'by the skin of your teeth' or 'to fall flat on your face'. Such expressions did not draw on vernacular English but, rather, were literal translations imposed upon and eventually taken up by the vernacular. In this sense, the *Bible* helped to form and codify the English language as we now know it. Equally, and central to this enterprise, the *King James Bible* was part of the process which made English-speaking cultures into cultures of the word or Word. Unlike the predominantly visual cultures of Catholic countries, English-speaking countries have an obsession with the written word. Some have even argued that by removing the hierarchy of priests and bishops from the equation, the translation of the *Bible* enabled the British to entertain a direct relationship with God, a fact which fostered a sense of their own importance and led to the democratisation of the country much earlier than happened elsewhere.

Further Reading

Jasper, David and Prickett, Stephen (eds), *The Bible and Literature: A Reader*. London: Blackwell Publishers, 1999. This book shows the *Bible* in action, with passages from it placed in conjunction with extracts from the canon of literary works which display its influence.

Norton, David, *A History of the English Bible as Literature*. London and New York: Cambridge University Press, 2000. This revised version of Norton's own book is rapidly becoming a classic in its own right. It examines the changing critical fortunes of the *Bible* over the years and shows how it went on to become the most important book in English.

BILLY BUDD, SAILOR (1886–1924)
by Herman Melville

Struck dead by an angel of God! Yet the angel must hang!

HERMAN MELVILLE wrote *Billy Budd* during the last five years of his life, but it was not published until 35 years after his death. Set at the end of the eighteenth century, this short novel tells the story of Billy Budd, an innocent young sailor who is coerced into killing a senior officer and is consequently hung.

Summary

When the novel opens, Billy Budd is a well-loved sailor on board the British Merchant Navy ship the *Rights-of-Man* (named after the book by THOMAS PAINE). However, the ship is soon boarded by an officer of the British Royal Navy vessel, H.M.S. *Bellipotent* (some editions of the novel follow Melville's first suggestion that the ship is called the *Indomitable*, where others prefer to call it the name he

finally settled on – the *Bellipotent*). The officer of the *Bellipotent* chooses to impress (or take into service by the threat of force) Billy Budd. The master of the *Rights-of-Man* professes that Billy is the best sailor he has because his simple, good nature keeps everyone from quarrelling, although he warns that if provoked Billy is able to use his muscular physique to potent effect.

Billy uncomplainingly joins the *Bellipotent* and takes to his work and his new crewmates with good heart. After witnessing a flogging given to a fellow sailor who went absent at his post, Billy undertakes to be particularly vigilant in his work. It thus puzzles him that he is subject to constant threats from some of the ship's corporals for causing minor infractions of the rules himself. Wanting to know why this is, Billy seeks the counsel of the Dansker, an old and experienced sailor with whom Billy has struck up a good rapport. The Dansker tells Billy that the reason for his problems lies with Claggart, the ship's master-at-arms, who has taken a dislike to Billy. Billy himself fails to believe this because Claggart is always pleasant to his face and, indeed, goes out of his way to be so.

A few nights later, Billy is woken from his sleep by an unidentified sailor who attempts to sign him up to a mutiny of the impressed men on the ship. Billy, who suffers from a strong stutter when he is upset, begins stammering at this point and threatens the unknown sailor with violence until he runs off. Unable to understand this event, Billy once again consults the Dansker. The incident confirms in the Dansker's mind that Claggart is after Billy, but he offers no advice to him and for his part Billy refuses to believe it.

Using a series of biblical allusions, *Billy Budd* tells the story of how an innocent young sailor is executed after being coerced into killing an officer.

Following this incident, Claggart informs the Captain of the ship that he thinks Billy is set to raise a mutiny. Having observed Billy's simple good nature before now, he is not convinced by Claggart's accusations but he nevertheless calls Billy to his office where Claggart repeats the charge. Billy is shocked at what he hears and is unable to speak. The Captain, sensing Billy's propensity to stammer at moments of extreme stress, commands him to explain himself in his own time. This kindness inflames Billy's emotions even more and he lashes out at Claggart with his fist and knocks him over dead.

No one believes that Billy maintained any evil intent towards Claggart or that he intended to kill him. However, as the Captain points out, at a time of war, and following a period of mutinies, there is no room for leniency and Billy is sentenced to death. The Captain tells Billy of his fate but it is clear that 'the condemned one suffered less than he who mainly had effected the condemnation'. When the chaplain arrives to bless Billy, it is clear that Billy is already at peace and he ends by blessing the chaplain. At Billy's death, the whole crew repeat his last words, 'God bless Captain Vere!' Ironically, when the Captain dies shortly afterwards, his last words are, 'Billy Budd, Billy Budd.' Soon a legend grows up around Billy and the spar from which he was hung is treated as a holy object, so that 'a chip of it was as a piece of the Cross'.

THEMES AND TECHNIQUES

One of the most striking aspects of the novel is the use of religious symbolism. In particular, Billy's story is associated with the Passion of Christ. These references range from subtle remarks that echo passages in the BIBLE, to more telling descriptions of Billy's confrontation with Claggart as a 'crucifixion' and to the spar upon which he is hung as the 'Cross'. As potent as these *New Testament* references are, they are also joined by allusions to the *Old Testament*, where Billy is compared to 'Adam' and Claggart is compared to a 'snake'. In the end, the novel defies any straightforward correspondence between the events and figures of the *Bible*, but it uses them to convey the plight of innocence in a corrupt world. Given the imagery, it is perhaps not too strong therefore to suggest that *Billy Budd* is about the way in which evil triumphs over innocence and how society itself is complicit in this by framing laws which leave little room for individual conscience.

Further Reading

Parker, Hershel, *Reading 'Billy Budd'.* Illinois: Northwestern University Press: Garland, 1990.

Hershel Parker is one of the world's foremost Melville scholars and here he brings his expertise to work on understanding *Billy Budd*.

Yannella, Donald (ed.), *New Essays on 'Billy Budd'.* Cambridge: Cambridge University Press, 2002. This book provides a number of critical essays on *Billy Budd*, looked at from a series of different angles.

BLEAK HOUSE (1852–53)
by Charles Dickens

It is a melancholy truth that even great men have their poor relations.

Bleak House could well lay claim to being the most comprehensive of DICKENS's novels as it presents a portrait not so much of a few characters but of the whole of Victorian society. Many of these stories are woven around the central figure of the never-ending law suit of Jarndyce and Jarndyce.

Summary

Bleak House does not so much begin as emerge from the fog of Victorian London and, particularly, the all-encompassing mist of the Chancery, the court of the Lord Chancellor (where in real life Dickens had been a court reporter). Here is heard a long-running law suit named Jarndyce and Jarndyce, a 'case so complicated that no man alive knows what it means'. This law suit will touch on many lives in the novel, one of them being John Jarndyce. Jarndyce is the guardian of Esther Summerson, 20 years old when the novel begins and the narrator of half of it (the rest of the story being told by an omniscient narrator).

Unbeknownst to Esther, she is the illegitimate child of Lady Dedlock and Captain Hawdon. Lady Dedlock is married to Sir Leicester Dedlock and they lead a respectable existence, somewhat removed from the struggles of real life. At the beginning of the novel, their personal attorney, Tulkinghorn, returns from attending the latest instalment of the Jarndyce and Jarndyce case and happens to show Lady Dedlock some legal documents copied out in a hand that she recognises.

When she asks Tulkinghorn about the handwriting, he takes it upon himself to find out who wrote the documents. He soon discovers that they were written by a man named 'Nemo', a friendless man living in poverty in a rag and bottle shop owned by the aptly named Krook (who goes on to die in literature's most celebrated instance of spontaneous combustion). When Tulkinghorn goes to interview Nemo, he finds that the man is already dead, possibly from an opium overdose.

> Probably Dickens's greatest novel, *Bleak House* uses the conceit of a never-ending law suit to explore the labyrinthine relations between the different strata of Victorian society.

Further investigations lead Tulkinghorn to Jo, a crossing sweeper who knew Nemo. In the meantime, Lady Dedlock has also tracked down Jo, knowing that Nemo was, in fact, her old lover Captain Hawdon. Disguised as her maid, Mlle Hortense, Lady Dedlock is shown where Hawdon is buried by Jo. Unfortunately for her, Hortense dislikes Lady Dedlock and is willingly persuaded by Tulkinghorn to betray her mistress. He is unwittingly aided in this by the otherwise estimable detective, Inspector Bucket. Tulkinghorn then lets Lady Dedlock know that he knows she is the mother of Esther. Shortly afterwards, Tulkinghorn is found shot dead.

Bucket investigates the case, and Lady Dedlock becomes one of the prime suspects. However, Bucket soon discovers that Hortense, who is also his lodger, actually killed Tulkinghorn after she felt abused by him. Not knowing this, Lady Dedlock flees the house leaving a valedictory note for Sir Leicester. Sir Leicester only receives the note after he has already suffered a stroke. He recovers sufficiently to hire Bucket to search for his wife and to convey his full forgiveness to her. Bucket finds a handkerchief with Esther's name on it in Lady Dedlock's possessions and goes to Jarndyce's house in order to use her as a way of placating Lady Dedlock when he finds her.

In the meantime, Esther has been working in Jarndyce's house as a chaperone to two of Jarndyce's other wards, Ada Clare and Richard Carstone. Clare and Carstone are in love and secretly marry when she reaches 21. However, Carstone is obsessed with the Jarndyce and Jarndyce case, out of which both he and Clare stand to inherit money. Esther had set her heart on marrying a young doctor, Allan Woodcourt, but she contracts smallpox from Jo and is left with a scarred face. Feeling unworthy to marry Woodcourt, she accepts Jarndyce's offer of marriage. She is also finally informed that she is the daughter of Lady Dedlock and is therefore eager to accompany Bucket on his mission to find her. After an exhaustive investigation, they find Lady Dedlock lying dead in the snow at the same cemetery where Captain Hawdon is buried. The Jarndyce and Jarndyce case subsequently finishes but the legal costs account for all the remaining funds and, heartbroken, Carstone dies. Ada gives birth to his son shortly afterwards. At the same time, Esther conspires with Woodcourt to give up her engagement with Jarndyce and to marry the young doctor instead.

THEMES AND TECHNIQUES

The labyrinthine and complicated plot of *Bleak House*, of which the above represents only the central strand is, for all its variety and scope, quite a claustrophobic affair. Each character has some relationship with everyone else, be it via the Jarndyce and Jarndyce case, an oft-visited location in the novel, or, in the case of Esther, Lady Dedlock and Mlle Hortense, even their shared appearance. So that even when characters do not know it, Dickens shows by this device that each part of society is connected to and responsible for the other parts. In this regard, it is no accident that Jo, the lowly crossing sweeper, actually holds the key to the fate of Lady Dedlock, a member of the aristocracy. Indeed, one of the themes of the novel is that characters so little realise their relative positions in society, that those who do manage to seek out these secrets, such as Tulkinghorn and Bucket, are able to achieve degrees of power according to the extent of their information.

The society thus depicted is, to some degree, a sick and incestuous one, and the novel's obsession with uncleanliness and dirt underlines this. In this context, the dual narration by an unnamed omniscient narrator and Esther starts to make sense. While the unnamed narrator is cynical and as fully mired in world-weary corruption as the characters he depicts, Esther is naïve, even bland, but certainly dirt-free. She acts as a counterpoint to all the bleakness, overcoming the ugliness of the world and enabling Dickens to end the novel with some degree of hope where, in contrast to the futile outcome of the Jarndyce case, Esther gives birth to two daughters.

Further Reading

Allan, Janice, *Routledge Literary Sourcebook on Charles Dickens' 'Bleak House'.* London and New York: Routledge, 2004. This book offers a thorough guide to the history of the novel's criticism, as well as looking in depth at key passages, and cross-referencing Dickens's text with contexts of the time.

Shatto, Susan, *The Companion to 'Bleak House'.* London: Unwin Hyman, 1988. This book provides a rich source of historical information bearing on the novel.

CALL OF THE WILD, THE (1903)
by Jack London

As token of what a puppet thing life is the ancient song surged through him and he came into his own again.

The Call of the Wild is a novel about the natural instincts of a dog called Buck. It follows his adventures as he is forced to leave his comfortable existence as a pet and answer the call of the wild.

Summary

When the novel opens, Buck, a large crossbreed between a St Bernard and a sheep dog, lives a comfortable life at Judge Miller's home in California. There he has the run of the place and complete dominance over the other house pets. However, Buck's carefree life soon comes to an end when a gardener working for Miller kidnaps Buck and sells him to pay off a gambling debt. Buck is sent north. After attacking several of the people that move him, he finally learns the 'law of the club' when he is beaten senseless by a man wielding a club. From that point on Buck realises that his easy days are over, but at the same time he senses the first stirrings of his primitive nature.

Eventually, Buck and a bitch called Curly are bought by a French Canadian and they are shipped north to where Buck encounters snow for the first time. Buck's new home immediately strikes him as brutal, a fact confirmed when Curly is torn to pieces by a pack of huskies after she goes to ground in a fight. Buck vows to himself never to go to ground once he is in a fight. He also learns how to scavenge for food and how to sleep warmly in the snow. On top of this, Buck is trained as a sled dog, a physical job which he soon accepts. When they start out on the trail, the lead dog is Spitz, a dog for whom Buck has already developed an antipathy after he seemed to laugh at Curly's death.

> Following the adventures of a dog called Buck, *The Call of the Wild* is a parable about the primacy of instincts over civilisation.

Relations between Spitz and Buck worsen as time progresses and, after a number of brief skirmishes are broken up by their owners, the two dogs finally become involved in a fight to the death. To begin with, Spitz's fighting experience means that he is barely scathed while Buck is badly torn. However, just as Spitz moves in for the kill, Buck feints and manages to break Spitz's legs. Spitz is then killed, leaving Buck as the top dog. With Buck in the lead position, Buck's sled becomes the quickest in the area. When Buck's owners are ordered to go elsewhere, the team is then sold to a mail carrier who makes the dogs pull far bigger loads, wearing them out to the point where one of the dogs has to be shot.

What remains of the team is then sold to a group of gold prospectors. However, the prospectors have little understanding of survival in the wilderness and, after chronically mismanaging the sled team, they soon find themselves without food. By the time the sled draws into the camp of John Thornton, a more experienced prospector, there are only five dogs left alive. Buck himself is exhausted and starved at this point. Thornton advises the prospectors not to continue their journey because the ice is beginning to melt, but they insist anyway. However, Buck senses danger ahead and he refuses to move, despite being beaten by one of the prospectors. Unable to stand by watching this maltreatment, Thornton intervenes and cuts Buck free. The rest of the team are led out of camp but, barely a quarter of a mile later, the ice breaks and the dogs and the humans all drown.

In Thornton, Buck finds a man who embodies the visions he has been having of a primal relationship with humankind. Thornton treats him well and is rewarded for this by Buck's fierce loyalty. This shows on two occasions where Buck saves Thornton's life, as well as when Buck wins Thornton a large bet that he could pull a 1,000 pound sled on his own. When Thornton settles down to excavate a new mine, Buck is left with little to do until, one night, he hears a call from the forest and encounters a timber wolf. His experience with the timber wolf leads him to accept a dual identity, one as a wild dog and the other as Thornton's sled dog. However, returning one day from the forest, Buck finds that Thornton has been killed by Yeehat Indians. Buck revenges Thornton by killing several of the Yeehat, but after that he is freed from the human world and he answers the call of the wild, joining the pack of timber wolves and becoming their leader.

THEMES AND TECHNIQUES

London's novel draws on two philosophies popular in the late nineteenth century. The first of these is Charles Darwin's law of adaptation, a law sometimes misleadingly termed the 'survival of the fittest'. At the beginning of the novel Buck is thrown into a new environment. Curly, who is with him, is unable to adapt and quickly dies, but Buck learns the rules of his new world, such as how to find warmth and how to fight, and he survives. The novel also draws upon another misrepresented theory, that of Friedrich Nietzsche's 'will to power'. In its populist version this theory promotes mastery over others as the supreme good. In *The Call of the Wild*, Buck spends much of the novel trying to achieve mastery

over others, firstly with the other dogs and then with humans. This mastery is really only a means to establishing his own freedom, the freedom that he finally achieves when he joins the pack of timber wolves. What the book seems to suggest is that this form of mastery is actually our natural state of being. Buck's visions of primitive life imply that his progress through the book is a matter of recalling his innate state, returning to the true way of his ancestors.

Further Reading

Nuernberg, Susan M. (ed.), *The Critical Response to Jack London*. Westport: Greenwood Press, 1995. London's work has always been controversial, tackling moral issues in a populist but robust manner. This book presents a series of essays, arranged in chronological order, which show critical reactions to London through the years.

Tavernier-Courbin, Jacqueline, *The Call of the Wild: A Naturalistic Romance*. New York: Twayne Publishers, 1994. This book examines the reception, context and interpretation of *The Call of the Wild*.

CANTERBURY TALES, THE (1386–1400)
by Geoffrey Chaucer

At night was come into that hostelrye
Wel nine and twenty in a compaignye
Of sundry folk, by aventure yfalle
In felaweshipe, and pilgrims were they alle.

The Canterbury Tales is a collection of stories told to pass the time by pilgrims travelling together from south London to Canterbury. The stories are largely told in verse and are connected by the commentary of an unnamed narrator.

Summary

The *Tales* begin with *The General Prologue* where the narrator recounts how he meets all the other pilgrims at the Tabard Inn in Southwark. He identifies all 29 of them individually and sketches their characteristics. At the end of these descriptions, the Host, Harry Bailey, devises a competition for the pilgrims. Each pilgrim will tell two stories on the way to Canterbury and two on the way back and he will judge whichever is the best and then provide the winner with a free meal at the Inn. They all agree and draw lots to see who will tell the first tale. It is the Knight who draws the short straw.

The Knight's Tale is set in Athens during the reign of Theseus and his Amazonian queen Hippolyta, both of whom will reappear as characters in WILLIAM SHAKESPEARE's *A MIDSUMMER NIGHT'S DREAM*. Having been imprisoned by Theseus, two knights, Arcite and Palamon see Hippolyta's sister, Emelye, from their prison window and fall in love with her. When they are free, both knights fight each other over Emelye until Theseus arranges a tournament between them with Emelye as the prize. Arcite wins but he is thrown from his horse and dies, leaving Palamon to marry Emelye.

Having heard this story of chivalry, the drunken Miller then jumps in to tell his more ribald tale of a student called Nicholas. In order to spend the night with his landlord's wife, Nicholas persuades his landlord that the world is going to be flooded again and that he should spend the night in a tub suspended from the ceiling. During the night, Nicholas and the landlord's wife, Alison, are interrupted by another suitor whom Alison puts off by getting him to kiss her backside in the dark. Humiliated by this rebuttal, the suitor returns with a hot iron and begs for another kiss. This time Nicholas offers his backside as a joke but when he is burnt by the iron he cries for water and the landlord, assuming this is the signal for the flood, cuts the ropes and falls to the ground breaking his arms.

Annoyed by the aspersions cast on the carpentry trade by the Miller, *The Reeve's Tale* is a story of a cheating miller whose wife and daughter are seduced by two students. *The Cook's Tale* which follows this is meant to be a yarn told at the expense of the Host, but it is left unfinished by Chaucer.

The Man of Law's Tale is a complicated and lengthy story following the fortunes of Constance, the daughter of a Roman emperor betrothed to the Sultan of Syria. It is also notable for the introduction to it in which the Man of Law declares his admiration for the storytelling skills of the poet Chaucer.

The Wife of Bath's Prologue is perhaps the most famous part of *The Canterbury Tales* and it recounts the Wife's opinion on women's relations with men following her five marriages. Her tale is of a knight who can only save his life by finding out what women want. An old crone reveals the secret on condition that he marry her. He agrees but confesses he finds her repulsive. She then says she can be young, beautiful and unfaithful, or old, ugly and faithful. He says the choice is hers whereupon she confirms that as she has achieved mastery she will be both young and faithful.

> Largely told in verse, *The Canterbury Tales* is a collection of stories told by pilgrims as they travel together to Canterbury. Although many of the stories are borrowed from other sources, Chaucer makes them his own with his lyrical use of the English language.

The Friar and the Summoner then tell tales at the expense of each other's profession. Their narratives are followed by *The Clerk's Tale*, in which he recounts the story of a virtuous peasant called Griselde. When she marries her husband, he decides to test her virtuous character by pretending that her two children have to be murdered and that they must be divorced. She accepts all this and then, finally, he tells her to help prepare for his wedding. At the wedding she finds out that he has been testing her and the family is happily reunited.

The Merchant then compares Griselde with his own wife and, unsurprisingly, finds her wanting. His tale tells of an old blind knight who marries a beautiful young wife against the best advice. Unhappy with his constant sexual attention, she commences an affair with his squire. The gods seek to alert the knight to this by restoring his sight, but even when the knight catches his wife and squire together, the wife assures him that he is still blind and he accepts it as the truth.

The Squire's Tale concerns a number of magical gifts given to a king, but it is left unfinished when the Franklin interrupts. The Franklin narrates the story of a knight's wife who departs to England from France. She worries that his ship will be dashed on the rocks when he returns so she promises another man that she will give her body to him if he can clear the rocks. He then asks a magician to create the illusion that the rocks have been moved. When the knight returns and hears of this he tells his wife that she must stick to the bargain. Impressed by the knight's honour, the young man refuses to go through with it and the magician, in turn, waives payment for his services.

The Physician's Tale records a legend in which a Roman soldier cuts his daughter's head off rather than have her dishonoured. The Pardoner then admits that his profession is largely fraudulent and narrates a cautionary fable in which three youths try to cheat each other out of some gold but end up killing themselves. *The Shipman's Tale* tells of a wife who repays a monetary debt to her husband with sexual favours. The Prioress follows this up with a story about a group of Jews who murder a choirboy. The choirboy continues singing after his death and the Jews are found out and executed. The Host then tasks the narrator to tell a story, but his verse is so bad the other pilgrims stop him and he tells another tale in prose instead about forgiveness.

Detail taken from the Ellesmere manuscript of *The Canterbury Tales*. Credit: Huntington Library and Art Gallery, San Marino, CA, USA and The Bridgeman Art Library

The Monk does not so much tell a story as illustrate the theme of falling from grace with several examples from history. *The Nun's Priest's Tale* tells of a rooster outwitting a fox, while the Second Nun recounts the life of the martyr St Cecilia. The Canon and his Yeoman then join the pilgrimage and wish to tell a tale. However, the Yeoman continually betrays the secrets of the Canon's fraudulent work and so the Canon leaves in shame, whereupon the Yeoman relates a tale of a cheating canon. After criticising the drunken Cook, the Manciple then recounts the story of how Phoebus is informed by a white crow that his wife is cheating on him. Phoebus promptly kills his wife and plucks the crow, cursing his feathers with blackness. Finally, the Parson provides the pilgrims with a sermon on the Seven Deadly Sins.

CHAUCER then ends the unfinished manuscript with a retraction asking its readers to forgive him for anything that causes offence, while praising Jesus for anything in the *Tales* that pleases them.

THEMES AND TECHNIQUES

For generations of writers who came after him, Chaucer is the font of English poetry, and *The Canterbury Tales* the source from which all else flows. For example, T.S. Eliot began *The Waste Land*, the most important poem written in English in the twentieth century, with the following lines:

> *April is the cruellest month, breeding*
> *Lilacs out of the dead land, mixing*
> *Memory and desire, stirring*
> *Dull roots with spring rain.*

In so doing, Eliot was consciously referring to and inscribing himself in a tradition of poetry that begins with Chaucer's opening lines to the *General Prologue:*

> *When that April with his showres soote*
> *The droughte of March hath perced to the roote,*
> *And bathed every veine in swich licour,*
> *Of which vertu engendred is the flowr.*

Perhaps surprisingly, then, part of Chaucer's own skill lies in the way he assimilated and rephrased existing materials to complete *The Canterbury Tales*. For instance, very few of the tales are actually thought to have been his own inventions, and nor was the device linking the stories together uniquely Chaucer's conception. What is Chaucerian about the *Tales*, however, and what distinguishes his poetry from the tradition of assimilated work, is their extraordinary lyricism, the way Chaucer used the English language to create a fluent, speech-like verse hitherto unknown.

Chaucer's achievement in creating an English verse to match the predominant forms of French, Latin and Italian poetry is augmented by the fact that he also created a certain model of England too. Whereas most writers at the time tended to concentrate on the aristocracy, Chaucer peoples his *Tales* with the whole of society, from knights to yeoman, from cooks to wives, discussing everything from chivalry and saints to sex and farts. No part of humanity is alien to *The Canterbury Tales*. This all-inclusive style, or 'streaky well-cured bacon' as CHARLES DICKENS characterised it, set the standard for the English imagination in the centuries that followed. Indeed, we can see a similar mix of characters and topics in the work of such great writers as Dickens himself, as well as WILLIAM SHAKESPEARE.

Further Reading

Chaucer, Geoffrey, *The Riverside Chaucer.* Edited by F. N. Robinson. Oxford: Oxford Paperbacks, 1988. This book is the standard edition of Chaucer's works and includes *The Canterbury Tales*. Each part is introduced by an explanatory essay and the difficult words are glossed throughout.

Hirsh, John C., *Chaucer and 'The Canterbury Tales': A Short Introduction.* London: Blackwell Publishers, 2002. As well as providing an instructive look at previous interpretations of Chaucer's work, this examines the *Tales* as a non-realist work of fiction.

Phillips, Helen, *An Introduction to 'The Canterbury Tales': Reading, Fiction, Context.* London: Palgrave Macmillan, 2000. This book looks at each of the tales in turn and provides the historical context, as well as interpreting the stories using a variety of modern techniques.

CASTLE OF OTRANTO, THE (1764)
by Horace Walpole

But what a sight for a father's eyes! – He beheld his child dashed to pieces, and almost buried under an enormous helmet, an hundred times more large than any casque ever made for human being, and shaded with a proportionable quantity of black feathers.

The Castle of Otranto is widely regarded as the first Gothic novel. On reading the book, the poet Thomas Gray complained to Walpole that he was too frightened to go to bed. The novel tells the story of Manfred and his attempts to maintain his family's dynasty against both natural and supernatural foes.

Summary

The preface of the novel urges us to believe that what follows is a translation from the Italian that was found in the library of an ancient Catholic family. It suggests that the story was probably based on an actual incident that occurred between 1095 and 1243.

The story itself opens with Manfred, Prince of Otranto, preparing for the wedding of his sickly young son, Conrad. However, before the wedding can take place, Conrad is discovered crushed to death beneath a giant helmet. A peasant points out that the helmet has come from the statue of Alfonso the Good, one of Manfred's ancestors. This fact greatly perturbs Manfred and, having imprisoned the peasant beneath the helmet, he resolves to marry Conrad's intended bride, Isabella, himself. As he is still married, Isabella is upset by this proposition and hides herself in the church next to the Castle of Otranto.

The next day Friar Jerome informs Manfred that Isabella is staying in the church. Manfred declares that Jerome must facilitate a divorce between Manfred and his wife, and then marry Manfred to Isabella in order that they may have an heir and save the principality of Otranto. The friar pretends to agree and plays for time by diverting Manfred's attention to the peasant's relationship with Isabella.

Enraged, Manfred orders the execution of the peasant but a mark on the peasant's body reveals him to be Theodore, the son of Jerome. Jerome, it transpires, is also the Count of Falconara. Deaf to the entreaties of Jerome to save his new-found son, Manfred only changes his mind about Theodore's execution when he sees the plumage on the giant helmet wave in time to the sound of approaching trumpets.

Centred around the attempts of Manfred, Prince of Otranto, to establish a dynasty, *The Castle of Otranto* is widely regarded as the first Gothic novel, setting the conventions for the genre that are still in place now.

The trumpets announce the arrival of a knight who comes to challenge Manfred over who is the rightful Prince of Otranto. While the mysterious knight is in conversation with Manfred, it is announced that Isabella has fled the church. Upon hearing this, the knight departs in search of Isabella. Meanwhile, she has taken sanctuary in some caves where Theodore vows to protect her. Assuming the knight to be sent by Manfred, Theodore defeats him in battle, only for the knight to reveal himself as Frederic, Marquis of Vicenza, Isabella's long-lost father. Thinking that Isabella intends to wed Theodore rather than himself following this, Manfred then steals up on her in the dark and stabs her. However, he quickly discovers that he has actually killed his own daughter instead. The Castle of Otranto then crumbles into the dust to reveal a giant vision of Alfonso the Good, who insists that Theodore is actually the true Prince of Otranto. Everyone agrees on this and Theodore eventually marries Isabella.

THEMES AND TECHNIQUES

The Castle of Otranto was an enormously influential book that inspired a whole generation of novelists to follow in its wake. In its use of the fake manuscript device, the frenzied pace, supernatural and paranormal events to resolve the plot, gloomy medieval setting and aristocratic subject matter, Walpole's novel established a set of conventions that subsequent authors would either employ in straight

imitation or at least pay ironic homage to. Indeed, the very tone that Walpole uses throughout *The Castle of Otranto*, hovering as it does somewhere between the serious and the satirical, was picked up by other novels that sought to emulate its success. However, then, as now, Walpole's Gothic melodrama was not received with universal critical acclaim. Some argued that the novel broke with the recently established rules set for the genre in that it failed to demonstrate a moral purpose. Even the preface to the book admits that the moral it does offer ('the sins of fathers are visited on their children to the third and fourth generation') is neither particularly 'useful' nor particularly believable. Instead of moral guidance, then, Walpole offers his readers a pure entertainment, one that presages the development of all art since in that it asks to be valued only for itself.

Further Reading

Botting, Fred (ed.), *Gothic*. London and New York: Routledge, 1996. Including a discussion of Walpole's novel, this book examines the wider meaning of Gothic within both literature and culture generally.

Punter, David, *The Literature of Terror*. London: Longman, 1996. This is the standard account of the history of Gothic fiction.

COMMON SENSE (1776)
by Thomas Paine

The cause of America is in a great measure the cause of all mankind. Many circumstances hath, and will arise, which are not local, but universal, and through which the principles of all lovers of mankind are affected, and in the event of which, their affections are interested.

Common Sense is a pamphlet setting forth the argument for an America independent of Great Britain. At the time it was published, representatives of the American colonies were still uncertain as to whether to commit to a war for independence. The huge success of the pamphlet was one of the decisive factors in persuading them to make that commitment.

Summary

Common Sense is composed of a series of arguments. These arguments move from the general case for independence to the specific cause of America. PAINE's plea for self-governance begins with the assertion that governments generally are an unfortunate necessity. He proposes that if people were always and everywhere able to restrain themselves, there would be no need for governments to do it for them. He contrasts that with the notion of society, which is what he defines as the exercise of our talents and affections to mutual benefit. The existence and scope of government are therefore an index of our own deviation from the path of a proper society. In this sense, 'government, like dress, is the badge of lost innocence; the palaces of kings are built on the ruins of the bowers of paradise'.

Paine then describes an imaginary scenario in which a group of people settle an unpopulated part of the earth. He depicts the manner in which they will quickly move from their state of 'natural liberty' into forming associations with one another and how, from this rudimentary society a system of government will inevitably spring up in order to supplant 'the defect of moral virtue'. Paine contends that in this case the best form of government is one that retains a common sympathy with the people that elected it. The parable here clearly refers to America and its distant governance by Great Britain. Paine then addresses himself directly to the British form of government. The constitutional monarchy, he argues, is merely 'the base remains of two ancient tyrannies, compounded with some new republican materials'. In particular, Paine attacks the idea of the monarchy and hereditary succession. If all men are born as equals, then the distinction between a monarch and its subjects is an unnatural distinction. Furthermore, the fitness of a monarch to rule in no way bestows that suitability upon the monarch's offspring.

Paine next attends to the specifics of American independence. He contends that America would have grown more vigorously without British intervention, and that such intervention as was undertaken by Britain was done so in its own interests. To prove the point, Paine goes on to argue that if America were independent, its trade would not suffer every time Britain went to war with another European country. He also looks to the personal sufferings of those Americans who suffered at the hands of the British colonial army. Having concluded his arguments in favour of America's independence, Paine then proposes the form of representative democracy that should replace British rule. Finally, he recommends that the time for action is now. Not only could America build a navy of similar power to the apparently all-conquering navy of the British fleet, but if it did so now it would have the resources to pay for it and would then be able to protect its own international trade. He also notes that America is both big enough to take on Britain in a war, but not so big as to lose a sense of unity and purpose as it might well do in the future.

One of the great democratic tracts, Thomas Paine's *Common Sense* helped to set the agenda for the Declaration of Independence and for America for many years afterwards.

THEMES AND TECHNIQUES

Paine's *Common Sense* set the agenda for the War of Independence. Its comparatively plain-speaking style enabled it to reach and persuade a mass audience in America, and thus helped to promote its arguments at a time of crucial national decision. *Common Sense* also set the agenda for America and its literature for many years afterwards. Drawing upon established techniques from political philosophy and the *BIBLE*, Paine sketches out the American national psyche as he sees it. It is a psyche that values its independence from government generally, but from the rule and influence of the Old World in particular. It is a psyche that understands and promotes the importance of commerce, and it is a psyche that, above all, values its own identity, distinct from any vision imposed upon it by others.

Further Reading

Paine, Thomas, *Thomas Paine – Political Writings*. Edited by Bruce Kuklick. Cambridge: Cambridge University Press, 2000. This offers

Paine's three most important works in one volume – *Common Sense, Rights of Man*, and *The Age of Reason*. It also provides an introduction to each and a short chronology of Paine and the events in his lifetime.

Liell, Scott, *46 Pages: Tom Paine, Common Sense, and the Turning Point to American Independence.* Philadelphia: Running Press, 2003. Written in the spirit of the style of Thomas Paine, this book provides the historical context for *Common Sense* and describes how it helped to sway the population from reconciliation to rebellion.

COMPLETE POEMS OF EMILY DICKINSON, THE (1960)
by Emily Dickinson

Because I could not stop for Death–
He kindly stopped for me

Virtually unknown during her lifetime, EMILY DICKINSON's poems were published long after her death in 1886. Her spare, but boldly moulded verse is as modern in form as it is in sentiment, making her poetry some of the most popular ever written.

Summary

When Dickinson's poems were first published after her death, they were arranged under various topic headings – Life, Love, Nature, Time and Eternity. These headings are broad enough to include most subjects, and in so doing they are faithful to the wide remit Dickinson gave to her poetry. For although Dickinson herself rarely left the confines of her own room, she was happy and able to submit to verse most aspects of life. Indeed, in poem No. 632 (Dickinson did not give titles to her own poems and so the numbers are those assigned for convenience by Thomas Herbert Johnson, her most faithful editor), Dickinson makes a claim for the expansiveness of her life:

The brain–is wider than the Sky–
For–put them side by side–
The one the other will contain
With ease–and You–beside–

Here she expresses her belief that the universe of the mind can easily enclose the universe itself because the imagination is infinite in its options. This gives us a clue to Dickinson's poetry as a whole, for it too celebrates the inner life – the life of the emotions and thoughts, and of the soul. But it does so in a way that is never insular because the personal tends to lead to the universal, while the inner world is often expressed in terms of the outer world. In this way, although the poems of Dickinson are never very long, and sometimes seem quite fragile, they are never small in scope or subject.

THEMES AND TECHNIQUES

In an introduction to a collected edition of her poetry written by her niece, Martha Dickinson Bianchi, it is argued that Dickinson's poems are poems for people who do not read poetry. She seems to speak directly to readers, unhampered by esoteric language or reference, and by-passing some of the poetic conceits that waylay those not schooled in the reading of poetry. There is a frankness about the metres and rhyme schemes she employs, many of which draw on the forms of hymns she learnt as a child. Equally, the diction she employs is mainly in the vernacular and rarely requires a gloss.

Described as 'the poetry for those who do not read poems', Dickinson's work was largely unknown during her lifetime but has succeeded in becoming some of the most popular verse ever written.

Furthermore, even though the final reference for her images may sometimes be a matter of interpretation, the images themselves are never elusive so that we, as readers, often appreciate her point at an intuitive level if we may not initially follow it at the level of meaning. In No. 341, for example, heartbreak assumes a funereal guise:

After great pain, a formal feeling comes–
The Nerves sit ceremonious, like Tombs–

The 'great pain' of a heartbreak is here superseded by the point where the emotion itself is dead and buried and the nerves that once conveyed that emotion serve now, 'like Tombs', only to mark its burial. The feeling, or rather the detachment from feeling, is autonomous, it 'comes' as of its own volition. As readers here we are being asked to understand one common situation, the sober aftermath of a destructive passion, in terms of another, the ceremonies attending death. Both are familiar to us, but in bringing them together, Dickinson manages to create a fresh approach to both.

Further Reading

Dickinson, Emily, *The Complete Poems of Emily Dickinson*. Edited by Thomas Herbert Johnson. London: Faber & Faber, 1976. This is the authoritative collection of Dickinson's 1,775 poems.

Farr, Judith (ed.), *Emily Dickinson: A Collection of Critical Essays*. London: Prentice Hall International Paperback Editions, 1996. This is an interesting compendium of essays which includes a number of modern critical views on Dickinson's poetry.

CONFESSIONS OF AN ENGLISH OPIUM EATER (1821–56)
by Thomas De Quincey

What really calls for excuse, is not the recourse to opium, when opium had become the one sole remedy available for the malady, but those follies which had themselves produced that malady.

Probably the best-known of a series of Victorian books professing to be confessions, THOMAS DE QUINCEY's book also established the drug addiction genre and became one of the first books to deal seriously with dreams. More or less an autobiography up to the point of writing, *Confessions* tells of how De Quincey ran away from a privileged upbringing and ended up living on the streets only to succumb to a life of drug-addled lassitude.

Summary

The *Confessions* is essentially split into three main parts. The first part of the book deals with De Quincey's early life. He informs the reader of his father's death when De Quincey is only 7 years old and tells how his affairs are then administered by four guardians. One of the guardians ensures he is sent to Manchester Grammar School where, despite apparently blending in with the other students, De Quincey decides to run away. He first goes to North Wales where his family allows him a brief respite to go walking in the hills. However, kept in place by a small allowance he then runs away to London. There he wanders the streets for two months, sleeping rough, before finding bleak accommodation with a disreputable lawyer. He also makes the acquaintance of an unnamed child and a prostitute known only as Ann.

One of the first works to explore dreams in any depth, *Confessions of an English Opium Eater* is Romanticism's emblematic autobiography. It tells the story of Thomas De Quincey's addiction to opium and its terrible effects upon his life.

After five months of this, he meets a friend on the street who gifts him some money. While De Quincey uses the money to secure a loan in Eton, Ann disappears and he does not see her again, although he is haunted by her fate and continues to search for her over the succeeding years. De Quincey is then reconciled to his family and attends Oxford University. While there he suffers a toothache that leaves him in pain for 20 days. On the 21st day he is recommended to use opium and it relieves his pain. For the next eight years De Quincey becomes a sporadic user of the drug, but while he is living in the Lake District he finds that he is completely addicted and is taking huge quantities of laudanum, which is opium dissolved in alcohol. Thereafter, in the final part of the book, De Quincey describes the horrors of his addiction from his dreadful depressions to the terrifying nightmares that blight his sleep. Finally he records how he escapes his habit and attempts to resume a normal life.

THEMES AND TECHNIQUES

Confessions of an English Opium Eater is perhaps most remarkable for its range of subject matter and complexity of voice. Ostensibly it is an educational book designed to inform an ignorant public of the true character of opium addiction. However, it is also something of a self-help manual for drug addicts. Indeed De Quincey remarks at one point that 'the moral of the narrative is addressed to the opium-eater; and, therefore, of necessity, limited in its application'. The supposedly limited application of the book is, in turn offset by the fact that it is also an autobiography, yet an autobiography of a particular type. Several key parts of De Quincey's story are left out of the book, but these are factual points and, as is befitting a Romantic autobiography, De Quincey's focus is more on his subjective experience – the 'confessions' of the title. In particular, he provides an extraordinary record of his dreams and drug-addled sensations. Much of this record is written in an astonishingly vivid prose style, one that adds to the compendium of styles used throughout the book as he moves from the dry ironies and self-lambasting prose of his school days through to the pedantic and scholarly footnotes and on to the pathos and sober descriptions of life on the streets. In this regard, *Confessions* is one of the most eclectic books in the literary canon, as fitful and engaging as its author.

Further Reading

Levin, Susan M., *The Romantic Art of Confession: De Quincey, Musset, Sand, Lamb, Hogg, Fremy, Soulie, Janin*. London: Camden House, 1998. This advanced volume, which includes an analysis of De Quincey's book, examines the genre of confessional literature, looking both at its religious origins and at its outcast narrators.

North, Julian, *De Quincey Reviewed: Thomas De Quincey's Critical Reception, 1821–1994*. London: Camden House, 1997. As the title suggests, this book reviews the history of critical reception to De Quincey's work and suggests that it provided the focus for many key Victorian debates.

CULTURE AND ANARCHY (1869)
by Matthew Arnold

The whole scope of the essay is to recommend culture as the great help out of our present difficulties; culture being a pursuit of our total perfection by means of getting to know, on all the matters which most concern us, the best which has been thought and said in the world, and, through this knowledge, turning a stream of fresh and free thought upon our stock notions and habits, which we now follow staunchly but mechanically, vainly imagining that there is a virtue in following them staunchly which makes up for the mischief of following them mechanically.

MATTHEW ARNOLD's influential book, *Culture and Anarchy*, is a strongly argued polemic in favour of the value of culture, a term he defines as 'the study of perfection'. In making his case, Arnold set the terms of debate for many years to come, particularly in his charge that the middle classes were essentially 'Philistines'.

Summary

Arnold begins his argument by challenging those people who consider culture either as a way of distinguishing one person from another, and one class from another, or as a manifestation of mere curiosity. More than either of these, Arnold contends that culture is in fact 'the study of perfection'. Not only does this involve a much wider remit than that generally afforded the term 'culture', but it also expands the meaning of 'study' too. For in Arnold's sense of the word, 'culture' is not just theoretical, as 'study' might suggest, it is also practical. Endowed with 'worthy notions of reason and the will of God', culture is, for Arnold, a reliably informed mode of self-improvement. Culture makes us better people and closer to the state of perfection that Arnold would wish for us.

Arnold contrasts this state of perfection

with the 'mechanical' society he sees about him in Victorian Britain. He argues that machinery is increasingly becoming an end in itself and that the material life is steadily winning over the spiritual, inner world. The people who value such a material life, Arnold terms 'Philistines'. Philistines value machinery because it makes them wealthy and they value wealth because it gives them freedom. But, according to Arnold, freedom is for them merely an end in itself too, or, worse, the excuse to make more machinery. What compounds this problem for Arnold is the fact that the working classes have also now adopted the principle of 'doing as one likes'. Devoid of proper moral leadership from the Philistine middle classes, the working classes happily riot when they are aggrieved and refuse to submit to conscription.

> Arnold's *Culture and Anarchy* set many of the parameters for the debate on modern culture. In particular, he claimed that the middle classes were Philistines who could only find spiritual salvation in the new religion of culture, or as he called it, 'the pursuit of sweetness and light'.

In opposition to this state of near anarchy, Arnold proposes that we institute the values of culture. These values he summarises in the phrase 'sweetness and light', a phrase he borrows from a fable in JONATHAN SWIFT's *Battle of the Books*. In Swift's book, anarchy is the product of the spider who spins on its own axis, making only cobwebs, whereas sweetness and light are essentially the products of the bee. Working together, bees travel across great distances to collect the materials for producing honey (or sweetness) and candles (or light). In Arnold's terms, 'sweetness' refers to a reasonableness of temper while 'light' designates enlightenment or education, and together they make up a cultured person. If we were to adopt these values, Arnold maintained, we would become more like the ancient Greeks, the society whose culture he most admired.

THEMES AND TECHNIQUES

A prominent theme of Victorian literature is the death or absence of God. As prominent as church-going was, the grip of organised reli-

gion upon the middle classes was loosening. With their minds newly invigorated by the apparently unstoppable powers of science, the middle classes experienced a loss of faith in the moral orthodoxies established by the clergy. Equally, the enormous changes enacted upon the population and the landscape by industrialisation disrupted many of the traditions and customs which had provided the bedrock of British life for centuries. People were becoming, in the opinion of Arnold as in the opinion of many others, spiritually rudderless. The answer to this problem was culture. Culture could supplant the traditional religions which, he argued, operated on too narrow a front and failed to ennoble life to its fullest capacity. Culture, on the other hand, was suffused with both scientific reason and the glory of God. It could add finesse to the bleak industrialism which gummed the national vistas while instilling some machine-bred tenacity into a flailing moral resolve. In other words, culture offered the best of everything, and made everything to its best.

Further Reading

Arnold, Matthew, *Culture and Anarchy*. Edited by Samuel Lipman. London and New Haven: Yale University Press, 1994. This edition of the text also includes a number of essays that examine Arnold's book from a modern perspective.

DAVID COPPERFIELD (1849–50)
by Charles Dickens

Annual income twenty pounds, annual expenditure nineteen six, result happiness. Annual income twenty pounds, annual expenditure twenty pounds ought and six, result misery.

David Copperfield is a semi-autobiographical novel which tells the story of the eponymous hero from his birth through to his successful years as an adult. A favourite with many Dickens readers, *David Copperfield* is also the work which led the author to comment, 'Of my books, I like this the best.'

Summary

David Copperfield's early life is a country idyll spent with his widowed mother and their maid Peggotty. However, after returning from a trip to see Peggotty's brother in Yarmouth, David finds that his mother has remarried to a miserably oppressive man called Murdstone. Shortly afterwards, Murdstone's sister moves in with her brother and between the two of them they bully David and his mother. David does his best to rebel against the Murdstones, but, after biting his stepfather on the hand, he is sent to a boarding school where he is forced to sport a sign advising people that he bites. While there he also becomes friends with some of the other students, including the unfortunate Tommy Traddles, and his idol James Steerforth.

Dickens's favourite novel, *David Copperfield* is also his most autobiographical. It tells of the triumph of Copperfield over those who conspire against him and his endearing cast of friends.

After a period of time, David is forced to leave when his mother and her new baby both die. Peggotty is subsequently fired by Murdstone and she marries a wagon driver called Barkis. David, at the age of just 10, is sent to work for Murdstone in his wine-bottling business. This proves to be as miserable an occupation as the company of Murdstone, but it is relieved, at least intermittently, when David gets to know Micawber and his family, with whom he lodges. When Mr Micawber is forced to leave London in order to assuage his ever-present debt problems, David decides to leave as well and try to seek out Betsey Trotwood, his father's sister and sole remaining relative. Trotwood, and her simple friend Mr Dick, quickly warm to David and when the Murdstones come to claim him, she refuses to hand David over.

Trotwood then sends David to school again, and, from there, to London where he studies the law under Mr Spenlow. David soon falls in love with Spenlow's daughter, Dora. He also meets up with Traddles again, who is lodging with the Micawbers, and Steerforth, who has fallen in love with Mr Peggotty's adopted daughter, Little Em'ly. After Barkis dies, Little Em'ly breaks off her engagement with Mr Peggotty's adopted son and elopes with Steerforth. Meanwhile, Trotwood is forced to move in with David after she is ruined financially by her lawyer, Wickfield, the man with whom David lodged while at school the second time around. Wickfield appears to be increasingly under the influence of his evil clerk, Uriah Heep.

When Spenlow dies, David is finally able to marry Dora. However, as neither of them is rich, and as Dora proves to be incapable of managing their domestic affairs, David turns to writing to help earn some more money. He soon meets with some success. Micawber, who is by this time employed by the nefarious Heep, works with David and Traddles to expose him and, by so doing, helps to unearth Trotwood's lost money. She then offers Micawber a loan to enable him and his family to start a new life in Australia, where he eventually proves to be extremely successful. The Micawbers are joined in Australia by Mr Peggotty and Little Em'ly; the latter returns after she is abandoned by Steerforth. Shortly after her return, Steerforth himself drowns in a terrible storm at sea, but not before Ham dies trying to rescue him. Just before this, Dora dies too, following a stillbirth, and after travelling abroad and writing of his experiences, David returns and marries Agnes, the daughter of Wickfield whom he has secretly loved for a long time. They have a family and live happily ever after.

THEMES AND TECHNIQUES

It is hard not to read *David Copperfield* in terms of Dickens's own life. The miserable child that is forced to work at Murdstone's bottling plant could as well have been Dickens when he was sent to work at Warren's shoe blacking factory. Similarly, while David is an orphan, Dickens certainly felt like one, and both work with an incredible determination to overturn the disadvantages bequeathed to them and become successful authors. But this is not to suggest that *David Copperfield* is merely a private matter in which Dickens gets to settle accounts in his imagination. On the contrary, in writing *David Copperfield*, Dickens touches upon some universal themes, most notably that of the relations between parents and children. The excessive and over-indulgent parents, such as the mothers of Heep and Steerforth, corrupt their sons whereas as the parental figures who are moderate, like Trotwood, provide for a balanced upbringing. In this regard, it is worth noting Dickens's declaration that, 'like many fond parents, I have in my heart of hearts a favourite child. And his name is David Copperfield.'

Further Reading

Dunn, Richard J., *Routledge Literary Sourcebook on Charles Dickens' 'David Copperfield'.* London and New York: Routledge, 2003. This book offers a thorough guide to the history of the novel's criticism and its dramatisations, as well as looking in depth at key passages, and cross-referencing Dickens's text with contexts of the time.

Storey, Graham, *'David Copperfield': Interweaving Truth and* Fiction. New York: Twayne Publishers, 1991. This book looks at one of the most interesting aspects of the novel which is the split in the point of view between the adult David and the child David about whom he writes.

DOCTOR FAUSTUS (1590–93)
by Christopher Marlowe

Was this the face that launched a thousand ships
And burnt the topless towers of Ilium?

Doctor Faustus tells the story of the eponymous German scholar who sells his soul to the Devil in exchange for 24 years of power on Earth. It was one of the most popular plays of the Elizabethan era and its story has been told by many writers and artists since.

Summary

When the play opens, Doctor Faustus is already an esteemed scholar, but, having mastered the traditional forms of knowledge, he

rails against their petty constraints. He wishes to be able to raise the dead and command great power. Upon declaring this he is visited by a Good Angel and a Bad Angel. The Good Angel pleads with him to desist from pursuing these thoughts any further in case he should incur the wrath of God, while the Bad Angel encourages him to become master of the world. Following the Bad Angel's advice, Faustus consults with Valdes and Cornelius, two scholars who encourage Faustus and help him to learn the black arts.

> One of literature's most enduring myths, Marlowe's play *Doctor Faustus* tells the story of a German scholar who sells his soul to the Devil in return for 24 years of power on Earth.

Faustus then uses his new powers to summon a devil, Mephistopheles. In a conscious echo of Faustus's story, Mephistopheles advises him that Lucifer came to be in hell because of his 'aspiring pride and insolence' and that he is never able to leave it. Despite this warning, Faustus resolves to make a pact with Lucifer and sends Mephistopheles to arrange it. Before Mephistopheles returns, Faustus is once again visited by the Good and Bad Angels as he debates whether or not it is a good idea to be eternally damned. Deciding that it is, he agrees to sign his soul over to Lucifer using his own blood drawn from his arm. However, his blood is initially reluctant to run freely enough for him to sign in it. When he does manage to complete the transaction, the blood on his arm appears to say '*Homo fuge!*' – 'Fly, man!' Faustus ignores this advice and, after Mephistopheles has distracted him with a troupe of performing devils, he hands over the signed document promising his soul to Lucifer in exchange for having Mephistopheles as his servant for a period of 24 years.

Having assumed his new powers, Faustus then sets about trying them out. His first target is the Pope in Rome upon whom he plays a series of childish tricks after making himself invisible. Becoming famous for his knowledge and skill, Faustus is summoned to the court of Charles V. For Charles's delight, Faustus conjures up the image of Alexander the Great defeating the King of Persia. He also causes horns to grow out of the heads of a group of knights that mock him. The rest of Faustus's 24 years are spent in similar petty pursuits.

As the deadline for delivery of his soul approaches, Faustus continues to indulge his appetites and idly entertains his friends, at one point having Mephistopheles conjure up a spirit in the shape of famed beauty Helen of Troy. An Old Man enters Faustus's study and almost makes him repent but Mephistopheles appears and threatens to tear Faustus to pieces. In order to appease his mind, Faustus requests to see Helen of Troy one more time. After this, Faustus confesses to his friends what he has done and they leave him. The two angels return to him one final time. The Good Angel informs him that he is now lost to God, while the Bad Angel tells him of the terrors to come. Faustus then spends the hour before midnight begging for mercy, but it is too late and at the stroke of the hour devils appear to carry his soul into hell. The next day, Faustus's body is found torn to pieces.

THEMES AND TECHNIQUES

Like all of MARLOWE's plays, *Doctor Faustus* centres upon the theme of over-reaching. The Prologue reminds us of the Greek myth of Icarus, the man who flew too near the sun and, when his wings melted, fell into the sea and drowned. A similar fate awaits Faustus who over-reaches himself in not being satisfied with merely being a man. This is a repetition of the fate of all humankind following the Fall of Adam and Eve in their defiance of God, which, in turn is a repetition of the fate of Lucifer, who exceeded himself by challenging God and was condemned for eternity as a result. All of these stories would have seemed very real to an Elizabethan audience and mysterious happenings and sightings of devils were not uncommon at performances. Faustus's dilemma would also have been pressing because it represented the problem facing all of Elizabethan society as it struggled to come to grips with the modern world. Faustus implicitly rejects the traditions of mediaeval life at the beginning of the play when he signs up for the kind of unlimited knowledge which was then becoming available to Renaissance scholars. In this regard, *Doctor Faustus* represents a conservative response to a rapidly expanding world which offered new treasures, pleasures and forms of knowledge. On the other hand, some of the most beautiful poetry in the English language seems to revel in these new riches, suggesting that Marlowe had one eye on convention and another on the thrill of the new.

Further Reading

Jump, John D. (ed.), *Marlowe's 'Doctor Faustus': A Casebook*. London: Palgrave Macmillan, 1969. Edited by one of the foremost scholars of Marlowe's play, this volume offers a solid introduction to the history of the play and provides a series of essays looking at different aspects of it.

McAlindon, T., *'Doctor Faustus': Divine in Show*. New York: Twayne Publishers, 1994. This book provides a comprehensive look at the play, including both its source and its influence.

DR JEKYLL AND MR HYDE (1886)
by Robert Louis Stevenson

Whereas, in the beginning, the difficulty had been to throw off the body of Jekyll, it had of late gradually but decidedly transferred itself to the other side. All things therefore seemed to point to this: that I was slowly losing hold of my original and better self, and becoming slowly incorporated with my second and worse.

Dr Jekyll and Mr Hyde is a short novel which explores the concept of duality in humankind. It tells the story of Dr Jekyll and his discovery of a potion which enables him to unleash his other self – the conscience-free Mr Hyde.

Summary

The story begins with a lawyer, Mr Utterson, being informed by his cousin, Mr Enfield, of a strange incident in which a deformed man, Mr Hyde, trampled a young girl. On tracing Hyde, Enfield pressed him to pay damages to the girl's family, a request to which he readily acceded by handing over a cheque bearing the signature of Dr Jekyll. Utterson knows Dr Jekyll and so, when he returns to his chambers, he checks the will Jekyll has recently made in which he transfers his inheritance to Hyde in the case of his disappearance. Puzzled by these events, Utterson tracks down Hyde and follows him to Jekyll's abode. Jekyll tells him not to worry about Hyde.

Partly conceived as an attack on Victorian hypocrisy, *Dr Jekyll and Mr Hyde* explores the concept of the duality of human nature.

A year later, however, witnesses spot Hyde beating a Member of Parliament to death with his cane. Utterson points the police in the direction of Jekyll's house but Jekyll assures Utterson that he has forsaken all contact with Hyde and produces a note from Hyde to prove it. Nevertheless, Utterson's clerk spots that the handwriting of Hyde is almost the same as Jekyll's handwriting, and so Utterson remains suspicious. His suspicions are heightened when a mutual friend of theirs, Dr Lanyon, dies shortly after attending a dinner party at Jekyll's house. When Jekyll's butler seeks out Utterson, complaining of the fact that Jekyll has locked himself in his laboratory, Utterson goes to the laboratory and breaks down the door. Inside he finds Hyde's dead body in Jekyll's clothes. There is also an envelope addressed to him explaining that Jekyll had discovered a potion which enabled him to transform into the evil Hyde. However, after a while of changing back and forwards at will, Jekyll found that he involuntarily turned into Hyde upon falling asleep. Fearing that he would eventually and irrevocably become Hyde, and worrying that he would continue to murder, he decided to kill himself and save the world from any more carnage.

THEMES AND TECHNIQUES

Dr Jekyll and Mr Hyde represent what Stevenson considered to be the two sides of human nature. One the one hand is the good Dr Jekyll, and on the other is the evil Mr Hyde. However, Stevenson complicates this simple picture. For while Jekyll is good, he is also the one who gives birth to Hyde in the first place. He also enjoys being Hyde in a way that he does not enjoy being Jekyll. Furthermore, Stevenson asks the question of whether Hyde's character is not merely Jekyll shorn of his Victorian morals. Indeed, there is a sense in which Hyde is a regression from Jekyll. Hyde is Neanderthal-like in appearance and operates by animalistic instinct rather than reason, but at the same time he understands that he is flouting society's conventions. For his part, Jekyll instinctively understands that what he does as Hyde is wrong. However, his faculty of reason, which he uses as a scientist, is, like that of FRANKENSTEIN, precisely what leads to the horror of Hyde in the first place.

Further Reading

Veeder, William and Hirsch, Gordon (eds), *Dr Jekyll and Mr Hyde after One Hundred Years.* Chicago: University of Chicago Press, 1988. Celebrating the centenary of Stevenson's novel, this generous collection of essays examines a variety of different aspects of the work and its subsequent influence.

DON JUAN (1818–24)
by Lord Byron

'Tis strange, but true; for truth is always strange,–
Stranger than fiction.

Immensely popular when the first parts of it were published, despite the fact that women were not supposed to read it, *Don Juan* is a comic masterpiece in verse which owes more to the work of ALEXANDER POPE than WILLIAM WORDSWORTH. Unfinished at BYRON's death, it meanders through the life of Don Juan, poking fun at the hypocrisy and sanctimoniousness of the age.

Summary

After the death of his noble but lascivious father, Don Juan's learned mother, Donna Inez decides to take his education in hand. She is keen that he does not follow in his father's footsteps and so deliberately keeps him from the facts of life while all the while schooling him in the arts and sciences. Despite this, however, Don Juan is a handsome young man and soon becomes involved in cuckolding a husband with the upshot that he is forced by his mother to go travelling for four years. Juan sets off from Spain for Italy but his boat sinks on the way. Drifting in a lifeboat, the survivors eat shoe leather out of desperation and then finally turn to cannibalism, eating Juan's private tutor. Before they have chance to eat anyone else, the lifeboat is broken up on a reef and Juan is borne to shore on the tide, while all the other survivors drown. When Juan wakes up he finds himself under the care of Haidée, the daughter of a Greek pirate. Knowing that her father will disapprove of Juan, Haidée keeps his existence quiet by leading him to a secret cave.

> Based upon already popular sources, Byron's *Don Juan* was a success all across Europe. It tells the meandering story of the eponymous Don using a scathing wit which is the very antithesis of Romanticism's more self-regarding verse.

The couple soon fall in love and secretly marry. When Haidée's father, Lambro, is reported missing at sea, Haidée assumes it is safe to bring Juan into the open and they move into Lambro's house together. However, Lambro is still alive and when he returns he orders his men to capture Juan. During the ensuing fight, Haidée collapses and within a fortnight she is dead. Lambro then sells Juan as a slave in Constantinople. He is bought by Gulbeyaz, one of the sultan's wives, who disguises him as a woman and has him installed in the harem, in order that he can be her lover. Juan eventually escapes from Constantinople and finds himself caught up in the war between the Turks and the Russians. Juan joins the Russian army and fights heroically. At one point he even saves a young Turkish girl, Leila, from being murdered by some Cossacks.

In the light of his heroic behaviour, Juan is selected to go to St Petersburgh to inform Empress Catherine of the victory. Juan takes Leila with him. Catherine proves unable to resist Juan's charm and falls under his spell, granting him wealth and anything else he desires. Juan soon becomes a little dissipated enjoying such a luxurious life and eventually he falls ill. Assuming it is the cold weather that ails him, Catherine reluctantly arranges for Juan to be sent on a diplomatic mission to England.

Once again Juan takes Leila with him and, when he arrives in England, he settles her with Lady Pinchbeck. Meanwhile, the handsome and daring Juan is feted all over England. He is invited to the country retreat of Lord Henry Amundeville, where he becomes the object of passion for several different women. Juan resists their advances and is promptly haunted by the ghost of a monk. On the second night of being haunted, Juan attacks the ghost only to find that it is actually Lady Fitz-Fulke, one of his pursuers. The next day Juan looks wan and worn, and that is where the story abruptly ends.

THEMES AND TECHNIQUES

As Byron admits at the beginning of the poem, *Don Juan* is an 'ancient friend'. The name of 'Don Juan' and the character of a swashbuckling and serial seducer had been used by a number of different authors before Byron put him to work. He was probably first invented by the Spanish dramatist Tirso de Molina for his play *El Burlador de Sevilla* in 1630. The Austrian composer Wolfgang Amadeus Mozart then used him as the central character in his opera *Don Giovanni* in 1787, and the Italian and French dramatists Carlo Goldoni and Molière also placed him in notable plays. By the time that Byron centred his epic poem around Don Juan, he was writing for an audience that already loved the character. Just as importantly, he was writing for an audience that was European, rather than just British; indeed it may be said that, Byron became the only Romantic poet who successfully exported to Continental Europe. Unlike most other works of Romanticism, *Don Juan* is also funny. Indeed, it parodies the self-regard inherent to the project of Romanticism, puncturing the pomp of self-obsession with scathing moments of anti-climax. In doing so, the poem is also a criticism of Byron's own image as being a man, in the famous words of Lady Caroline Lamb, 'mad, bad and dangerous to know'. Also like Byron, *Don Juan* is cut short, left unfinished by its author who planned to kill his hero off in Revolutionary France, but was unable to do so before he was himself killed in the Greek Revolution.

Further Reading

Haslett, Moyra, *Byron's 'Don Juan' and the Don Juan Legend*. London: Clarendon Press, 1997. This advanced book looks at Byron's *Don Juan* in terms of the Don Juan legend.

Johnson, Thomas Herbert (ed.), *Romanticism and Male Fantasy in Byron's 'Don Juan': A Marketable Vice*. London: Palgrave Macmillan, 1999. This book examines the moral indignation that greeted the publication of Byron's poem, and traces the poet's battle with contemporary censorship.

DRACULA (1897)
by Bram Stoker

Ah, it is the fault of our science that it wants to explain all; and if it explain not, then it says there is nothing to explain. But yet we see around us every day the growth of new beliefs, which think themselves new; and which are yet but the old, which pretend to be young – like fine ladies at the opera.

Depicting one of the greatest monsters in any literature, *Dracula* is a novel that follows the attempts of a group of nineteenth-century men to destroy the eponymous vampire.

Summary

Jonathan Harker, a young English lawyer, is despatched to Transylvania from his office in England where he is supposed to assist Count Dracula, a local nobleman, to buy an estate in England. On his way to the Count's castle, Harker is continually warned by the locals about some non-specific threat which seems to issue from around Dracula's lands. Undeterred, Harker meets Dracula whom he immediately takes to be a friendly and cultivated man. This initial impression soon wears off when he finds that he is all but a prisoner in the Count's castle. Harker's unease is compounded when he spies Dracula scampering up and down walls and when he is attacked by three voluptuous females who appear to be in the power of Dracula.

Meanwhile, back in England, Harker's fiancée, Mina Murray, confides her worries over Harker's safety to her friend Lucy Westenra. For her part, Lucy worries which of her three suitors she is to accept in marriage – Dr Seward, Arthur Holmwood or Quincey Morris. When Lucy accepts Holmwood, Mina joins her in the seaside town of Whitby. While they are there, a ship is wrecked off the coast. All the crew are missing apart from the captain who is strapped, dead, to the wheel. On board are 50 boxes of earth from Dracula's castle and a giant black dog who leaps to shore and runs away. Shortly after this, Lucy begins to exhibit strange behaviour, growing thin and pale. One night, after following Lucy as she sleepwalks to the cemetery, Mina sees a pair of glowing eyes bent over her friend but when she advances, the eyes depart.

When Mina hears that Harker has been found in a dazed state in Budapest, she travels there to nurse him better. Lucy's condition worsens and Holmwood calls upon Seward to advise about her medical condition. Baffled, Seward asks his mentor Professor Abraham Van Helsing to help him cure Lucy. Van Helsing immediately seems to know what is wrong with Lucy and covers the room with garlic cloves. This stems the problem until Lucy's mother removes them because of the bad odour. Lucy's condition worsens and the men try to help her with a series of blood transfusions. This works until a wolf breaks into the house, ultimately resulting in the death of both Lucy and her mother.

> In a time increasingly dominated by technology, *Dracula* depicts a world beyond the ken of modern science. The monstrous Dracula is a form of anti-Christ, forcing his opponents to re-engage with their Christian faiths if they are to survive.

Van Helsing convinces Holmwood, Seward, and Morris that Lucy is now one of the Undead and when they see her preying upon a child, they help to kill her by driving a stake through her heart, cutting her head off and filling her mouth with garlic. They pledge to destroy Dracula and join forces with Harker and Mina who, now married, have returned to England. Using Seward's mental asylum as a refuge, they attempt to track down Dracula and his 50 boxes of earth. Unbeknownst to them, one of Seward's patients is a disciple of Dracula and he lets the count in to prey upon Mina. When they discover this, they realise they have only a limited time before she too becomes a vampire.

The men then manage to sanctify all but one of the chests of earth in which Dracula has to sleep, forcing him back to Transylvania. Following him there, the group splits up. Van Helsing and Mina go to the castle where they purge it of the three vampires. The others finally catch up with Dracula's box, and, after a brief struggle with his helpers, they manage to exterminate Dracula before the sun sets, although Quincey is mortally wounded in the action.

THEMES AND TECHNIQUES

Dracula is not told from a single perspective. Rather, it is composed of various fragments from letters, diaries, telegrams, newspapers and journals, all written by different characters in the novel. Apart from affording the narrative a semblance of being recorded history, this mixture of sources suggests that such a story exceeds the ability of a single viewpoint. In this regard, they are like Dracula's unreflecting image in the mirror. For Dracula is, in one sense, beyond the ken of modern understanding. He represents the parts of the world for which modern science cannot account, which is why, before the arrival of Van Helsing, Seward, the progressive doctor, is unable to diagnose Lucy's illness. As Harker earlier notes, 'the old centuries had, and have, powers of their own which mere modernity cannot kill.'

This excessive element to life is largely represented in the novel by religion. Many of Dracula's actions, for example, like those of Faustus in DOCTOR FAUSTUS, are reversals of Christian rites and symbols. Whereas in Communion, wine symbolising the blood of Christ is drunk to facilitate the eternity of the life of the soul, Dracula drinks actual blood to facilitate the eternity of his physical life at the expense of the death of his soul. The value of Christian symbols, such as the cross, to those pursuing Dracula lies not just in their ability to oppose the Count, but also in the way they reverse his reversals and affirm the Christian heritage forsaken by modern science.

Further Reading

Byron, Glennis (ed.), *Bram Stoker's 'Dracula': A Casebook*. London: Palgrave Macmillan, 1999. This volume offers a wide-ranging and incisive introduction to the history of the novel, as well as providing a series of essays examining different aspects of it.

Stoker, Bram *'Dracula': Complete, Authoritative Text with Biographical, Historical, and Cultural Contexts, Critical History, and Essays from Contemporary Critical Perspectives*. Edited by John Paul Riquelme. London: Palgrave Macmillan, 2002. A comprehensive review of the novel.

EDUCATION OF HENRY ADAMS, THE (1919)
by Henry Adams

A friend in power is a friend lost.

Awarded a Pulitzer Prize following its posthumous publication, ADAMS's book offers an autobiographical account of life in America and Britain at the end of the nineteenth century. As Adams mixed in the very highest circles, this autobiography also includes inside commentary on politics and the arts, as well as Adams's own theory of society.

Summary

Describing the birth of Henry Adams in 1838, the narrator of the book begins with the assertion that, 'Probably no child, born in the year, held better cards than he.' Displaying these cards, Adams is revealed as the great-grandchild of one President, John Adams, and the grandson of another, John Quincy Adams. He spends his early life alternating between his home in Boston and the family's summer house in Quincy, but he soon comes to question his life of privilege. He begins to realise, through a snowball fight with some slum children, that poorer people have morals and principles too. By the age of 16, Adams 'had as yet no education at all,' a state of affairs which he claims is not improved by then attending Harvard. Adams then travels to Europe to study in Berlin, Dresden and Rome. However, he finds he becomes nothing but a tourist and returns to America to study as a lawyer.

These studies also fail to come to fruition and he eventually becomes his father's private secretary. When his father becomes Minister to England, Adams joins him and, by so doing, completely misses the Civil War. He undertakes some journalism while he is in England and, when he returns in 1868, he leaves his father to become a freelance reporter. After the death of his sister, Adams is invited to teach at Harvard, a post he accepts. He becomes an assiduous innovator, introducing the seminar system and student evaluations.

> Although *The Education of Henry Adams* takes the form of an autobiography, Adams's real object of study was not himself but the various educations he received, both scholastic and worldly.

Then the book simply omits the 20 years between 1872–92, the years where his life is severed in half by the death of his wife. By the time we rejoin him, Adams is sadder but wiser. His great preoccupations remain politics and history and he combines them both in his writing, for example in the development of his dynamic theory of history. He ends the book in 1905, aware that his generation is slowly dying off but hopeful of the era to come which he suspects might be one which 'sensitive and timid natures could regard without a shudder'.

THEMES AND TECHNIQUES

Despite ostensibly being an autobiography, *The Education of Henry Adams* is not told in the first person (the 'I', or what Adams called the 'perpendicular pronoun'), but the third person ('he'). Adams describes himself as if he were writing about a character, rather than writing about himself. The distancing effect of this approach is compounded by the fact that Adams very rarely describes or discusses his thoughts and emotions. For example, Adams skips almost 20 years of his life during the period when he was married to Marian

Hooper and following her suicide in 1885. Rather than focusing on Henry Adams then, the book centres on the education he receives. Indeed, Adams describes himself as a manikin upon which he hangs various forms of education to see what their effects are. As he says, 'the object of study is the garment, not the figure'. Nor is the garment in question necessarily what we might think of as relating to education. For Adams does not refer just to schools and colleges when he talks about education, but to the schooling he receives from the various experiences of his life too. Much of this part of his education is a lesson in compromise, as Adams learns that his ideals are not always attainable in the world of *Realpolitik*.

Further Reading

Adams, Henry, *Education of Henry Adams: An Autobiography*. Edited by Henry Cabot Lodge. Whitefish: R. A. Kessinger Publishing Co., 2003. This is a heavily annotated version of Adams's book.

Rowe, John Carlos (ed.), *New Essays on 'The Education of Henry Adams'*. New York: Cambridge University Press, 1996. This short collection of essays examines the canonical status of Adams's work and argues for its continuing relevance.

> ## ETHAN FROME (1911)
> ## by Edith Wharton
>
> *Almost everybody in the neighbourhood had 'troubles', frankly localized and specified; but only the chosen had 'complications'. To have them was in itself a distinction, though it was also, in most cases, a death warrant. People struggled on for years with 'troubles', but they almost always succumbed to 'complications'.*

Ethan Frome is a short novel set at the end of the nineteenth century in New England. It tells the story of a farmer, Ethan Frome, and the unhappy relationship he has with his wife and her cousin.

Summary

After hearing that the appearance of a man, Ethan Frome, is due to a 'smash-up' he had 23 years ago, the narrator's curiosity is only piqued. No one in the town of Starkfield is able to provide him with an explanation of the look on Ethan's face which, he believes, 'neither poverty nor physical suffering could have put there'. Needing someone to drive him to and from his own work, the narrator hires Ethan as his driver. One evening, a snow storm interrupts their journey and the narrator is forced to spend the night at Ethan's farm. It is while there that he begins to put together Ethan's story.

The novel then turns back in time to when Ethan was a young man. It is again a snowy night and Ethan meets his cousin Mattie Silver on her way home from a dance. Mattie is employed as a maid at Ethan's farm. They both entertain an unspoken regard for each other, but, unfortunately for them, Ethan is already unhappily married to Zeena. Zeena is a bitter hypochondriac who is always seeking cures for her maladies. She rightly harbours suspicions about the relationship between Ethan and Mattie.

Ethan Frome depicts the unhappy love affair between a farmer and his maid. Constrained by the moral pressures of society, their love is consummated in tragedy.

One day, Zeena leaves the farm to take a cure and stays overnight with relatives. Spending the night alone together, the romantic tension between Ethan and Mattie grows. At one point, Ethan smashes Zeena's favourite dish but the tension remains unbroken in any other way. The next day, when Zeena returns she announces that she has hired someone else to look after her in her illness. The result of this is that Zeena decides to sack Mattie. Ethan is shocked but feels unable to stop it. When he informs Mattie they kiss for the first time. Shortly afterwards, Zeena discovers the broken dish and, when Mattie admits to breaking it, she becomes even more determined to rid herself of her.

The next day, Ethan insists on driving Mattie to the station. On the way, they stop to enjoy a moment sledding down a hill. After a first try where they narrowly miss a large elm tree at the bottom of the hill, Mattie suggests they go again, but this time they should deliberately aim for the tree in order to end their lives together. Ethan eventually consents to this and they set off again, this time driving directly into the elm. The action of the novel then resumes in the present day where the narrator discovers that the bitter-sounding woman he heard on his arrival at the farm is actually Mattie. She is now paralysed and under the care of the sour Zeena, while Ethan broods unhappily with them both.

THEMES AND TECHNIQUES

Like much of EDITH WHARTON's work, *Ethan Frome* is a novel in which individual characters battle against strictures placed on their lives by society. Ethan's love for Mattie is unwavering, yet any manifestation of this is constantly stifled by the oppressive reminders of his socially sanctified marriage to Zeena. Whereas THOMAS HARDY's characters actually commit acts of social transgression and are punished for them, Wharton's characters are forestalled at source and tend to suffer internally. For example, Ethan's conscience prohibits him from fully enjoying his one night alone with Mattie, or from deceiving his neighbours in order that he might procure the money to escape. Because Ethan struggles mainly with his conscience, rather than an external force, Wharton has to use symbols and images to portray this inner life. One of the most vivid ways in which she does this is by employing colours. The oppressive white of the winter snows, which imprison the inhabitants of Starkfield for half of every year, contrast vividly with the reds associated with Mattie. Her red scarf and ribbon draw on strong associations with passion and vitality, as well as on a literary heritage where red, as in *The Scarlet Letter*, is an expression of adultery.

Further Reading

Smith, Christopher (ed.), *Readings on 'Ethan Frome'*. San Diego: Greenhaven Press, 2000. As the title suggests, this volume offers a variety of interpretations of *Ethan Frome*, looking at everything from the autobiographical sources of the novel to its imagery.

Springer, Marlene, *'Ethan Frome': A Nightmare of Need*. New York: Twayne Publishers, 1993. This book takes a close look at the autobiographical relevance of the novel to the author's own troubled personal life.

FAERIE QUEENE, THE
(1590–96)
by Edmund Spenser

Through thick and thin, both over bank and bush,

In hope her to attain by hook or crook

SPENSER referred to *The Faerie Queene* as a 'dark conceit'. It is ostensibly a set of tales about chivalric knights, but was also designed to work as both a moral and historical allegory.

Summary

Spenser completed six books of *The Faerie Queene* (he had originally planned 12), each one of which is 12 cantos long, with each canto containing roughly 50 stanzas of nine lines. Although the structures of the individual books vary, they all have in common a central character engaged in a quest. The plot of Book One is exemplary in this regard. It tells the story of the Redcrosse Knight, the knight of Holiness. Travelling with Una, a 'lovely Ladie', and a 'Dwarfe', Redcrosse has been tasked by Gloriana, the 'greatest Glorious Queene of Faerie Lond', to slay a terrible dragon. During a storm Redcrosse enters the den of Error, a fabled beast whom he manages to slay. The travellers are then given shelter by a hermit who turns out to be Archimago, an evil sorcerer. While they sleep he conjures up sprites who fool Redcrosse into thinking Una has forsaken her honour. Disgusted, the next morning Redcrosse leaves Una behind and soon after encounters Sansfoy, another knight. The two fight and Redcrosse kills Sansfoy leaving him to claim Fidessa, the woman travelling with Sansfoy. However, Fidessa is actually Duessa, an evil witch.

Meanwhile, Una sets off in search of Redcrosse. She believes she finds him, although it is actually Archimago in disguise. Sansloy, brother of Sansfoy, seeks revenge and attacks the disguised Archimago. About to be killed, Archimago soon reveals his true identity and lets Sansloy take Una as a prize. The real Redcrosse is led by Duessa to a great palace called the House of Pride. When the dwarf discovers that people of pride have died there, he and Redcrosse leave. They are followed by Duessa who stops a giant, Orgoglio, from killing Redcrosse. Orgoglio then claims Duessa as his own and throws Redcrosse into a dungeon. Escaping from the dungeon, the dwarf then seeks out Una, who escaped from Sansloy when he was accosted by a satyr knight. Una then encounters King Arthur and ask for his help. He rides to Orgoglio's castle, kills the giant, frees Redcrosse and shows him the true identity of Duessa.

> Although only half of the planned 12 books were ever completed, *The Faerie Queene* remains one of the most richly symbolic and densely textured poems in the English language.

Arthur then explains that he has come to Faerie Land to seek out its queen with whom he has fallen in love. He continues on his quest and Redcrosse and Una return to theirs. Already weakened, Redcrosse almost succumbs to taking his own life in the cave of Despair, but Una intervenes and takes him to the House of Holiness. There, attended by, among others, Fidelia, Sperenza, and Charissa (or Faith, Hope and Charity), Redcrosse is reinvigorated. He also learns that his real name is George and that he is destined to be a great saint in England. He and Una leave for the castle of her parents, which has been seized by the dragon Redcrosse is supposed to kill. On the first day of the battle between Redcrosse and the dragon, the knight is injured but falls into a well with magic powers which heal him and stiffen his sword. A similar thing happens the next day, and by the third day Redcrosse is able to kill the dragon. Having saved her parents, Redcrosse is expected to marry Una but he states that he can only do this after serving the Faerie Queene for another six years in her battle against an evil king.

THEMES AND TECHNIQUES

In a letter to Sir Walter Ralegh, Spenser declared his intention to make *The Faerie Queene* an allegorical work. As an allegorical work, the stories of each book make sense on a surface level but they can also be read on a symbolic level too. In particular, Spenser wished to make all of the 12 principal heroes and heroines in the books represent a particular virtue. Redcrosse, for example, represents Holiness. In the other completed books, the five protagonists represent Temperance, Chastity, Friendship, Justice and Courtesy. Taken together, Spenser hoped that the 12 virtues would make the perfect person.

What is interesting about these allegorical attributes is that the characters do not necessarily represent them all the way through their respective stories, but they have to earn these qualities. Redcrosse, for example, suffers many trials, including entering the den of Error, the house of Pride, and the cave of Despair, before his Holiness is established and he is able to defeat the evil represented by the dragon. This moral allegory is also complemented by a historical and political allegory. The Faerie Queene herself, for example, is Queen Elizabeth I, while many of the villains in the poem represent Roman Catholicism against whom representatives of English Protestantism, such as Redcrosse or St George, set themselves. These multiple layers of meaning give *The Faerie Queene* a density and richness that make it one of the greatest poems ever written in English.

Further Reading

Erickson, Wayne, *Mapping 'The Faerie Queene': Quest Structures and the World of the Poem.* London: Garland Publishing, 1996. This book examines the geography of Spenser's poem, linking it both to political events of the day and to the classical scheme of the quest.

Suzuki, Mihoko (ed.), *Critical Essays on Edmund Spenser.* New York: G.K. Hall and Co., 1995. This collection of essays mostly examines *The Faerie Queene* from a variety of modern perspectives.

FAR FROM THE MADDING CROWD (1874)
by Thomas Hardy

A resolution to avoid an evil is seldom framed till the evil is so far advanced as to make avoidance impossible.

Far from the Madding Crowd is a novel set in the nineteenth century in southern England. It tells the story of the relationship between Bathsheba Everdene and the three men who love her.

Summary

Gabriel Oak is a steady young shepherd who has built up his flock by dint of hard work and his own skill. He falls in love with the capricious Bathsheba Everdene, a beautiful young woman, but although she initially entertains the idea of marriage, ultimately she rejects him. When she moves away Oak is heartbroken. Oak's heartbreak is compounded when his dog runs his sheep over a cliff, killing them all and ruining him. His only compensation is that at least he has not reduced Bathsheba to poverty too.

Oak then travels to nearby Weatherbury where he is able to save a local farm from fire. He then takes the opportunity to ask the owner if he could be employed as a shepherd. The owner turns out to be Bathsheba who has inherited the farm from her uncle and, reluctantly, she agrees to employ her one-time suitor. Meanwhile, an ex-servant at the farm, Fanny Robin, tries to marry the dissolute Sergeant Troy, a soldier in the local barracks. However, Fanny ends up at the wrong church and Troy, who is left waiting and embarrassed, resolves not to bother himself with her again.

Mr Boldwood, a rich and reserved farmer, expresses paternal concern for Fanny and attempts to seek her out. In so doing, he meets Bathsheba who divines that he presents a challenge to her skills of seduction. She then sends him a valentine with an invitation to marry her stamped on it. From that point on, Boldwood becomes smitten with Bathsheba and tries to persuade her to marry him. She is hesitant at first, but, on the point of finally agreeing to his proposal, Bathsheba meets Troy. Despite Oak's advice to the contrary, and Boldwood's attempts to bribe Troy into leaving the area, Bathsheba marries the soldier.

One evening, Troy and Bathsheba encounter Fanny. Not knowing the truth of their relationship, Bathsheba pays for an elaborate funeral for the young woman when she hears that she has died the next day. Troy, however, finally reveals his love for Fanny to Bathsheba, and, despite Oak's best efforts to hide the fact, Bathsheba learns that Fanny had just had a baby with Troy. Troy leaves the farm in shame and is assumed drowned when his clothes are found on a beach. Bathsheba then agrees to marry Boldwood in seven years, at which time Troy will be declared legally dead.

> Set in rural southern England, *Far from the Madding Crowd* is the story of Bathsheba Everdene and the three men who love her in their different ways. Although, like most Hardy novels, it is touched by tragedy, *Far from the Madding Crowd* finishes with an unusually optimistic conclusion.

However, one evening, Troy returns to claim Bathsheba, a move that so distresses Boldwood that he shoots the soldier dead. After attempting to turn the gun on himself, Boldwood resigns himself to spending the rest of his life in prison. Distraught after all that has happened, Bathsheba falls ill and is nursed back to health under the supervision of Oak. When she is better Oak declares his wish to leave the farm. Realising that she will be left all alone, Bathsheba begs Oak to stay and asks him to marry her. Oak, steady to the last, agrees to the request and the couple are married in a secret ceremony.

THEMES AND TECHNIQUES

One of the key themes in *Far from the Madding Crowd*, as well as in HARDY's novels generally, is the relationship between people and nature. Hardy saw that the traditional methods of working, methods based upon a symbiotic rapport with the natural environment, were fading away. Oak is the character who represents the old ways of working. As piteous as his fate becomes at times, such as when he loses his entire flock, he stoically accepts his fate and maintains a fidelity to tradition. Such sentiments find expression in the poem, 'Elegy Written in a Country Churchyard' by

Thomas Gray (a friend of HORACE WALPOLE), from which Hardy took the title of the novel:

> *Far from the madding crowd's ignoble strife,*
> *Their sober wishes never learned to stray;*
> *Along the cool sequestered vale of life*
> *They kept the noiseless tenor of their way.*

Oak is the one constant in the book, the one whose 'sober wishes' (his love for Bathsheba) never stray. Whereas the other characters become caught up in fickle and heady passions, such as Boldwood's desperate love for Bathsheba, or Bathsheba's foolhardy infatuation with Troy, or his careless fervour for Fanny, Oak is steadfast in his love for Bathsheba, neither succumbing to desperation when it fails nor forgetting his responsibilities when it succeeds at the end. That, Hardy seems to suggest, is the measure of true love.

Further Reading

Morgan, Rosemarie, *Cancelled Words: Rediscovering Thomas Hardy*. London and New York: Routledge, 1992. This book examines the original manuscript of *Far From the Madding Crowd*, and identifies what was excluded because of censorship, and what it discloses about Hardy's working methods.

FRANKENSTEIN (1818–31)
by Mary Wollstonecraft Shelley

Learn from me, if not by my precepts, at least by my example, how dangerous is the acquirement of knowledge, and how happier the man is who believes his native town to be the world, than he who aspires to become greater than his nature will allow.

Named for its eponymous hero, *Frankenstein* is a short novel telling the story of one scientist's pursuit of the secret of life. On finding the secret, Frankenstein creates a monster who ends up killing and destroying all that is dear to him.

Summary

On a ship journeying to the North Pole, Robert Walton sends letters to his sister describing the progress of his ship. This progress halts when the ship becomes stuck in pack ice. While stuck, Walton and the crew see a large man pulling a sled across the ice. A short time later they encounter another man close to death, also traversing the ice by sled. Taking him aboard, Walton helps to nurse him back to health. When the man gets better he introduces himself as Dr Frankenstein. Frankenstein becomes alarmed at Walton's insistence on exploring the reaches of the North Pole at any cost and proceeds to tell him his own story of seeking after knowledge whatever the price.

> *Frankenstein* is a moral fable about the terrible consequences of unlimited power. Obsessed with the pursuit of knowledge, Dr Frankenstein takes the ultimate step by creating life itself. The life he creates is deemed a monster by society and, shunned, it wreaks a terrible revenge.

Frankenstein is born into a wealthy Swiss family where he spends an idyllic childhood. In particular he enjoys the company of Elizabeth Lavenza, his adopted sister/cousin. His parents encourage them to be close and, on her deathbed, Frankenstein's mother presses her hopes that the two will marry. Frankenstein then departs to Ingolstadt, where he will study at the university with his friend Henry Clerval. Initially, Frankenstein's studies go well, but he soon develops a consuming interest in trying to find the secret of life itself. Spending day and night in his laboratory, Frankenstein ignores his family and friends, until, one day he thinks he has finally discovered the secret.

Piecing together a giant creature from the body parts of dead people, Frankenstein creates a monster who comes alive. He is horrified by the ugliness of the monster and runs out of the laboratory to collect Clerval. When the pair return, the monster has disappeared. Frankenstein is distraught at what he has done. Deciding to return to Geneva, Frankenstein receives a letter informing him that his younger brother has been murdered. On his way back to his home, Frankenstein passes through a wood where he is seized by a sense of disquiet. He sees the monster lit up in a flash of lightning and realises who it was that murdered his brother. However, he feels unable to confess what has happened, even when a faithful family servant is accused of the murder, convicted and executed.

In order to escape from the results of his actions, Frankenstein takes a holiday in the mountains. While there, he is confronted by the monster who explains what has happened to him. He says that he hid in a shed adjoining the home of some French exiles. From them he learnt how to speak and read, as well as something of the culture of humans. However, when he showed himself, he proved so hideous that he was driven away. Filled with hatred for the creator who had abandoned him, the monster decided to revenge himself on Frankenstein and subsequently killed his brother and framed Justine. He pleads with Frankenstein to create him a mate so that he may leave human society forever.

Frankenstein initially agrees, but when his creation is nearly complete, he destroys the female monster, causing the male monster to declare revenge. Soon afterwards, Clerval is found torn to pieces. Frankenstein is charged with the crime but let off and he returns home to marry Elizabeth. However, on their wedding night the monster kills her. Frankenstein's father promptly dies of grief, leaving Frankenstein alone and embittered, vowing to pursue the monster across the world. This is what he was doing when he encountered Walton. Frankenstein then dies in his sleep. A little later, Walton encounters the monster weeping over Frankenstein's body, wracked with remorse at what he has done. He promises Walton that he will now hide in the northernmost part of the world and burn himself on a funeral pyre so that no one will ever discover him.

THEMES AND TECHNIQUES

Frankenstein is a fable about the terrible consequences of unlimited power. The novel's alternative title – *The Modern Prometheus* – hints at SHELLEY's concern. Prometheus was a Titan in Greek mythology who stole fire from Mount Olympus to give to humankind. He, like Frankenstein, and even *DOCTOR FAUSTUS*, are classic over-reachers, and all of them end up being punished for assuming power that they should not have. In this case, the power is the power to create life and, as the references to JOHN MILTON's *PARADISE LOST* make clear, Frankenstein is a form of surrogate God, creating his Adam in the monster. On the one hand, MARY SHELLEY seems to be suggesting that science displays an irresponsible arrogance in searching after the secret of life itself, a secret that should be left to God. On the other hand, the monster may well be considered the most eloquent and pitiful character in the novel, and Frankenstein, his effective God, the least sympathetic because of the way he abandons the monster. In this regard, Shelley foreshadows the concerns of literature since the turn of the nineteenth century, which has often focused on the difficulty of living in a world where God is said to have abandoned humankind.

Further Reading

Bann, Stephen (ed.), *Frankenstein, Creation and Monstrosity*. London: Reaktion Books, 1997. This book takes an advanced look at some of the themes in *Frankenstein*, including a detailed account of its literary legacy.

Levine, George and Knoepflmacher, U.C. (eds), *The Endurance of 'Frankenstein': Essays on Mary Shelley's Novel*. Berkeley: University of California Press, 1982. This book includes a number of interesting essays on *Frankenstein*, including ones looking at the film adaptations of the novel.

Morton, Timothy (ed.), *A Routledge Literary Sourcebook on Mary Shelley's 'Frankenstein'*. London and New York: Routledge, 2002. As the title suggests, this book looks at the history of *Frankenstein*, from its sources to its reception at the time and since. It also examines key passages in the text.

G

GREAT EXPECTATIONS (1860–61)
by Charles Dickens

Pip, dear old chap, life is made of ever so many partings welded together, and as I may say, one man's a blacksmith, one's a whitesmith, and one's a goldsmith, and one's a coppersmith. Divisions among such must come, and must be met as they come.

Photo credit: *Illustrated London News*

Great Expectations is a novel set in the nineteenth century which relates the story of Pip, an orphan from the Kent marshes. It describes how he unexpectedly becomes the beneficiary of an unknown benefactor and subsequently develops 'great expectations' at enormous personal cost.

Summary

The novel begins with the child Pip looking at his parents' gravestones in the local cemetery. While there, an escaped convict assails Pip and demands that he bring him some food and a file to break his irons. Frightened, Pip does as he is told, taking a file from Joe Gargery, a blacksmith who is his sister's husband, and some food from his sister's pantry, the woman who now looks after Pip. Pip takes the provisions to the prisoner who thanks him for his troubles and disappears. He is later caught, but he takes the blame for the items missing from Pip's house.

> *Great Expectations* is the bearer of the sober message that wealth neither makes you happy nor leaves you a superior moral being.

Pip then forgets about this incident when he is requested to go and 'play' at 'Satis House', the dilapidated home of Miss Havisham. There he meets Estella, a young girl with whom he falls in love. She treats him in a derogatory fashion, much to Miss Havisham's amusement, particularly remarking on Pip's coarse appearance. Pip concludes that there must be something wrong with him and yearns to become a gentleman of the kind that he thinks would impress Estella. One day Miss Havisham shows Pip a room with her wedding feast still displayed in it, now decayed and rotten, from the time years before when she was left at the altar. Miss Havisham then dismisses Pip and pays for him to become an apprentice to Joe.

Pip is disheartened by this as he had hoped to become a gentleman, but he sticks to his task until he is unexpectedly visited by a lawyer, Jaggers, whom he once saw at Miss Havisham's house. Jaggers informs Pip that he is to be sponsored by a benefactor who wishes to remain anonymous, although Pip assumes that it is Miss Havisham and she lets him think the same. Pip then sets off on the road to becoming a gentleman, by moving to London and learning from his friend Herbert. During this period, Pip sees little of Joe and only returns to his home when his sister dies. He does, however, continue to nurture hopes that he and Estella will one day be married, even though Herbert informs him that Miss Havisham has brought Estella up to break the hearts of men.

On his twenty-fourth birthday, Pip is once again confronted by the convict that he met as a child. This time the convict, called Magwitch, reveals that he is actually Pip's secret benefactor, a role he had undertaken in gratitude for the help that Pip had given him all those years before. Pip is initially appalled by Magwitch, but grows to like him and vows to protect him from the police and from his old partner in crime, Compeyson. Compeyson, it transpires, was the man who jilted Miss Havisham on her wedding day. Even more startling, Pip learns that Magwitch is Estella's real father and that her mother is Jaggers' maid. When Pip goes to confront Miss Havisham with all he has learnt, she finally repents and begs his forgiveness. Pip agrees, noting that he needs to seek forgiveness for his own behaviour. Shortly afterwards, Miss Havisham catches fire and is badly burnt, as is Pip when he saves her.

Meanwhile, Pip and Herbert try to help Magwitch escape by boat but Compeyson tips the police off and they are interrupted. In the confusion on the water, Compeyson drowns and Magwitch is sentenced to death. In prison, Magwitch falls ill and dies, finally at peace with the world after Pip tells him about Estella. Pip himself then falls ill and Joe comes up to London to look after him. When Pip is better, he asks for Joe's forgiveness and it is duly granted. Joe then happily marries Biddy, the woman who has been looking after him since his first wife fell ill and died. Miss Havisham dies, leaving a large part of her fortune to Herbert's family. Pip then goes abroad, working in the mercantile trade. One day, upon his return, he visits the remains of Satis House. There he finds Estella, who is now a widow. Together they leave the house for the last time. Pip sees 'no shadow of another parting from her'.

THEMES AND TECHNIQUES

Great Expectations tenders the relatively straightforward message that being wealthy does not make you happy. Pip harbours 'great expectations' for himself from an early age. Left dissatisfied with an ordinary working life following his infatuation with Estella, Pip's moral growth is stunted just as his material life

takes off. He makes great social advances in ways that would no doubt have appealed to Dickens's increasingly socially mobile readership, but he does so at the expense of forgetting and alienating his origins. Furthermore, the 'uncommon' class he aspires to join is seemingly populated with characters warped by their ability to use money to divorce themselves from common life. Compeyson and Miss Havisham are the measure of this class, and it is only when Pip is left all but penniless again that he resumes his moral education and comes to appreciate the value of an uncommon soul over and above an uncommon set of clothes. Indeed, Dickens originally wished to leave Pip in a more chastened condition at the end of the novel by having Estella marry someone else. He was, however, persuaded that Pip had suffered enough and rewrote it to leave his hero sober but happy.

Further Reading

Carlisle, Janice (ed.), *Case Studies in 'Great Expectations' by Charles Dickens*. New York: St Martin's Press, 1995. This book includes a number of interesting analyses of *Great Expectations*, including a look at the alternative endings of the novel.

Tredell, Nicholas (ed.), *Charles Dickens – 'Great Expectations'*. London: Palgrave Macmillan, 2000. This book examines the history of criticism of the novel from its publication up until the 1990s.

GULLIVER'S TRAVELS (1726)
by Jonathan Swift

For, it is plain, that every word we speak is in some degree a diminution of our lungs by corrosion; and consequently contributes to the shortening of our lives. An expedient was therefore offered, that since words are only names for things, it would be more convenient for all men to carry about them, such things as were necessary to express the particular business they are to discourse on.

The novel *Gulliver's Travels* follows the adventures of Lemuel Gulliver, a ship's surgeon, as he travels to unknown places around the globe. All of the various places Gulliver visits offer a satirical bearing upon the world of human beings, both in the eighteenth century and now.

Summary

Told from the hero's point of view, *Gulliver's Travels* begins with Gulliver being shipwrecked. When he awakes, he finds that he is pinioned to the ground with innumerable threads. He soon discovers that he is in Lilliput, a land whose inhabitants are tiny. As Gulliver is, by comparison, a giant he is treated with some degree of reverence by the Lilliputians; indeed, after the Lilliputians have established a strict set of rules to govern Gulliver's conduct, he becomes an honoured member of their society. His status only increases when he goes into battle against the Lilliputians' equally diminutive foes – the people of Blefuscu. Having helped to defeat Blefuscu, he then helps to secure them better terms of peace. This makes him unpopular in Lilliput, an unpopularity which is compounded when he puts out a fire at the royal palace by urinating on it. For this crime he is sentenced to be shot in the eyes with poisoned arrows. Gulliver escapes to Blefuscu, and from there to England.

> Written with a caustic wit, *Gulliver's Travels* is a satire of the human condition as much as it is an allegory of eighteenth-century politics. The madness of the world that Gulliver discovers is summed up by the famous scientist who 'had been eight years upon a project for extracting sunbeams out of cucumbers, which were to be put into vials hermetically sealed, and let out to warm the air in raw, inclement summers.'

Anxious to return to his adventures, Gulliver soon joins another ship. This time, after an eventful voyage he find himself in Brobdingnag. Here the people are all giants to him and he is effectively a Lilliputian. After spending a short time as the amusing pet of a farmer, Gulliver is sold to the royal court where he leads a fairly comfortable life. However, he is sickened by the physicality of the Brobdingnagians whose size magnifies features, such as their mole hairs, to an enormous extent, making them unbearable to Gulliver. He is also constantly under threat from the wildlife of the country and, while planning an escape, he is picked up in his box by a bird and dropped into the sea. After a short while, he is rescued by an English boat and taken home again.

Despite his wife's entreaties to stay at home, Gulliver soon sets off on another voyage. After becoming entangled with some pirates, Gulliver finds himself hauled up to the floating island of Laputa. Run by academics, the inhabitants of this island are so distracted they require 'flappers' to hit them on the mouth and ears to remind them to continue any conversation in which they are engaged. Gulliver soon tires of them and travels to the neighbouring Balnibarbi, where the scientists are engaged in useful activities like extracting sunshine from cucumbers and reducing human excrement to its original food components. He then sails to Glubbdubdrib, where the inhabitants are magicians who can call up the dead to serve them, and from there to Luggnagg, where a proportion of the population grow old but never die. After this, Gulliver sails to Japan and then returns home to England.

He is then asked to become captain of a ship and sets sail for the final time. However, Gulliver's crew soon mutiny against him and, after a short imprisonment, set him down in an unknown land. Here he encounters the Houyhnhnms, horses who rule the land, and the Yahoos, ape-like people who scavenge around the Houyhnhnms. Gulliver soon learns that the Houyhnhnms are blessed with grace and wisdom and, after learning their language, he explains to them the institutions and practices of England while they share knowledge of theirs with him. However, as he is not a Houyhnhnm, he is asked to leave their country and he makes a canoe and travels to a nearby island where he is picked up by a Portuguese ship and eventually taken home. When he returns, Gulliver finds that people remind him too much of Yahoos and that he now prefers the company of horses.

THEMES AND TECHNIQUES

In *Gulliver's Travels*, SWIFT sets himself the mammoth task of dissecting the human condition itself. Although many of the scenarios in the novel are allegories relating to eighteenth-century politics (Lilliput and Blefuscu, for example, can be read as England and France respectively), they can also be read as more general portraits of any society. The diminutive size of the Lilliputians is a literal realisation of the pettiness of certain types of politics, the very type of politics that leads them into a war with people who break their eggs open at the small end. On the other hand, the enormous size of the Brobdingnagians is expressive of human generosity. Contrasted with both of these are the Laputan scientists, whose concerns are so esoteric that they need reminding when to speak and listen. Swift offsets these theoretical concerns with the ever-pervasive images of excrement, reminding us that however rational and high-minded we might become, like the Houyhnhnms, we are always also grounded in our own bodies, like the Yahoos, and are thus human in a material sense that precedes our ability to extract sunshine from cucumbers.

Further Reading

Knowles, Ronald, *'Gulliver's Travels': Politics of Satire*. New York: Twayne Publishers, 1996. This book examines the nature of the satire in Swift's novel.

Swift, Jonathan, *Jonathan Swift's 'Gulliver's Travels'*. Edited by Albert J. Rivero. New York: W.W. Norton, 2002. This edition of the novel takes the authoritative 1726 text as its basis. It also provides a valuable compilation of contextual documents, as well as a collection of critiques of the novel.

HAMLET, PRINCE OF DENMARK (1600–01)
by William Shakespeare

To be, or not to be: that is the question:
Whether 'tis nobler in the mind to suffer
The slings and arrows of outrageous
fortune,
Or to take arms against a sea of troubles,
And by opposing end them?

Hamlet is one of the greatest and most popular plays ever written in the English language. It is often said to have heralded a change in the way drama was written, marking the point at which fully rounded characterisation took over from stereotypes. At its heart, it is a revenge tragedy following the fortunes of Hamlet, the young Prince of Denmark, in the aftermath of his father's murder.

Summary

Hamlet begins with a sighting of the ghost of Hamlet's father on the castle ramparts of Elsinore. Hamlet's father was the King of Denmark until he died, apparently by the bite of a poisonous snake. His brother Claudius now rules in his stead and has even married his wife, Queen Gertrude. Hamlet, Gertrude's son, is extremely unhappy that she has married Claudius so soon after his father's death. When Hamlet eventually gets to speak to the ghost, he is told that Hamlet's father was in fact murdered by Claudius. The ghost then instructs Hamlet to seek revenge on his father's behalf in order that his spirit may find peace.

Hamlet agrees to exact vengeance but almost immediately begins to meditate upon his mission, rather than following it through. Hamlet's overly thoughtful and melancholic disposition causes Gertrude and Claudius to suppose that Hamlet is in fact in love with Ophelia. Ophelia is the daughter of Polonius, the pompous Lord Chamberlain, and the sister of Laertes, who is sent to study in France. Although there is some lingering affection between Hamlet and Ophelia, Hamlet is so bitter about his mother's marriage to his uncle that he rebuffs Ophelia and advises her to join a nunnery.

When a group of travelling actors comes to Elsinore, Hamlet pays them to perform a short play in front of Claudius imitating the way his father was really killed. At the moment of the murder, Claudius gets up and leaves, thus confirming Hamlet in his belief that his uncle actually did kill his father. Pursuing Claudius to his chamber, Hamlet is prepared to slay the king but finds him at prayer and he therefore decides that Claudius would go to his death at peace with the world, unlike his father, and he leaves him for another time. Claudius, now fearful of his nephew's madness, determines to send Hamlet to England where he plots to have him killed. In the meantime, Hamlet goes to his mother's bedroom to confront her. Hearing a noise behind the curtain, Hamlet believes it to be the king and stabs at him with his sword. It is actually Polonius and Hamlet has killed him. Hamlet is dispatched to England for this crime. Ophelia, meanwhile, is driven to despair by her father's death and drowns in the river.

> Arguably the greatest play ever written, *Hamlet* is a revenge tragedy in which the eponymous Prince of Denmark seeks retribution for the murder of his father. Charged with passion, intrigue and treachery, it is a play that questions what we know and how we know it.

Upon hearing of his father's death, Laertes returns from France and finds that his sister is dead as well. When Claudius learns that Hamlet has escaped from his death-trap in England and is about to return to Denmark, he takes advantage of Laertes' anger at these deaths and persuades him to exact revenge on Hamlet. His plan is to challenge him to a fencing match using poisoned swords. As a back-up, Claudius also poisons a goblet which he aims to offer to Hamlet. When the fencing begins, Laertes stabs Hamlet with the poisoned rapier but then a scuffle ensues in which he exchanges swords with Laertes who is himself then wounded by the poisoned sword. During the fight, Claudius offers Hamlet the poisoned goblet but Gertrude takes it instead and is almost immediately killed. At her death, Laertes confesses to the plan and in response Hamlet stabs Claudius with the poisoned sword and then makes him drink from the goblet too. Claudius dies instantly, followed shortly by Laertes and finally Hamlet himself.

THEMES AND TECHNIQUES

Although *Hamlet* is a revenge tragedy, the actual act of revenge is famously delayed right until the end of the play. What concerns Hamlet and the other characters in the interim is the question of certainty. The play begins with a moment of uncertainty – 'Who's there?' – and continues in the same questioning vein thereafter. Is the ghost really the old king? Was he really murdered by Claudius? Can Hamlet discern Claudius's guilt just by observing him? All these questions centre upon what can be known for sure. In their quest for certainty, most of the characters in the play indulge in acts of espionage of some sort, from Hamlet spying on Claudius at prayer, to the tragic eavesdropping of Polonius on Hamlet in Gertrude's chamber. The only certainty in the play is that no one is ever alone. Even Hamlet's private thoughts, expressed in the most famous soliloquy of all time ('To be or not to be'), are actually overheard by those 'lawful espials' Claudius and Polonius. All this spying, however, fails to yield the knowledge that the spies seek. Even the greatest certainty of them all – death – reveals itself to be an 'undiscovered country' in which, as Hamlet's father proves, one can both be dead and somehow alive at the same time.

The structure and language of *Hamlet* is built upon a series of doublings. Apart from the more obvious pairs of characters, such as the interchangeable Rosencrantz and Guildenstern, or Cornelius and Voltemand, or the two clowns, there are also roles which are doubled up. For example, both Hamlet and Laertes are sons of murdered fathers seeking revenge. Similarly, the role of Hamlet's father is played both by his actual father and by Claudius – 'my cousin Hamlet, and my son' he avers at one point. Even the very atoms of dust double up, being at one moment Alexander the Great, and the next a stopper in a beer barrel. This structural doubling is joined by a similar effect at the level of language. Either the actual words are repeated (for example, 'one may smile, and smile, and be a villain') or a word is part of a pair joined by a conjunction (such as, 'slow *and* stately', 'true *and* good'). This compulsive doubling in the play may ultimately find its cause in the incestuous role of Gertrude. As Claudius comments, she is 'our sometimes sister, now our queen'. It is a problem that perplexes Hamlet and he spends proportionately more lines musing on the questionable role of his mother than he does on the death of his father. As he notes before he sails for England, 'My mother – father and mother is man and wife, man and wife is one flesh, and so, my mother.'

Further Reading

Cantor, Paul Arthur, *Shakespeare: Hamlet*. London and New York: Cambridge University

Press, 1989. This interesting volume examines the delay in Hamlet's revenge in its cultural context, as well as looking at the techniques in the play, and its overall reception.

Coyle, Martin, *New Casebook Studies: 'Hamlet'*. London and New York: Palgrave Macmillan, 1992. This advanced volume brings together a series of essays looking at *Hamlet*. It compares and contrasts older ways of analysing the play with newer, more theoretically inclined models.

Skakespeare, William, *Hamlet*. Edited by Harold Jenkins. London: The Arden Shakespeare, 2001. This is one of the best available editions of the play. It includes a fascinating introduction to the history of the play and a very detailed set of notes.

HARD TIMES (1854)
by Charles Dickens

Now what I want is, Facts. Teach these boys and girls nothing but Facts. Facts alone are wanted in life. Plant nothing else, and root out everything else. You can only form the minds of reasoning animals upon Facts: nothing else will ever be of service to them.

Hard Times is DICKENS's most biting critique of Victorian working conditions. The novel tells the story of Stephen Blackpool and Louisa Gradgrind and how their lives are altered by a society that values wealth over well-being.

Summary

The novel begins with Thomas Gradgrind espousing his philosophy of rationalism and hard fact. Gradgrind is a leading citizen of Coketown, a northern industrial city, and he has five children, including Tom and Louisa, whom he has brought up to disregard imagination and emotion, and respect only facts. Catching Tom and Louisa at the circus, he blames one of their schoolmates, Sissy Jupe. As Sissy's father has run away, he offers to become her guardian and thereby save her from a life of fancy. Josiah Bounderby, a factory and bank owner in the town, disagrees with Gradgrind's offer to Sissy. He constantly reminds people how he was nothing but a poor deserted child who worked his way up to wealth and how indulging poor people sends them rotten.

As Bounderby and Gradgrind are friends and as Bounderby is similarly devoid of sentiment, Gradgrind tenders a deal with Bounderby whereby he will marry Louisa and Tom will work in his bank. Everyone seems happy with this idea apart from Louisa, but her father dismisses her objections as fanciful. A year after the marriage, the aristocratic James Harthouse comes to Coketown to work for Gradgrind's political party. Harthouse divines that all is not perfect between Bounderby and Louisa, and he attempts to seduce her.

Meanwhile, one of the factory workers, Stephen Blackpool, is in love with Rachael, another worker. However, the two are obliged to remain apart while Stephen is still married to his wife, a dissolute woman who disappears for months at a time. When Stephen asks Bounderby about whether he may get a divorce, Bounderby advises him that such things are only for the wealthy. Stephen's troubles are compounded when he learns that the other factory workers want to form a union to strike. He refuses to join, but he also refuses to spy on his workmates when Bounderby asks him. The result of this is that he is sacked by Bounderby and disowned by his friends. When Louisa hears of this she is impressed by Stephen's integrity and seeks him out to give him some money. Tom accompanies Louisa to see Stephen and, when she has left the room, advises him to wait outside the bank every night for the next few nights in the hope of good fortune.

When nothing happens, Stephen leaves Coketown. Shortly afterwards, the bank is robbed and Stephen becomes the prime suspect because he was seen waiting outside over the previous few nights. Louisa suspects Tom, but in the meantime she is overcome at the failure of her marriage to Bounderby and her relationship with Harthouse. Throwing herself on her father's mercy, she regales him with bringing her up as an automaton, disconnected from her emotions and devoid of imagination. Distraught at what he has done to his daughter and at the failure of his philosophy, Gradgrind resolves to take her in. Sissy then goes to Harthouse and persuades him to leave Coketown and put Louisa behind him.

Stephen, meanwhile, tries to return to Coketown in order to clear his name but falls down a disused mine shaft. Rachael and Louisa find him and organise a rescue effort, but Stephen dies anyway. An employee of Bounderby drags in an old woman who knew Stephen for questioning but Bounderby recoils when he sees her because it is actually his mother. It transpires that she did not desert him as a child, but that he had forbidden her to visit him. Elsewhere, realising that Tom is actually the culprit responsible for robbing the bank, Gradgrind, Louisa and Sissy help him escape abroad using Sissy's contacts in the circus. Tom eventually dies there, never seeing his family again. Gradgrind devotes himself to charitable works while Bounderby dies alone. Only Sissy ends up happy with a loving family, although Louisa becomes a favourite visitor doing her best to rediscover her imagination.

> *Hard Times* was Dickens's most direct attack on the form of capitalism which dominated Britain at the time and which gave rise to the kind of massive inequities that scar his characters.

THEMES AND TECHNIQUES

Perhaps more so than with any other of his novels, the reader of *Hard Times* is left in no doubt as to what Dickens thinks of his characters and their actions. He rails against the industrialisation of Victorian England, which leaves such a large percentage of the population living and working in a form of grimy, inane hell, and, more particularly, he launches a scathing (if ultimately conservative) attack on the philosophies that support such rampant capitalism. The most hated of these philosophies is the sort of rational utilitarianism advanced by Gradgrind and Bounderby, where the only things that matter are facts, and specifically facts which can be put to the service of making money. The structure of *Hard Times* invites us to see what happens when a generation is raised on a form of thought which values quantity over quality. At the beginning of the novel, the part entitled 'Sowing', we are shown this ruthless form of

thought being inculcated into children. In the following two parts, 'Reaping' and 'Garnering', the novel depicts the harvest that comes from such an education and it is almost uniformly grim, leaving most of the characters either dead or in a state of permanent repentance.

Further Reading

Dickens, Charles, *Charles Dickens' 'Hard Times'*. Edited by Fred Kaplan and Sylvere Monod. New York: W.W. Norton, 2000. This new edition of the novel provides a valuable compilation of contextual documents, as well as a collection of critiques of the novel.

Simpson, Margaret, *The Companion to 'Hard Times'*. New York: Greenwood Publishing, 1997. This book is a fascinating companion to Dickens's novel, enabling you to cross-reference it with explanations about everything from the meaning of contemporary phrases and politics, to foods and fashion.

HEART OF DARKNESS (1901)
by Joseph Conrad

The horror! The horror!

CONRAD's short novel recounts the story of Marlow, the captain of a boat sent deep into the Belgian Congo. While there, Marlow meets Mr Kurtz and through him encounters the 'heart of darkness'.

Summary

The story begins with Marlow on a boat in the River Thames, waiting for the tide to turn. He recounts a story from his own time as a seaman. While looking for a ship one time, Marlow is directed towards a Belgian company trading ivory in Africa. He is offered the job of piloting a steamboat on a river and, after having taken a medical, he sets off for his new job. When Marlow arrives in Africa he is struck by the brutality of the conditions the Europeans impose upon the Africans working for them. He is appalled by what he sees as a 'flabby, pretending, weak-eyed devil of a rapacious and pitiless folly' and is inclined to think of it as a warning of what is to come.

While waiting at the first company station for a caravan to take him upriver, Marlow meets the company's chief accountant. Marlow is impressed by him because amidst all the death, disease and general lassitude, the accountant manages to keep wearing starched collars and properly ironed shirts. The accountant also gives Marlow his first hint as to the nature of Mr Kurtz. Kurtz is apparently an agent who sends as much ivory downriver as the rest of the company's agents combined. He is apparently 'a remarkable person'.

> Intended as an attack on the system of imperialism, Conrad's *Heart of Darkness* also created one of the most potent figures of modern fiction in the character of the atavistic Kurtz.

After fifteen days struggling through the jungle on foot, Marlow arrives at the Central Station. He is immediately informed that the steamer which he was supposed to captain lies at the bottom of the river. The general manager, a man who keeps his post because he is the only one who can also keep his health, informs him that Kurtz may well be sick. It is imperative that Marlow retrieves the boat from the bottom of the river and fix it as soon as possible. This, however, takes some time and Marlow is increasingly filled with foreboding about the journey he will soon undertake.

When he is finally able to depart for the Inner Station, Kurtz is more of a myth than a man to Marlow but he finds himself inexplicably drawn to him. He is therefore devastated when the boat is attacked from the shore by arrows being shot from amidst the trees and everyone assumes that Kurtz has been killed by a similar attack. However, just before the manager orders the boat to turn back, they stumble onto the Inner station. There they are greeted by a Russian dressed as a harlequin who informs them that the attack on the boat was organised in the hope that they would leave Kurtz alone, assuming he was dead.

When Marlow finally meets Kurtz, it soon becomes clear that Kurtz is very ill. He is obsessed with his plans and often delirious. However, after trying to run away, Kurtz is put aboard Marlow's boat and they set off for the Central Station. After entrusting his papers to Marlow, including a document on civilising the indigenous population (which ends with the phrase, 'Exterminate all the brutes!'), Kurtz dies. His last words are, 'The horror! The horror!' When Marlow returns to Europe, he visits Kurtz's fiancée. Despite declaring a hatred for lies, Marlow tells her that Kurtz's last words were actually her name.

THEMES AND TECHNIQUES

Heart of Darkness is based, to some degree, on CONRAD's own experience in the Belgian Congo Free State, one of the foulest and most corrupt regimes ever installed. In this regard, his book stands as an indictment not just of that particular colony, but also of the whole project of imperialism. Initially believing in the justness of the European colonial mission, Marlow soon finds that the imperial cause is hollow to the core, wreaking a brutal cost on the indigenous populations of Africa. Thus as Marlow travels deeper and deeper into the heart of the mystery of Africa, he finds not enlightenment, or the just results of a cause, but increasing darkness. Darkness is a pervasive symbol in the novel, often referring to malevolence. As the lack of a definite article (a 'the') in the title suggests, the 'heart' of darkness cannot be easily located and confined to one place, for it is everywhere. The darkness of the terrible deeds performed in Africa in the name of European civilisation return to Europe and render that dark too. Interestingly, Conrad's own critique of imperialism has been turned against him since he wrote the novel. In particular, the great Nigerian author Chinua Achebe has charged Conrad with treating Africans in the novel as though they were primitive beings lacking their own culture.

Further Reading

Conrad, Joseph, *'Heart of Darkness': An Authoritative Text, Backgrounds and Sources, Criticism*. Edited by Robert Kimbrough. New York: W.W. Norton, 1988. This edition (which sometimes goes under other names) of *Heart of Darkness* provides a valuable compilation of contextual documents, as well as a collection of critiques of the novel, including Achebe's influential assessment.

Conrad, Joseph, 'Heart of Darkness' and Selection from the Congo Diary. Edited by Caryl Philips. New York: Modern Library, 1999. This edition of the novel also includes a selection from Conrad's diary, recording his impressions of the Congo when he worked there.

HOUSE OF THE SEVEN GABLES, THE (1851)
by Nathaniel Hawthorne

Man's own youth is the world's youth; at least he feels as if it were, and imagines that the earth's granite substance is something not yet hardened, and which he can mould into whatever shape he likes.

Initially set in Puritan New England, *The House of the Seven Gables* is a novel that tells the story of a building seemingly fated with ill-luck. Each successive generation apparently bequeaths its own bad fortune on to the next until the cycle is finally broken.

Summary

The house of the seven gables is a property originally built by Colonel Pyncheon. It is erected on land that the Colonel acquired by accusing its former owner, Matthew Maule, of witchcraft. As Maule is preparing to be executed, he curses the Colonel. Ignoring this, the Colonel continues with his plan to build the house with the seven gables, even using Maule's son to help him. When it is finished, the Colonel holds a big party at which he is found dead in his study. After his death, it is discovered that an enormous land deed is missing from the Colonel's effects. From that moment onwards, the Pyncheon family is doomed, each successive generation placing its hopes on finding the missing deed.

The present generation of Pyncheons is already suffering from bad luck when the novel begins. Clifford Pyncheon is in prison for murdering his uncle, although there is a suggestion that his conviction is unfounded, and Hepzibah is now too poor to live the life of a lady and is forced to open a shop selling cheap goods. She also has a lodger in the house of seven gables, a daguerreotypist, or early photographer, called Holgrave. They are soon joined by Phoebe, an optimistic and good-natured teenager who is Hepzibah's cousin. One day he tells Phoebe about the Pyncheon family history.

In particular, Holgrave tells Phoebe the story of Alice Pyncheon. She was the daughter of Colonel Pyncheon's grandson, Gervayse Pyncheon. At one time he had summoned the grandson of Matthew Maule, also called Matthew Maule, in order to tell him what had happened to the lost land deed which Gervayse claimed the younger Matthew Maule's father had hidden in revenge for the death of his father, the original Matthew Maule. The younger Matthew Maule agrees to help but only if the land originally belonging to the Maule family is returned to him. Maule then asks Gervayse to see his daughter Alice, whom he then hypnotises and through her contacts the spirit of Colonel Pyncheon. However, Pyncheon is prevented from revealing the secret by the ghosts of Maule's father and grandfather, so the deal is cancelled. Nevertheless, Alice remains under Maule's spell and he mistreats her, causing her to catch pneumonia and die. When Holgrave finishes telling the story, he realises he has hypnotised Phoebe, but he immediately snaps her out of it.

Hawthorne's *House of the Seven Gables* examines the power of fiction to change lives by showing how a curse is continually blamed for the misfortunes of several generations of the same family.

Shortly afterwards, Judge Pyncheon, the effective reincarnation of Colonel Pyncheon, comes to visit the house to see Clifford. Clifford has been let out of prison but after so long inside he is close to a mental breakdown. Hepzibah refuses to let the intimidating Judge see Clifford, but he threatens to have Clifford locked up again if she does not relent. She tries to find Clifford but when she returns to the Judge, he is dead and Clifford is there too. Thinking that Clifford will be imprisoned again, Hepzibah flees the scene with him. However, when they return, Holgrave assures them that the Judge, like his forebears, died of a stroke. He also reveals that he is a descendant of Matthew Maule and can produce the deed everyone has been looking for. As the Judge's son is dead, Clifford, Hepzibah and Phoebe become the rightful heirs to his fortune and are finally able to leave the house of the seven gables behind.

THEMES AND TECHNIQUES

At first sight the central theme of *The House of the Seven Gables* seems fairly clear: the sins of one generation will be visited upon the next. Colonel Pyncheon's greed causes him to be cursed with a bloody death and every succeeding generation feels the consequences of it. However, Hawthorne undermines this notion by highlighting the way in which the generations meet their doom. They all suffer because they are essentially covetous of that which they do not have. Gervayse's life is perfectly happy until he attempts to find the missing deed and ends up indirectly causing the death of his daughter. Similarly, the deaths of the Pyncheon men are caused by a hereditary disposition towards strokes, not a blood curse. What the novel points to therefore is the discrepancy between facts and the stories used to explain them. HAWTHORNE declares in the preface to *The House of the Seven Gables* that it is more of a romance than a novel because it does not adhere strictly to the truth but brightens the light and deepens the shade a little more than a novel would. In other words, it is about the power of stories to change the meaning of events. In the same way as Hepzibah's scowl makes her appear to be miserable when really she just suffers from poor eyesight, so the story of the curse changes the way events appear to the characters, causing them to misinterpret their own lives.

Further Reading

Buitenhuis, Peter, *'The House of the Seven Gables': Severing Family and Colonial Ties*. New York: Twayne Publishers, 1991. This book examines the historical context of Hawthorne's novel, as well as offering a detailed look at its structure and meaning.

Rosenthal, Bernard (ed.), *Critical Essays on Nathaniel Hawthorne's 'The House of the Seven Gables'*. New York: Macmillan, 1995. This collection of essays follows the critical fortunes of *The House of the Seven Gables* since its publication.

IMPORTANCE OF BEING EARNEST, THE (1895)
by Oscar Wilde

I dislike arguments of any kind. They are always vulgar, and often convincing.

The Importance of Being Earnest is a witty comedy set in the drawing rooms of late nineteenth-century England. It follows the progress of Jack and Algernon as they use the name of 'Earnest' in order to get married.

Summary

The play opens with Algernon Moncrieff at home. While he awaits for the arrival of his aunt, Lady Bracknell, and her daughter, Gwendolen, he is unexpectedly visited by Ernest Worthing. Ernest announces his intention of proposing to Gwendolen, with whom he is in love. However, Algernon declares that as her guardian, he cannot allow her to marry Ernest until he can explain the inscription inside Ernest's cigarette case: 'From little Cecily, with her fondest love to her dear Uncle Jack'.

Ernest declares that he is, in fact, called Jack. He pretends to be Ernest when he goes to town, but he is Jack in the country. He does this because he is guardian to Cecily Cardew in the country and wishes to set a good example to her. In order to pursue a more dissolute life, he invented a younger brother called Ernest who gets into terrible scrapes thereby requiring Jack to travel into town where he is free from the constraints of being Cecily's guardian. Algernon informs Jack that he is a 'Bunburyist'. Bunbury is the name of Algernon's fictitious friend who is permanently invalided, thereby allowing Algernon an excuse to go to the country whenever he wants.

When Lady Bracknell and Gwendolen arrive at Algernon's flat, Jack seizes the opportunity to propose to Gwendolen. She agrees, partly on the basis that his name is Ernest, which she mistakenly believes it to be. Lady Bracknell, however, does not consent to the marriage because Jack was found in a handbag at a railway station and therefore cannot prove his parentage.

The action then moves to Jack's house in the country. Despite Jack refusing to give him the address, Algernon goes to Jack's house pretending to be his dissolute brother Ernest in order that he might meet Cecily. When Jack returns from the town, he announces that Ernest has died before he realises that Algernon is there pretending to be his recently deceased brother. Angry with Algernon, Jack demands that he leave. Algernon agrees but only if Jack changes out of his mourning clothes first. This gives Algernon just enough time to propose to Cecily who accepts, but largely because his name is Ernest. Temporarily left alone, Cecily encounters Gwendolen and they quickly realise that they are engaged to the same Ernest. When Jack and Algernon return, they explain that they have both lied. The women then retreat into the house to await the arrival of the 'real' Ernest.

> Despite being, as Wilde described it, a play 'written by a butterfly for butterflies', *The Importance of Being Earnest* also manages to turn all its wit to account by highlighting the inverted value system of Victorian social codes.

Inside the house, the men explain that they are willing to get themselves re-christened as 'Ernest' and this seems to satisfy Cecily and Gwendolen. By the time the vicar arrives, however, Lady Bracknell has intervened to stop the wedding from progressing. As he himself cannot marry, Jack refuses Cecily permission to marry Algernon. The vicar then announces he has an appointment with a Miss Prism, Cecily's tutor. Intrigued by the name, Lady Bracknell calls the woman in and declares that she had been the maid to her sister. It transpires that Prism had accidentally left Jack in a handbag in Victoria Station. Jack is therefore really Algernon's elder brother and his real name is also Ernest. There are now no further obstacles to the marriages.

THEMES AND TECHNIQUES

Wilde described *The Importance of Being Earnest* as a play 'written by a butterfly for butterflies'. It certainly displays a sustained interest in

superficiality, but, by doing so, it makes a serious point about social mores. For, throughout the play, Wilde contrasts the importance attached to how things appear with the value of the thing itself. The most obvious example of this is the name of 'Ernest'. Both Gwendolen and Cecily agree to marry because they are inspired by the soundness of the name, rather than the value of either of the bearers of the pseudonym. The inference Wilde wished us to take here may well be that upper-class Victorian society was earnest about the wrong things. In Wilde's case, one of those things was marriage itself. His own marriage was a sham to conceal the homosexuality which would eventually land him in prison. Some more recent readings of the play argue that 'Bunburying' is a coded reference to the dual existence lived by homosexuals at a time when being gay was illegal.

Further Reading

Raby, Peter, *'The Importance of Being Earnest': A Reader's Companion*. New York: Twayne Publishers, 1996. Written by one of the leading experts on Wilde and this play in particular, Raby's book examines the historical context of *The Importance of Being Earnest*, as well as offering a detailed look at its structure and meaning.

Siebold, Thomas (ed.), *Readings on 'The Importance of Being Earnest'*. San Diego: Greenhaven Press, 2001. This book includes a biography of Wilde as well as a number of critical essays on the play.

INCIDENTS IN THE LIFE OF A SLAVE GIRL (1861)
by Harriet Jacobs

> *Reader, my story ends with freedom; not in the usual way, with marriage. I and my children are now free! We are as free from the power of slaveholders as are the white people of the north; and though that according to my ideas, is not saying a great deal, it is a vast improvement in my condition.*

JACOBS's short book is a semi-autobiographical account of her life as a slave. It tells the story of Linda Brent from her birth to her escape and freedom just before the commencement of the Civil War.

Summary

Although Linda Brent is born in slavery to slaves, it is only when she is 6 years old that she realises that she actually is a slave. At that age, her mother dies and Linda is taken into the home of her mother's mistress. Unusually, she is taught to read and write, but when Linda is not quite 12 her mistress dies, and she is bequeathed to her mistress's niece, a child of only 5 years of age. This places Linda under the control of the girl's father, Dr Flint. As Linda grows to adulthood, Flint continually threatens her with his unwanted sexual advances, advances which she evades by ever more ingenious means. For his part, Flint refuses to countenance the idea of Linda marrying the man that she loves. On top of this, Linda is also subject to the spite of Flint's wife who is piqued with jealousy at her husband's interest in Linda. The fraught bondage of Linda to Flint eventually comes to the notice of an unmarried lawyer, Mr Sands. His interest in Linda is encouraged by her as a defence against Flint. The two of them begin to have a relationship and, in desperation, Linda bears him two children, Ellen and Benny.

> *Incidents in the Life of a Slave Girl* is a thinly disguised autobiographical account of the experiences of Harriet Jacobs as a slave and as a fugitive. Designed to persuade people of the evils of slavery, Jacobs's work was unusual in its emphasis on the female experience of slavery.

All this time Flint continues to threaten and abuse Linda, refusing to sell her to Sands. Infuriated by her refusal to accept his offer of living in a lonely cottage at his whim, Flint finally sends her to a plantation to be 'broken in'. Linda manages to escape and hides at her grandmother's house in exceedingly cramped conditions. During this time she is not able to have proper contact with her children, even when Benny is savaged by a dog, because they are constantly subject to the blandishments of Flint, as he tries to bribe or cajole them into

revealing what they know of her whereabouts. For seven years she watches the world through a tiny hole, only coming out on rare occasions, on one of which she is nearly caught.

Eventually, Flint gives up looking for Linda and sells her children to Sands. Linda then escapes by boat with a friend to the Free States in the north of America. Life is better if far from perfect in the North until the government introduces the Fugitive Slave Law, allowing bounty hunters to pursue escaped slaves that much more aggressively. Linda is forced to leave New York for a while as she hears Flint is still looking for her, but eventually Linda's employer, Mrs Bruce, buys Linda's freedom from Flint's daughter's husband. Although unhappy that she has to be bought at all, Linda is at last free and feels a great burden lifted from her shoulders.

THEMES AND TECHNIQUES

Slavery was the dominant issue of nineteenth-century America, and one that featured prominently in all the major works of the time, including MARK TWAIN's THE ADVENTURES OF HUCKLEBERRY FINN and HARRIET BEECHER STOWE's UNCLE TOM'S CABIN. Slave narratives (stories told by slaves about slavery) were designed to promote an awareness of the conditions of slavery in the north of America and in Great Britain, where slavery was outlawed. In particular they were designed to persuade white people of the terrible suffering imposed by slavery. Part of the value of Jacobs's narrative lies in the way it addresses women specifically. Through the whole account, Jacobs foregrounds the moral challenges of being a female slave and being subject to the lust of a male slave owner. She also highlights her concern for her children, the sacrifices she is prepared to make for them, and how she suffers during the seven-year period she spends in hiding not being able to be with them. In doing this, Jacobs makes a clear and effective distinction between her torment and the life of white women of the time.

Further Reading

Garfield, Deborah and Zafar, Rafia (eds), *'Incidents in the Life of a Slave Girl: New Critical Essays.* London: Cambridge University Press, 1996. This collection of essays provides a modern look at the book, including analyses of gender and spirituality.

Harriet, Jacobs, *Incidents in the Life of a Slave Girl*. Edited by N. Y. McKay and F. Smith Foster. New York: W.W. Norton, 2001. This edition of the novel also includes a selection from Jacobs's letters, a chronology, contemporary responses to the book and criticism since.

IN MEMORIAM (1850)
by Alfred Lord Tennyson

Nature, red in tooth and claw.

Written for the early death of his friend Arthur Hallam, *In Memoriam* is the poem which established TENNYSON's reputation with both the public and the critics. It details Tennyson's feelings of loss for Hallam and develops them into a broader theme as the poet struggles to maintain his faith in the face of such needless death.

Summary

In Memoriam is perhaps unique in the canon of English literature. It is a collection of 131 poems which combine to recount the development of Tennyson's grief for his friend Arthur Hallam, who suddenly died when he was only 22 years old. Indeed, Hallam was more than just Tennyson's friend, he was also his sister's fiancé and a strong supporter of Tennyson's poetry. When Hallam died, therefore, Tennyson not only began to doubt the concept of a benevolent design to the universe, but he also lost faith in his own poetic talent without Hallam to champion it. *In Memoriam* records Tennyson's struggle with his misgivings about the world and his eventual triumph over those qualms and fears. In this sense, the collection of poems that make up *In Memoriam* are essentially progressive, moving towards a point where things change for the better. However, there is great deal of vacillation before this point is reached and the poems move back and forth across different shades of despair.

The structure of *In Memoriam* is also underwritten by a loose chronology. The initial shock and grief following Hallam's death is overtaken by a consideration of the practicalities of death as Hallam's body is brought back from Vienna on the River Danube and then buried in Somerset on the River Severn.

Tennyson even realises he was writing a letter to Hallam at the moment his friend died. The rest of *In Memoriam* is based around the three Christmases following Hallam's death. In the first Christmas, starting in section 28, Tennyson wonders 'how dare we keep our Christmas eve'. By the following year, and having been through perhaps his keenest moments of doubt in the intervening period, Tennyson finds that, in section 78, he is once more able to participate in the festive routines. This does not mean that his sorrow has waned, but rather that 'with long use her tears are dry'. By the third Christmas after Hallam's death, beginning in section 104, Tennyson and his family have moved house and with the sound of unfamiliar bells pealing to commemorate the birth of Christ, Tennyson has a sense of being freed from reminders of the past and of beginning again. This new dawn comes to a culmination with the wedding of his sister to Edmund Lushington, a ceremony Tennyson records in an Epilogue in which he looks forward to the birth of their child.

> Written in the wake of the death of his close friend Arthur Hallam, *In Memoriam* is a collection of 131 poems recording the different stages of Tennyson's grief. Deeply personal as well as embracing universal concerns, this was the work that established Tennyson as the foremost poet of his generation.

THEMES AND TECHNIQUES

Like JOHN MILTON's *Lycidas*, *In Memoriam* is essentially an elegy, or a poem dedicated to lamenting the memory of someone. This intensely personal type of poem is almost confessional. For Tennyson announces his deepest fears here and shows himself struggling to accept the order of a universe in which his young friend can be so suddenly and unexpectedly taken from him. The muffled sound of the bells in the first Christmas section reveals how estranged Tennyson felt from his faith. However, by the time of the Epilogue and his sister's wedding, Tennyson is able to articulate with confidence once again the divine purpose which informs both the death of Hallam and the birth of his expected nephew. At the same time, this deeply personal form of address is developed by Tennyson into an exploration of more universal themes. In particular, Tennyson was one of the first writers to tackle the new scientific theories of geology and evolution which undermined the story of creation in the BIBLE. Navigating his way through these difficult spiritual waters, Tennyson nevertheless finds not only a positive affirmation of his faith, but also an affirmation of the process of doubt and loss too. This triumph is perhaps summed up early in the poem in its most famous lines:

'Tis better to have loved and lost
Than never to have loved at all.

Further Reading

Peltason, Timothy, *Reading 'In Memoriam'*. New York: Princeton University Press, 1985. This extended essay examines the themes and techniques of Tennyson's poem.

Tennyson, Alfred, *In Memoriam*. Edited by Erik Gray. New York: W.W. Norton, 2003. This edition of the poem also includes extensive annotations in the text, as well as 13 critical essays and an extract from the leading Tennyson biography.

IVANHOE (1819)
by Sir Walter Scott

For he that does good, having the unlimited power to do evil, deserves praise not only for the good which he performs, but for the evil which he forbears.

Ivanhoe is a novel about chivalry and romance in the twelfth century. It tells the story of Ivanhoe, a Saxon knight seeking glory, justice and the hand of his beloved.

Summary

When the novel opens, England is being torn apart by a power struggle between the Saxons and the Normans. After the success of William the Conqueror in 1066, the French Normans retain control of the throne under King Richard. Richard is known as the Lion-Hearted, a fair and just king, but while returning from fighting in the Holy Land he is captured and imprisoned by the Austrians. Meanwhile, his brother, John, sits on the throne and allows the Norman barons to seize the property of the indigenous Saxons, throw them in prison and steal their titles. A leading Saxon, Cedric, is furious at the treatment meted out to his countrymen and vows the destruction of the Normans. He also disinherits his son, Ivanhoe, because Ivanhoe has declared allegiance to Richard and followed him to war. Ivanhoe also threatened his plans to marry Rowena, a descendant of Alfred the Great and Cedric's ward, to Athelstane, the last of an old Saxon royal family.

Unbeknownst to Cedric, Ivanhoe returns to England in disguise as the Disinherited Knight. He attends a jousting tournament at Ashby-de-la-Zouche and, with the help of the mysterious Black Knight, manages to win, naming Rowena as his Queen. However, Ivanhoe proves to be badly injured and is taken care of by Rebecca and her father Isaac. Ivanhoe, Rebecca and Isaac are then captured with Cedric, Rowena and Athelstane. John has heard that Richard has escaped from his Austrian prison and plots to stop him from re-assuming the throne. Part of the plot involves one of his advisors, Maurice de Bracy, marrying the regal Rowena. Brian de Bois-Guilbert, another of John's henchmen, hopes to marry Rebecca. However, both men are unable to persuade either of the women to accept their proposals.

Meanwhile, the Black Knight joins forces with Robin of Locksley, better known as Robin Hood. Between the two of them they manage to storm the castle where the captives are being held and free them before it burns to the ground. Nevertheless, de Bois-Guilbert manages to escape with Rebecca. He takes her to the stronghold of the Knights Templar where he is informed that she is probably a witch because she is Jewish. She is condemned, but calls for the right to a trial by combat. Against his will, de Bois-Guilbert is forced to fight against Rebecca's sponsor. If he wins, she dies, and if her sponsor wins then he dies. Ivanhoe eventually turns up to champion Rebecca, but he is still badly wounded and de Bois-Guilbert defeats him easily. However, at the crucial moment, de Bois-Guilbert drops dead and Rebecca is saved.

In the meantime, the mysterious Black Knight reveals that he is actually King Richard. He then sets about reconciling Cedric and Ivanhoe and, when Cedric agrees and Athelstane removes himself as an obstacle, Rowena and Ivanhoe are married. Rebecca expresses her gratitude for Ivanhoe's part in saving her life and subsequently departs with Isaac for Grenada, where they hope to start a new life. Richard punishes many of John's henchmen, although he lets John alone. Ivanhoe lives out the rest of Richard's regime pursuing acts of valour and heroism.

> *Ivanhoe* was one of a number of historical novels with which Sir Walter Scott made both his name and his fortune. It helped to popularise the kind of complex characterisation and densely plotted narratives which persist in novels today.

THEMES AND TECHNIQUES

SIR WALTER SCOTT is often charged with developing the modern historical novel. He popularised the techniques of detailed description, complex characterisation and densely-plotted narratives. In so doing, he threw off the more two-dimensional style of his predecessors in the genre, such as HENRY FIELDING and Samuel Richardson. It is therefore a little odd that *Ivanhoe*, his most popular novel, should be so concerned with matters of chivalry and romance, the very subjects which hark back to previous forms of writing. However, Scott returns to these topics with a critical eye which is happy to chastise Richard for his overseas adventuring, as much as it is keen to undermine the hypocritical rituals of chivalry, such as the bloody and pointless tournament. Indeed, what Scott's novel proposes, to some degree, is the value of a society based on merit, rather than blood. Richard, for example, is one of the Normans whose duplicity is clearly foregrounded, yet he is accepted even by the arch Saxon Cedric because of what he does, rather than who he is. Such a meritocratic approach to society would have been popular with the emergent middle classes who made up the larger part of Scott's readership and who themselves were busy dismantling Britain's aristocratic privileges.

Further Reading

Degategno, Paul J., *'Ivanhoe': The Mask of Chivalry*. New York: Twayne Publishers, 1994. This book examines the role of chivalry in Scott's work and looks at some of the novel's telling historical inaccuracies.

> ### JANE EYRE (1847)
> by Charlotte Brontë
>
> *Reader, I married him.*

Jane Eyre is a witty and dark novel about the life and loves of an orphan at the beginning of the nineteenth century. It tells the story of Jane Eyre from her childhood to the time when she finally marries her beloved Mr Rochester.

Summary

When the novel opens, Jane Eyre is an orphan living with her aunt and cousins. Her aunt is continually hostile to her and Jane's only source of enjoyment is talking to Bessie, a servant. One day Jane is locked up in a room after getting in a fight with her older and larger male cousin. This is the room where her uncle died and Jane believes she sees his ghost and promptly faints with fear. Later, the apothecary who helps bring her round suggests that Jane be sent to school. Jane is keen to go and her aunt concurs, glad to be rid of her.

However, the school she attends, Lowood, is run by a cruel and forbidding man named Mr Brocklehurst. He lets his charges live and work in austere conditions while indulging in no small degree of luxury himself. Eventually, conditions deteriorate to the point where there is an outbreak of typhus which alerts the authorities to Brocklehurst's insalubrious practices and he is removed as headmaster. However, Jane also loses her first childhood friend, Helen Burns, who dies of consumption. Following Brocklehurst's departure, conditions in the school improve markedly and

Jane spends another six years there as a pupil and two more as a tutor.

Jane then finds employment at Thornfield, a large house owned by the fiery Mr Rochester. She works there as a governess to Adèle, a ward of Rochester's, although it is some time before she finally gets to meet him. When they do finally meet, she finds herself falling in love with him. One night, Jane saves the house from burning down. Rochester blames the fire on Grace Poole, a servant who works on the third floor, but Jane is not convinced. Nevertheless, she continues to fall more deeply in love with Rochester until it is announced that he will marry Blanche Ingram, a beautiful but mercenary woman. Rochester, however, is clearly aware that Blanche wants to marry him only for his money and he asks Jane if she will marry him instead.

> By turns witty and moving, *Jane Eyre* tells the story of the eponymous heroine's life from her miserable childhood to her happy marriage.

Jane accepts, but as the wedding is about to go ahead, a man called Mason introduces himself as the brother of Rochester's already existing wife. Rochester then reveals that Grace Poole is employed to look after Bertha Mason, the woman who lives in the attic and who caused the fire Jane put out. Bertha is mad and scrabbles about on all fours. Distraught, Jane leaves Thornfield and is quickly reduced to the status of a beggar. In this state, she is rescued by two sisters and a brother of the Rivers family. One day, Jane learns that she has inherited a large amount of money from her uncle and that she is, in fact, related to the Rivers family. She immediately decides to share out the money between them. The brother, St John, asks if Jane will accompany him on missionary work to India as his wife. However, Jane does not love him and instead she decides to seek out Rochester once more. Returning to Thornfield, she finds that it was burnt down in a fire that killed Bertha and that Rochester was severely injured. Jane is not put off, however, and the two end by marrying and having children.

THEMES AND TECHNIQUES

One of the most interesting aspects of *Jane Eyre* is the character of Bertha Mason. Before we know who she is, Bertha figures as a vague threat in the novel, a mysterious presence that results in the initial fire associated with Grace Poole. However, when we find out who she is, Bertha reveals a side to Rochester that we may not have expected, and she also serves as a warning to Jane of what may happen to her if she marries Rochester and completely surrenders to him. The time she spends away from Rochester is therefore essential as she becomes a woman of independent means who will return to him as an equal, even functioning as his eyes until he partially regains his sight. Some critics have read Bertha more symbolically. Locked up in the attic, she represents the wild side of Jane's emotions which she must keep in check. Indeed, both Jane's emotions and Bertha are associated with fire. Bertha's imprisonment could also be said to represent the constrictions placed on women by society at the time. Given Bertha's origins in the colonies, other critics have extended the metaphor to suggest that she represents the horrors of imperialism that Britain at the time had to ignore in order to continue building the Empire. Indeed, one of the greatest novelists of recent years, Jean Rhys, has written *Wide Sargasso Sea*, the story of this repression told from Bertha's (or Antoinette's) point of view.

Further Reading

Bloom, Harold (ed.), *Charlotte Brontë's 'Jane Eyre'*. Broomall: Chelsea House Publishers, 1991. This book provides a collection of essays about Brontë's novel.

Gilbert, Sandra M. and Gubar, Susan (eds) *The Madwoman in the Attic: The Woman Writer and the Nineteenth-Century Imagination*. New Haven: Yale University Press, 1979. One of the most important critical works of the past 50 years, this feminist classic was inspired by and discusses the figure of Bertha in *Jane Eyre*. Always controversial, this is well worth a read.

Rhys, Jean, *Wide Sargasso Sea*. London: Penguin, 2000. This edition of the novel, wonderfully edited and introduced by Angela Smith, fills in the gaps of Bertha's life and explains how she came to be Rochester's wife.

JUDE THE OBSCURE (1896)
by Thomas Hardy

You are Joseph the dreamer of dreams,
dear Jude, and a tragic Don Quixote.
And sometimes you are St Stephen, who
while they were stoning him, could see
Heaven opened. O my poor friend and
comrade, you'll suffer yet!

Infamous almost from the moment of its publication, *Jude the Obscure* was HARDY's last novel. It tells the story of Jude and how, unable to pursue the education of which he dreams because of his social and economic status, he becomes trapped in a loveless marriage only to fall in love with Sue, similarly trapped herself.

Summary

When the novel begins, Jude Fawley is still a boy living in the village of Marygreen with his aunt Drusilla. When the local schoolmaster, Richard Phillotson, moves to the university town of Christminster in order to get a degree, Jude begins to teach himself Latin and Greek so that he might one day go there too. In the meantime, Jude also learns the trade of stonemasonry to enable him to pay his way once he goes. One day, at the end of his teenage years and just before he departs for Christminster, Jude meets Arabella Donn, the daughter of a pig farmer. Arabella soon claims to be pregnant and Jude feels compelled to marry her. However, once they are married Arabella reveals that she is not pregnant and Jude believes he is trapped in a loveless marriage. Returning home one day, Jude discovers that Arabella has left for Australia with her parents.

After a few more years, Jude travels to Christminster with the intention of entering the university. When he arrives he meets his cousin, Sue Bridehead, a headstrong and refined woman who seems the exact opposite of the coarse Arabella. Jude falls in love with Sue but he cannot pursue his interest in her because he is still married. When she is about to leave Christminster, Jude introduces her to Phillotson, his old teacher.

Phillotson is still teaching after failing to get a degree. He agrees to take Sue on as an apprentice teacher, although soon they are more than just colleagues. Unhappy at this, Jude feels completely dejected when all the colleges to which he has applied reject him. He returns to Marygreen where he undertakes to become a licentiate in the church. From Marygreen he travels to Melchester in order to be closer to Sue who is training there as a teacher. However, when Sue and Phillotson marry, he is unable to stand living in Melchester any longer and returns to Marygreen.

> Hardy's novel *Jude the Obscure* tells the story of the many compromises which blight the lives of Jude and Sue and how they eventually lead to tragedy. The reception to Hardy's analysis of society was so condemnatory that he never wrote another novel again.

When Sue comes to Drusilla's funeral, Jude realises his feelings for her are incompatible with his becoming a minister, so he abandons his training. Sue then leaves Phillotson and seeks a divorce from him while Jude seeks a divorce from Arabella. When they both finally are divorced, however, Sue initially insists on living with Jude only as a companion. Arabella then announces that she was pregnant by Jude at the time she left for Australia and that her parents can no longer afford to keep the boy. Sue agrees to take on the boy, named Little Father Time, and they have two other children together. However, because of their unmarried status few people will let them rooms or give Jude employment. Hearing of their difficulty, Little Father Time hangs himself and the other two children. Sue believes this calamity is a punishment for her behaviour in leaving Phillotson and she returns to him and they remarry. Jude is then cajoled into remarrying Arabella. Knowing he is ill, Jude visits Sue one last time and she admits she still loves him. Jude then returns home where he dies alone shortly afterwards.

THEMES AND TECHNIQUES

Jude the Obscure was highly controversial when it was published. Hardy recalls in a postscript to the novel written some 16 years later that it was even burnt by a bishop – 'probably in his despair at not being able to burn me'. Part of this furore was caused by people's reactions to the unswerving portrait of Jude and Sue's respective marriages. In each case marriage is shown to be a compromise that traps one or both parties into a perpetual unhappiness. Even when Sue is freed from her marriage by divorce, she feels still beholden to Phillotson and eventually returns to him, persuaded by her undeserved guilt at the death of Little Father Time. This, then, ties in with the larger theme of the work which is that of the compromise between the individual and society. Jude's life is compromised throughout the novel, by his poverty, his class, his education, his marriage to Arabella, his relationship with Sue, and his children. Each of these factors chips away a little at his aspirations, whether it is his marriage to Arabella which forestalls his relationship with Sue, or his class which stops him from being accepted at Christminster. In this regard, *Jude the Obscure* is a novel that foreshadows the individualism of modern novels. For Jude is not so much set against society as he is left outside of it, unable to access its education system and unable to justify his love for Sue in public. His is a thoroughly modern alienation in which he is estranged from an unyielding and unsympathetic world. This mirrored Hardy's own position after the publication of the book and so, perhaps unsurprisingly, it became his last prose work, just as it is now often cited as the first novel of the twentieth century.

Further Reading

Boumelha, Penny (ed.) *New Casebook on 'Jude the Obscure'*. London: Palgrave Macmillan, 1999. This collection of essays looks at Hardy's novel from a number of different modern perspectives.

Hardy, Thomas, *Jude the Obscure*. Edited by Thomas Page. London and New York: W.W. Norton, 1999. This edition of the text also includes a number of essays that examine Hardy's book from a modern perspective, as well reviews from the time of its publication.

KING LEAR (1605–06)
by William Shakespeare

The worst is not
So long as we can say, 'This is the worst.'

One of SHAKESPEARE's greatest tragedies, *King Lear* follows the fortunes of the eponymous hero when he decides to split his kingdom between his three daughters.

Summary

When the play begins, King Lear is an old man. In his dotage he wishes to split his kingdom between his three daughters – Goneril, Regan and Cordelia. In order to satisfy his vanity, Lear decides he will first put his daughters' devotion to a public test. He asks them to declare how much they love him. Goneril and Regan, who are both well-versed in flattery, succeed in placating Lear's need for sycophancy by making extravagant claims about the depth of their love for their father. Cordelia, however, answers in a straightforward and unembellished manner. This sends Lear into a frenzy and he disinherits her, dividing his kingdom instead between only Goneril and Regan. Kent, a nobleman loyal to Lear, steps in to defend Cordelia but Lear is so consumed with his own disappointment that he banishes Kent. The Duke of Burgundy, who had been a suitor to Cordelia, relinquishes his interest in her once he realises that she will come with no dowry. However, her other suitor, the King of France, remains loyal to Cordelia and she leaves the country with him.

Meanwhile, Edmund, the illegitimate son of the Earl of Gloucester, plots to oust his legitimate half-brother, Edgar, from their father's affections. Deceiving his father, Edmund fabricates a letter from Edgar in which it appears that Edgar asks Edmund for help in overthrowing their father. Gloucester is naturally outraged and sends for Edgar. However, Edmund gets to Edgar first, claiming he should leave for some other reason. When he has gone, Edmund wounds himself and then shows Gloucester, who promptly sends out his men to capture Edgar. When Goneril and Regan arrive at Gloucester's castle, they too believe the story and pledge allegiance to Edmund.

Despite being banished by Lear, Kent returns to serve him in disguise. He is therefore able to witness at first hand the cruel treatment meted out to him by Goneril and Regan. Between them they rob Lear of his retinue of knights, deprive him of all authority and then let him leave in the middle of a stormy night with only Kent and a Fool for company. Wandering on a heath, Lear starts to lose his grip on sanity, although he is persuaded out of his worst notions by Poor Tom, Edgar disguised as a beggar. When Gloucester hears of Lear's treatment he is appalled and, after confiding in Edmund, he goes off to help him. When Edmund informs Regan and her husband Cornwall of this, they have Gloucester arrested and deliberately blinded. During the process of blinding Gloucester, a loyal servant fatally wounds Cornwall before he is also killed. When they have finished, Gloucester is also thrown out into the storm.

> One of Shakespeare's four great tragedies, *King Lear* focuses on one of his most abiding themes – the crisis of authority. This crisis is precipitated by Lear himself when he attempts to divide his kingdom between his three daughters.

Out on the heath, Gloucester encounters Poor Tom, and, not knowing that it is his son, he asks him to lead him off a cliff. Tom tricks him by leading him off an imaginary cliff which does much to bring Gloucester to his senses. Meanwhile, Cordelia has landed at Dover with the French army, where she is reunited with Lear. She is eager to seek retribution for her father's poor treatment. Edmund, playing off the jealousy between Goneril and Regan, has become the leader of the English army and leads them to victory over the French. Cordelia and Lear are captured and Edmund secretly orders their execution. Edgar and Edmund end up in a duel during which Edmund is mortally wounded. He confesses that he ordered the deaths of Lear and Cordelia. In the meantime, Goneril poisons Regan through jealousy over her relationship with Edmund and then kills herself out of shame. Edmund's confession coming too late, Lear then carries in the dead body of Cordelia and promptly dies of grief himself.

THEMES AND TECHNIQUES

King Lear is perhaps Shakespeare's finest expression of one of his most enduring themes – the crisis of authority. Here, the failure of authority is most clearly figured in the character of Lear who misplaces the authority vested in him by using it to extract pointless confessions of love from his own children by which measure he then proceeds to apportion his power. Having literally misplaced his authority in the hands of Goneril and Regan, Lear learns how baseless his own power is. For he soon has neither a position as head of the family, or as head of a retinue of knights, or as head of the country. Through physical suffering, half-naked in a raging storm that represents the turmoil of the kingdom's disorder, Lear comes to learn the painful mental truth that he was a deluded and vain old fool when he gave away the throne to his scheming daughters. Having finally restored sense to a position of authority in his own personal kingdom, Lear learns that he is too late and that the disorder he has created has led to the death of Cordelia and, ultimately, to his own. Order is only really restored when Edgar, Cordelia's equivalent in the play's sub-plot, takes over the realm of the kingdom.

Further Reading

Drakakis, John (ed.), *Shakespearean Tragedy*. London: Longman, 1992. This collection of theoretical essays puts *King Lear* into the wider context of both Shakespearean tragedy and criticism.

Halio, Jay L. (ed.), *Critical Essays on Shakespeare's 'King Lear'*. London: G.K. Hall & Co., 1996. This collection of essays provides a number of different approaches to the play, as well as looking at the play's revision by Shakespeare.

Ioppolo, Grace (ed.), *A Routledge Literary Sourcebook on William Shakespeare's 'King Lear'*. London and New York: Routledge, 2002. This comprehensive collection of essays also includes a selection of detailed analyses of the text, a list of sources, and a range of critical responses.

LAMIA, ISABELLA, THE EVE OF ST AGNES AND OTHER POEMS (1820)
by John Keats

Already with thee! tender is the night.

One of the singlemost remarkable collections of poems ever published, KEATS's reputation rests almost solely on *Lamia, Isabella, The Eve of St Agnes and Other Poems*. The 'other' poems it contains include his most famous works – 'Ode to a Nightingale', 'To Autumn' and 'Ode on a Grecian Urn'.

Summary

'Ode to a Nightingale' was written when Keats lived with his friend Charles Brown in London. In the spring of 1819, a nightingale had built a nest near their house and Keats 'felt a tranquil and continual joy in her song'. Inspired by this, he composed the 'Ode' one morning while sitting under a plum tree. The speaker of the poem begins by stating that he feels as if he has drunk a poison that has drugged his senses. This sense he ascribes to listening to the nightingale sing and being too happy in its happiness. The speaker wishes for oblivion and to escape from the cares of being human 'where but to think is to be full of sorrow'. He enjoins the nightingale to fly away and declares that he will join it, borne aloft by his own imagination. The speaker then asserts that he would quite happily die right there and then while listening to the nightingale sing, although he concedes that if he did he would no longer be able to hear the bird's song. This self same song, he concedes, is not subject to the laws of human artistic production in which successive generations tread all over the work of their forbears; rather, it is an eternal song heard as equally now as it was by 'emperor and clown'. However, the speaker is soon brought back to his senses and is no longer sure if he dreamt the scenario or if it was real.

Keats returned to the question of the timelessness of art in 'Ode on a Grecian Urn'. Here the speaker addresses the figures in sculpted relief on an imaginary pot. He wonders what stories inspired the men, maidens and gods chasing each other and who the figures might be. Looking at another scene on the urn, the speaker spies a piper and two lovers. He delights in the fact that he cannot hear the tune of the piper because unheard melodies are sweeter. Similarly, the speaker consoles the frozen lovers that even though their love cannot be consummated, though it is ever so near, it will, for this reason, last forever and never fade. Likewise, the trees under which they play will never lose their leaves. The next scene the speaker contemplates is one where a priest leads a heifer to be sacrificed. He wonders what little town has been emptied of people who follow the priest and laments the fact that it will be empty for ever more. This melancholy thought brings the speaker back to himself and causes him to recollect the fact that when his generation have all died, the urn will still be there passing on its eternal message: 'Beauty is truth, truth beauty'.

One of the most remarkable poetry collections ever published, *Lamia, Isabella, The Eve of St Agnes and Other Poems* is invested throughout by Keats's very real concerns about mortality.

THEMES AND TECHNIQUES

Keats's life was remarkably short and, during its span, he was ever aware of death encroaching upon him. This very real sense of his own mortality brought into sharp relief the conflict between his own fleeting existence and the eternity he hoped for the poetry he created. We can see this battle between mortality and immortality throughout his poetic oeuvre. In 'Ode to a Nightingale', the nightingale's song offers itself up as a relief from the day-to-day pains of living – 'the weariness, the fever, and the fret'. Typically, the here and now is charged with unhappiness while the ecstatic beauty of the nightingale's song is timeless. In 'Ode on a Grecian Urn', Keats finds a consolation in the fact that all the figures' actions and emotions are suspended in a sculptural aspic. They are frozen in time and thus free from its effects, effects which, Keats is apt to remind us, are always corrosive. For while the figures live on unchanged, never to suffer a disappointed love or a naked tree, the speaker of the poem is filled with melancholy at the thought that his own generation will soon perish. Of course, Keats did not just write about these themes; he also enshrined them with his attempts to become a great English poet before he died. Sadly consumed with the thought that his poems had failed to achieve immortality, he penned the following misguided epitaph for his own tombstone: 'Here lies one whose name was writ on water'.

Further Reading

De Almeida, Hermione (ed.), *Critical Essays on John Keats*. New York: G.K. Hall and Co., 1990. This is a collection of recent essays which looks at all aspects of Keats's work.

Keats, John, *Lamia, Isabella, The Eve of St Agnes and Other Poems*. London and New York: Penguin Books, 1999. A recent edition of Keats's book reprinted in its original 1820 format.

LAST OF THE MOHICANS, THE (1826)
by James Fenimore Cooper

The pale-faces are masters of the earth, and the time of the red-men has not yet come again.

Part of a series of books following the variously named Hawkeye, this novel shows him caught up in the American war between France and Britain.

Summary

Some time during the late 1750s, the frontier west of New York is the scene of the French and Indian wars. Setting out from Fort Edward, Alice and Cora Munro attempt to visit their father, Colonel Munro at Fort William Henry. They are accompanied by Major Duncan Heyward. To guide them through the dangerous forests, they take Magua, a Huron guide. On the way, they encounter Hawkeye, a white forest dweller, and his two companions, Chingachgook and Uncas, the last surviving members of the Mohican tribe. When Hawkeye asks Heyward where they are going, he realises that Magua has led them astray. Despite an attempt to capture him, Magua escapes. Hawkeye and the Mohicans know that Magua will call upon the Huron to help him attack the travellers so they agree to try and lead them out of harm's way.

The Last of the Mohicans is one of a series of novels about the variously named Natty Bumppo which established the reputation of James Fenimore Cooper.

The travellers soon become trapped by the Huron and Hawkeye, also known as Natty Bumppo, Chingachgook and Uncas temporarily leave Heyward and the women so that they might return to rescue them later. When Heyward attempts to convert Magua to the British cause, he learns that Magua was treated badly by Colonel Munro and that this is his revenge. Magua offers to release Alice safely as long as Cora agrees to marry him, but, with the consent of the others, she refuses. Shortly afterwards, Hawkeye, Chingachgook and Uncas invade the Huron camp and rescue the travellers, although, once again, Magua manages to escape. Hawkeye then leads the group through the French army besieging Fort William Henry and Colonel Munro greets his daughters. However, there is little time for rejoicing because Munro learns that he is not about to receive any reinforcements and that he therefore has to surrender to the French.

Upon surrendering to the French, many of the British are subject to an attack by the Huron who wish to unleash their bloodlust. In the confusion, Magua is able to recapture Cora and Alice. Setting off in pursuit, Heyward, Munro, Hawkeye, Chingachgook and Uncas learn that Alice has been sent to one camp and Cora to another. By disguising themselves in a number of ways, the group manage to free Alice from her captors. However, they are unable to release Cora and she departs with Magua. A chase follows in which most of the fleeing Huron are killed, but not before Cora also dies. In attacking her assassin, Uncas exposes himself to an attack from Magua who stabs him in the back. Although Magua tries to escape, Hawkeye shoots him. The dead are then properly buried.

THEMES AND TECHNIQUES

In *The Last of the Mohicans*, Cooper uses the natural surroundings, which had so inspired him as a child, in a number of different ways. The forests, hills and rivers of the frontier provide a tough, physical challenge to his characters. For the Europeans, the terrain is a visible reminder of the difference between the Old and New Worlds, figuring almost as a barrier to their colonial exploits. Without any indigenous allies, the British come to look upon the environment almost as an enemy in its own right. Within this context, COOPER employs the natural world as a proving ground for his characters. Hawkeye's respect for the frontier, for example, is proof of his wisdom and guile, whereas Heyward's impatience with it suggests that he is unnecessarily arrogant, unable to yield to his subordinate position on the new continent. Chingachgook and Uncas, as part of the indigenous population, move with ease and grace through the landscape and by so doing confirm their status as the natural inheritors of the land. This inheritance is what the novel laments at the end when Uncas, the last of the Mohicans, dies, for with his death, as Cooper knew, the landscape was also partially doomed.

Further Reading

Peck, Daniel (ed.), *New Essays on 'The Last of the Mohicans'*. New York and London: Cambridge University Press, 1992. This collection of essays offers a number of different approaches to the novel, with a particular emphasis on the relation of Cooper's book to history.

LEAVES OF GRASS (1855–81)
by Walt Whitman

I celebrate myself,
And what I assume you shall assume,
For every atom belonging to me as good
belongs to you.

Photo credit: © Bettmann/CORBIS

Despite being derided as indecent when it was first published, the ever-evolving *Leaves of Grass* established WHITMAN as America's national poet. More a collection of poems than a single poem, it celebrates Whitman's premise that 'the United States themselves are essentially the greatest poem'.

Summary

Leaves of Grass was a work that Whitman developed over the course of his entire poetic career. In many ways, it was Whitman's poetic career, comprising, as it did, almost the entirety of his output. Less one poem than a group of poems that form more than the sum of their parts, the title 'Leaves of Grass' was originally printed as the title of each poem. When Whitman published the first edition in 1855 it contained just 12 poems. Over the following years he revised the existing poems and added to them, putting together several new editions during this period. By the time he published the final so-called 'deathbed' edition in 1892, the collection contained more than 150 poems, each by now individually titled.

Leaves of Grass established Walt Whitman as America's First Poet. As Whitman himself declared in reviewing his own book: 'An American bard at last!'

Probably the most famous poem in *Leaves in Grass*, and the one that established Whitman as a genuinely new poetic voice when it was first published in 1855, is 'Song of Myself'. If the title of the poem suggests that it is autobiographical, a sense of precisely how it is autobiographical can be gleaned from the title changes it endured down the years. After originally being granted the anonymity of the name of 'Leaves of Grass', by the second edition it was called the very specific 'Poem of Walt Whitman, an American'. After this it took on the more simple title 'Walt Whitman'. Finally, in its last version it took on the title by which we now know it, 'Song of Myself'. As these changes suggest, the emphasis of the poem moved from the biography of someone defined by the precepts of society, that is someone with a name and a nation and so forth, to someone defined in terms of their spiritual and physical being. In other words, this meandering and abstract poem explores Whitman in his most generic form, as a 'self'. The poem traces the boundaries of the self and finds them to be both distinctive and indistinguishable all at the same time. One aspect of this is the sexual union in which two people become one but still remain two people. In this sense, as egotistical as the title sounds, the poem is really a celebration of the interconnectedness of humanity, an interconnectedness that the poem ultimately finds in the all-pervasive spirituality of God.

THEMES AND TECHNIQUES

Leaves of Grass received mixed reviews when it was first published. One of the more enthusiastic reviews came, perhaps not surprisingly, from Whitman himself who, writing pseudo-anonymously, greeted the book with the declaration, 'An American bard at last!' If this might appear a slightly conceited assertion, it does at least announce the terms in which Whitman wanted his work to be understood. He felt that America was a new land, distinct from the lands of Europe whose peoples had colonised it and that, as such, it required a new and distinctive poetry. In order to reflect the America that Whitman saw around him, this new poetry had to be free and democratic. To this end, Whitman developed his own version of free verse, which was long-lined and not rhyming and catalogued the abundant treasures of the new world in long lists where no element has the upper hand over the other. Whitman also drew on the history of English-speaking vernacular poetry, writing his poems in an idiom and a diction that everyone could understand. If this is the form of the new America, Whitman celebrates its democratic spirit in his subject matter too, claiming kinship with everybody as 'one of the great nation, the nation of many nations – the smallest the same and the largest the same.'

Further Reading

Hindus, Milton (ed.), *Leaves of Grass: One Hundred Years After – New Essays*. London: Oxford University Press, 1955. This is a small collection of essays written in order to commemorate the 100th anniversary of the first publication of *Leaves of Grass*.

Miller, James E. *Leaves of Grass: America's Lyric-Epic of Self and Democracy*. New York: Twayne Publishers, 1992. This extended essay examines the themes, techniques and meaning of Whitman's epic.

LIFE AND OPINIONS OF TRISTRAM SHANDY, THE (1759–66)
by Laurence Sterne

I wish either my father or my mother, or indeed both of them, as they were in duty both equally bound to it, had minded what they were about when they begot me.

Unique and very popular in its own time, STERNE's novel has had many imitators in recent years, although few manage to mix its inventiveness and humour with such exuberance. Ostensibly it tells the tale of the life of Tristram Shandy, but it is really concerned with a series of comic digressions, many of which concern his immortal Uncle Toby.

Summary

Tristram Shandy consists of nine separate volumes. The first volume opens with a description of the moments surrounding Tristram's conception. He laments the fact that his parents did not focus on what they were doing and then embarks upon a lengthy digression that will lead up to his birth on 5 November 1718. This digression introduces us to Parson Yorick, Dr Slop and Uncle Toby, as well as Tristram's warring parents. Walter, Tristram's father, forces his mother to have the baby at home rather than in London. She then calls for the midwife while Dr Slop remains downstairs with Toby and Walter. By the end of volume two, the action of the novel has not advanced at all.

In volume three Dr Slop is finally called into the delivery room where he uses his new instrument – forceps – to deliver baby Tristram. While this is happening and Toby and Walter are asleep, the author composes the Preface to the book. Toby and Walter are finally awoken with the news that the forceps have squashed Tristram's nose. Walter is distraught because a history of small noses has held his family back over the years. He attempts to counteract this deficiency by giving his newly born son a great name – Trismegistus. Unfortunately, by the time it gets to the christening, the name is relayed incorrectly and the baby is christened

Tristram instead. Walter proves to be philo-sophical on this point when he inherits £10,000. Tristram is also happy because his elder brother dies leaving him the heir to the estate.

In volume five, Walter devotes himself to his remaining son's education by writing a book on it and neglecting his actual educa-tion. During this period of neglect a sash win-dow falls down and accidentally circumcises Tristram.

> One of the funniest books in the canon of English literature, the unique *Tristram Shandy* also remains one of the most influ-ential. Obsessed with the process of its own writing, Sterne's novel prefigures many modern works of fiction.

Volume six announces that Uncle Toby falls in love with Widow Wadman. The follow-ing volume gives itself over almost entirely to a digression in which Tristram describes his travels through France. Volume eight returns us to Toby's love affair with Widow Wadman. She uses the ruse of having something in her eye to get Toby's notice after 11 years of wait-ing for him to make a move. Under the watch-ful eye of Mrs Shandy, and with numerous digressions and two blank chapters on the way, Toby finally asks Widow Wadman to marry him. She, however, is reticent to accept because of Toby's war wound in the groin which she suspects leaves him impotent. Toby is badly disillusioned when he finally learns of her concerns, while Walter is annoyed on his brother's behalf. The novel ends with a famous cock and bull story.

THEMES AND TECHNIQUES

SAMUEL JOHNSON declared of *Tristram Shandy* that, 'Nothing odd will do long.' Obviously he was wrong so far as its longevity is concerned, but he is certainly correct about its singularity. *Tristram Shandy* defies the reader's expectations throughout its nine volumes. The supposed writer of the book, Tristram, introduces all kinds of quirks into the conventional form of the novel. He misses a chapter and then recounts what would have been in the chapter, digresses even from his digressions, leaves a page blank, another black, quotes from other writers and then complains about plagiarism, describes parts of the manuscript being used for curling papers, prints his laundry list, and even starts a story in one volume, breaks off for another volume to describe something else and then resumes the story again, in the process destroying all notion of chronological time.

Many of these quirks produce a comic effect which chimes in nicely with the richly comic characters which people its pages. Recently, many critics have found the book to be of interest because it prefigures modern lit-erature in that it is obsessed with the process of its own writing. Tristram constantly refers to what he has written, how and where he has written it and what he intends to write, as well as discoursing upon many other different forms of writing, including the cock and bull story which appropriately ends the novel.

Further Reading

New, Melvyn, *Tristram Shandy: A Book for Free Spirits*. New York: Twayne Publishers, 1995. This book examines the themes and tech-niques of Sterne's novel.

Sterne, Laurence, *Tristram Shandy: An Authoritative Text, The Author on the Novel, Criticism*. Edited by Howard Anderson. New York: W.W. Norton, 1980. This edition of the novel also includes extensive annotations in the text, as well as critical commentaries from the time.

> ## LIFE OF SAMUEL JOHNSON, THE (1791)
> ### by James Boswell
> *Patriotism is the last refuge of a scoundrel.*

Often cited as the greatest biography ever written in the English language, BOSWELL's book created the JOHNSON we now know. It tells the story of Johnson's life but focuses on the latter part of his days when he is already an established writer, conversationalist and wit.

Summary

The Life of Samuel Johnson, as the name sug-gests, follows the influential writer from his birth through to his death. Boswell only met Johnson when he was 54, so much of the early part of the biography is based on Johnson's own testimony or on the recollection of acquaintances and friends. As Boswell points out, it was not always possible to press Johnson on some of the more sensitive issues in his life, such as his poor background, and so Boswell is forced to surmise in more concise terms about Johnson's early years.

After 1763, the notable year in which Boswell met Johnson, the *Life* offers fuller accounts of the lexicographer's life. Indeed, it offers fuller accounts of life in England at the time on a broader stage, revealing interesting portraits of such leading personalities as King George III, the painter Sir Joshua Reynolds, the novelist OLIVER GOLDSMITH and the actor David Garrick. All of these dramatic encounters are, however, centred around Johnson, who dominates proceedings with his sheer physical bulk, his wit and erudition.

THEMES AND TECHNIQUES

Boswell's task in creating *The Life of Samuel Johnson* was enormous. He had spent 20 years off and on in Johnson's company and had, almost from the start, used this time with the great man with the express purpose of recording and collecting material for the biography. He devised a form of shorthand to help him document Johnson's sparkling conversation, and he also trained his memory to remember what his shorthand could not recall. He would then spend each evening writing up his notes and editing the dialogue to retain its original charm. As he himself admitted after the publication of the *Life*, 'the stretch of mind and prompt assiduity by which so many conversations are preserved, I myself, at some distance of time, contemplate with wonder.' On top of this, Boswell also had to sort through Johnson's voluminous correspondence, as well as his work, and the remembrances of Johnson's friends and acquaintances.

Boswell's attention to detail and his devotion to the truth were unremitting. He recalls at one point traipsing across London to secure the accuracy of a date. Such objective grounding for the *Life* allowed Boswell to flaunt a form of partiality towards Johnson, displaying him in different and most often beneficial lights in order to reveal the literary and humane genius that Boswell believed him

to be before he even started to write. Indeed, it is a measure of Boswell's own humanity that he repeatedly played the fool in order to allow Johnson to demonstrate his facility for witticisms.

Largely responsible for the impression we have today of Johnson as the leading wit of his time, Boswell's *Life of Samuel Johnson* also set the standard for modern biographies in terms of research and the rich portrayal of its subject.

Further Reading

Sisman, Adam, *Boswell's Presumptuous Task: The Making of 'The Life of Dr Johnson'*. New York: Farrar Straus & Giroux, 2001. This book is essentially a biography of the biography, exploring the story of Boswell's great endeavour.

LYRICAL BALLADS (1798–1800)
by Samuel Taylor Coleridge and William Wordsworth

Water, water, every where,
Nor any drop to drink.

The publication of *Lyrical Ballads* changed the landscape of British poetry. Opening with COLERIDGE's 'Rime of the Ancient Mariner' and closing with WORDSWORTH's 'Lines Composed a Few Miles Above Tintern Abbey', the book introduced the English-speaking public to a Romantic poetry where personal feelings and style triumphed over the impersonal representation of situations and the deft deployment of rhetoric.

Summary

Possibly the most memorable poem in *Lyrical Ballads* is the collection's only ballad, Coleridge's 'Rime of the Ancient Mariner'. It is also one of the book's most obvious collaborations, for although this poem was written by Coleridge, Wordsworth was originally going to contribute a number of verses himself and offered several ideas for it. The poem begins with the Ancient Mariner accosting a Wedding-Guest as he is about to enter a wedding. Transfixing the Wedding-Guest's will, the Ancient Mariner proceeds to tell him the story of a voyage on which he was a sailor.

The ship leaves the harbour with the crew in good spirits, but after a while it is overtaken by storms until eventually it drifts into the ice floes around the South Pole. Surrounded by glaciers, the ship is immobilised until an Albatross flies through the fog and is hailed by the crew. The bird proves to be a good omen for, after circling the ship several times, the ice begins to crack and the wind gets up enough to break them free.

> *Lyrical Ballads* was the most influential volume of poetry published in its day. Written by Samuel Coleridge and William Wordsworth, it espoused a new kind of poetry that came to be associated with Romanticism.

For reasons that are unexplained, the ancient Mariner then shoots down the Albatross with his crossbow. When the ship then becomes becalmed, the crew hold the Ancient Mariner responsible and hang the dead bird around his neck in place of a cross. Stranded and surrounded by water they cannot drink, the crew grow closer to death until a ship approaches. It soon becomes apparent that it is a ghost ship manned only by Death and Life-in-Death. The two cast die to see who decides the crew's fate and Life-in-Death wins the Ancient Mariner. His 200 crew mates all drop dead one by one, cursing him as they go until he is the only one left. Eventually, the Ancient Mariner turns to prayer and it is only then that the Albatross drops from around his neck and into the sea.

The Ancient Mariner is then finally able to sleep again, and as he does so it rains once more. The bodies of the dead crew are then reanimated by angelic spirits and they work the ship as normal. The ship is propelled by a variety of unnatural means back to the native country of the Ancient Mariner, where the angels leave the bodies of the dead men behind them. The Pilot, the Pilot's boy and the Hermit all row out to meet the ship but

before they get there it sinks. The Ancient Mariner is saved by the Pilot, whereupon he asks the Hermit to grant him absolution for his sins. The Hermit does so and the Ancient Mariner is temporarily relieved. However, over time the guilt comes back until he retells his story. He is thus condemned to wander the world looking for the person to whom he can tell his tale. Having told his story, the Ancient Mariner leaves the Wedding-Guest who wakes the next morning 'a sadder and wiser man'.

THEMES AND TECHNIQUES

Lyrical Ballads is often seen in terms of the Preface that Wordsworth wrote for a second edition of the book. This Preface outlines a programme for a new kind of poetry – the kind that we today think of as Romantic poetry. However, it would be a mistake to read Coleridge's, and even all of Wordsworth's, contributions to *Lyrical Ballads* in the light of the theory that Wordsworth outlines. For example, Wordsworth writes of his intention to compose verse about 'incidents and situations from common life' using 'the real language of men in a state of vivid sensation'. Coleridge's 'Rime of the Ancient Mariner', however, clearly recounts a fantastical story outwith the parameters of everyday life , and it does so using words not taken from the common stock, even after Coleridge's later amendments removed some of the earlier archaisms. In doing so, 'Rime of the Ancient Mariner' remains faithful to the approach adopted by Coleridge throughout his career. For his best works, such as 'Ancient Mariner' and 'Kubla Khan', celebrate the creative powers of the imagination and revel in their free rein. Indeed, Coleridge later complained that his main criticism of 'Ancient Mariner' was that its moral intruded too obviously upon a work that was intended as one of pure imagination.

Further Reading

Cronin, Richard (ed.), *1798: Year of the 'Lyrical Ballads'.* New York: St Martin's Press, 1998. This fascinating book pieces together the context in which *Lyrical Ballads* was written, re-creating the literary culture of the time.

Wordsworth, William and Coleridge, Samuel Taylor, *Wordsworth and Coleridge: Lyrical Ballads,*

1798. Edited by W.J.B. Owen. London: Oxford University Press, 1969. This version of the text includes both of Wordsworth's prefaces, as well as a critical commentary and an introduction.

MACBETH (1606)
by William Shakespeare

Tomorrow, and tomorrow, and tomorrow
Creeps in this petty pace from day to day,
To the last syllable of recorded time;
And all our yesterdays have lighted fools
The way to dusty death. Out, out, brief
candle!
Life's but a walking shadow, a poor
player
That struts and frets his hour upon the
stage
And then is heard no more. It is a tale
Told by an idiot, full of sound and fury,
Signifying nothing.

Macbeth is one of SHAKESPEARE's four great tragedies, along with *Hamlet*, *Othello* and *King Lear*. The play tells the story of how Macbeth and his wife seize the Scottish throne and are ultimately overthrown themselves.

Summary

Returning from a victorious battle defending Scotland from invaders, two distinguished generals, Macbeth and Banquo, meet three witches on a blasted heath. The witches prophesy that Macbeth shall be made Thane of Cawdor and then become King of Scotland, and that Banquo, while not destined to sit on the throne himself, shall nevertheless beget sons who will be kings. This all seems improbable to Macbeth and Banquo but, before they can be questioned, the witches disappear into thin air. Shortly afterwards, two of King Duncan's men tell Macbeth that he has been made Thane of Cawdor following the treach-

ery of the previous holder of the title. With half of the prophesy already true, Macbeth begins to think that he might also be King of Scotland. When he tells his wife, Lady Macbeth, she is sure that he will sit on the throne but worries that Macbeth is 'too full o' the milk of human kindness'. She therefore invokes spirits to 'unsex' her and fill her with the 'direst cruelty' so that she may assist her husband in fulfilling the prophesy.

> *Macbeth* is one Shakespeare's four great tragedies. It tells the story of Macbeth, a man who illegitimately seizes the Scottish throne and pays for it with his life.

That night, Lady Macbeth persuades her husband to murder Duncan while he sleeps. After getting the chamberlains guarding Duncan to drink themselves into a stupor with wine, Macbeth steals into the King's room and stabs him to death. As soon as he has accomplished the deed, he is struck by regret, and begins to hear strange murmurings and shrieks in the air. Macbeth planted bloody daggers on the two chamberlains and so the next morning, when Duncan's body is found, it is assumed they are guilty of the murder and Macbeth kills them pretending to be consumed with rage. Duncan's two sons, Malcolm and Donalbain, then flee to England and Ireland respectively in case they too become victims. Suspicions fall on them for the murder of Duncan, and Macbeth is presently made King.

Macbeth next identifies Banquo and his son Fleance as the only threat to his power, so he hires a group of killers to ambush and kill them. The assassins manage to kill Banquo but Fleance escapes. That night, at a banquet, Macbeth is visited by Banquo's ghost. As no one else can see him, he appears to be raving at thin air, thus fuelling the doubts that have already begun to form about his kingship. Increasingly anxious, Macbeth revisits the three witches who inform him that he should beware of Macduff. However, Macbeth also hears that he is safe from any man 'of woman born' and that he will have nothing to fear as long as Birnan Wood does not move to Dunsinane Hill. Feeling confident after this, Macbeth then orders the slaughter of

Macduff's family after Macduff has fled to England.

Macduff joins Malcolm in England, where he has raised an army to attack Macbeth. Before they arrive, the English army cut down Birnan Wood to use as camouflage. When Macbeth hears this he is shaken. His doubts are compounded when Lady Macbeth, who has been sleepwalking, plagued by stains on her hand that only she can see, kills herself. Macbeth fights on, confident that he cannot be killed by a man not born of woman. However, he eventually encounters Macduff, who informs Macbeth that he was 'untimely ripped' from his mother's womb (i.e., he was born by Caesarean section). Fearful at this news, Macbeth is soon slain by Macduff and Malcolm becomes King.

THEMES AND TECHNIQUES

As with many other tragedies, *Macbeth* is a story about ambition and how those who over-reach themselves generally meet an unhappy ending. Macbeth places his own ambition before his loyalty to the King and, although he temporarily gains power, he loses his life as a result of his greed. Shakespeare reinforces the illegitimate status of Macbeth's kingship in a variety of ways, not the least of which is referring to him as a 'tyrant' rather than a king. Shakespeare also associates Macbeth's reign with unnatural acts, such as an eclipse of the sun, or when Duncan's horses eat each other. The most unnatural image of them all is Lady Macbeth, who unsexes herself, or becomes masculine, in order to accomplish the murder of Duncan. She is then troubled by unnatural visions of blood on her hands that she cannot wash off. Blood is used here as a visible indication of guilt, but it is also joined by other images of a sick body which deck the descriptions of Macbeth's corrupt reign. This is a favourite image of Shakespearean drama and, in this play, images of disease are matched in number only by those alluding to the strangeness of time. Time is never at ease with itself – it is either too quick or too slow, becoming day when it is night and night when it is day, as both the Macbeths find when they try to sleep. Indeed, the disjointedness of time is ultimately their fault because, as Duncan points out, Macbeth is 'so far before' himself, while Lady Macbeth is too willing to 'feel now the future in the instant'.

Further Reading

Schoenbaum, Sam (ed.), *'Macbeth': Critical Essays*. New York and London: Garland Science, 1991. This is an interesting collection of essays, ranging from work by Samuel Johnson to classic essays of the last century.

Shakespeare, Williams, *Macbeth*. Edited by Kenneth Muir. London: The Arden Shakespeare, 2001. One of the best editions available of the play, this book fully glosses the text and offers an introduction to its history.

MAC FLECKNOE (1679–82)
by John Dryden

Sh— alone my perfect image bears,
Mature in dullness from his tender years:
Sh— alone, of all my sons, is he
Who stands confirmed in full stupidity.

Written at the expense of a literary and political opponent, *Mac Flecknoe* is a mock-heroic poem. It tells the story of Sh— , the adopted heir of Flecknoe, the ruler of an empire of dullness.

Summary

The poem begins by describing Flecknoe, the absolute monarch of the 'realms of Nonsense' as he approaches the end of his life and thus the end of his reign 'in prose and verse'. Like Augustus, the first Roman Emperor, Flecknoe decides to adopt an heir. Casting around for a suitable successor, Flecknoe alights upon Sh—, Thomas Shadwell, a writer who, 'mature in dullness' most resembles Flecknoe. While some writers may try and be witty, or even try to make sense, Sh— never deviates from his own foggy night of senselessness. Sh— even has the bulk 'designed for thoughtless majesty'. Taking all this into account, Flecknoe believes that he has only really paved the way for the true genius of Sh—. In fact, Flecknoe can imagine him sailing majestically down the Thames, borne along upon the sewage. He then loses himself in 'silent raptures' contemplating quite how wonderfully dull Sh—'s work is, especially his plays.

Flecknoe then sets about building a throne suitable for Sh— near the Nursery, a training school for actors, in a district of London known for its low-life. As Sh—'s coronation approaches, the way is lined with the limbs of mangled poets, neglected authors and unsold copies of Sh—'s work. Sh— then swears to maintain his dullness until his death, while forever waging war on wit and sense. He holds a mug of ale in one hand, a copy of a bad Flecknoe play in the other, while poppies are sprinkled on his head. After 12 owls have landed on Sh—'s left arm, Flecknoe then pronounces his hopes for his adopted son's reign. He hopes that Sh— will take dullness to new levels, suffering 'pangs without birth, and fruitless industry.' He further trusts that no one will dare to compare him to BEN JONSON, a writer who did not have the talent to comment on things he did not understand, or to promise a play that turned out to be a farce, or to steal lines from other playwrights. Still making his speech, Flecknoe sinks beneath the stage, leaving his mantle for Sh— to wear.

Dryden's *Mac Flecknoe* is a mock-heroic poem. It satirises one of Dryden's literary rivals, Thomas Shadwell, with whom Dryden had had a long-running dispute.

THEMES AND TECHNIQUES

Dryden was more than proficient in most forms of writing, but he excelled in satire, such as in *Absalom and Achitophel*, and, here, in *Mac Flecknoe*. *Mac Flecknoe* stems from a long-running dispute Dryden had with the writer Thomas Shadwell, whose identity is supposedly protected in the poem by being reduced to the cryptic Sh—. Shadwell held that he was the natural heir to Ben Jonson, the playwright who wrote comedies of humours. If Dryden was not persuaded of the value of Jonson's 'humour' plays, he was certainly less than enamoured by Shadwell's inferior imitations.

At some stage, Dryden decided to take their argument to another level and wrote *Mac Flecknoe*, in which he satirises Shadwell, describing him as the son (the 'Mac' of the title) and heir to the prolific but dull writer Richard Flecknoe who had recently died. Written in 1679, it was initially only distributed

amongst friends, but when Dryden and Shadwell became political as well as literary rivals, a publisher decided to put it to press in 1682.

The central conceit of the poem is the mock-heroic coronation of Shadwell as the new monarch of dullness. The mock-heroic technique involves using a heroic style to deride airs and affectations. In this instance, the coronation of Shadwell is referred to in terms of majestic and important events in the past. For example, a comparison is made between Flecknoe foreshadowing Shadwell in the same way as John the Baptist foreshadowed Jesus. The discrepancy between the two sides of the comparison blights rather than favours its object, leaving Shadwell well and truly belittled.

Further Reading

Hammond, Paul and Hopkins, David (ed.), *John Dryden: Tercentenary Essays*. Oxford: Clarendon Press, 2000. This collection of essays marking 300 years since Dryden's death, looks at all aspects of his work, including his relationships with other writers, such as Shadwell.

MAGGIE: A GIRL OF THE STREETS (1893)
by Stephen Crane

She speculated how long her youth would endure. She began to see the bloom upon her cheeks as valuable.

Maggie is a short, uncompromising novel about the terrible waste of human potential caused by poverty. It tells the story of Maggie, a beautiful and naïve girl who is forced to become a prostitute.

Summary

The novel opens with Jimmie, Maggie's brother, deep into a fight with some neighbouring boys in the Bowery district of New York. Pete, an older boy, breaks up the fight and takes Jimmie home with his casually vicious father. There they are met by Maggie and her younger brother Tommie. Mary, their mother, beats Jimmie for fighting again and he runs away to get beer for his friendly neighbour. Maggie's father retires to the pub while Mary sinks into a drunken slumber. This is a typical evening in the life of Maggie's family. Soon Maggie's father and Tommie are both dead. As Jimmie grows up he becomes as mean as his father. One day he warns Maggie that she will become a prostitute if she does not get a job. Maggie takes up an offer of work in a collar and cuff factory.

> Written as a counterpoint to the myth of prosperity described in mainstream novels of the time, Crane's *Maggie* was poorly received because of its gritty portrayal of a woman forced to become a prostitute.

She is also reintroduced to Pete who is now a bartender. She believes that he is special because he wears gaudy clothes and takes her to various entertainments, such as dance halls and melodramas. Mary, however, condemns Maggie as a whore, announcing that she has gone 'to deh devil'. Jimmie concurs with this opinion and smashes up Pete's bar as a form of retribution. Maggie moves in with Pete but it is only temporary because, one evening, Pete is himself seduced by Nellie, a more cunning woman than Maggie. When Maggie goes to see Pete at his bar he tells her that she has to stay away because the manager wants to keep the place respectable. Maggie finds that everyone seems to look at her differently and so, inevitably, she becomes a prostitute. One day Jimmie goes home to Mary and informs her that Maggie is dead. Mary is urged by her neighbours to forgive Maggie, which she finally does.

THEMES AND TECHNIQUES

When Crane first wrote *Maggie*, it was rejected by publishers because of its unflinching realism. Even when Crane published it at his own expense, the novel was considered scandalous by some critics and too dour by others. However, Crane was reacting to the popular novels of the time which, to his mind, sentimentalised the world and ignored the seamier underside of society. During the 1890s, America enjoyed a previously unknown level of prosperity and much of the literature of the

time seemed to revel in that. Crane, however, not only showed an alternative to the prosperity myth, he also suggested that people's lives were largely determined by their circumstances. Born into a poor family with alcoholic parents, the good-looking but naïve Maggie is almost doomed to become a prostitute. This is an uncomfortable alternative to the American Dream, which advises people that as long as their aspirations are exceeded by their efforts, they will succeed. In this regard Crane pioneered a form of social realism that would come to dominate both the form of the American novel and its ever more cynical tone.

Further Reading

Crane, Stephen, *Maggie: A Girl of the Streets*. Edited by Thomas Gullason. New York: W.W. Norton, 1980. This edition of the novel also offers background material and various critical essays.

MAJOR BARBARA (1905)
by George Bernard Shaw

You cannot have power for good without having power for evil too. Even mother's milk nourishes murderers as well as heroes.

Major Barbara is a polemical play that deals with the question of poverty. It follows Major Barbara of the Salvation Army as she struggles to reconcile herself to the logic of her father and his deadly armaments business.

Summary

The play opens at Lady Britomart's house some time in January 1906. Britomart advises her son, Stephen, that she can no longer bear the burden of the family affairs and that, as a grown man, he must take responsibility himself. It soon transpires that the family finances are not in a good condition. Stephen has two sisters – Sarah and Barbara. Sarah has a fiancé but he is immature and he will not come into funds for ten years. Barbara is a major in the Salvation Army and she is engaged to a professor of Greek. The only recourse they have is to their father, Andrew Undershaft. Britomart tells Stephen that she separated from Undershaft because he disinherited Stephen when he was a baby.

Undershaft is descended from a long line of foundlings stretching back to James the First. The first Undershaft was adopted by an armourer and gun-maker and, when he succeeded to the business himself, out of gratitude he passed it on to another foundling, whom he named Andrew Undershaft too. This became a tradition that the cannon business was always left to an adopted foundling named Andrew Undershaft. The present Undershaft has disinherited Stephen for just this reason. However, he is still willing to pay for their living expenses and so, despite telling Stephen he is in control, Britomart has already invited Undershaft to see them this evening. When he arrives, he and Barbara soon clash over the morality of the arms business. In order to settle their differences, Undershaft agrees to spend a day with Barbara at the Salvation Army shelter where she works, and the following day she will join him at his munitions factory.

At the shelter, Undershaft watches his daughter work and is impressed with her approach. He suggests that she would be the very person to take over his factory. However, when he attempts to donate a couple of pennies to the charity, Barbara refuses his money because it is tainted. Undeterred, when Undershaft learns that the shelter is in danger of closing unless it can match a £5,000 grant offered by Lord Saxmundham, he agrees to get the money. Barbara wants to refuse her father's help but she is overruled and so, dispirited, she pins her army badge on Undershaft's collar. The next day Barbara appears without her uniform. When they tour the factory the group learn that Barbara's fiancé, Cusins, is in fact a foundling of sorts and that he is entitled to inherit the factory. As he and Undershaft have struck up a mutual understanding, it only remains for Barbara to be convinced. She admits that she now understands how the world works and that money and power are not intrinsically evil but may be used for good too. Cusins promises to use his new position to change the world and Barbara

decides to return to the Army, fired up with her new convictions.

THEMES AND TECHNIQUES

Major Barbara is less about developing a plot in terms of action, than it is about developing an argument. That argument is given its fullest realisation in the character of Undershaft. SHAW declares in the 'Preface' he wrote to the play that Undershaft represents a man who understands 'that the greatest of our evils, and the worst of our crimes is poverty, and that our first duty, to which every other consideration should be sacrificed, is not to be poor.' Shaw terms this the 'Gospel of St Andrew Undershaft' and much of the play is given up to showing how ineffective many of the arguments against it are. In the end, even Barbara is converted to the cause. She sees that when Undershaft is able to keep the shelter going, that his creed gives him the power to alter things for the better. She is then able to return to the Salvation Army disabused of the notion that poverty is blessed.

> Less concerned with advancing the plot than it is with developing an argument, *Major Barbara* is a polemical play in which Shaw examines the evil caused by poverty.

Further Reading

Bloom, Harold (ed.), *George Bernard Shaw's 'Major Barbara'*. Broomall: Chelsea House Publishers, 1988. This is a solid collection of critical essays arranged in order of publication.

MEN AND WOMEN (1855)
by Robert Browning

Make them forget there's such a thing as flesh.
Your business is to paint the souls of men.

Reflecting his enjoyment of Italy, *Men and Women* is probably BROWNING's best loved collection of poetry. It contains many of his most memorable poems, including 'Andrea del Sarto', 'A Toccata of Galuppi's', and 'Fra Lippo Lippi'.

Summary

One of Browning's most famous pieces of work from the collection *Men and Women* is 'Fra Lippo Lippi'. Based on the Italian Renaissance painter of the same name, it tells the imaginary story of Fra (Brother) Lippi, a monk, returning home drunk and his interrogation by the local guards. It is a dramatic monologue in which we only hear Lippi's voice. Once he has revealed the fact that he is a monk and a painter whose patron is the ruler of Florence, 'Cosimo of the Medici', the guards release their grip of him. Lippi then begins to look at the guards' faces as possible models for his religious paintings. The one who held him by the throat could be a model for Judas, while another could stand in for the slave who held John the Baptist's head. Lippi then explains that he was painting when he heard revelling in the streets, and being much taken with the spring air, he made a knotted ladder from the sheets in his room and let himself down to the ground.

Written in Italy during a period of great happiness, Browning's collection of poems *Men and Women* proved to be very influential. In particular, many of the book's poems feature the dramatic monologue, a technique favoured by several leading modern poets.

He goes on to recount to the guards how, as a child, he had been left an orphan in the streets and how he became a monk, taking advantage of the opportunity offered him to become a painter. However, when he painted a cloister wall, the images were too close to the likenesses of real people for his superiors' liking and he was ordered to start again. Now, however, his new way of painting is appreciated and because he has a powerful patron, he can paint what he likes. He argues that as God has made everything, then to paint anything in its truest likeness is a form of homage to God. Lippo says he will make amends for his behaviour by painting a picture which the guards will be able to see in six months' time in Sant Ambrogio's church. Pleased at this thought, he thereupon leaves the guards as the dawn is about to break.

THEMES AND TECHNIQUES

Lippo Lippi was a Florentine painter who lived and worked in the fifteenth century at the dawn of the Italian Renaissance. He was part of a wave of painters who inaugurated a new style of more realistic painting, using, for example, depth and perspective to create the illusion of an accurate portrayal of landscapes and people, as opposed to the more iconic, two-dimensional form of painting that predominated in medieval times. Browning has the character of Lippi advance a theory of realism in the course of his dramatic monologue, advising us that, in so doing, he discloses 'the value and significance of flesh'.

Such an argument could equally be applied to the form of the poem, the dramatic monologue, which imitates a realistic portrayal of speech. The dramatic monologue is a form of poetry (or prose) in which the speaker of the poem is a character addressing a silent or implied audience. In this case, the audience for Lippi's address are the guards who have stopped him. The readers of the poem take the place of the implied audience in listening to Lippi. From what he says, we are also able to infer the situation in which he finds himself, that of coming home late and drunk. Typically, the character making the address in a dramatic monologue also makes an argument. Here, the argument is about the nature and purpose of art.

In poems like 'Fra Lippo Lippi' Browning developed the technique of the dramatic monologue. Dismissed as esoteric in his own time, it is the technique for which he was later lauded by poets such as W.B. Yeats and T.S. Eliot.

Further Reading

Browning, Robert, *The Poetical Works of Robert Browning: Volume 5 – Men and Women*. Edited by Ian Jack and Robert Inglesfield. Oxford: Clarendon Press, 1995. Rapidly becoming the standard edition of Browning's poetry, this version of *Men and Women* is replete with a detailed introduction to each poem.

Watson, J.R. (ed.), *Casebook on Browning's 'Men and Women' and Other Poems*. London: Macmillan, 1974. This is a generous collection of essays looking at a number of different aspects of Browning's poetry, including the dramatic monologue.

MERCHANT OF VENICE, THE (1596–97)
by William Shakespeare

If you prick us, do we not bleed? If you tickle us, do we not laugh? If you poison us, do we not die? And if you wrong us, shall we not revenge? If we are like you in the rest, we will resemble you in that. If a Jew wrong a Christian, what is his humility? Revenge. If a Christian wrong a Jew, what should his sufferance be by Christian example? Why, revenge. The villainy you teach me, I will execute, and it shall go hard but I will better the instruction.

The Merchant of Venice is one of Shakespeare's strangest tales, in which carefree comedy mixes with an anguished humanism. It tells the story of Shylock, the moneylender, and his desire to exact revenge upon Antonio by taking a pound of his flesh.

Summary

When the play opens, Bassanio, a young Venetian, is short of money. He needs the money in order to woo Portia, a wealthy young woman from Belmont. If he succeeds in winning her hand then he will be rich once again and able to pay off the debts he owes to Antonio, his friend and a merchant of Venice. Antonio, who is plagued by an inexplicable sadness, agrees with Bassanio's plan but is unable to loan him the funds himself because all his money is tied up in ships at sea. He therefore suggests that Bassanio secure a loan using Antonio's name as a guarantor of credit. Meanwhile, Portia complains to her servant, Nerissa, of the will left by her father which stipulates that she can only marry the man who picks the correct casket from three – gold, silver or lead. The only man of whom they talk fondly is Bassanio when he visited her as part of the company of another suitor.

Back in Venice, Antonio and Bassanio go and see Shylock, the Jewish moneylender. Shylock dislikes Antonio because he continually berates both Shylock and Jews generally.

Nevertheless, he agrees to the loan on condition that if Antonio is unable to pay it back on time, then Shylock is entitled to a pound of Antonio's flesh, cut from whatever part of the body pleases Shylock. Despite Bassanio's misgivings, Antonio agrees to the deal. Later, in the night, Shylock's daughter, Jessica, elopes with one of Antonio's friends, Lorenzo. They take some of Shylock's money with them. Meanwhile, in Belmont, Portia has suffered two suitors who have chosen the gold and the silver caskets unsuccessfully. When Bassanio arrives with Graziano, his friend, Portia informs Bassanio that he must choose the correct casket or forever forgo the right to marry. Bassanio agrees and wanders between the three chests, and then, based on the reasoning that 'outward shows be least themselves' he picks the lead casket. It is the correct choice for inside it is a picture of Portia.

Their happiness is doubled when it is revealed that Graziano and Nerissa are also in love, and it is tripled when they are joined by Jessica and Lorenzo. However, the celebrations are cut short when news reaches them that Antonio's ships have sunk and that he is now liable to Shylock for a pound of flesh. Bassanio and Graziano leave for Venice immediately, and they are quickly followed by Portia and Nerissa, disguised as men. At the trial in Venice, Shylock refuses any other form of compensation for the contract and demands instead the pound of flesh. The Duke presiding over the trial then calls a legal expert who, it turns out, is actually Portia in disguise. She concurs that the contract is legally binding, but that Shylock is not entitled to any blood. Furthermore, as the contract would result in Antonio losing his life if executed, it contravenes a law stating that foreigners are not allowed to conspire against the life of a Venetian. Shylock is forced to become a Christian, pay a heavy fine and leave his entire fortune to Jessica and Lorenzo, but escapes with his life. Back in Belmont, Portia reveals to Bassanio that she was the legal expert. They also learn that several of Antonio's ships have not sunk and that he will be wealthy again, leaving them to celebrate their happiness together.

THEMES AND TECHNIQUES

At the centre of most debates about *The Merchant of Venice* is the character of Shylock.

Many commentators argue that because Shylock is indissolubly linked with his own Jewishness, and that because Shylock is essentially a mean character, the play itself, and by association SHAKESPEARE, is anti-Semitic. This is undoubtedly a possibility. Anti-Semitism was rife at the time the play was written following the execution for treason of a prominent Jew, as well as a popular play by CHRISTOPHER MARLOWE, *The Jew of Malta*, the central character of which is a villainous Jew who loses his daughter.

The Merchant of Venice is Shakespeare's most controversial play. Many critics argue that through Shakespeare's characterisation of Shylock, the play is fundamentally anti-Semitic. Others argue though that it was actually written as a riposte to anti-Semitic sentiments popular at the time.

Other critics, however, contend that Shakespeare's Shylock is written as a riposte to Marlowe's Barabas. For example, Shylock is not the straightforward money-grabber of legend. This is perhaps most obvious in the fact that Shylock forgoes the money owed to him in order to exact revenge upon Antonio for all the insults he has heaped on him and also for the loss of his daughter. Conversely, the Christian Bassanio initially only wants to marry Portia so he can secure enough money to pay off his debts. The play therefore allows different possible readings and performances. Indeed, it is important to remember that this is a play and that it is finally the performance which determines whether Shylock is played as a villain or a tragic hero or some combination of the two.

Further Reading

Mahon, John W. and Mahon, Ellen McLeod (ed.), *'The Merchant of Venice': Critical Essays*. London and New York: Routledge, 2002. This is a fascinating collection of essays that deals with many different aspects of the play, including its relationship to Marlowe's work and how to render it acceptable to a modern audience.

Shakespeare, William, *The Merchant of Venice*. Edited by J.R. Brown. London: The Arden

Shakespeare, 2000. This is a very good edition of the text which not only fully glosses the play, but also deals with the issue of the play's position in a post-Holocaust world.

MIDDLEMARCH (1871–72)
by George Eliot

Your pier-glass or extensive surface of polished steel made to be rubbed by a housemaid, will be minutely and multitudinously scratched in all directions; but place now against it a lighted candle as a centre of illumination, and lo! The scratches will seem to arrange themselves in a fine series of concentric circles around that little sun. It is demonstrable that the scratches are going everywhere impartially, and it is only your candle which produces the flattering illusion of a concentric arrangement, its light falling with an exclusive optical selection. These things are a parable. The scratches are events, and the candle is the egoism of any person now absent.

Middlemarch is GEORGE ELIOT's masterpiece and one of the most intelligent novels ever written. It centres on the mental and spiritual ambitions of Dorothea Brooke and Dr Lydgate, following them in their troubled marriages and social relationships in and around the provincial town of Middlemarch.

Summary

When the novel opens, Dorothea Brooke decides to marry Isaac Casaubon, a dry and passionless scholar, against the advice of her family. She has intellectual ambitions herself and hopes that she will be ably matched in that regard with Casaubon. However, when they travel on their honeymoon to Rome, Casaubon devotes himself to his studies and neglects Dorothea. She then spends a lot of time with Will Ladislaw, Casaubon's cousin and a man he despises. When Casaubon and Dorothea return to Middlemarch, the two become more and more distant and the intellectual stimulation Dorothea craves is entirely absent. Indeed, Dorothea starts to disrespect Casaubon's work, fearing that the great project he works on has all been done elsewhere.

Meanwhile, another Middlemarcher, Fred Vincy, is a dissolute young man with a large gambling debt. He persuades Caleb Garth to sign for the debt, but when Vincy's uncle Featherstone gives him the money to pay it off, Fred wastes it all, thus temporarily ruining the prospects of his beloved (and Garth's daughter) Mary. As Featherstone is dying, Fred hopes that he will be served favourably by the will, but he, like the rest of the scavenging relatives, are disappointed when Featherstone leaves his fortune to his illegitimate son. After exploring a number of avenues, Fred eventually begins to work for Garth and becomes a responsible man whom Mary is finally able to marry.

Fred's vain sister, Rosamond, decides to enslave the town's new doctor, Tertius Lydgate. Lydgate uses new methods and proves to be controversial among the town's older medics. In order to ease his position, Lydgate becomes friendly with Bulstrode, an influential man in Middlemarch. Without really meaning to, Lydgate finds himself engaged to Rosamond. They too had been warned that they were unsuited to each other, and it soon becomes apparent that Rosamond has little sympathy with Lydgate's intellectual ambition, nor any understanding of his budgetary constraints. One day, Casaubon falls ill and Lydgate treats him. Shortly afterwards, Casaubon dies leaving a condition in his will that if Dorothea marries Will, she will forfeit all Casaubon's property.

Will Ladislaw has moved to Middlemarch to work on a newspaper and support a career in politics. He proves to be a distraction to Rosamond who flatters herself that he wishes to marry her. However, when Ladislaw learns of the clause in Casaubon's will he is incensed and leaves for London. Will returns some time later and the two are almost reconciled until Dorothea catches Will with Rosamond. Rosamond is, by this stage, very unhappy, particularly as Lydgate's financial situation is deteriorating. Desperate, Lydgate accepts some money from Bulstrode. It is ostensibly a loan but to some people it looks like money paid to keep Will quiet after a man blackmailing Bulstrode is found dead in his house and Will declares it to be death by natural causes.

Bulstrode is forced to leave Middlemarch because of the scandal, but, with Dorothea's support, Lydgate is able to stay. Having helped to pay off Lydgate's loan, Dorothea decides she does not want to be beholden to money and, accepting the clause in Casaubon's will, she decides to marry Will and live in London. There, Will is elected to Parliament and they are finally happy. Lydgate and Rosamond eventually also move to London where he runs a practice for rich people until he meets an early death, leaving Rosamond a wealthy woman.

Virginia Woolf described *Middlemarch* as 'one of the few English novels written for grown-up people'. It examines the psychological responses of characters to the brakes placed on their ambitions.

THEMES AND TECHNIQUES

Middlemarch is a dense and complex novel, and the plot outlined above touches on but a part of it. Nevertheless, certain themes are dominant in all the interwoven stories, not the least of which is thwarted ambition. Eliot shows how everyone has to either adapt themselves to the constraints imposed upon them or fight them. Dorothea is constrained throughout the novel, firstly by conventions which dictate what a woman can and cannot do, then by a passionless marriage, and finally by a will. While she is helped out of the marriage by circumstance, and out of the will by her relationship with Ladislaw, she has to adapt more subtly to the conventions dictated to Victorian women, by establishing herself as a charity worker, performing unnamed, small acts of kindness rather than one large dramatic act. On the other side of the coin, the boldness which eludes Dorothea is shown, in the case of Lydgate, to be the cause of its own limitations. For Lydgate's failure to negotiate the social niceties of Middlemarch means that his pioneering practice is all but destroyed by the conservative forces of the town. Equally, the demands placed upon him by the responsibilities of being a husband prove to be too onerous and he has to curb his ambition to suit, ending up as a conventional doctor and dying young.

Further Reading

Hornback, Bert G. (ed.), *'Middlemarch': A Novel of Reform*. New York: Twayne Publishers, 1988. This book offers an introduction to the novel's history, as well its themes and types of characterisation.

Peck, John (ed.), *New Casebook on 'Middlemarch'*. New York and London: St Martin's Press, 1992. This is an interesting collection of contemporary critical essays on Eliot's novel.

MIDSUMMER NIGHT'S DREAM, A (1595)
by William Shakespeare

The course of true love never did run smooth.

A Midsummer Night's Dream is one of SHAKESPEARE's most popular comedies. It follows the fortunes of a group of Athenians as they sort out their tangled love lives in an enchanted forest.

Summary

When the play opens, Theseus, the Duke of Athens, is contemplating his impending marriage to Hippolyta, the Amazon Queen whom he has recently conquered. Their reverie is interrupted by Egeus, a prominent Athenian and father to Hermia. He has Hermia with him, as well as two young men, Demetrius and Lysander. Egeus explains that he wants Hermia to marry Demetrius, as does Demetrius himself. However, Hermia and Lysander are already in love with each other. Egeus asks Theseus if he can invoke the ancient privilege of Athens which allows a father to decide the future husband of his daughter or seek her death. Theseus concurs, although he allows Hermia the option of becoming a nun instead. She is given until the next new moon to think about her response.

Lysander and Hermia then hatch a plan. The following night they will elope to Lysander's aunt's house some seven leagues away. As it is outside the jurisdiction of Athenian law, they will be able to marry each other safely. They recount their plan to Helena, Hermia's best friend. She has long been in love with Demetrius and decides that if she tells him the plan he will love her for it. However, when Demetrius hears of the plan, he sets off in pursuit of Lysander and Hermia and enters a forest near Athens. This forest is also the home of Titania and Oberon, the King and Queen of the fairies. They are engaged in an argument over who should have a little changeling boy Titania has brought back from India. Oberon asks his sprite, Puck, to help him get revenge and sends him to secure a potion that can make anyone who is spotted with it fall in love with the first person they see when they wake. When Oberon spies Helena, who has followed Demetrius into the woods, being abused by him, he instructs Puck to apply some potion to Demetrius's eyes so he will fall in love with Helena.

One of Shakespeare's most popular comedies, *A Midsummer Night's Dream* intertwines the worlds of myth and magic with the more commonplace loves of a group of Athenian citizens.

Mistakenly, Puck puts the potion on Lysander's eyes. When he awakes he falls in love with Helena, who is the first person he sees. Realising his mistake, Puck later puts the potion on Demetrius' eyes, causing them both to be in love with Helena. Now Hermia is enraged at Helena and the two men are on the point of fighting until Puck manages to separate them with some trickery. Meanwhile, the potion is also used on Titania. When she awakes she falls in love with Bottom, a simple craftsman, who now has the head of a donkey, thanks to Puck. This continues until Titania gives Oberon the changeling and he reverses the charm. Puck does the same for Lysander. The next day, the lovers are discovered in the forest. When it transpires that Demetrius no longer loves Hermia, but Helena instead, Theseus overrules Egeus and the two couples join the Duke and Hippolyta for their wedding. At the wedding they are entertained by an unintentionally comic version of the tragic love story about Pyramus and Thisbe, performed by Bottom and his incompetent friends.

THEMES AND TECHNIQUES

As with all of Shakespeare's plays, *A Midsummer Night's Dream* is not quite as straightforward as it might appear. For although the play is a comedy with a seemingly light-hearted tone throughout it, it also has a sinister side. This can be seen most clearly in the play's most prominent theme – love. The triple wedding feast at the end of the drama seems to be a celebration of love, but it is somewhat undermined by the route to that ending. Hippolyta, we are informed, is wedding Theseus because he conquered her people with his sword. Hermia loves Lysander, but only because he has wooed her with all the flattering tricks culled from that insincere form of love known as courtly love. Meanwhile, Demetrius only loves Helena because he is still under the influence of Puck's drug. Elsewhere in the play, the example of the already married couple of the fairy King and Queen is tarnished when Oberon drugs Titania so he can get his own way. Even Egeus's fatherly love is hardly inspiring, demanding as he does that his daughter either be killed or sent to a nunnery.

Further Reading

Halio, J.L., *'A Midsummer Night's Dream': Shakespeare in Performance*. Manchester: Manchester University Press, 2003. This is a very interesting title that examines the different ways in which the play has been produced, particularly in the twentieth century.

Kehler, Dorothea (ed.), *'A Midsummer Night's Dream': Critical Essays*. London and New York: Garland Science, 1998. A comprehensive collection of essays that deals with many different aspects of the play, including its critical and performance history.

MILL ON THE FLOSS, THE (1860)
by George Eliot

More helpful than all wisdom is one draught of simple human pity that will not forsake us.

The Mill on the Floss, one of ELIOT's earliest novels, finds her once again exploring the 'dead level of provincial existence'. The story follows Maggie Tulliver as she struggles to reconcile herself with rural society.

Summary

Maggie Tulliver is an energetic, lively and intelligent child, devoted to her elder brother, Tom. She lives with her parents at Dorlcote Mill on the River Floss. Despite the fact that Maggie is apparently much brighter than Tom, Mr Tulliver decides to pay for Tom to take extra schooling so that he does not need to work in the mill when he grows up. This causes a degree of family friction because Mr Tulliver owes his wife's sister a large amount of money already. Despite the fact that his own sister owes him roughly the same amount, he refuses to call in the loan. Against this background, Mr Tulliver is involved in a protracted law suit with Lawyer Wakem over the use of the Floss.

When Maggie goes to visit Tom, she meets Philip Wakem, Lawyer Wakem's crippled son, who is studying at the same place as Tom. She immediately strikes up an accord with Philip, all the while knowing that she is really consorting with the enemy. This fact is brought home to her when she is withdrawn from school following Lawyer Wakem's victory in the law suit. Her father is bankrupted and falls ill and Tom also returns home. Eventually, Wakem buys the mill himself and hires Tulliver to run it. This unhappy turn of events is relieved with the arrival of Tom's friend, Bob Jakin.

Jakin buys Maggie books and encourages her intellectual and spiritual development. Soon afterwards, she begins to see Philip again, meeting in secret. Eventually they declare their love for each other, but when Tom finds out, he makes Maggie promise not to see Philip again. Working with Jakin, Tom manages to accrue enough money to pay off the family's debts. However, on the same day that this is accomplished, Tulliver attacks Lawyer Wakem, falls ill and dies.

Several years later, Maggie is working as a teacher. On a visit to her old home town to see her cousin, Lucy, and her fiancé, Stephen Guest, Maggie once again meets Philip. After receiving Tom's permission, Maggie renews their relationship. Philip confesses his love for Maggie to his father, who not only adds his consent but also concedes that he will sell Dorlcote Mill to Tom. However, these blessings are diffused by Maggie's realisation that she is hopelessly attracted to Stephen, and he to her. She resolves to leave him behind her but, through a series of mistimings, they end up alone on a boat together. When they return the next day, Maggie is treated as a harlot and shunned by almost everyone, including Tom. She stays with the Jakin family and is eventually forgiven by both Philip and Lucy. Stephen, however, still pleads with her to marry him, but she refuses, despite the distress it causes her. One day, the Floss breaks its banks. After warning the Jakin family, Maggie rows a boat to Dorlcote Mill in order to rescue Tom. She manages to reach the trapped Tom, but, once he is onboard the boat, it capsizes and they both drown in each other's embrace.

The Mill on the Floss offers an intimate portrait of a rural way of life that was vanishing at the time. The characters, struggling to come to terms with modernisation, find that history and tradition serve as the only reliable moral compasses.

THEMES AND TECHNIQUES

The Mill on the Floss is a historical novel in several senses. Firstly, insofar as it faithfully records a certain type of English rural life in the first half of the nineteenth century. Eliot's beautifully rendered descriptions of St Ogg's and the surrounding area offer us a vivid picture of a way of life which has vanished with the advent of modernisation. Indeed, it is precisely the process of modernisation which Eliot addresses here. The second sense in which *The Mill on the Floss* is historical is the value it places on history. History and tradition function as a form of moral gravity for the novel's characters. Right from the beginning this is apparent in the smallest of ways. We see, for example, the young Maggie struggle to cope with her brother's censorious attitude because she has yet to gain the perspective that previous experience will afford her. However, Tom, in his entrepreneurial endeavours, and Stephen, in his pursuit of Maggie, at various times express their need to live only for the present, disregarding the larger

perspective. It is precisely this larger perspective which informs Maggie's final decision to save Tom. Not only is this based on a lifetime's worth of filial love, but also upon the legend of St Ogg, whom she emulates by rowing to save her brother regardless of her own safety.

Further Reading

Shuttleworth, Sally (ed.), *The Mill on the Floss*. London and New York: Routledge Publishers, 1991. This edition of the novel comes with a fascinating commentary which looks at Eliot's use of gender and the assumptions of realism which underpin it.

Yousaf, Nahem and Maunder, Andrew (eds), *New Casebook on 'The Mill on the Floss' and 'Silas Marner'*. New York and London: St Martin's Press, 2002. This is a solid collection of contemporary critical essays about both *The Mill on the Floss* and *Silas Marner*.

MISCELLANEOUS POEMS (1681)
by Andrew Marvell

Had we but world enough, and time,
This coyness, Lady, were no crime.

MARVELL published very little poetry during his own lifetime, and this collection was printed posthumously by a woman pretending to be his wife in order to gain his pension. It contains most of the poems by which we now know him, including 'To His Coy Mistress' and 'The Definition of Love'.

Summary

Marvell's most famous poem is 'To His Coy Mistress'. It is essentially a plea from the speaker of the poem for his mistress to succumb to his sexual advances. He argues that the woman's diffidence in this matter would only be acceptable if they had unlimited time at their disposal. They could spend their days on opposite sides of the world from each other, her in India and he in Hull, writing complaints or love poems of deep yearning. If this were the situation, then he would quite happily love her in this chaste manner from near the beginning of time to near the end. He would spend a 100 years praising her eyes, 200 years on each breast, and 30,000 years for the rest of her. Indeed, he argues that if this were the case, he could not love her in less time because that is what a lady such as her demands.

However, the speaker of the poem points out that they do not have all the time in world, and that, conversely, time is a constant pressure. Time not only flies by, but once it has gone, it leaves the two of them in a blank eternity in which only the worms will keep her company in her tomb and all her honour will turn to dust anyway. As he points out, once she is dead she will be embraced by no one. He therefore suggests that they take advantage of their youth while they still have it. In particular, he argues she should make the most of her youthful ardour and eat up the time making love rather than having the time eat them up by not doing anything. At least that way, although they will not be able to stop time, they will be able to keep it on the run.

Marvell's poems were only collected and published after he was dead; this was undertaken by his landlady in the hope that she might profit from his pension. Many of the works in *Miscellaneous Poems* are typically metaphysical in that they are based around elaborate metaphors and similes.

THEMES AND TECHNIQUES

In 'To His Coy Mistress' the speaker's plea is centred around three basic ideas that would have been familiar to Marvell's audience at the time. The first of these is the notion that 'time flies' (*tempus fugit*). With 'time's winged chariot' at their backs, they have very little time in which to act before the moment disappears forever. The second idea upon which the speaker bases his argument is the reminder of their impending death (*memento mori*). The speaker paints an image of the woman's eventual grave, where her virginity will turn to dust anyway and she will be confined to a 'fine' (or narrow) and 'private' (or deprived) place for eternity. The final idea, leading on from the previous two, is that in

the light of the fact that they are both speeding towards death they should seize the day while they can (*carpe diem*). In this regard they could, he proposes, rightly indulge themselves in a frenzied and animal-like here-and-now, living life to the fullest.

Further Reading

Brett, R.L. (ed.), *Andrew Marvell: Essays on the Tercentenary of His Death*. London: Oxford University Press, 1969. This book contains a selection of essays to mark the 300th anniversary of Marvell's death.

Pollard, Arthur (ed.), *Casebook on Andrew Marvell's Poems*. London: Palgrave Macmillan, 1980. This collection of essays looks at Marvell's poetry from a variety of different perspectives.

MOBY DICK (1851)
by Herman Melville

Call me Ishmael.

The encyclopaedic and mythical *Moby Dick* is one of the greatest novels in any language. Told by Ishmael, a sailor on board the *Pequod*, the novel follows Captain Ahab's relentless pursuit for Moby Dick, the great white whale which cost him his leg.

Summary

At the beginning of the novel, Ishmael, a young sailor looking for adventure, arrives in New Bedford. Here he teams up with Queequeg, a cannibal and expert harpooner and together they set off for Nantucket, the capital of the whaling industry. There they negotiate with the owners of a boat, the *Pequod*, and are signed up for a year's voyage. They meet several other members of the crew, including Starbuck, the first mate, but there is no sign of Captain Ahab, the ship's captain about whom they have already been warned. The ship leaves on Christmas Day, but it is several days before Ahab emerges from his cabin. When he does come out, he eventually reveals that the purpose of the voyage is to kill Moby Dick, a legendary white whale who caused him to lose one of his legs, a leg which is now replaced with whale bone. Ahab nails a gold coin to the mast and offers it to the first man to spot the whale. He has even smuggled aboard a group of men, led by Fedallah, specifically designed to hunt Moby Dick.

Moby Dick is one of the greatest stories about obsession ever told. It describes Captain Ahab's unrelenting pursuit of the seemingly indestructible and insatiable whale Moby Dick.

The *Pequod* encounters a number of other ships on its voyage around the globe, including the *Jeroboam*. On board the *Jeroboam* a prophet called Gabriel warns of the disaster facing the *Pequod*. Ishmael has already been warned about the ship's impending doom, and, when this is combined with Starbuck's concerns about Ahab's mental state, he starts to feel some concern. Nevertheless, the crew of the *Pequod* continue to hunt for whales during this period with varying degrees of success. On one occasion, the cabin boy becomes fearful and jumps out of one of the whaling boats. Having been warned about this behaviour before, he is left behind. Although he is later picked up, the incident sends him insane. This is considered to be another bad omen and it is compounded when they encounter another ship, the *Samuel Enderby*, whose captain has lost an arm to Moby Dick and advises Ahab to forget his quest, but Ahab is not to be deterred.

As the ship approaches the Pacific waters which Moby Dick is known to frequent, Ahab gives up all pretence of ordinary whale hunting. At this stage Queequeg falls sick and orders the ship's carpenter to make him a coffin. He recovers just in time for Ahab to take the *Pequod* into a vicious storm which results in the death of another crew member. Next, they meet the *Rachel*, a ship which has just encountered Moby Dick. They learn how the whale caused the loss of the captain's son. Hearing this, Ahab's zeal for Moby Dick becomes maniacal and, shortly afterwards, he sights the great white whale himself. For the following three days the crew of the *Pequod* fight the massive creature. In the process, Fedallah is killed and Ahab loses his false leg. However, he continues to attack Moby Dick until the whale rams the *Pequod* and the ship starts to sink. Ahab makes one last lunge at the whale but his neck is caught up in his own line and he is pulled under, the rest of his crew being sucked into the vortex caused by the sinking *Pequod*. Only Ishmael escapes being sucked under, floating on the open sea in Queequeg's coffin until he is picked up by the *Rachel*, still searching for the captain's son.

THEMES AND TECHNIQUES

Moby Dick is almost the book that ate everything. Like Queequeg, it is cannibalistic in its nature, devouring seminal texts from other cultures, including everything from the BIBLE to KING LEAR, through to Greek tragedy and previous American literature. It displays a vast encyclopaedic knowledge and is surely one of the widest-ranging novels ever written, traversing global literature in much the same way as the *Pequod* traverses the world's seas. However, in being such a knowledgeable text, *Moby Dick* also points to the limit of what we can know. In this regard nothing is more poignant than Moby Dick itself.

Ishmael, the novel's narrator, begins the book with a series of quotations about whales in order to show how these sublime creatures infiltrate every field of learning. As the *Pequod* progresses on its journey, great swathes of pages are given over to trying to explain all there is to know about whales. However, Ishmael ultimately has to admit defeat in this endeavour and it is Moby Dick that represents that failure. For the giant whale, like death, is ultimately unknowable and its ways finally mysterious. Any attempt to explain it is as fruitless as Ahab's attempt to overthrow and kill it. Beginning and ending the novel in a coffin, the two book-ends of Ishmael's narrative are bordered by the final frontier of what we can know – representations of death itself.

Further Reading

Brodhead, Richard H. (ed.), *New Essays on 'Moby Dick'*. Cambridge: Cambridge University Press 1986. This is a collection of essays that deals with several different aspects of the novel, including its critical history and its place in the American canon.

Olson, Charles, *Call Me Ishmael*. Baltimore: Johns Hopkins University Press, 1997. First published in 1947, this is a classic of modern criticism. Beautifully written by the Black Mountain poet Charles Olson, it addresses the influence of Shakespeare on Melville amongst other issues.

MOLL FLANDERS (1722)
by Daniel Defoe

The moral, indeed, of all my history is left to be gathered by the senses and judgement of the reader; I am not qualified to preach to them. Let the experience of one creature completely wicked, and completely miserable, be a storehouse of useful warning to those that read.

Moll Flanders is a novel masquerading as an autobiography. DEFOE tells the story of Moll and how she survives in eighteenth-century London by any means possible, foul or fair, as a prostitute, a wife, a thief and a felon.

Summary

Moll Flanders begins her life in Newgate Prison, where she is born to a criminal. When her mother is transported to Virginia for her crimes, Moll is left alone in the world. Taken in by some gypsies, she leaves them when she is 3 years old and is given a place with a parish nurse. At the age of 8 she is supposed to start work, but she protests that she wishes to be a gentlewoman. Some of the ladies of the parish find this amusing and support her until she is 14 and her nurse dies.

Moll then goes to live with one of these ladies and becomes an adopted member of the household. As she grows up, she becomes very attractive and is soon subject to the blandishments of the house's eldest son. With a mixture of flattery and deception, he seduces Moll and continues to have sex with her for some time. Moll soon finds that the youngest son of the house is in love with her and wants to marry her. Although Moll is in love with the eldest son, he encourages her to marry his younger brother and, eventually, they become husband and wife. Moll bears him two children but he dies within five years, and they are sent to live with his parents.

Relatively rich from all the money given to her by her first lover, Moll casts about for a suitable husband. She finally settles on a draper but he turns out to be a profligate spender. He is soon arrested and sent to prison but then escapes and flees to France. Effectively husbandless again, although actually still married, Moll finds that in her poorer condition she is less of a catch this time so she lies about her wealth. This leads to her marrying a plantation owner. When he finds that Moll is not so rich herself, they are forced to move to his plantation in Virginia and live with his family. There Moll is quite happy until, little by little, she realises that her husband's mother is also her mother and that she is, in fact, married to her half-brother. Despite her mother's suggestion that she let things lie, Moll is unable to countenance committing further incest on top of the bigamy she is already committing, and so she returns to England.

After losing most of her goods in a storm, Moll moves to Bath where she meets and befriends a wealthy man. As his wife is insane, Moll ends up living with the man as a *de facto* wife until he suffers from a religious epiphany and gives up Moll, although not until she has extracted as much money from him as possible. After meeting a banker whom she promises she will consider marrying if he obtains a divorce, Moll then falls for Jemy, a man she supposes to be rich. He, meantime, supposes Moll to be rich but it is only after they are married that the double fraud comes to light and they separate. After giving birth to a child resulting from her union with Jemy, Moll returns to London to marry the banker, who has now secured a divorce. They marry and Moll lives happily for five years until the banker loses a deal of money and suddenly dies.

Impoverished once again, Moll turns to a life of crime and finds that she is, in fact, a very good thief. Eventually, however, she is arrested and sent to Newgate Prison to await her execution. While there she becomes truly repentant for her crimes and has her sentence commuted to transportation to America. She also meets Jemy in prison and he agrees to join her on her voyage to Virginia. When they arrive, Moll chances upon her son and finds that her mother is now dead. Knowing that her mother promised to provide for her in her will, Moll encourages her son to send her the annual income without letting Moll's brother know. When Moll's brother dies, she confesses everything to Jemy and introduces him to her son, intimating that she and Jemy are just recently married. Freed from all the lies that have dogged her life, Moll finally returns to England at the age of 70, truly repentant at last.

> Daniel Defoe's *Moll Flanders* is one of the earliest forms of what we now call the novel. It tells the story of the eponymous heroine and her various escapades as a prostitute, thief, wife and felon.

THEMES AND TECHNIQUES

Moll Flanders is one of the earliest forms of what we now call the novel. It draws upon the tradition of criminal biographies that were popular at the time, such as Defoe's own bestseller, *The True and Genuine Account of the Life and Action of the Late Jonathan Wild*. But it adds to this genre a sense of psychological depth which we eventually come to associate with the novel form. We know what Moll thinks and what motives lie behind her actions; we do not just see, as we might in a play, what she does. Nevertheless, *Moll Flanders* is essentially a picaresque, that is, a narrative detailing a series of adventures. There is no great thematic core holding the novel together above and beyond Moll's life and, more pertinently, Moll's character. In a genre dominated by male characters, Moll Flanders stands out as one of literature's most resourceful, witty and interesting heroines, matched only by CHAUCER's Wife of Bath (in *THE CANTERBURY TALES*) in the way that she works a system designed solely to benefit men.

Further Reading

Backscheider, P.R., *'Moll Flanders': The Making of a Criminal Mind*. New York: Twayne Publishers, 1990. This is an extended analysis of Defoe's novel, examining both the context in which it was written and the effect of the text itself.

Defoe, Daniel, *Moll Flanders*. Edited by Edward Kelly. New York: W.W. Norton, 1981. This edition of the novel also includes an account of the critical reactions to the book over the years.

NARRATIVE OF THE LIFE OF FREDERICK DOUGLASS (1845) by Frederick Douglass

My long-crushed spirit rose, cowardice departed, bold defiance took its place; and I now resolved that, however long I might remain a slave in form, the day had passed forever when I could be a slave in fact. I did not hesitate to let it be known of me, that the white man who expected to succeed in whipping, must also succeed in killing me.

Narrative of the Life of Frederick Douglass is an autobiographical work, telling the story of an escaped slave. It follows Douglass's life from his birth on a plantation in Maryland to his bid for liberty in the Free States.

Summary

Unsure of his exact date of birth, Douglass only knows that he is born into slavery. His mother was a slave and his father may well have been his master, Captain Anthony, on the plantation where he lives, a large farm run by a wealthy slave owner, Colonel Lloyd. Life is extremely brutal for the slaves and Douglass witnesses his own aunt being whipped until she is bloody, as well as another slave who is immediately shot for refusing to obey an order. As Douglass is only a child, he works in the house and therefore escapes the harshest side of the regime underneath the cruel overseers, Severe and Gore. However, when Douglass reaches the age of 7, he is handed over to Captain Anthony's relative, Hugh Auld.

Auld lives in the city, where conditions are generally less onerous to slaves. Douglass is particularly pleased because Auld's wife, Sophia, teaches him how to read. However, when Auld discovers this, he reprimands Sophia and henceforth she becomes much crueller towards young Douglass. Thinking that Auld must have something to hide by keeping him from reading, Douglass continues to teach himself how to read and, eventually, how to write, and in the process he learns all about the anti-slavery movement. He vows one day to become a free man. In the meantime, however, following the death of Captain Anthony, Douglass is passed from one member of the family to another until finally he is sent back to the country to live with Captain Thomas Auld.

The *Narrative* is an autobiographical account of Douglass's hard life as a slave and how he finally escaped to freedom.

Captain Auld is convinced that city living has spoiled Douglass and so he sends him to Edward Covey, a farmer with the reputation of being a 'slave breaker'. Within six months, Covey has beaten and bullied Douglass so much that his spirit is all but crushed. However, one day, after a particularly severe beating, Douglass decides to fight back. The two men then struggle with each other for two hours and when it is over, Douglass determines that from that point onwards his spirit will be free and that he will kill anyone who tries to crush him. For his part, Covey never touches Douglass again. When his time with Covey is up, Douglass is hired out for a couple of years to William Freeland.

Freeland is kinder than Covey or Auld, but he still uses slaves and Douglass decides to try and escape. Douglass helps to educate many of his fellow slaves in the neighbourhood in which he works and, with three of them, he formulates an escape plan. However, the group is betrayed to Freeland and they are sent to jail. Captain Auld then decides to send Douglass back to Hugh Auld in order for him to learn the ship-caulking trade. This Douglass does and, after working overtime, he manages to save enough money to make an escape feasible. Douglass goes to New

York and from there he moves to Massachusetts where he settles down and marries, devoting his free time to the anti-slavery movement.

THEMES AND TECHNIQUES

One of the many themes that run through *Narrative of the Life of Frederick Douglass* is the relationship between knowledge and power. From the very beginning, Douglass is put at a disadvantage because he does not know his own birth date or even who his father is. When he learns to read and write, he does so because he rightly believes that if he is forbidden to do it, then there must be some benefit which accrues to him if he does so. This benefit comes in the form of finding out about the anti-slavery movement. However, the awareness this brings to his own condition does not actually set him free, but rather contrasts that new-found notion of freedom with his own slavery. In this sense, Douglass's knowledge is as much a source of anguish as it is a source of empowerment.

This split in Douglass is matched in the *Narrative* by the split in his voice. At one and the same time, Douglass is telling his story but having to do so in as objective a voice as possible in order to make it persuasive. He also has to maintain an empathy with the other slaves about whom he writes, but, as he is also no longer a slave when he writes the book, he is also distinct from them. Finally, Douglass is not writing the book for slaves, he is writing it for educated white people, so he must assume a voice that is closer to theirs than his own. The result is that the *Narrative* strikes a masterly balance between several competing voices.

Further Reading

Andrews, William L. *Critical Essays on Frederick Douglass*. New York: G.K. Hall, 1991. This selection of essays traces the critiques of Douglass's work from the time of publication to the present day.

Sundquist, Eric (ed.), *Frederick Douglass: New Literary and Historical Essays*. New York: Cambridge University Press, 1990. This collection of essays evaluates the impact of Frederick Douglass and his books during and after his lifetime.

NATURE (1836)
by Ralph Waldo Emerson

To go into solitude, a man needs to retire as much from his chamber as from society. I am not solitary whilst I read and write, though nobody is with me. But if a man would be alone, let him look at the stars. The rays that come from those heavenly worlds, will separate between him and vulgar things.

EMERSON's mind has been described as America's mind. If that is the case, then it is certainly a unique mind because this slim volume defies easy categorisation. As much as it is a work of philosophy, it is also a manifesto for respecting the divinity of nature and as such is almost more relevant today than when it was written.

Summary

Nature begins by asking why the present generation should not 'enjoy an original relation to the universe'. Assuming that it should, Emerson proposes two different definitions of nature, nature being the object about which all science wishes to find a theory. The first definition of nature is the common one and 'refers to essences unchanged by man'. The second definition is broader and he sums it up as all that is 'not me'. He advises us that any confusion between the two is immaterial. He then describes the state of ecstasy he sometimes feels being in nature, submitting himself to it until he enjoys his own sense of being negligible.

Emerson finds that the ultimate purposes of nature can be classified in four ways: Commodity, Beauty, Language and Discipline. Under Commodity, Emerson ranks 'all those advantages which our senses owe to nature'. Under Beauty, he asserts how we derive pleasure from observing nature in its simplest forms, from identifying nature as a sign of divinity, and from our intellectual appreciation of it. In terms of Language, Emerson proposes that nature is quite simply the vehicle of thought, while in terms of Discipline, it provides the parameters within which both thought and action have meaning.

Emerson goes on to tackle the claim of idealist philosophy, that the existence of nature cannot be proved beyond the realm of the mind. He explains the prevalence of this view by noting that 'all culture tends to imbue us with idealism', separating humanity's soul from its senses. However, he avers that we should not forget that 'God never jests with us'. Indeed, above all else, nature is a reminder of the presence of the absolute, like 'a great shadow pointing always to the sun behind us'. Until man returns to the appreciation of nature, seeing the divine in the mundane, he will remain merely 'a god in ruins'.

Nature was accepted as one of the basic texts of the Transcendentalist movement based in Concord. It is part philosophical tract, part prose poem and part manifesto.

THEMES AND TECHNIQUES

Nature is a multi-faceted work that can be considered in a number of ways. In one way, it is a work of philosophy dealing with some of the most basic questions known to the discipline, such as the existence of a divine being, and the oneness or duality of man and nature. It is also a staggering work of poetic prose, one that sustains a level of inventiveness far beyond the length of most poems. It glories in its subject and attempts to share that glory by depicting the experience of nature in all its form through a lyrical and elegiac style of writing. Both these elements, the philosophic and the poetic, combine to give power to the third aspect of the work which is its manifesto-like promptings to submit to nature and become one with the divine force that motivates it. Indeed, Emerson finishes the book by suggesting that we take inspiration from the creation of nature by building our own worlds and creating our own small universes.

Further Reading

Sealts, Merton M. Jr and Ferguson, Alfred R. *'Nature' – Origin, Growth, Meaning.* Carbondale: Southern Illinois University Press, 1979. This is the standard work on Emerson's book and it examines the many ways in which *Nature* can be read.

One of the first to be written, but one of the last to be published, *Northanger Abbey* is one of AUSTEN's liveliest works. It tells the story of Catherine Morland and how her obsession with Gothic fiction leads to her imagination running riot before she finally settles down and marries.

NORTHANGER ABBEY (1818) by Jane Austen

There seems almost a general wish of descrying the capacity and undervaluing the labour of the novelist, and of slighting the performances which have only genius, wit, and taste to recommend them.

Summary

The novel begins with 17-year-old Catherine Morland accepting an invitation from family friends, the Allens, to stay with them in Bath. There she is introduced to Henry Tilney, a young clergyman whom she immediately finds attractive. Before they meet again, Catherine is introduced to Isabella Thorpe, who is only slightly older than Catherine. The two of them get on well and Isabella introduces Catherine into the social world of Bath. They are soon joined in Bath by Catherine's brother, James, and Isabella's brother, John. Isabella immediately finds James attractive and begins to court his favours. In order to complete the symmetry of the situation, John shows a keen interest in Catherine, but she finds him boorish and, when she sees Henry again, she is reminded of his good qualities and of her preference for him.

Increasingly abandoned by Isabella who is pursuing her relationship with James, Catherine begins to forge a friendship with Eleanor, Henry's sister. To Catherine's delight, she discovers that both Henry and Eleanor are avid readers of the novels that she likes. Eleanor then invites Catherine to stay with the Tilneys at their home in Northanger Abbey. Catherine accepts and is unduly excited at the prospect of residing in such an atmospheric setting. She imagines all sorts of mysterious happenings during her time there, including that General Tilney, Eleanor's father, has murdered his wife. In the meantime, James and Isabella have become engaged. This is broken off, however, when Isabella discovers how poor James is in contrast to Captain Frederick Tilney, Henry's elder brother with whom Isabella then begins to consort.

Taking a wry look at the popularity for Gothic fiction current at the time, *Northanger Abbey* tells the story of Catherine Morland and her overactive imagination.

When Frederick leaves town with his regiment, Isabella's attentions return to James. Catherine is already annoyed at Isabella for encouraging John into thinking that Catherine loved him, but she is doubly annoyed with Isabella now that her brother is being so badly treated. Catherine's mind is distracted from this problem, however, when the General returns home one day and orders Eleanor to send Catherine home. As the General had previously encouraged Catherine to marry Henry, this is a shock. In time, it transpires that John had misled the General into first thinking that Catherine is very wealthy, and then that she is very poor. Upset that his son might marry a poor woman, the General had sent Catherine away. However, once Eleanor has married a rich man, and the true, moderate condition of Catherine's finances is ascertained, the General consents to Henry and Catherine marrying.

THEMES AND TECHNIQUES

Northanger Abbey is often described as a parody of Gothic literature. It mocks the dark romanticism of such popular works at the time as Ann Radcliffe's *The Mysteries of Udolpho* and M.G. Lewis's *The Monk*. Setting the cool, ironic voice of Austen's narrator against Catherine's more febrile imaginings provides a delicious contrast. We see, for example, how she builds up a gloomy and bloody history around the General based on the supposition, advanced in many Gothic fictions, that he has murdered the late Mrs Tilney. Of course, this is nonsense and Catherine is duly censored for her dangerous fantasy by Henry.

However, while *Northanger Abbey* parodies Gothic fiction, and, indeed, could be justifiably cited as a conservative attack on the dominant culture of Romanticism, the parodies of Gothic fiction are there for the purposes of characterisation too. Catherine is rather bookish in the novel but, practically speaking, she is also rather naïve and misses out on the truth of situations, such as Isabella's superficiality. Like many of Austen's heroines, she has to stop painting the world in black and white (here represented by Gothic fiction) and learn to appreciate the subtle shades of meaning from which the adult world is made. When she has successfully made this transition, as Elizabeth does in *Pride and Prejudice*, she is ready to marry and does so.

Further Reading

Southam, Brian Charles (ed.), *'Northanger Abbey' and 'Persuasion': Casebook Studies*. London: Palgrave Macmillan, 1991. This collection of essays evaluates both *Northanger Abbey* and *Persuasion*, examining their relationship with their social, historical and literary contexts.

OLIVER TWIST (1837–39)
by Charles Dickens

Please, sir, I want some more.

DICKENS's second novel and the one that cemented his place in the public's affections, *Oliver Twist*, is also perhaps his most famous work. It follows the fortunes of the orphan Oliver as he eventually triumphs over poverty, danger and desperation.

Summary

The novel begins with an unknown woman giving birth to Oliver Twist. She dies shortly afterwards and Oliver is brought up in an orphanage where he is maltreated and malnourished. When Oliver is 9 years old, he is transferred to a workhouse where a new policy ensures that there is little food for the occupants. When Oliver asks for more gruel

because he is so hungry, he is beaten and put up for sale as an example to everyone else. While he waits for someone to pay the £5 necessary to buy him, he is locked away in solitary confinement. After several days, a chimney-sweep comes to buy him, but Oliver is so terrified that he does not go and he is apprenticed instead to a local undertaker, Mr Sowerberry. When Sowerberry's other apprentice abuses Oliver's mother, Oliver attacks him and he is once again locked up. This time, Oliver decides he would be better on his own so he runs away to London.

When he arrives in London, Oliver meets a lively boy his own age, Jack Dawkins, or the Artful Dodger. The Artful Dodger introduces him to Fagin, a man who runs a gang of boys who work as thieves. Horrified at this, Oliver nevertheless assents to being trained as a pickpocket. One day, during his training, he is arrested while picking the pocket of Mr Brownlow. Brownlow is so taken with the terrified young Oliver that he not only has the charges dropped but brings Oliver into his house and looks after him. The first time Oliver leaves Brownlow's house, however, he is seized by Nancy and Bill Sikes, two associates of Fagin, and taken back to Fagin's hideout. There he is appraised to be the perfect size to help Sikes commit a robbery, and so he accompanies Sikes to the Maylies' house. The robbery is interrupted and Oliver is wounded. He is taken in by the kindly Maylie family and looked after by Mrs Maylie and her niece Rose.

Oliver Twist is one of Dickens's most popular novels. Its hero, the orphan Oliver, established the archetype for all the abandoned children that populate Dickens's oeuvre.

The Maylies attempt to find Mr Brownlow in order to help Oliver, but their attempts fail. Meanwhile, Fagin is now keeping company with a mysterious man named Monks. He seems determined to destroy any evidence of Oliver's parentage. When Nancy, who always had a soft spot for Oliver, hears them talking about the boy, she realises that Monks is Oliver's half-brother and is attempting to keep him from his inheritance. Nancy decides to contact Rose Maylie to warn Oliver. Rose finally finds Brownlow and they meet up with Nancy.

However, Fagin has had Nancy followed and when she returns, he incites Sikes to beat her so badly that he murders her. After two days on the run, Sikes accidentally hangs himself while trying to escape from the police. Fagin is sentenced to death for his crimes and his gang is scattered. Brownlow forces Monks to reveal that Oliver's mother was also Rose's sister, so Oliver is left with wealth and a family. Monks disappears to America and dies in prison.

THEMES AND TECHNIQUES

Although it is his second major work, *Oliver Twist* is really Dickens's first novel. *The Pickwick Papers*, Dickens's first book, is more of a picaresque, having a narrative that follows the random adventures of the group surrounding the remarkable Mr Pickwick. *Oliver Twist*, on the other hand, is tightly designed, all the elements combining into a thematic whole, such as when Rose turns out to be Oliver's aunt when all the while they have had a familial relationship anyway. Equally, the novel touches much more explicitly on the themes that will obsess Dickens for the rest of his writing career. In particular, the orphan Oliver stands as the archetype for all the disowned and abandoned children that populate his novels, from David Copperfield and Pip through to Esther and Little Nell. Each of these characters are innocents who fall on hard times through no fault of their own and then find that society is pitiless and indifferent to their plight. If it is essentially the same story in each case, it is nevertheless told with urgency and conviction, for Dickens believed it to be his own story too.

Further Reading

Dickens, Charles, *Oliver Twist: Authoritative Text, Backgrounds and Sources, Early Reviews, Criticism*. Edited by Fred Kaplan. New York: W.W. Norton, 1993. Edited by one of the leading Dickens scholars in the world, this edition of the novel comes with a variety of contextual sources.

Dunn, Richard J. (ed.), *'Oliver Twist': Whole Heart and Soul*. New York: Twayne Publishers, 1993. This short book offers a brief history of the critical reception to the novel, as well as a chronology of Dickens and an examination of the themes of *Oliver Twist*.

OTHELLO (1603–04)
by William Shakespeare

Then must you speak
Of one that loved not wisely but too well,
Of one not easily jealous but, being wrought,
Perplexed in the extreme; of one whose hand,
Like the base Indian, threw a pearl away
Richer than all his tribe; of one whose subdued eyes,
Albeit unused to the melting mood,
Drop tears as fast as the Arabian trees
Their medicinable gum.

Othello is often cited as one of SHAKESPEARE's greatest tragedies. It tells the story of how the great warrior Othello is fooled by one of literature's most villainous characters, Iago, into killing his wife, the innocent Desdemona.

Summary

The play opens one night in Venice. Roderigo is upset because Desdemona has eloped with Othello, a Moor general in the service of Venice. He complains to Iago. Iago is also bitter at Othello, having been passed over for promotion by him in favour of the less experienced Cassio. Admitting to the audience that he is a self-serving liar, Iago agrees to help Cassio win back Desdemona in order that he might ruin Othello. While Iago slopes off, Cassio wakes Brabantio, Desdemona's father and a Venetian senator. Shocked at his daughter's elopement, Brabantio goes to the senate and demands that it be annulled on the grounds that Othello used witchcraft to lure his daughter into marriage. However, Othello successfully defends his cause, saying he used stories of derring-do to win Desdemona's hand. The senate then orders Othello to go to Cyprus to defend it against an impending attack by the Turks.

Before Othello manages to arrive in Cyprus, the Turkish fleet is destroyed by a great storm. Othello's ship arrives unscathed and he orders that a feast be laid on for the victory. Meanwhile, Iago persuades Roderigo that Cassio is his main rival for Desdemona's affections and that he should attack him that night. Having got Cassio drunk, Iago lets Roderigo incite a quarrel with him, during the course of which, Montano, the Governor of Cyprus is stabbed by Cassio. When Othello learns of this, he demotes Cassio. Distraught at this, Cassio eagerly accepts Iago's advice that the best way to retrieve his position is by asking Desdemona to plead his cause for him. Meanwhile, Iago reveals that he will try to make Othello believe Cassio is having a secret affair with Desdemona.

Othello is one of Shakespeare's four great tragedies. In Iago it features one of the most notorious villains in literature, the character who manages to manipulate all those around him until they succumb to his treacherous design.

Desdemona quickly agrees to ask her husband if Cassio can have his job back. However, when she does this, she is unaware that Iago has already planted the seeds of doubt in Othello's mind regarding her fidelity. Knowing that only visible proof will ultimately persuade Othello of Desdemona's guilt, Iago manages to get his wife, Emilia, to retrieve the handkerchief Othello had first given to Desdemona. He then ensures that Cassio is caught with the handkerchief in view of Othello. Othello asks Iago to murder Cassio while he will kill Desdemona. Iago then convinces Roderigo to kill Cassio, but Cassio successfully defends himself and Iago, pretending to be on Cassio's side, murders Roderigo in revenge.

Upon hearing Cassio's cry, Othello assumes Iago has murdered him and prepares himself to kill Desdemona. Desdemona pleads her innocence, but he fails to believe her and smothers her with a pillow until she is dead. When Emilia enters, Othello explains that he killed her because she was having an affair with Cassio. Emilia realises that Iago has caused all this when she gave him the handkerchief and she tells Othello this. Upon discovering that he has been duped, Othello tries to kill Iago, but Iago escapes

after having killed Emilia. He is then brought back by Montano and Othello stabs him. Seemingly disarmed, Othello then produces a secret dagger, kisses Desdemona and kills himself. Cassio assumes command of the troops and Iago is sentenced to death.

THEMES AND TECHNIQUES

It has been suggested that, despite the tragedy bearing his name, Othello is not the hero of the play – rather it is Iago. A great soldier, Othello is made great by the same warrior passions that eventually bring him low. In this regard he is an almost two-dimensional character compared to the scheming and duplicitous character of Iago. It is Iago who seems to dominate almost every other character in the play, using them for his own purposes as if he were some grand puppeteer, or, perhaps more appropriately, a writer. Iago's treachery, however, depends upon his machinations being invisible, a feat which he is able to accomplish by appearing to support others' prejudices and fears and otherwise subordinating himself to their desires. In this regard, Iago is particularly able to exploit Othello's status as a Moor, that is as an outsider to Venetian society. Taking advantage of the suspicion the Venetians have of the Moor, and the Moor of the Venetians, Iago is everybody's friend and nobody's but himself at the same time. Indeed, Iago's position in relation to Othello is most tellingly alluded to in those parts of the play which hint at Othello's shortsightedness. Unable to make things out quite as clearly as he would like, Othello often has recourse to Iago to confirm the truth of an image for him. In other words, he becomes Othello's spectacles, the lens through which the world is distorted and which leads him to see something that is not there, ultimately leading to Desdemona's untimely death.

Further Reading

Kolin, Philip (ed.), 'Othello': New Critical Essays. London and New York: Routledge, 2001. This is a generous collection of essays that examines everything in the play from jealousy to race.

Shakespeare, William, *Othello*. London: The Arden Shakespeare, 1997. Edited by E.A.J. Honigman. This edition of the play offers a full gloss of the text, as well a history of its various incarnations, and a look at some of the tragedy's more pressing issues.

P

PARADISE LOST (1667)
by John Milton

Of Man's First Disobedience, and the Fruit

Of that Forbidden Tree, whose mortal taste

Brought death into the World, and all our woe,

With loss of Eden, till one greater Man

Restore us, and regain the blissful Seat.

Paradise Lost is MILTON's epic poem about the Fall of Adam and Eve from Paradise. It follows the trials of Adam and Eve from their creation by God to their undoing by Satan and the resulting pain of all humankind.

Summary

When the poem opens, Satan and the other rebel angels are chained to a lake of fire in Hell. Freeing themselves, they set about building Satan's palace, called Pandemonium. There they hold a council meeting in which all the leaders of the supporters of Satan confer on how to proceed against God. It is decided that they will not tackle God directly, for they are frightened of his power. Instead Satan will try to corrupt God's new creation and thus hurt him indirectly. The new creation of which they speak is humankind, Adam and Eve. In order to leave Hell, Satan moves to its gates, guarded by Sin and Death and they let him out into the chaos from which God has fashioned the universe. Disguising himself as a cherub, Satan manages to sneak past Uriel, the archangel guarding the Earth. However, when he enters Paradise, Satan is pained at what he has lost, an ex-

pression that gives him away to Uriel who calls on the other angels to try and help find him.

> Probably the greatest epic written in the English language, *Paradise Lost* was designed by Milton to 'justify the ways of God to men'. In so doing it tells the story of the Fall of Adam and Eve from Paradise.

Eventually, Gabriel finds Satan and with God's help throws him out of Paradise. Nevertheless, Satan still manages to whisper into Eve's ear about eating from the Tree of Knowledge, the one thing that God has forbidden her and Adam to do. Worried about his creation, although already knowing that they are doomed, God sends Raphael down to Paradise to warn Adam and Eve about Satan's intentions to corrupt them. While he is there, Raphael tells Adam and Eve about how Satan found himself in Hell in the first place. He explains that Satan challenged God's power and that a mighty battle took place in which the forces of God, led by Gabriel and Michael, took on Satan's legions. Winning at first, Michael and Gabriel were forced back until God sent the Son into battle for him and he cast Satan down into Hell. Raphael then explains that God created Adam to fill the gap left by the fallen angels. He also re-affirms God's injunction not to eat from the Tree of Knowledge and warns Adam not to want to find out too much.

A short time later, Satan returns to Paradise, this time disguised as a talking snake. Finding Eve alone, he tells her that God wants her and Adam to eat from the Tree of Knowledge and that he is really testing their courage. Persuaded by this, Eve bites an apple from the Tree of Knowledge. As soon as she has done so, she regrets it. When Adam finds out, he realises that she will be thrown from Paradise and, deciding that he does not want to be alone, he takes a bite too so that they are condemned together. Satan returns to Pandemonium to receive the plaudits of his legions, while God sends the Son to punish Adam and Eve. Eve he condemns to the pain of childbirth, and Adam he condemns to till the less fruitful land. Michael then leads them out of Paradise, showing Adam a vision of humankind's future, largely as it is laid out in the BIBLE. Adam and Eve leave Paradise hand in hand, weeping at what they have lost.

THEMES AND TECHNIQUES

Milton describes his intent behind *Paradise Lost* as an attempt to 'justify the ways of God to men'. Following the *Bible*, but also adding to it, Milton conceives the Fall of humankind as a repetition of the fall of Satan and his devils. However, whereas Satan rebels against God and fails to repent, thereby condemning him to an eternity in Hell, Adam and Eve contravene the law of God but very quickly repent of their wrong-doing. They are thus offered the possibility of claiming redemption through the sacrifice of the Son. This act of God's mercy is so great, according to Milton, that he has Adam declare it to be a happy fault that he caused the Fall of humankind in the first place, for without it, no one would appreciate how tender is God's love in offering forgiveness to sinners. Many critics have argued, however, that because Milton was unable to render the unknowable splendour of God, he fails to catch the imagination of readers to the same extent that Satan does. The poet WILLIAM BLAKE even suggested that Milton 'was of the Devil's party without knowing it'.

This is ironic given the interpretation of some critics who propose that *Paradise Lost* is a coded reference to Milton's invidious political position following the Restoration. They conjecture that Satan, with his 'courts and palaces', is actually a representation of the newly enthroned king and therefore the very enemy of Milton, who was strongly anti-Royalist. From this point of view, the poem does not so much 'explain the ways of God to men' for all time, but for the present of its writing, following the failure of the Commonwealth after the death of Oliver Cromwell. Such an explanation suggests that the vision of humankind restored to Paradise, or a new Commonwealth if we read the poem allegorically, is held to be all the sweeter after the reign of the king is over.

Further Reading

Milton, John, *Paradise Lost*. Edited by Scott Elledge. New York: W.W. Norton, 1993. This is an excellent edition of the text, including an

extensive number of notes to explain Milton's notoriously allusive text.

Zunder, William (ed.), *New Casebook on 'Paradise Lost'*. London: Palgrave Macmillan, 1999. This book contains a number of essays looking at Milton's poem from various modern standpoints.

PILGRIM'S PROGRESS, THE (1678–84)
by John Bunyan
He that is down needs fear no fall.

Written while the author was in prison, *Pilgrim's Progress* is one of the most popular allegorical works in the English language. It tells the story of a journey through a Christian life.

Summary

The Pilgrim's Progress was published in two parts. Part One tells the story of Christian, while Part Two tells the story of his wife, Christiana. The book opens with the author recalling a dream in which he sees a man called Christian. Christian is weighed down by troubles and cares and does not know what to do. He is advised by Evangelist to seek out the glory of God in the Celestial City.

Heartened by this advice, Christian sets out for the Wicket Gate and the beginning of his journey. He is initially joined by his neighbours, Pliable and Obstinate. They both try to deter Christian from going but he perseveres, even when he enters the Slough of Despond. He soon enters the village of Morality where he is tempted to settle, but he dreams of eternal salvation and so continues on his journey until he reaches the Wicket Gate. There he is told to follow the straight and narrow path to the Celestial City.

Christian accepts this instruction and continues on his way to the cross, where the weight of his burden is miraculously relieved. Next he comes to Difficulty Hill where Formalist and Hypocrisy advise him to take short cuts. Christian disowns this advice and is wise to do so because Formalist and Hypocrisy both perish. After resting in the Palace Beautiful and traversing the

Valley of Humiliation, Christian is awed by having to cross the Valley of the Shadow of Death. He finally manages to do so with the aid of a friend, Faithful. However, when the pair enter Vanity Fair and refuse to succumb to its materialism, Faithful is executed while Christian only just escapes. He meets Hopeful and the two are then kidnapped by Giant Despair in Doubting Castle. They manage to break out when Christian recalls he has the Key of Promise. Next, the pair cross the Delectable Mountains, pass the Flatterer and the Enchanted Ground until they finally reach the shores of the Dark River. Hopeful buoys up the nervous Christian as they cross over and into the Celestial City. Christiana largely repeats the same journey and is also accepted into the Celestial City.

For many years, *The Pilgrim's Progress* was second only to the *Bible* in terms of its popularity. It records the spiritual journey of Christian as he makes his troubled way to the Celestial City.

THEMES AND TECHNIQUES

Once a household book, *The Pilgrim's Progress* was so popular because it is rooted in the commonplace. The basic premise, that of the journey, is familiar to most people. Similarly, the places along the journey, from hills to meadows and fairs, are well known to most people too. As with the parables in the BIBLE, BUNYAN then invests these everyday settings with a spiritual significance which can be readily understood, such as the Slough of Despond. Rather than use complex psychological characters, the book is populated more with abstract figures who represent one particular trait. Ignorance, for example, represents nothing more than his name. Even Christian, who is the most complex and character-like of the figures in the book, is really no more than an Everyman figure, someone bowed down by sin and seeking salvation. Readers are meant to recognise themselves in the figures of Christian and Christiana and, like them, turn towards God. In this regard, *The Pilgrim's Progress* is an unusual book because it tries to make its readers do something beyond merely entertaining them.

Further Reading

Hofmeyr, Isabel, *The Portable Bunyan: A Transnational History of 'The Pilgrim's Progress'*. New York: Princeton University Press, 2004. This fascinating book examines the history of Bunyan's book, looking at its effect across the world and examining the changes wrought by translation.

POEMS, CHIEFLY IN THE SCOTTISH DIALECT (1786)
by Robert Burns

But Lord, remember me and mine
Wi' mercies temporal and divine!
That I for grace and gear may shine,
Excell'd by nane!
And a' the glory shall be thine!
Amen! Amen!

Also known as the 'Kilmarnock edition' because of its place of publication, *Poems, Chiefly in the Scottish Dialect* established ROBERT BURNS as a poet of the first order. It features many of his most popular works, including 'To A Mouse' and, in its second edition Burns's most famous poem 'Tam O'Shanter'.

Summary

'Tam O'Shanter' is a bawdy narrative poem that tells the tale of the eponymous hero's encounter with a witches' coven. It begins in Ayr on a market day where Tam, a farmer from Carrick, has been conducting his business. He lingers late into the night, sitting by the fire getting drunk with his friend Souter Johnny, despite the warning of his wife Kate who has advised him to ride home before it falls to the witching hour. Eventually, in the darkest hour of the night, Tam mounts his horse, Meg, and sets off for home, crooning to himself as he goes. It is a dismal night but Tam soon reaches the Kirk-Alloway, or local church. The place is reputed to be haunted and on this particular night it appears to Tam to be on fire.

Emboldened by the whisky he has drunk, Tam urges the reluctant Meg towards the blaze so he can have a closer look. There he sees warlocks and witches dancing jigs and reels under the watchful eye of 'auld Nick, in shape o' beast', lighted by corpses holding candles. Tam watches them for a while and is particularly taken with the appearance of one witch whose smock is too short for her. At one point he unthinkingly shouts out in admiration of her and as soon as he has done so, the whole place goes dark and he is forced to flee for his life. The witches fly after him and Tam heads for a running stream, knowing that witches cannot pursue anyone across such a natural barrier. He all but makes it across before one of the witches throws herself at him. However, the only part of him still on the same side of the stream as herself is the horse's tail which comes off in the witch's hand. The tailless horse ever after serves as a warning to other Carrick farmers not to tarry too long drinking on a market day.

Poems, Chiefly in the Scottish Dialect was the collection of poetry that first brought the work of Robert Burns to public attention. It contains many of his most popular poems, including the inimitable 'Tam O'Shanter'.

THEMES AND TECHNIQUES

'Tam O'Shanter' was originally composed by Burns on the request of the antiquary Francis Grose. Burns had asked Grose if he would make a drawing of Alloway-Kirk, the burial place of his father, when he came to Ayrshire. Grose agreed to this request after Burns had enticed him with stories of the place's association with witches, but only on the proviso that Burns provide him with a witches' story to accompany its publication. Burns consented to this and supplied Grose with three such tales, 'Tam O'Shanter' being the second. The poem was then duly published in the 1791 edition of Grose's *Antiquities of Scotland* before it was reprinted in an expanded edition of Burns's *Poems, Chiefly in the Scottish Dialect*. Burns claimed the story of the poem was based on local folklore and was 'authentic'. Whatever the truth of the story, there is no doubt about the quality of the poem itself which mixes a high adrenaline narrative with mock-heroic descriptions in a style adapted

from the work of ALEXANDER POPE, whom Burns greatly admired. However, while there are similarities between this and, for example, THE RAPE OF THE LOCK, part of Burns's skill lies in earning our affection for his drunken hero. Whereas the narrator of *The Rape of the Lock* condescends towards the characters of the poem, the narrator of 'Tam O'Shanter' describes Tam as more of an endearing rascal than as a mean or stupid villain. Indeed, this is characteristic of all of Burns's poems as they display their humanity before their skill, concealing the proficiency with which they are written beneath their wit and empathy.

Further Reading

Burns, Robert, *The Kilmarnock Poems: Poems, Chiefly in the Scottish Dialect*. Edited by Donald A. Low. London: Everyman's Library, 1985. Edited by one of the foremost scholars of Burns, this is a fine edition of Burns's 1786 book.

Low, Donald A. (ed.), *Robert Burns: The Critical Heritage*. London: Routledge 1974. This is an impressive collection of essays charting critical reaction to Burns's poems from their publication to more recent times.

POEMS OF THE PAST AND THE PRESENT (1902)
by Thomas Hardy

So little cause for carolings
Of such ecstatic sound
Was written on terrestrial things
Afar or nigh around.

Following the censorious reception given to JUDE THE OBSCURE when it was published in 1896, HARDY gave up writing novels and returned to his first love – poetry. *Poems of the Past and the Present* was Hardy's second and most generous collection, and one that helped establish him as one of the greatest poets of the twentieth century.

Summary

One of Hardy's most famous pieces from the collection *Poems of the Past and the Present* is 'The Darkling Thrush'. Composed in four stanzas and written in the past tense, it begins with the speaker of the poem leaning on a gate in the countryside at the end of a winter's day. The bare tree branches remind the speaker of broken lyre strings and, with such a sight, he imagines that everyone else is at home by a fire. Compounding the sense of desolation, the land about seems to the speaker to be the corpse of the dead nineteenth century. The clouds are like a crypt and the wind is like a dirge, mourning the dead. Even the cyclical pattern of birth and death appears to have stalled on the latter, lending the world a sense of lifelessness.

Suddenly, the speaker hears a joyful voice breaking through the bleakness. It comes from above and is an 'aged thrush, frail, gaunt, and small.' Despite its advancing years, it throws caution to the wind and is happy to 'fling his soul' onto the darkening day. However, the speaker is unable to comprehend why the thrush is singing so ecstatically and he compares the thrilled birdsong with the earthly misery he sees around him. The only reason that the speaker can think to ascribe to the song of the darkling thrush is that the bird knows of some kind of hope of which the speaker is completely unaware.

THEMES AND TECHNIQUES

'The Darkling Thrush' is a typical Hardy poem, describing personal and public sadness in terms of natural imagery. The meaning of the poem centres around the tension between the 'blessed Hope' of the thrush's song and the relentless desolation of the landscape. The thrush's song may at first seem triumphant. This can be seen in the development of the images of sound in the poem. In the first stanza, the aural landscape is discordant ('the strings of broken lyres'), while in the second stanza it is more harmonious but still depressing ('his death-lament'). The arrival of the thrush in the third stanza, however, creates a chiasmus in the mood as the sound is not only harmonious ('evensong'), but happy too ('Of joy illimited'), a feature which in the final stanza reaches the heights of the 'ecstatic sound' of 'carolings' which herald the birth of Christ. Nevertheless, in spite of this, the outlook for the persona remains bleak as he is 'unaware' of the reason for 'Hope'. Such bleakness is emphasised

both by the sense of inevitability produced by the rhyming couplets of the poem and by the unchanging rhythm, neither of which deviates from the beginning of the poem to the end, so not changing the poem's mood. As the poem is written in the past tense, it also can be assumed that had the 'Hope' come to fruition, the ending would have been changed to take account of that.

> Hardy's second and most generous collection of poetry, *Poems of the Past and the Present*, continues his use of natural imagery to convey personal and public emotions.

Further Reading

Hardy, Thomas, *Thomas Hardy: The Complete Poems*. Edited by James Gibson. London: Palgrave Macmillan, 2002. This book includes the collection *Poems of the Past and the Present*, as well as extensive notes.

Orel, Harold (ed.), *Critical Essays on Thomas Hardy's Poetry*. London: G.K. Hall and Co., 1995. This is a solid collection of essays looking at a number of different aspects of Hardy's poems.

PORTRAIT OF A LADY, THE (1881)
by Henry James

Money's a horrid thing to follow, but a charming thing to meet.

The Portrait of a Lady is often proposed as one of HENRY JAMES's greatest novels. It tells the story of how Isabel Archer negotiates a male-dominated world by rejecting two suitors and marrying a third.

Summary

When the novel opens, Isabel Archer is already renowned as a strong-minded young woman within the genteel circle of 1860s Albany society. Her mother died when she was a child. When her father dies, she is visited by Mrs Touchett, her wealthy aunt now living in Europe. Mrs Touchett suggests she join her in returning to England and Isabel agrees. It gives her the opportunity to turn down an offer of marriage from Caspar Goodwood until she has spent a year travelling round Europe. She fears that if she gets married she will lose her independence.

When they arrive in England, Isabel is introduced to Mr Touchett and his dying son Ralph. Ralph immediately becomes fond of Isabel and he is joined in this by Lord Warburton, the Touchetts' neighbour. Warburton proposes to Isabel, but, once again, she turns him down for fear of losing her autonomy. She already feels constricted by the social rules governing interaction in polite society. However, she soon gains her financial independence when Mr Touchett dies and leaves her half his fortune at Ralph's request. The new-found wealth invites the interest of Serena Merle, Mrs Touchett's friend. Merle is poor but socially graceful and charms Isabel, introducing her to Gilbert Osmond, a man devoted to art who lives in Florence.

> One of the most beloved novels by Henry James, *The Portrait of a Lady* follows the fortunes of Isabel Archer as the integrity of her principles is tested to breaking point.

While in Italy, Isabel learns that Osmond is widowed with a daughter, Pansy, who attends a convent. Isabel soon succumbs to the charisma of Osmond and agrees to marry him, despite the fact that no one apart from Merle seems to approve of the match. They have a child together who dies after six months and then fall into an habitual dislike for each other. She dislikes his attempts to control her and he dislikes her sense of independence. Nevertheless, Isabel considers it her duty to remain committed to the marriage and so she does not leave him. However, Warburton has not given up on Isabel and, in order to get closer to her, he begins to show an interest in Pansy.

Pansy, meanwhile, has already fallen in love with Edward Rosier, an art collector lacking in either wealth or social standing. Osmond forbids the match for these reasons and, instead, encourages the suit of Warburton. Distressed by this, Isabel eventually points out to Warburton that Pansy is in love with Rosier and Warburton admits the real reason for his interest and leaves. Osmond is furious at Isabel's interference, as, suspiciously, is Merle. Isabel then realises that not only are Merle and Osmond lovers, but also that Pansy is their illegitimate love-child. Shocked, Isabel returns to England in time to attend Ralph on his death-bed. After the funeral, Goodwood proposes to Isabel again, but Isabel decides to return to Osmond instead.

THEMES AND TECHNIQUES

Typically, James pushes his characters into a situation that is harder and harder for them to escape from without a terrible sacrifice of principle. The situation then becomes something of a testing ground for their fortitude and moral resilience, enabling James to demonstrate the psychological nuances of his creations at a quite minute level. In the case of *The Portrait of a Lady*, James creates the essentially independent Isabel Archer. She is defined by her sense of autonomy, from the time as a child when she is given practically free rein to educate herself, to when, as an adult, she is freed from the financial insecurities which would have pressured so many women of the Victorian age into a marriage for reasons other than just love. Having defined Isabel in this way and shown her rejecting two other offers of marriage as a matter of principle, James then has her accept the advances of Osmond and marry him. Osmond treats Isabel as if she were one of his art objects and curbs her independence at every available opportunity, but Isabel refuses to leave him as a matter of principle. She stays with him because 'certain obligations were involved in the very fact of marriage, and were quite independent of the quantity of enjoyment extracted from it.' As things get worse and worse, the value of her integrity escalates until it reaches a point where it is beyond the empathy of most readers. This then becomes the natural point at which to end the novel and James duly does so, having once again shown us how unhappy an inflexible character leaves everyone.

Further Reading

Porte, Joel (ed.), *New Essays on 'The Portrait of a Lady'.* London: Cambridge University Press, 1990. This is an interesting collection of essays which examines James's novel from a number of angles, including a look at the book's sense of morality and its relation to the history of novels.

Powers, Lyall H. *'The Portrait of a Lady': Maiden, Woman, and Heroine.* New York: Twayne Publishers, 1992. This small book analyses the central themes of James's novel as well as its critical history.

PRELUDE, THE
(1799–1850)
by William Wordsworth

Bliss was it in that very dawn to be alive,

But to be young was very Heaven!

Photo credit: © Bettmann/CORBIS

Often proposed as the best epic poem to have been written in English since JOHN MILTON's PARADISE LOST, *The Prelude* is, in contrast, a search for significance in a secular world. It is essentially an autobiographical poem, recording WORDSWORTH's impressions of his early life.

Summary

As the subtitle to the poem suggests, *The Prelude* is about the 'growth of a poet's mind'. The poet in this case is Wordsworth and *The Prelude* largely tells his autobiography. However, it is not an autobiography in any traditional sense, but one that traces, as Wordsworth wrote in another poem ('My heart leaps up'), the way in which 'The Child is father of the Man'. That is to say, *The Prelude* looks at the influences of his youth which affect him as a man. The poem thus darts about from one moment in time to another but, with this proviso in mind, it is still possible to discern a broad chronological progression to the work. It begins by looking at Wordsworth's childhood and school days and then moves on to his time spent at St John's College in Cambridge University. Book Four describes his various pastimes during the summer vacation. He then expounds upon the influence of books in his life and gives vent to his fear that all books will be one day be destroyed in a paper Armageddon.

> *The Prelude* is essentially an autobiographical poem. It records the early years of William Wordsworth, tracing his development as a poet and a person.

Book Six of *The Prelude* opens with Wordsworth's recollections of his trip through Switzerland and France with fellow mountaineer Robert Jones. He remembers his disappointment at finding he has crossed the Alps when he still expects to continue climbing. Wordsworth then returns to London and partakes of the variety of life there at St Bartholomew's Fair. He also discerns the way in which his earlier love for nature leads to the development of, and love for, an abstract concept of the goodness of man. Such goodness is what he first sees in the French people during his visit to Revolutionary France. Wordsworth states his admiration for the cause but then moves towards a gradual disillusionment with the carnage and the hypocrisy of it all.

When he returns to England for the last time he suffers a breakdown. Wordsworth then records his recovery from this and how he developed once more his creative powers, but this time in a way attuned to ordinary people rather than grand events like the French Revolution. He finishes the poem with a recollection of an earlier climb up Mount Snowdon in Wales, once more with his friend Robert Jones.

THEMES AND TECHNIQUES

The Prelude was not published in Wordsworth's lifetime. He began work on it in 1799, when it was just two parts and thereafter revised it until in 1805 he had 13 books of material. For the next 34 years he continued to tinker with it until, by 1839, his last major revision, he had established a 14-book version of the poem. This was the poem that he authorised his executors to release after his death in 1850.

Wordsworth's executors did publish *The Prelude*, but not without adding their own revisions. There are some editors who have done their best to re-edit the text to reveal the poem that Wordsworth is supposed to have intended, a text that is only 13 books long. What these editorial problems suggest is quite how far removed Wordsworth was from the received image of the romantic poet as someone who just poured forth emotions onto paper in their natural order. Rather, as the poem suggests, Wordsworth's ideas, and thus his understanding of his own life, changed over time. *The Prelude* begins and ends with literal journeys which become metaphors for Wordsworth's journey into himself. He recovers his earlier lost selves, such as the Wordsworth who held a preconceived image of Mont Blanc in his head, only to have it destroyed by the majesty of the real thing. In doing this, Wordsworth developed a way of dealing with and expressing personal experience whose influence remains with us to this day.

Further Reading

Harvey, William John and Gravil, Richard (eds), *Casebook on William Wordsworth's 'The Prelude'*. London: Palgrave Macmillan, 1972. An extended selection of essays that deal with many different aspects of Wordsworth's poems.

Wordsworth, William, *'The Prelude': Authoritative Texts, Recent Critical Essays, Context and Reception*. Edited by Jonathan Wordsworth, M.H. Abrams and Stephen Gill. New York: W.W. Norton, 1980. This book contains all three versions of Wordsworth's epic from 1799, 1801, and 1850, as well as essays and background material.

PRIDE AND PREJUDICE (1813)
by Jane Austen

It is a truth universally acknowledged, that a single man in possession of a good fortune must be in want of a wife.

Probably AUSTEN's most popular novel, *Pride and Prejudice* is a light and witty comedy of manners. It tells the story of the relationship between Elizabeth and Darcy and how they throw up obstacles to their own union.

Summary

Beginning with the most famous opening line in English literature, the novel introduces us to the genteel world of the Bennet family, some time during the Napoleonic wars. There is much excitement in the household because a wealthy bachelor, Charles Bingley, has moved in nearby and Mr and Mrs Bennet have five unmarried daughters for whom they are seeking partners. At a local ball, Bingley and the eldest Bennet, Jane, begin to court each other, much to the disdain of Fitzwilliam Darcy, Bingley's friend. He also refuses to dance with Elizabeth, the next eldest Bennet daughter, and disparages her appearance. Elizabeth overhears this and condemns him as rude and arrogant. The next time they meet, Darcy expresses an interest in Elizabeth, but she refuses to dance with him.

With the relationship between Bingley and Jane progressing, she is invited to tea at Bingley's house by his sister, Caroline. On the way over, Jane is caught in a torrential downpour and falls ill, forcing her to stop there while she recovers. Elizabeth then walks to the house to look after her sister. She soon divines that Caroline is only feigning friendship with Jane and, in fact, regards the Bennet family as too poor and vulgar. During this time, Elizabeth encounters Darcy on several occasions. She treats him with irony and a cool detachment which only seems to inflame his interest in her. When Jane and Elizabeth return home, they meet Mr Collins, the man who will inherit their father's property when he dies. Collins is an insufferable bore, but he is nevertheless attracted to the Bennet girls and proposes to Elizabeth. She turns him down. A little later, Elizabeth hears that her friend, Charlotte, has married Collins for financial reasons. She also learns from a handsome soldier, Wickham, that Darcy treated him badly.

When Bingley returns to London in the winter, Jane is distraught that her relationship with him is over. In the spring, Elizabeth visits Charlotte and Collins, and she meets Darcy's aunt and also Darcy. Darcy unexpectedly proposes to Elizabeth in a famously inappropriate manner and she refuses, citing his arrogance, his treatment of Wickham, and his attempts to put Bingley off Jane. Darcy then writes to her a letter in which he explains everything to her satisfaction, including the fact that Wickham tried to elope with his sister. While visiting Darcy's magnificent estate with family friends, Elizabeth hears that Wickham has eloped with her sister, Lydia. This could heap untold disgrace upon the Bennet family, but Wickham agrees to marry Lydia in return for an annual income. It eventually transpires that Darcy has paid this money. Now realising that Darcy is just about perfect, Elizabeth agrees to his next proposal and they join Bingley and Jane, who have also been reunited, in getting married.

> Originally entitled 'First Impressions', *Pride and Prejudice* centres upon Elizabeth and Darcy overcoming their poor first impressions of each other.

THEMES AND TECHNIQUES

The essence of any great love story, such as *Pride and Prejudice*, is to prevent the principal characters from forming a contented union before the end of the book. Lovers must be impeded and blocked from realising their love be that because of external forces, such as in *Romeo and Juliet*, or because of the characters of the lovers themselves, as in this case. Indeed, it would not be totally inaccurate to conclude that what keeps Elizabeth and Darcy apart, at least initially, is the fact that they do not even know they are attracted to each other. The reason for this may well be found in the novel's original title – *First Impressions*. Elizabeth quickly surmises that Darcy is a haughty and arrogant man, while Darcy perceives Elizabeth to be merely 'tolerable'. Armed with these prejudices, it takes much of the rest of the novel for both characters to overcome their pride in the validity of their observations. The development of their characters comes from this process of overcoming. Elizabeth learns that first impressions are often more useful with a second opinion, while Darcy learns the value of making what he appears to feel match what he actually feels.

Further Reading

Austen, Jane, *Pride and Prejudice*. Edited by Susan J. Wolfson and Claudia L. Johnson. London: Longman Publishing Group, 2002.

This edition of the novel is fully annotated and comes with a lively introduction, as well as a contextual matrix.

Powers, Lyall H., '*Pride and Prejudice*': A Study in Artistic Economy. New York: Twayne Publishers, 1988. This small book examines the central themes and types of characterisation in Austen's novel.

> ## PROMETHEUS UNBOUND (1820)
> ### by Percy Bysshe Shelley
>
> *My soul is an enchanted boat,*
> *Which, like a sleeping swan, doth float*
> *Upon the silver waves of thy sweet singing;*
> *And thine doth like an angel sit*
> *Beside a helm conducting it,*
> *Whilst all the winds with melody are*
> *ringing.*

Prometheus Unbound is a poetic drama in four acts. SHELLEY takes up the ancient story of Prometheus who stole fire from the gods and was chained to Mount Caucasus as a punishment, condemned to have his liver pecked out afresh by a vulture every day.

Summary

Prometheus Unbound continues the story of *Prometheus Bound*, a play by the dramatist and father of Greek tragedy, Aeschylus. In *Prometheus Bound*, Prometheus steals fire from the gods and is punished by Zeus. It is reported that Aeschylus composed a sequel to his play, also called *Prometheus Unbound*, in which Prometheus is reconciled with Zeus. However, like many of Aeschylus's plays, only fragments of it remain and so Shelley's version is largely original. When the play begins, Prometheus is wracked with pain and still bound to an 'eagle-baffling mountain', devoid of life and hope. Prometheus has already cursed Jupiter but no one will dare to repeat the curse for fear of what Jupiter will do to them.

Uncertain of what he has said, Prometheus is forced to call on the Phantasm of Jupiter to repeat Prometheus's words. This the Phantasm does and it causes Prometheus to affirm his view that Jupiter should be pitied for any hurt that is inflicted upon him. As a punishment for uttering the curse, Jupiter sends a group of Furies to taunt Prometheus with visions of the destructive potential of humankind. To counteract this, Spirits of the Earth show the noble potential of humankind. Asia, from whom Prometheus has been parted, and her sister Panthea, then descend into the underworld of Demogorgon, a figure of blind necessity. Asia and Panthea question Demogorgon, but he does not understand himself the powers that control him and he can only answer in riddles, except to confirm the power of eternal love. Asia then transfigures into a 'diviner' state of being. Meanwhile, Demogorgon rises from his underworld and deposes Jupiter. Hercules unbinds Prometheus and he is reunited with Asia. While they retire to a cave, the Spirit of the Hour describes a vision in which the world is renewed and humankind exists in a state where 'None fawned, none trampled'.

Continuing the story from Aeschylus's Greek tragedy *Prometheus Bound*, *Prometheus Unbound* is a poetic drama which encourages the practice of Christian love as an answer to the divisions of the world.

THEMES AND TECHNIQUES

Shelley thought of *Prometheus Unbound* as 'a poem of a higher character than anything I have yet attempted and perhaps less an imitation of anything that has gone before it'. As may be inferred from a summary of the plot of *Prometheus Unbound*, the story is not always paramount in this lyrical drama. Rather it is a philosophical and political work in which the idea is more important than the narrative that displays it. Shelley was careful to distance his play from the idea of it being a didactic work: 'didactic poetry is my abhorrence' he announces in the preface. Nevertheless, there is a sense in which *Prometheus Unbound* remains resolutely political in so far as it encourages people to practise the brotherly love of Christ in the Sermon on the Mount. In so doing, Shelley advises us, we will be able to overcome the larger ills of society which are nothing but the manifestation of personal hatreds. These personal hatreds are the very things that trouble Prometheus and divide him from Asia before he gives himself over to

mercy and forgives Jupiter for the tortures he has visited upon him.

Further Reading

Flagg, John Sewell, *'Prometheus Unbound' and 'Hellas': An Approach to Shelley's Lyrical Dramas*. New York: Edwin Mellen Press, 1972. This book compares and contrasts Shelley's two major lyrical dramas – *Prometheus Unbound* and *Hellas*.

Lewis, Linda M., *The Promethean Politics of Milton, Blake and Shelley*. Columbia: University of Missouri Press, 1992. This book examines the figure of Prometheus in the work of Shelley, Milton and Blake, unearthing his ambiguous political significance for these writers.

PURLOINED LETTER, THE (1844)
by Edgar Allan Poe

Perhaps the mystery is a little too plain?

Already responsible for developing both the Gothic short story, in tales such as 'The Fall of the House of Usher', and modern science fiction, in tales such as 'MS. Found in a Bottle', POE also all but invented the detective story in three tales centred around C. Auguste Dupin. *The Purloined Letter* is the third and most famous of these tales. It follows Dupin as he solves a case of blackmail.

Summary

When the story begins, the unnamed narrator and C. Auguste Dupin are sitting and smoking in contemplative silence when Monsieur G—, the Prefect of the Parisian police, enters in order to seek the assistance of Dupin. He explains that a letter has been stolen, most likely from the Queen. This letter would be highly damaging to the Queen if its contents were known by a third person whom we assume to be the King. However, the letter was stolen from the Queen when she was reading it one day and the King entered the room. Forced to leave it out in the open, the letter was spotted by the Minister D—. In full view of the Queen, the Minister D— swapped the letter with one of his own, but she was unable to comment upon this act because the King was still present. Since that time the Queen has been blackmailed for political purposes by the Minister D—. Monsieur G— then explains that he and his men have systematically searched the Minister's apartment every night for many weeks but they have been unable to find the letter. They have also searched Minister D— himself, but to no avail. Dupin advises him to make another search.

A month later the Prefect returns. He still has not found the letter and informs Dupin that the reward has increased. Dupin says he will hand over the letter if the policeman gives him his reward right there and then. G— agrees and Dupin hands over the letter. G— is so delighted that he does not even wait to hear how Dupin managed to secure the document, but the narrator is more eager for an explanation. Dupin says the key to finding it, as well as the key to solving any case, is 'an identification of the reasoner's intellect with that of his opponent', in this case Minister D—. Dupin declares that he is very clever and will pretend to be listless although he is, in fact, very energetic and animated when no one is looking. Equally, Dupin reasons that he would conceal the letter by 'not attempting to conceal it at all'. Indeed, when Dupin visits D—, he spies the letter in another envelope in plain view. Dupin then makes a copy of the envelope, returns to D— and swaps the letter when D— is distracted by a noise outside his window which Dupin arranged for earlier.

THEMES AND TECHNIQUES

Dupin was the first of the classic amateur detectives, and the three stories written by Poe which feature him, *The Murders in the Rue Morgue*, *The Mystery of Marie Roget*, and *The Purloined Letter*, established the conventions of the detective story genre. Having written a highly unlikely 'whodunit' in *The Murders in the Rue Morgue*, Poe here writes a 'howdunit'. For having established the identity of the criminal from the start of the story, the intrigue of the story rests on explaining how to retrieve the situation. Dupin's answer to this problem is fundamentally simple: the only way to solve a crime is to repeat it. Dupin merely does to D—, what D— did to the Queen.

In describing the nature of detection in this way, Poe identifies the character of most detective stories since. For detective fiction is based on disclosing or repeating the story of a crime. Poe also established another conven-

tion in this story with the letter. While every other example of textual evidence in the story is quoted, the letter is merely paraphrased. This is because it does not matter what is in it, but only where it is. The letter merely becomes the excuse for the plot rather than something with intrinsic value of its own. In this regard the letter is rather like a knife – there is nothing significant about it in itself, it only becomes interesting if it is in someone's back.

The Purloined Letter was the third tale written by Edgar Allan Poe about the amateur detective C. Auguste Dupin. This pioneering work helped to establish the generic conventions of crime fiction.

Further Reading

Muller, John P. and Richardson, William J. (eds), *The Purloined Poe: Lacan, Derrida, and Psychoanalytic Reading*. Baltimore: Johns Hopkins University Press, 1988. This very demanding text is a classic of modern criticism. Using Poe's story as springboard for debate, two of the most influential thinkers of the twentieth century argue over the nature of meaning.

Silverman, Kenneth (ed.), *New Essays on Poe's Major Tales*. New York: Cambridge University Press, 1993. Slightly less demanding, this short collection of essays examines various aspects of Poe's work, including his preoccupation with death.

RAPE OF THE LOCK, THE (1712–14)
by Alexander Pope

What dire offence from amorous causes springs!
What mighty contests rise from trivial things!

The Rape of the Lock was occasioned by a contemporary incident at a party, where a girl's hair was cut. This led to a mighty dispute between the parties concerned which Pope then strove to deflate by writing his account of the incident in the form of a mock epic poem.

Summary

After a dedication to the real person upon whom the heroine of the poem is based, Arabella Fermor, *The Rape of the Lock* begins with an account of a dream dreamt by the wealthy Belinda. It transpires that the dream is the work of Belinda's guardian Sylph, Ariel, a gentle spirit who, with many other such spirits, looks after Belinda and helps to guard her chastity. He warns her that he has seen the portents of some 'dread event' for her this very day, but he does not know exactly what it will be. All he can advise is to 'beware of man'.

Having heard this in her dream, Belinda is then awoken by her lapdog, Shock, and forgets all about the dream while she gets dressed for the day. Once dressed, Belinda sets off on a boat down the River Thames to a party at Hampton Court Palace. She looks resplendent, particularly her two shining locks of hair that hang down over her neck. These ringlets are objects of devotion for the Baron who, earlier in the day, constructed a sacrificial pyre to pray for success in stealing them. Ariel, aware of the impending threat, orders an army of Sylphs to guard various parts of the blissfully unaware Belinda.

Arriving at Hampton Court, Belinda then plays a game of cards. This is described in terms of a vast battle in which her cards are largely ranged against those of the Baron. She only just manages to win on the last turn of the cards. Next, while coffee is being served, the Baron procures a pair of scissors and attempts on three occasions to cut off Belinda's ringlets. The Sylphs keep intervening until Ariel discovers that 'an earthly lover' lurks in Belinda's heart and, amazed and confused, he retires from her defence and the Baron is finally able to cut off her hair. Umbriel, a melancholy sprite, then flies to the Cave of Spleen and fetches a bag of 'sighs, sobs and passions' with which he douses Belinda. On Belinda's behalf, Sir Plume asks the Baron to return the lock, but he refuses. Umbriel then releases a vial of 'soft sorrows, melting griefs, and flowing tears' onto Belinda who bemoans the fact that she ignored her

dream. A scuffle ensues and Belinda then throws snuff at the Baron. Defeated, the Baron consents to give up the stolen lock but no one is able to find it. It is surmised that the lock has ascended to the 'lunar sphere' where it will burn like a star, more envied than ever the lock was when it was attached to her head.

THEMES AND TECHNIQUES

The Rape of the Lock is based around an incident where Lord Petre cut off a lock of hair from the famous beauty Arabella Fermor. This relatively trivial episode set the respective families against one another. Pope was asked by his friend John Caryll to write a comic account of the occasion to help cool the families' respective tempers.

> Based upon an incident where Lord Petre cut off a lock of hair from society beauty Arabella Fermor, Pope wrote *The Rape of the Lock* in the hope that it would defuse the situation. To this end, he employed the form of the mock epic, using heightened verse to describe this essentially trivial incident.

Pope agreed to do this using the form of the mock-heroic epic. An epic is a vast poem that deals with vast themes, such as Homer's Iliad, or JOHN MILTON's PARADISE LOST. Constantly alluding to these works and others of their ilk, Pope's poem uses the same type of poetry to write about the trivial theme of the stolen ringlet. In this sense, Pope is not mocking the form of the epic, but rather using the form to mock the trivial nature of the incident. For what is at stake between Belinda and the Baron, or Fermor and Petre, is not of very great importance but it is treated by those involved as though it were. By comparing the heroic deeds of a true epic, in which people die and nations are destroyed, Pope hopes to show how petty is the whole conflict over a piece of hair. Society, he suggests, has lost its sense of proportion.

Further Reading

Pope, Alexander, *The Rape of the Lock*. Edited by Geoffrey Tillotson. London and New York: Routledge, 1990. This is an excellent edition of the text, including both versions of the poem as well as extensive notes and critical appendices.

Rousseau, G.S. (ed.), *'The Rape of the Lock': A Collection of Critical Essays*. New Jersey: Prentice-Hall, 1969. This short book contains a number of essays looking at Pope's poem from various standpoints.

RASSELAS (1759)
by Samuel Johnson

Marriage has many pains, but celibacy has no pleasures.

More of a fable than a novel, *Rasselas* is a prose narrative that follows the travels of Rasselas, the Prince of Abyssinia, and his trusty companions. It examines the question of what choice of life will bring us happiness, and, without giving any precise answers, it warns against the seductions of hope and illusion.

Summary

Rasselas begins with a description of the Abyssinian royal palace. Practically inaccessible and inescapable, the secluded palace is a kind of prison where every pleasure is fulfilled but no one is allowed to leave. All the princes seem happy with this arrangement except the 26-year-old Rasselas, for whom 'pleasure has ceased to please'. He admits that he wants nothing but want itself, and expresses a wish to see the miseries of the world in order that he might know his own happiness. Rasselas dreams of escaping to the outside world and even commissions an artist to construct him wings, but the project fails and he is left still more unsatisfied.

Eventually, Rasselas meets Imlac, a scholar and poet, who describes his travels in the outside world. With the help of Nekayah, Rasselas's sister, they tunnel through the mountain surrounding the palace, and escape into the outside world. It is very strange to them and Imlac takes great pains in making sure they do not give away their true identity. When Imlac is sure they are ready, the little group travels to Cairo where Imlac knows they will be able to see all forms of humanity, and from their observations, make their choice of life. Rasselas is then exposed to a variety of life styles, from the hedonistic to the ascetic, but

each one has its defects and leaves him dissatisfied. Nekayah too gives her consideration to various domestic arrangements and finds that marriage is very often based on the illusion that two people who are unhappy apart believe they will be happy together.

The group then travels to the pyramids, monuments whose pointlessness impresses upon them how even unlimited power and wealth cannot bring happiness. After this, Rasselas decides to devote himself to science. However, Imlac cautions him with the tale of an astronomer who was so taken with his own powers that he believed he could control the weather itself. Further discussions ensue in which they decide that the choice of eternity is more important than the choice of life. Having failed to fix upon a choice of life, the group determines to return to Abyssinia.

> *Rasselas* is a fable in which Samuel Johnson examines what constitutes a happy life. Given the straitened circumstances in which it was written, it is perhaps unsurprising that it expresses a pessimistic view of human nature.

THEMES AND TECHNIQUES

Rasselas was written by JOHNSON when he was still very poor. He wrote it quickly in order to raise some money that he might make his mother's last few days bearable, but she died before he was able to reach her. It is perhaps not surprising then that *Rasselas* express a profoundly pessimistic view of human nature. For, given the entire multitude of life and the ability to pick from any one mode of living, Rasselas is unable to find even one choice of life whose exponent is actually happy. This, in its way, may have been a comfort to the beleaguered Johnson, imagining others more fortunate than himself to be miserable too. However, what cannot have been of comfort is the unhappiness that he attributes to the faculty which, as a man of letters, he was clearly a master himself – the faculty of the imagination. The imagination, *Rasselas* seems to suggest, is perilously close to a mental disorder. It offers hope where there should be none, and trumps reason to the point of delusion and madness. Shorn even of the comfort of fictions, Johnson leaves Rasselas and company wiser (if not actually happier) in the knowledge that their goals cannot be obtained.

Further Reading

Johnson, Samuel, *'Rasselas' and Other Tales.* Edited by Gwin J. Kolb. New Haven: Yale University Press, 1990. Edited by a leading Johnson expert, this is an excellent edition of the text, and it includes an introduction and an extensive glossary.

RED BADGE OF COURAGE, THE (1894–95)
by Stephen Crane

He wished that he, too, had a wound, a red badge of courage.

The Red Badge of Courage is a novel about the American Civil War. It tells the story of the experience of Henry Fleming, a new recruit to the Union army.

Summary

When the novel opens, Henry Fleming, a new recruit to the Union army, is sitting with his regiment while they debate rumours of an impending battle. Henry sits apart from the others, contemplating his own bravery and whether or not he will cope under fire. Worried that he might be a coward, he asks a more experienced soldier, Jim Conklin, if he would ever run away. Jim does not think he will, but he cannot definitely say he will not. Eventually, Henry's regiment heads towards a battlefield. On the way, Henry's feelings range from fear that he will be killed to a kind of blood-lust.

When they reach the battlefield and await the enemy, Henry sees another regiment in front of them flee. He imagines that the enemy is a fierce monster, but when his regiment is charged he is too busy and too tightly packed in to run away. The enemy soon retreats and Henry feels a sense of satisfaction. However, this is short-lived and the enemy returns to the fight. This time Henry is overcome with fear and he drops his weapon and runs away. He feels that he is being chased by the monster and that those who have remained behind are fools who will all perish. It is not until he overhears an officer telling of the victory of his regiment that

Henry comes to regret his decision to run away.

Ashamed of his response and unwilling to take the jibes he imagines will attend his return, Henry disappears into a nearby forest. Coming out the other side, he stumbles upon a line of wounded men, retreating from the front. A tattered-looking soldier pesters Henry, asking him where he is wounded. Feeling guilty at his lack of a wound, Henry runs away from the soldier, only to bump into Jim who is returning from the fight seriously wounded. The tattered man offers his assistance in helping Jim but Jim falls over and dies. When the tattered man presses Henry once more about the location of his wounds, Henry leaves him staggering about in a field. He then meets a line of retreating men, but when Henry asks them what has happened, one of them hits Henry on the head with his rifle butt.

> Still hailed as one of the most realistic accounts of a soldier in battle, *The Red Badge of Courage* was written when Crane had never even seen conflict let alone experienced it first-hand. The novel follows Henry as he develops from a brash and frightened youth into a more considered and mature soldier.

Henry then makes his way back to his regiment at the front with the gash on his head. There he is treated as if he received a bullet wound to the head. A few soldiers jeer at him, but during the next fight, Henry is seized with a passion for fighting and excels himself. This happens again the next time he is caught up in fighting when he seizes the flag of his regiment after his colour sergeant is killed. Henry learns that he and his friend have been noticed as the two best fighters. However, his regiment had stopped short of achieving a memorable victory and so they are immediately thrust back into battle again and this time they manage to defeat the enemy and take four prisoners. Reflecting on his experiences, he believes he has survived and in the process come to a solid understanding of himself as a man.

THEMES AND TECHNIQUES

Crane's work is not dissimilar to the work of HENRY JAMES in the way that he puts a character into a highly pressured situation and then describes how they cope with it. The difference between Crane and James is that while James's characters may well suffer symbolic losses from these situations, Crane's characters are put into circumstances in which they may very well die. Nowhere is this more obvious than in *The Red Badge of Courage*. From before Henry has even seen a battle, he is haunted by his own reactions to his possible death. While his aspirations to be a hero are misplaced and borne from fiction, his apprehension of his own death is equally naïve. It is only when he sees a corpse for the first time that he begins to realise how normal and inevitable his own mortality is, despite his thoughts that it might in some way be special. Equally, it is only after he has actually fulfilled his earlier notion of being a hero by saving the flag that Henry comes to understand that heroism is a more considered affair, far from the brash imaginings of his youth. Indeed, so pressured is the situation in which Henry finds himself that the few short weeks in which the novel is set are enough for him to mature from being a callow, hysterical youth to a calmly confident man.

Further Reading

Mitchell, Lee Clark (ed.), *New Essays on 'The Red Badge of Courage'*. New York: Cambridge University Press, 1986. This short and accessible collection of essays considers in what ways Crane's novel represented a new form of writing, as well the subject of courage, amongst others.

Pizer, Donald, *Critical Essays on Stephen Crane's 'The Red Badge of Courage'*. Boston: G.K. Hall, 1990. This larger and more scholarly collection of essays offers a chronological look at the novel's reception, including reviews of the novel from the time of its publication.

RICHARD III (1593–95)
by William Shakespeare

Now is the winter of our discontent
Made glorious summer by this sun of York;
And all the clouds that lower'd upon our house
In the deep bosom of the ocean buried.

One of the most famous villains in literature, the hump-backed Richard III is the star of this history play. It charts his rise to the English throne through various schemes and murders until he is eventually toppled.

Summary

When the play opens, the War of the Roses between the royal houses of York and Lancaster has just been decided in favour of York. Edward IV is King and everyone is seemingly happy apart from Richard, his younger brother. Richard is restlessly ambitious and desires to sit on the throne himself. He therefore sets about creating the conditions in which he will be made King. He begins by creating conflict between his other elder brother, Clarence, who would have been next in line for the throne, and Edward. Clarence is imprisoned in the Tower of London and, on Richard's orders, murdered by assassins that go there under the assumption that it is Edward's bidding. Already ill, Edward falls sicker yet when he finds out what he has supposedly done.

Meanwhile, Richard decides he wishes to wed the wealthy Lady Anne, widow of the son of the late Henry VI, even though he is directly responsible for her being a widow in the first place. In an astonishing display of his rhetorical powers, Richard seduces Lady Anne and persuades her to marry him. Elsewhere, however, Richard is less well received. Edward's wife, Queen Elizabeth, is particularly worried that Richard has been named Protector of the Realm and will be guardian to her two sons, the next in line to the throne if and when Edward dies. During an attempt to effect a reconciliation between the two of them, it is announced that Clarence is dead. Shortly afterwards, Edward dies too. With the princes too young to take the throne, Richard is in temporary charge and he immediately arrests the Queen's brother and son.

With his co-conspirator, the Duke of Buckingham, Richard then sees to it that Edward, the Prince of Wales and king-in-waiting, and his brother, the Duke of York, are sent to the Tower of London for their safety. While they are safely locked away, Buckingham begins to persuade public opinion that the two boys are in fact illegitimate. The Lord Mayor then seems inclined to make Richard King in their stead. Seemingly reluctantly, Richard accepts and becomes Richard

III. After this, Richard moves quickly to consolidate his power, firstly by having the two princes murdered in the Tower, and secondly by murdering his own wife in order that he may marry Elizabeth's daughter and that way bolster his own legitimacy.

> *Richard III* follows the hump-backed Richard on his murderous path to becoming King and his subsequent loss of the throne. The character and acts of Richard were deliberately exaggerated by Shakespeare in order to please Elizabeth I, whose grandfather Henry VII defeated Richard.

Fearing for his life after he refused to murder the princes, Buckingham flees from Richard and builds up an army of his own to protect himself. Richard has little trouble in defeating it and when Buckingham is captured, he has him executed. However, Richard's biggest threat now appears to come from Henry of Richmond, the surviving heir of the Lancaster claim to the throne. He has built an army in France and invades England, ready for a final battle with Richard's forces. The night before the final battle, Richard is haunted by visions of all the people he has murdered who tell him he will die the following day. Richard also learns that Queen Elizabeth has secretly arranged for her daughter to marry Richmond, a match which would unite the two houses of York and Lancaster. During the battle that follows, Richard fights fiercely, attempting to find and kill Richmond, but (famously bereft of a horse), he is unable to prosecute his cause to the fullest and dies. Richmond is subsequently crowned Henry VII and the country is happy to succumb to an era of peace and prosperity.

THEMES AND TECHNIQUES

It is worth bearing in mind when you see this play that SHAKESPEARE did not write it in a vacuum. Composed comparatively early in his career, *Richard III* was performed when Queen Elizabeth was on the throne. Shakespeare not only had to avoid incurring her wrath, in case she shut down the theatre or had him arrested, he also had to curry her favour in the hope that she would offer his company some kind of patronage, however indirect.

To this end, *Richard III* celebrates a decisive moment in the history of the house of Tudor, Elizabeth's royal family – the moment when they assumed power in the form of Henry VII. In order to present Henry's ascension to power in the most glorious terms possible, while at the same time affirming his legitimacy as King at a time when there were competing claims to the throne, Shakespeare presents Richard III as highly corrupt and debased. Like Thomas More before him, Shakespeare exaggerated the stories of Richard's monstrous deformity, elaborated the story of the two princes' death and generally presented him as a divisive king. When the fair-minded Henry takes the throne from Richard, it is not therefore seen as a treasonable act of usurpation (as monarchs tended to view such matters) but as the rightful remedy to a malignant disease that was plaguing England. It is said that the victors write history and, in this case, our understanding of Richard III has been marred ever since.

Further Reading

Kendall, Paul Murray, *Richard III: The Great Debate*. New York: W.W. Norton, 2002. This book examines the myth of Richard III and the role of Shakespeare's play in creating it.

Shakespeare, William, *King Richard III*. Edited by Janis Lull. London and New York: Cambridge University Press, 1999. This edition of Shakespeare's play emphasises its translation onto the stage, looking at its history in production, including Sir Ian McKellen's recent brilliant film version.

> **ROMEO AND JULIET (1594–95)**
> by William Shakespeare
>
> *From forth the fatal loins of these two foes*
> *A pair of star-crossed lovers take their life;*
> *Whose misadventured piteous overthrows*
> *Doth with their death bury their parents'*
> *strife*

Written comparatively early in SHAKESPEARE's career, *Romeo and Juliet* is one of the most famous love stories ever told. It depicts the intense passion between Romeo and Juliet and dramatises their struggle to be together in the face of the hostility of their warring families.

Summary

The play is set against a long-standing feud between two families from Verona – the Montagues and the Capulets. In order to quell any further hostilities following the brawl with which the play starts, Prince Escalus, the ruler of Verona, imposes a sentence of death upon the next person to revive the quarrel. Meanwhile, Paris, a relation of the Prince, meets Capulet in order to ask for the hand of his daughter – Juliet – in marriage. Capulet is happy with the idea, but suggests to Paris that he wait for a couple of years as she is still only 13 years old, and that he must also gain her consent. Capulet is holding a feast that evening and invites Paris to join him.

Hearing of the feast, Benvolio and his cousin Romeo decide to go with their witty friend Mercutio. As Romeo is the son of Montague, they will go in disguise. While there, Romeo hopes to see Rosaline, the girl with whom he has recently been infatuated. However, he soon forgets Rosaline when he sees and instantly falls in love with Juliet. The attraction is mutual but both realise the difficulty of their position given the background of their warring families, so they resolve to have a secret wedding. With the help of Romeo's friend, Friar Laurence, and Juliet's nurse, the couple are married the next day. Meanwhile, Capulet's cousin Tybalt has sworn vengeance on Romeo after having seen him gatecrash the previous night's party. When he finally meets Romeo again, Romeo is unwilling to fight someone whom he now considers to be family. Unwilling to sit and do nothing while Tybalt taunts Romeo, Mercutio takes up Tybalt's challenge and is killed by him. In order to avenge his friend's death, Romeo then kills Tybalt. As a result, the Prince bans Romeo from Verona for the rest of his life.

When Juliet hears of Tybalt's death and her husband's banishment, she is heartbroken. However, things become worse when her father announces that Juliet must now marry Paris within two days. Juliet consults the Friar. He advises her to agree to the marriage and take a potion on the eve of her wedding which will make it seem as if she is dead when really she will be sleeping for 42 hours. In the meantime, the friar will contact Romeo in Mantua and he will return secretly to Verona and wait in the Capulet tomb for Juliet to awake. Tragically, the friar's messenger is waylaid by the plague and Romeo only hears that Juliet is dead. Suicidal, he buys some poison and makes his way to the Capulet tomb with the intention of seeing her one more time before he dies..When he gets there he encounters Paris and kills him. Inside the tomb Juliet appears to be dead and so Romeo takes the poison and kills himself. Shortly afterwards, Juliet awakes and finds Romeo dead by her side. Desperate, she takes a dagger and stabs herself to death. Finally, the Capulets and Montagues are united in grief.

> In Shakespeare's *Romeo and Juliet* love is a wild and unstable emotion. Traversing the feud between their two families, the passionate love of Romeo and Juliet, the 'pair of star-crossed lovers', results in a funeral rather than a marriage.

THEMES AND TECHNIQUES

In terms of its theme – love – *Romeo and Juliet* is actually a comedy with a tragic ending. It is similar to A MIDSUMMER NIGHT'S DREAM, at least in the first two acts, where real love is set against courtly love in order to show how shallow the latter is. However, whereas in *A Midsummer Night's Dream* everything is risked to no more account than a hangover, in *Romeo and Juliet* the gambles all turn out ill and many characters pay with their lives. Indeed, this play is perhaps the first of Shakespeare's plays in which love becomes a dangerous and essentially uncontrollable emotion, the kind that in later works, such as ANTONY AND CLEOPATRA, is capable of toppling whole dynasties and empires. The corpses that litter the stage at the end of the play also foreshadow the later works in which no sentiment is properly validated until it is marked by a dead body. Such an extreme view of the world prompted the nineteenth-century critic William Hazlitt to declare that 'Romeo is Hamlet in love'. Like the earnest young prince, Romeo's character is interested in only bold expression. Either he is delirious or wracked with misery, vitally alive or needlessly dead, and in that he personifies the violent love which causes him these emotions.

Further Reading

Halio, Jay L. (ed.), *Shakespeare's 'Romeo and Juliet': Texts, Contexts and Interpretations*. Newark: University of Delaware Press, 1996. Amongst other issues, this book describes the social and historical context of *Romeo and Juliet*, disclosing Shakespeare's indebtedness to sources current at the time.

Porter, Joseph A. (ed.), *Critical Essays on Shakespeare's 'Romeo and* Juliet'. New York: Twayne Publishers, 1997. This collection of essays looks at a variety of different interpretations of the play.

ROVER, THE (1677)
by Aphra Behn

The banished cavaliers! A roving blade!
A popish carnival! A masquerade!
The devil's in't if this will please the nation
In these our blessed times of reformation.

The first professional female writer, APHRA BEHN was also one of the most prolific dramatists of the Restoration. *The Rover* is her most popular play and it tells the story of the tangled love affairs of two sisters and their beaux.

Summary

The play opens in Naples during the carnival season. Two sisters, Florinda and Hellena, discuss Florinda's love for Belvile, an English colonel who saved Florinda and her brother, Don Pedro, from ill-treatment at the hands of the French. When Don Pedro arrives, he advises Florinda to pay her respects to Don Vincentio, a rich old man whom her father has decided she should marry. Florinda hates him and so Don Pedro devises a compromise in which she will marry his friend Don Antonio, the Viceroy's son. For her part, Hellena is set to become a nun against her wishes. Disguised as gypsies, Florinda and Hellena meet Belvile and Willmore (the rover or cavalier of the title) and arrange to meet later in the evening.

In the meantime, Don Pedro spots Don Antonio paying homage to Angellica, a famous courtesan, and, in disguise, he vows to avenge Florinda by challenging him to a duel set for the next day. Willmore too is taken by Angellica and she by him. He admits his undying love to her, but then falls for the charms of Hellena once more. Upon returning to Angellica's apartment, Willmore unknowingly wounds Don Antonio. However, Belvile is assumed to be the assailant and is taken away by Don Antonio's officers. Don Antonio asks Belvile to fight his duel for him as he is injured. Wearing the mask of Don Antonio, Belvile beats Don Pedro who, assuming him still to be Don Antonio, offers Florinda in marriage. Willmore inadvertently reveals the true identity of Belvile but Don Pedro is so disappointed at Don Antonio sending a replacement that he agrees to the marriage of both Belvile to Florinda, and Willmore to Hellena.

THEMES AND TECHNIQUES

The Rover ostensibly takes as its hero Willmore, the sea captain and 'rover' of the title. Willmore and the other members of the English party represent the Royalists who were exiled to Continental Europe during the reign of Oliver Cromwell between 1649 (the date of the execution of Charles I), and 1660 (the date of the Restoration of the monarchy). The theatre had been closed during Cromwell's reign, but one of Charles II's first acts upon assuming the throne was to grant licences to two theatres.

Written to appeal to the aristocratic tastes of the court of Charles II, *The Rover* unsurprisingly indulges in ribaldry and licentious wit.

The Rover was first performed at one of these theatres in front of Charles II and his courtiers and was designed to appeal to this audience. In this regard it is unsurprising that much of the play is given over to the pursuit of pleasure, as this echoed the infamously hedonistic court of the new King. However, *The Rover* is not just a play about male hedonists. Perhaps uniquely, and possibly because it was written by a woman, the play also features two female heroines whose wits make them more than a match for the cavaliers in the play. Indeed, some modern critics now argue that the play is invested with a specifically feminine type of sensibility, one that reveals itself in the plasticity of the characters' various identities and guises.

Further Reading

Day, Roger (ed.), *Shakespeare, Aphra Behn and the Canon*. London and New York: Routledge, 1996. This book compares and contrasts the fortunes of *The Rover* with three of Shakespeare's plays. It also includes an annotated version of *The Rover*.

Todd, Janet, *The Critical Fortunes of Aphra Behn*. New York: Camden House, 1998. This is a fascinating book that examines how Behn's status as a female writer has altered her reception from the beginning of her career to the present day.

S

SCARLET LETTER, THE (1850)
by Nathaniel Hawthorne

My fortune somewhat resembled that of a person who should entertain an idea of committing suicide, and, altogether beyond his hopes, meets with the good hap to be murdered.

The Scarlet Letter is a tale of adultery set in Puritan America. It follows Hester Prynne, who is punished for her adulterous behaviour by being forced to wear a scarlet 'A' embroidered upon her breast.

Summary

The novel begins with a lengthy prologue explaining how the narrator stumbles upon a rag of scarlet cloth and a number of accompanying documents which relate to the story that follows. The story that follows commences some 200 years earlier when Hester Prynne is led from a prison to a scaffold in the centre of town. Carrying a baby in her arms and bearing the scarlet letter 'A' emblazoned across her chest, she is being punished for the act of adultery which led to the creation of her baby. Her husband sent her to America ahead of himself, but it is believed that he has been lost at sea. She, meanwhile, has had an affair with someone else but exactly who, she will not reveal. While she stands on top of the scaffold being publicly shamed, she spots two people in the crowd – Arthur Dimmesdale, the local Puritan minister, and Roger Chillingworth, her husband.

When Chillingworth sees his wife being shamed in this way, he vows revenge upon the man that caused it. At the same time, acting in his capacity as a doctor, he is admitted to see Hester where he compels her to keep his identity a secret. Shunned by society, Hester and her daughter, Pearl, move to the outskirts of the town where they remain, Hester earning money by sewing. As Pearl grows up, however, she becomes a wild child and the town's governors suggest that she be taken away from Hester because Hester is clearly such a bad influence. Dimmesdale intervenes at this point and successfully makes the case that Pearl should stay with Hester as a reminder of her sin. Following this, Dimmesdale falls ill and Chillingworth, who has observed Dimmesdale's actions with interest, divines that Dimmesdale's illness is a result of the guilt he feels at fathering Hester's child. Chillingworth then moves into the same dwelling as Dimmesdale, ostensibly to nurse him back to health, but in reality to torment him for committing adultery with his wife.

One day, while Dimmesdale is asleep, Chillingworth observes Dimmesdale's chest and is shocked by what he finds there. Hester, increasingly worried about Dimmesdale's health, reveals to him that Chillingworth is in fact her husband and that he is bent on revenge. Furious with this, Dimmesdale is temporarily reinvigorated. He agrees with Hester's plan to escape the town by boarding a ship for Bristol on the day after Election day.

During the ceremonies for Election day, Hester learns that Chillingworth has booked himself on the same ship as Dimmesdale and Hester. Meanwhile, Dimmesdale delivers the most impressive sermon of his life. When he sees Hester and Pearl standing near the scaffold, he asks them to join him standing on top of it. With them next to him, and despite Chillingworth's protest, Dimmesdale then reveals the letter 'A' burnt into his chest. He collapses and subsequently dies in Hester's arms. Hester and Pearl leave the town for a while, but Hester later returns by herself, still with the 'A' emblazoned on her breast. It is assumed that Pearl has married into European nobility. Hester continues to live there until her death, when she is buried next to Dimmesdale, the two of them sharing a single tombstone bearing the letter 'A'.

THEMES AND TECHNIQUES

The scarlet letter that Hester is forced to wear as a punishment for her adulterous behaviour is clearly one of the keys to HAWTHORNE's novel. As a form of punishment, it readily identifies Hester to everyone in the town, showing her to be an outcast. This marginal social position is reflected in the position of her house on the outskirts of town. Despite this negative association with the scarlet letter, Hester begins to wear it with a degree of defiance. Not only does she refuse to leave town, where she would no longer have to wear it, but she is actively distressed when she is told that she may remove it and indeed continues to wear it right until she dies.

> *The Scarlet Letter* tells the story of Hester Prynne, who is forced to wear the embroidered letter 'A' on her clothing as a punishment for her adultery.

The reason Hester does this is that the letter becomes 'the symbol of her calling'. Her sinfulness, of which the letter is her badge, is the means by which she learns the sympathy which allows her to become so helpful to others in need. In fact, many of the townspeople come to interpret the letter as meaning 'Able', referring to her ability to be sympathetic with other misfortunate persons. Pearl even refuses to recognise Hester as her mother without the letter 'A' on her breast. These are just two of the ways in which the scarlet letter actually affords Hester multiple identities. Dimmesdale, in contrast, represses the admission of his sin, and is tormented for it, locked ever more firmly into a conception of himself as only an adulterer. So whereas Hester's 'A' is possible to remove, Dimmesdale's 'A' is actually seared into his flesh and impossible to

escape except by death. These two ways of expressing sinfulness symbolise religious approaches to Original Sin, the sin that every person is born with following the Fall of Adam and Eve from Paradise. On the one hand, Dimmesdale's approach suggests that such sin taints the flesh and torments the soul until death. On the other hand, Hester's approach involves an open admission of the knowledge of sin, which leads to a more sympathetic life while on earth.

Further Reading

Barlow, Jamie, *The Scarlet Mob of Scribblers: Rereading Hester Prynne*. Illinois: Southern Illinois University Press, 2000. This advanced book examines the influence of Hester Prynne as a symbol for women generally, and specifically for female scholarship.

Kesterton, David B. (ed.), *Critical Essays on Hawthorne's 'The Scarlet Letter'*. Boston: G.K. Hall, 1988. This collection of essays looks at many different aspects of Hawthorne's novel, including the meaning of the scarlet letter itself.

SILAS MARNER (1861)
by George Eliot

Even people whose lives have been made various by learning, sometimes find it hard to keep a fast hold on their habitual views of life, on their faith in the Invisible – nay, on the sense that their past joys and sorrows are a real experience, when they are suddenly transported to a new land, where by beings around them know nothing of their history, and share none of their ideas – where their mother earth shows another lap, and human life has other forms than those on which their souls have been nourished.

This was ELIOT's favourite novel, which she described as 'a story of old-fashioned village life, which has unfolded itself from the merest millet-seed of thought.' It relates the tale of

Silas Marner, a reclusive weaver who settles in the village of Raveloe, and who has his life changed by the chance adoption of a small child.

Summary

Silas Marner is a weaver in the village of Raveloe, just before the advent of industrialisation. Previously a highly religious man, he was evicted from his religious community at Lantern Yard after being falsely accused of a theft. He now lives a reclusive life in Raveloe, distrusted as an outsider, spending his days working at the loom and his nights counting his ever-growing pile of money. Meanwhile, the greatest man in Raveloe, Squire Cass, has two sons. Godfrey is the eldest son and he is in love with Nancy Lammeter, a wealthy landowner's daughter. However, he is already secretly married to a peasant girl, Molly Farren, with whom he has had a daughter. Squire Cass's youngest son, Dunstan, blackmails the good-natured but stupid Godfrey over the affair.

One day, Dunstan forces Godfrey to sell his prize horse, Wildfire, in order to get more money. Taking the horse to sell himself, Dunstan decides to indulge in a hunt before he has concluded the sale. In so doing, he accidentally kills Wildfire. Determined to get the money, Dunstan remembers the rumours about Silas's hoard of gold coins and decides to take it off him. When he arrives at Silas's cottage, he finds it unoccupied and promptly steals the weaver's entire 15 years' worth of savings. When Silas returns to discover the money missing, he is devastated. When he informs the villagers in the pub, they speculate that it was a peddler who took it. Dunstan does not return home that night.

Some time later, Silas awakes one night to find a small child in his house. He follows the child's tracks out into the snow and discovers Molly Farren lying dead in the snow. Rushing to Squire Cass's house to get help, Silas is met by Godfrey. Godfrey recognises the child as his, but does not say anything, realising that with Molly now dead he is free to marry Nancy. Silas adopts the child and calls her Eppie. He raises her with the help of Dolly Winthrop, a kindly villager, and finds a happiness that the gold never brought him.

Some years later, when Eppie is a young woman, a pit near Silas's house is drained. Dunstan's body and Silas's gold are recovered at the bottom of it, clearly from where Dunstan had stumbled into it in the dark on the night he stole the money. Hearing this, Godfrey fears what other discoveries may be made and admits to Nancy, now his wife, that he is the father of Eppie. As they have been unable to have children of their own, the couple determine to adopt Eppie. However, when they offer to do so, Eppie says she prefers to stay with Silas. With his faith in life renewed because of this decision, Silas returns to Lantern Yard to see about clearing his name from all those years ago. When he gets there though, the whole town has changed and Silas returns to Raveloe, content to let things be. The novel ends with Eppie marrying the son of Dolly Winthrop and them both moving to be with Silas in their newly enlarged home, paid for by Godfrey.

> *Silas Marner* tells the story of a reclusive weaver who has his life changed by the chance adoption of a small child. Unusually for George Eliot, the novel has an optimistic ending with Marner adapting to change rather than being overcome by it.

THEMES AND TECHNIQUES

Like many of the novels of the nineteenth century, *Silas Marner* deals with the effects of change upon characters' lives. Silas is forced out of his old home in Lantern Yard when he is accused of a crime he did not commit. When he moves to Raveloe, his established routine is firstly disturbed when his gold is stolen, and then again when Eppie arrives and transforms his life completely. In each case, the force that changes Silas's life is outside his control. It is possible to read such changes as symbolic of the wholesale disruption being wrought on Victorian society by the advance of modernisation. This was similarly outside most people's control and brought with it vast changes to their way of life.

Silas's initial reaction to the change in his life is a tortoise-like withdrawal into a miserable shell, refusing to go to church, or otherwise socialise, and establishing a fixed routine that keeps him hunched over his loom day in, day out, for over a decade. He is forced out of this insular life by further changes, particularly the arrival of Eppie, and this time he does not hide but deals with them head on. Silas finds happiness in doing this and it is significant that when he returns to Raveloe a second time, after visiting Lantern Yard, he is content to let things change as they will. By rendering Silas in this way, Eliot suggests that we will be happier accepting and dealing with change, rather than pretending it will go away.

Further Reading

Wiener, Gary (ed.), *Readings on 'Silas Marner'*. San Diego: Greenhaven Press, 2000. This book offers a biography of Eliot, as well as a contextual history of the novel and a series of readings.

Yousaf, Nahem and Maunder, Andrew (eds), *New Casebook on 'The Mill on the Floss' and 'Silas Marner'*. New York and London: St Martin's Press, 2002. This is a solid collection of contemporary critical essays about both *The Mill on the Floss* and *Silas Marner*.

SIR GAWAIN AND THE GREEN KNIGHT (1375–1400)
by Anonymous

Great wonder grew in hall
At his hue most strange to see,
For man and gear and all
Were green as green could be.

Probably the finest surviving English verse romance, this poem centres on the code of chivalry at the Court of King Arthur. It tells the story of the mysterious Green Knight and his challenge to Sir Gawain to hit him with an axe and then receive a hit in turn.

Summary

The poem opens at King Arthur's Court in Camelot where Arthur is holding a New Year's feast. The feast is interrupted by the arrival of a giant dressed all in green and known as the Green Knight. He challenges Arthur to give him a blow from his great axe on condition that he will be then allowed to return the blow in a year's time. As it would be a slur on his

honour to refuse the challenge, Arthur is just about to take up the mighty axe when Sir Gawain, one of his trusty knights, intervenes and takes the challenge upon himself. He grabs the axe and slices the head off the Green Knight with one stroke. To the astonishment of the assembled throng, the Green Knight picks up his head and leaves, reminding Sir Gawain as he goes that he must seek him out a year from now. As winter approaches in the following year, Sir Gawain sets off in order to find the Green Knight and fulfil his obligation to him.

> One of the finest surviving English verse romances, *Sir Gawain and the Green Knight* is typical in that it describes the code of chivalry at the court of King Arthur.

He travels for many weeks, battling various beasts and monsters, although nothing proves more vicious than the cold and the damp. Eventually, on Christmas Eve, he reaches a magnificent castle where he is welcomed by Bertilak, its lord. Sir Gawain learns that the Green Knight lives very close by and so he agrees to stay where he is for the next few days until he must submit to be hit. Bertilak suggests that during the wait Sir Gawain should save his strength by staying in the castle while he goes hunting. He proposes to Sir Gawain that he will give him everything he wins outside if Sir Gawain gives him everything he wins inside. Sir Gawain agrees to this and for the next two days he hands everything over that he wins. However, on the third day he wins a green silk girdle that protects the wearer from death. Thinking that it might come in useful, he breaks his word to Bertilak and keeps the garment for himself. The next day when he meets the Green Knight he bares his neck in preparation for a huge blow but actually only receives a nick from the axe. The Green Knight then reveals himself to be Bertilak in disguise and says he has merely been testing Sir Gawain. Sir Gawain then returns to Camelot wearing the green girdle on his arm as a mark of his shame at having cheated. However, to prove their solidarity, the other knights at Camelot agree to wear girdles on their arms too.

THEMES AND TECHNIQUES

Sir Gawain and the Green Knight was found in a manuscript with three other poems – *Patience*,

Cleanness and *Pearl*. Nothing is known about the author, although the dialect in which the manuscript is written suggests that the poems were written somewhere in the northwest midlands of England. Their content also suggests that the author was an educated personage, for much of the material is taken up from previous romances, particularly the French versions of the Arthurian legend.

What is at stake in the poem is the nature of the chivalric code. The pentangle emblem on Sir Gawain's shield represents the five virtues of franchise, fellowship, cleanness, courtesy and charity. Sir Gawain is bound to these virtues by his pledge as a chivalrous knight. The premise of the poem is that sometimes this pledge is more honoured in tales than in deeds. Sir Gawain proves to be brave in seeking out the Green Knight in the first place, but he lets himself down by keeping the girdle. By wearing the girdle ever after, the other knights of the Round Table are ever minded that even the smallest lapse is a breach of the chivalric code.

Further Reading

Borroff, Marie (trans.), 'Sir Gawain and the Green Knight', 'Patience' and 'Pearl': Verse Translations. New York: W.W. Norton, 2001. This book includes the standard translation of *Sir Gawain* into modern English, as well as two of the three other works by the anonymous author.

Putter, Ad, 'Sir Gawain and the Green Knight' and the French Arthurian Romance. Oxford: Clarendon Press, 1995. This book examines the connections between *Sir Gawain* and the tradition of French Arthurian romances.

SISTER CARRIE (1900)
by Theodore Dreiser

The novelty and danger of the situation modified, in a way, his disgust and distress at being compelled to be here, but not enough to prevent him from feeling grim and sour. This was a dog's life, he thought. It was a tough thing to have to come to.

Sister Carrie tells the stories of Caroline Meeber and George Hurstwood in an almost brutally simple fashion. While Meeber rises through life to become a successful actress, Hurstwood heads in the opposite direction, descending into suicide.

Summary

The novel begins in 1889 with the 18-year-old Caroline Meeber, or Carrie, leaving her home in Columbia City on a train going to Chicago. She has only a few dollars with her. On the train she strikes up a conversation with Charlie Drouet, a wealthy-looking businessman and they vow to meet again. When Carrie arrives in Chicago she goes to live with her sister, Minnie, and her husband. They live a poor life and Carrie has to find a job to pay for food and rent. After a dispiriting trudge around the city, she gets a job working in a shoe factory. The work is boring and exhausting and the pay she receives does not leave enough for her to buy clothes for the winter. In due course, Carrie falls ill and loses her job. While she is out looking for another job, she encounters Drouet.

Drouet lends her some money, then buys her clothes and then eventually has her move in with him. It is at this point that Drouet introduces Carrie to George Hurstwood, a friend of his and manager of one of Chicago's top bars. Carrie is impressed with Hurstwood and begins to compare him favourably with Drouet. For his part, Hurstwood begins to fall in love with Carrie, who seems much more attractive than his wife with whom he constantly argues. Unaware of their relationship, Drouet continues to support Carrie and finds her a part in a play where she proves to be a great success. Drouet then discovers the relationship between Carrie and Hurstwood and leaves her. At the same time, Hurstwood's wife finds out that he has been seeing Carrie, files for divorce and locks him out of the house, safe in the knowledge that the property is in her name. Learning that Hurstwood is married, Carrie does not want to see him anymore and begins to look for shop work again now that Drouet is no longer supporting her.

Increasingly desperate, Hurstwood finds that the bar safe is left unlocked one night and that there is ten thousand dollars inside. He takes the money and talks Carrie into getting on a train with him under the pretence that they are going to see Drouet in hospital.

Carrie soon realises that they are headed for Montreal and she acquiesces into marrying him. Hurstwood then returns most of the money to the bar owners but is unable to get his job back so the two move to New York. There, he uses what money he has left to buy a share in a bar, but this soon loses its lease and he fails to find another investment. After a while, Carrie regrets marrying Hurstwood. He is poorer than she imagined and increasingly apathetic about life.

> Although *Sister Carrie* was all but censored when it was first published, Dreiser's spare prose style proved to be highly influential, paving the way for a much more objective and documentary fiction.

When Hurstwood begins gambling, Carrie is forced into looking for work again and this time she returns to her dream of becoming an actress when she starts as a chorus girl. As she advances through the ranks to become a lead, Hurstwood deteriorates even further. He eventually gets a job working as a trolley driver during a strike, but when he is attacked he gives it up. Carrie thinks this is because of laziness and, leaving him 20 dollars, she moves in with her friend instead. Carrie soon becomes a famous actress, highly sought after for her comedic abilities and popular with men. Hurstwood reads about her success in the papers, but his own life falls apart and he ends up begging on the street. Eventually, he kills himself. Carrie, still searching for something she cannot define, never learns of Hurstwood's death.

THEMES AND TECHNIQUES

Sister Carrie was all but censored when it first was published, but it proved to be a highly influential novel. In particular, DREISER's non-judgemental and spare prose style set a standard that was often imitated, but only rarely bested by the likes of Ernest Hemingway. By cutting back the role of the narrator to that of reporter, Dreiser pioneered a much more objective approach to fiction, one that either seemed to lack the necessary confidence to judge its characters or, instead, held a greater confidence in its readers to judge properly for themselves.

What is at stake in *Sister Carrie* is very much

the American Dream itself. When Carrie leaves home, she is full of the promise of getting herself a better life. However, this idealism is very quickly tempered by the materialism inherent in the Dream and, shortly after meeting Drouet, she learns to judge people by the cost of their clothes and the money behind their manners. As the novel progresses, the ideals of all the characters are perverted by the lure of wealth and Dreiser shows that whether you end up poor, as in Hurstwood's case, or rich, as in Carrie's case, you can just as easily end up spiritually bankrupt too.

Further Reading

Pizer, Donald (ed.), *New Essays on 'Sister Carrie'.* New York: Cambridge University Press, 1991. This fascinating collection of essays looks at many different aspects of Dreiser's novel, including its naturalistic technique.

Sloane, David, *'Sister Carrie': Theodore Dreiser's Sociological Tragedy.* New York: Twayne Publishers, 1992. This book examines the novel both in terms of the social context of the time and the ideas informing Dreiser's critique.

SKETCH BOOK, THE (1819–20) by Washington Irving

They all stared at him with equal marks of surprise, and whenever they cast eyes upon him, invariably stroked their chins. The constant recurrence of this gesture, induced Rip, involuntarily, to do the same, when, to his astonishment, he found his beard had grown a foot long!

Photo credit: © Bettmann/CORBIS

The Sketch Book, a collection of tales and short stories, established WASHINGTON IRVING as the most influential American writer of his day. It contains two of the most famous short stories ever written – 'The Legend of Sleepy Hollow' and 'Rip Van Winkle'.

Summary

The story of 'Rip Van Winkle' is set in a village at the foot of the Kaatskill mountains in pre-Revolutionary America. Rip Van Winkle is a simple, good-natured man, loved by most people and hen-pecked by his wife, Dame Van Winkle. Always willing to help others, he is careless about his own fate and is thus harangued by Dame Van Winkle for being lazy. In order to escape his wife, Van Winkle one day ventures into the mountains where he is hailed by an antiquated-looking figure who gets Van Winkle to help him carry a barrel of ale to a group of similarly attired men playing at nine-pins. Happy to oblige, Van Winkle then serves the drink into flagons after which he drinks himself into a stupor and falls asleep. When he wakes up in the morning, the strange men have all gone, as has his faithful dog, and his rifle has rusted.

> *The Sketch Book* established Washington Irving as the First Man of American Letters. It contains two of the most popular short stories ever written – 'Rip Van Winkle' and 'The Legend of Sleepy Hollow'.

Making his way back to the village, Van Winkle finds that everything has changed. His family have disappeared, his house has been abandoned and he has somehow grown a huge beard. When he is interrogated by the locals as to his identity, it is soon established that he is Rip Van Winkle. He is reintroduced to his now fully grown daughter and son, who is the facsimile of Van Winkle, and he is informed that Dame Van Winkle has died of a fit of apoplexy. He also learns that the people he saw in the mountains were the ghosts of the explorer Henry Hudson and his crew who return every 20 years to the place that they discovered in the seventeenth century. As there seems to be no other explanation than that he has slept for 20 years, Van Winkle resumes his old habits of idling the day away. However, 'being arrived at that happy age when a man can do nothing with impunity', and no longer having a wife to harass him, Van Winkle now enjoys his life to the full.

THEMES AND TECHNIQUES

'Rip Van Winkle' is based upon a German folk tale originally pointed out to Irving by the British author, SIR WALTER SCOTT when he was in England. Despite this European lineage,

the tale as told by Irving is definitively American and became extremely influential in defining the early canon of American literature.

While seeming to describe the solution for a man plagued by his wife – if going to sleep until she is dead counts as such – 'Rip Van Winkle' also offers itself as an imaginary resolution to the problems of living in a rapidly changing world. As the list of changes that have happened to Van Winkle's remote village is relayed to him upon his return from the mountains, it is clear that Revolutionary America was a restless, ever mutating world that sometimes overtook its citizens, as we imagine our modern era does to us. Van Winkle's failure to embrace the change and instead become a point of stability himself, for which he is justly celebrated, mark him out as the antithesis of BENJAMIN FRANKLIN, the legendary self-made man who was forever instigating and profiting from personal and political revolutions. In this sense, Van Winkle is the first American anti-hero, a character whose determination *not* to succeed yields a failure which is ironically a form of success.

Further Reading

Aderman, Ralph M. (ed.), *Critical Essays on Washington Irving*. New York: G.K. Hall and Co., 1990. This generous collection of essays looks at all aspects of Irving's work, including 'Rip Van Winkle' and 'The Legend of Sleepy Hollow'.

> **SONGS AND SONNETS**
> **(1595–1635)**
> by John Donne
>
> *Busy old fool, unruly sun,*
> *Why dost thou thus*
> *Through windows and through curtains call on us?*
> *Must to thy motions lovers' seasons run?*

Although a widely circulated manuscript in his lifetime, *Songs and Sonnets* was not published until after DONNE's death. It contains many of his most popular works, including 'The Flea', 'The Sun Rising' and 'A Valediction: Forbidding Mourning'.

Summary

The scenario that Donne uses most often in his poems is one where the spiritual self has to battle with the physical self for supremacy. 'The Flea', one of Donne's most famous poems, provides an interesting example of this. The speaker, the 'I' of the poem, represents the carnal self, lusting after his prospective lover. In turn, the speaker's beloved represents the spiritual self, refusing to accede to the speaker's sexual advances. The speaker points to a flea who has sucked blood from both of them and in whom their blood mingles. This is not, the speaker argues, 'a sin, or shame, or loss of maidenhead' but rather a matter of very little account in a similar vein to that which she denies him. The speaker's beloved then moves to kill the flea but the speaker argues for its life, claiming that the flea represents their marriage as well as both of them and so, in killing the flea, she would also kill the three of them. In the final verse, the beloved kills the flea and claims that neither of them is the worse for it. The speaker then concurs, saying that she will lose nothing either if she yields to him.

John Donne's poems helped to inspire a generation of poets who became known as the Metaphysicals. They took their cue from his inventive and elaborate imagery in poems such as 'The Flea' and 'A Valediction: Forbidding Mourning'.

Another of Donne's most famous poems is 'A Valediction: Forbidding Mourning'. There are four valedictions in *Songs and Sonnets*. In many ways, the spiritual position of the speaker in this one provides a counterpoint to the carnality of the speaker in 'The Flea'. The poem is said to have been written for Donne's wife when he left for a trip to Europe, although it perhaps makes more sense if it is told from her point of view. The speaker here advises his beloved not to profess any great demonstration of grief because he has to leave her. Unlike love based only on physical attraction, the speaker contends that their love can stand them being apart because their two souls will still be one. He compares their love to gold beaten into 'airy thinness' but not breached. Should their souls be considered separately, they are only separate in the sense that the two legs of a compass are separate. While her soul stays where it is, his soul moves around it. Finally, the fixity of her soul allows him to describe a circle in which he comes back to the point from which he started.

THEMES AND TECHNIQUES

Donne is often cited as the inspiration for a generation of writers, including ANDREW MARVELL, who are known as the Metaphysical Poets. Although by no means a cohesive group, the point of comparison between these poets is their use, inherited from Donne, of what are called conceits. Conceits are elaborate and ingenious comparisons between objects which are not conventionally placed next to each other. The most famous conceit is the one employed by Donne in 'A Valediction: Forbidding Mourning', in which a pair of compasses is compared at length to a pair of separated lovers. The stationary compass leg, like the stationary lover is joined to the departing lover, and it 'leans and hearkens after it', becoming erect as the other comes home. The compasses, with their connotations of calculation and precision, also add a sense of intellectual purity to the description of the couple's love. SAMUEL JOHNSON, however, complained of the inventiveness of the image, declaring that it was too clever to be sincere. If that reflected some of the mood of Johnson's age, more modern times have found in the conceit precisely the kind of detachment and ingenuity that is demanded of sincerity.

Further Reading

Donne, John, *'The Elegies' and 'The Songs and Sonnets'*. Edited by Helen Gardner. London: Oxford University Press, 1965. This is a generous edition of Donne's poetry and includes an introduction and extensive notes.

Lovelock, Julian (ed.), *Casebook on Donne: Songs and Sonnets*. London: Palgrave Macmillan, 1973. This is a collection of essays that examines Donne's work from a variety of angles.

SONGS OF INNOCENCE AND SONGS OF EXPERIENCE (1789–94)
by William Blake

Tyger! Tyger! Burning bright
In the forests of the night.

Either disregarded or dismissed as insane during his day, BLAKE was a visionary artist who expressed himself in verse and pictures. Probably his best-known work, *Songs of Innocence and of Experience* contains such poems as 'The Sick Rose', 'The Tyger' and 'London'.

Summary

Originally published as *Songs of Innocence* in 1789, Blake added a number of new poems in 1794 and split the collection into two between the *Songs of Innocence* and the *Songs of Experience*. He intended that this division should show the 'two contrary states of the human soul'. In this way a number of the poems in *Songs of Experience* are counterparts of poems in *Songs of Innocence*. One of the most famous examples of such a pairing is the one between 'The Lamb' in *Songs of Innocence* and 'The Tyger' in *Songs of Experience*. Told from the point of view of a child using a childish metre, 'The Lamb' begins with a question, 'Little Lamb, who made thee?' Having repeated the question in an incantatory manner akin to a nursery rhyme, the speaker of the poem then answers the question for the lamb:

He is called by thy name,
For he calls himself a Lamb;
He is meek and he is mild,
He became a little child.

The reference here is to Jesus who is often symbolised as a lamb, representing his Christian qualities of humbleness and gentleness.

If this is one aspect of Christianity, Blake shows another aspect of it in 'The Tyger'. Here the poem is centred upon a single issue expressed in the first stanza:

What immortal hand or eye
Could frame thy fearful symmetry?

If the maker of the lamb in the first poem is 'meek and mild' and domesticated in the symbol of a lamb, here the maker is completely alien from human experience. For whoever frames the 'fearful symmetry' of the tiger is 'immortal', dwelling in 'distant deeps or skies' and capable of great power that is not easily frightened by 'deadly terrors'. Is it possible, the speaker of the poem asks, that he 'who made the Lamb make thee?' As the maker in question here is God, then the answer is 'yes', which is suggestive of the difference between the innocence of the first poem and the experience of the second. For in the first poem there are only certainties, whereas in the second poem there are only questions with no easy answers, marking how experience only opens us up to the mysteries of Creation rather providing us with answers.

THEMES AND TECHNIQUES

Blake's poems in *Songs of Innocence* and *Songs of Experience* are written in a deceptively simple fashion. The choice of words and the rhythms in which they are encased verge on the child-like at times. However, to infer from this that the poems themselves are unsophisticated is to ignore the highly compressed symbolism of his work, which allows meanings to multiply far beyond the ostensive sense of what is written on the page.

Songs of Innocence and *Songs of Experience* contain many of Blake's best-known poems, including 'The Sick Rose' and 'The Tyger'. Deceptively simple, these poems are packed with symbols and allusions.

This density of symbol and allusion is compounded in the *Songs* by the pairing of poems together within the framework of the themes of innocence and experience. In 'The Lamb' and 'The Tyger', for example, there is a subtle shift in the level of diction between the two poems which discloses the experience of the speaker in the second poem relative to the naïvety of the speaker of the first poem. Phrases like 'immortal hand' and 'fearful symmetry', for instance, would be out of place in 'The Lamb'. There is also a series of allusions in 'The Tyger' which index the presence of an educated speaker. The question 'On what wings dare he aspire?' refers to the myth of Icarus who flew too near the sun, for example, while the question 'What hand dare seize the fire?' references the myth of Prometheus who stole fire from the gods. The irony, and part of the complexity of the poetry, is that innocence allows for a certainty that experience, with all its classical references and expanded diction, seems to strip away. The more we know, Blake suggests, the less we understand.

Further Reading

Adams, Hazard (ed.), *Critical Essays on William Blake*. New York: G.K. Hall and Co., 1991. This collection of essays stresses the disparity between Blake's reception in his own time and now.

Paley, Morton D. (ed.), *Blake's 'Songs of Innocence and Experience': A Collection of Critical Essays*. London: Prentice-Hall, 1970. This is a short collection of essays that examines Blake's work from a variety of angles.

TALE OF TWO CITIES, A (1859)
by Charles Dickens

It was the best of times, it was the worst of times, it was the age of wisdom, it was the age of foolishness, it was the epoch of belief, it was the epoch of incredulity, it was the season of Light, it was the season of Darkness, it was the spring of hope, it was the winter of despair, we had everything before us, we had nothing before us, we were all going direct to Heaven, we were all going direct the other way – in short, the period was so far like the present period, that some sort of its noisiest authorities insisted on its being received, for good or for evil, in the superlative degree of comparison only.

Based on the events of the French Revolution in Paris and how they affected people in London, this is one of DICKENS's two great historical novels (the other being *Barnaby Rudge*). It tells the story of Lucie Manette and Charles Darnay as they struggle against the forces of history to keep their love alive.

Summary

When the novel opens it is 1775 and the avuncular Jarvis Lorry, an official from Tellson's Bank in London, helps Lucie Manette travel to Paris where she discovers that her father, Dr Manette, is actually still alive, although he had been presumed dead after spending 18 years in the Bastille prison. Driven to an early dementia by his long incarceration, Manette is cared for by his former servants, Ernest and Therese Defarge, and spends most of the day making shoes. The Defarges display revolutionary sympathies over what has been done to Manette, with Madame Defarge knitting a list of the enemies of the revolution. Lucie and Lorry remove Manette from this febrile atmosphere and take him back to London.

Five years later, Manette and Lucie are called as witnesses against Charles Darnay whom they met on their return from France. He is accused of being a French spy and looks set to be executed before Sydney Carton, an associate of Darnay's lawyer, Stryver, points out that he looks exactly like Darnay himself, and that the witnesses against Darnay could well be suffering from a case of mistaken identity. Darnay, it soon transpires, is an aristocrat from France who has renounced his title and now makes a living as a tutor in London. Carton despises Darnay because he is everything Carton wants to be, while Carton himself leads a wasteful and dissolute life. Both men fall in love with Lucie, but she is only really interested in Darnay. Despite this, Carton finds some sort of redemption in his love for Lucie and it puts new purpose into his life.

After several years, Darnay asks Manette if he may marry Lucie and he agrees provided that Darnay reveals his secret to him on their wedding day. Darnay pledges to do this and on the morning of their wedding, he reveals his secret to Manette. This seems to cause Manette to lapse back into his shoe-making behaviour for over a week, but then he recovers completely and burns his shoe-making equipment. Darnay and Lucie share a happy marriage and have a baby daughter. Even Carton comes to be friends with Darnay. However, the events of the 1789 Revolution in France soon catch up with Darnay when his old servant asks for aid after being locked up in the Bastille. Darnay ventures to France but is himself immediately arrested for being an emigrant.

Manette, Lucie and her faithful matriarchal maid Miss Pross head for Paris to try and save Darnay. Manette is able to use the credit he has with the revolutionaries after being locked up for 18 years to get Darnay an acquittal. However, Darnay is arrested again almost immediately, this time on charges put forward by the Defarges. At his trial it transpires that Manette was actually imprisoned by Darnay's father and uncle. Manette had been called by them to attend two of Madame Defarge's siblings after they were both fatally wounded by one of the aristocrats. Fearing that Manette might betray them, they had had him imprisoned. Now Darnay is to be convicted of their crimes and his execution is set for the following day. Meanwhile, Carton hears that Madame Defarge wants to execute Lucie and her daughter too so he organises for them to leave. When Madame Defarge goes to Lucie's apartment to arrest her, she meets, instead, Miss Pross who fights with Defarge and accidentally shoots her with her own gun. Carton then goes to the Bastille where he drugs Darnay and has him appear in Carton's clothes and taken out to safety by an associate. Carton, who looks exactly like Darnay, remains in his place and is executed the following day, knowing by his sacrifice that his life finally has meaning.

THEMES AND TECHNIQUES

Dickens himself declared that *A Tale of Two Cities* is 'the best story I have written'. He originally wrote it as a weekly story for his new journal, *All the Year Round*. *All the Year Round* resurrected Dickens's career in journals after he had pulled out of editing *Household Words*. It is perhaps not surprising then that the theme of resurrection figures so prominently in the story told to mark that rebirth.

The novel begins with *Book the First*, entitled 'Recalled to Life', the phrase that Lorry uses to mark the news that Manette, long thought dead, is actually alive after 18 years in the Bastille. It also applies to Darnay as he takes on a new life in England, renouncing his aristocratic heritage in France. However, the character to whom the resurrection theme

most clearly pertains is Carton. Carton sacrifices his own life in order to save Darnay from being executed. Having already been reinvigorated by his love for Lucie, he goes to the guillotine believing that he lives on in her memory and even as a name for her next child. In turn, Carton's sacrifice comes to symbolise the sacrifice of the French people who die during the Revolution in the hope of a better society. Carton envisages just such a rebirth as he is led to the scaffold, imagining 'a beautiful city and a brilliant people rising from this abyss'.

> Dickens considered *A Tale of Two Cities* to be 'the best story I have written'. Based on the events of the French Revolution, it recounts the struggle of Lucie Manette and Charles Darnay to maintain their love in the face of the overwhelming events of history.

Further Reading

Cotsell, Michael (ed.), *Critical Essays on Charles Dickens' 'A Tale of Two Cities'*. New York: Twayne Publishers, 1998. This fascinating collection of essays looks at many different aspects of Dickens's novel, including its relation to actual history and its fascinating dualism.

Sanders, Andrew, *The Companion to 'A Tale of Two Cities'*. Mountfield: Helm Information, 2002. Written by a leading expert on Victorian fiction, this fascinating companion to Dickens's novel examines its relation to historical sources, as well as glossing many of the references lost to modern readers.

> ## TALES OF SOLDIERS AND CIVILIANS (1894)
> ## by Ambrose Bierce
>
> *And so the clumsy multitude dragged itself slowly and painfully along in hideous pantomime – moved forward down the slope like a swarm of great black beetles, with never a sound of going – in silence profound, absolute.*

BIERCE's *Tales of Soldiers and Civilians* was based in large part on his experiences in the

American Civil War. It contains much of his best short story work, including the haunting 'Chickamauga' about a boy who stumbles upon the retreating injured of the Union army.

Summary

'Chickamauga' begins with an unnamed 6-year-old boy exploring the freedom of a forest. The boy is said to be endowed with the spirit of his ancestors who 'had conquered its way through two continents and passing a great sea and penetrated a third, there to be born to war and dominion as a heritage.' The boy's father has encouraged a military zeal in the child and the boy himself has responded by fashioning a wooden sword with which he pursues his imaginary enemies through the forest. Suddenly the boy is confronted by a rabbit and he takes flight, stumbling through the woods until, exhausted, he collapses sobbing to the floor and falls asleep. Meanwhile, we learn that the boy's parents are desperately searching for him.

Ambrose Bierce's groundbreaking *Tales of Soldiers and Civilians* was based in large part on his experiences in the American Civil War. The stories are told using a form of realism which records an individual's subjective responses to a situation.

When the child awakens he does not return the way he came but sets off deeper into the forest. He soon spies a moving shape which becomes a series of shapes which he distinguishes as men crawling on their hands and knees. The forest is full of them and their red and white faces remind the boy of clowns and he moves among them laughing. He doesn't realise they are dying soldiers. At one point he even climbs on to the back of a man like a horse, but the man, who has no chin, throws him off. Advancing to the front of these men, the boy leads them with his wooden sword, retreating over the ground they had originally passed on their way to battle. The boy comes across a blazing building upon which he throws his sword. He eventually recognises it as his home and sees in the wreckage caused by a shell a dead woman with her skull split

open. The boy, a deaf mute, utters an inarticulate cry.

THEMES AND TECHNIQUES

'Chickamauga' takes its name and its setting from the Battle of Chickamauga Creek. This was a battle fought in the American Civil War over two days in September 1863 where there were over 34,000 casualties. Although not injured, Bierce fought in this battle and later recorded his impressions of the fighting in 'A Little of Chickamauga'. In this article, he recalls his view that the Union forces, of which he was part, had advanced too far in pursuit of the retreating Confederate forces. In this regard, the boy echoes the actions of the army when, 'made reckless by the ease with which he overcame invisible foes attempting to stay his advance, he committed the common enough military error of pushing the pursuit to a dangerous extreme.' Like the attenuated Union army, the boy then has to turn tail and flee when he is met by a regrouped foe, in this case a rabbit.

The boy's terrified reaction to the rabbit and his subsequently joyous reaction to the dying troops illustrate the difference in approach between Bierce and STEPHEN CRANE towards the Civil War. For whereas Crane fashioned his descriptions of war to make them as realistic as possible, Bierce's technique of contrasting the boy's inappropriate reactions to the dead with that of a realistic reaction renders the whole scene unrealistic. This unreality, however, is in a sense more realistic than an objective account of the facts because it discloses the subjective, and therefore real, impressions of the war. The boy, with his wooden sword, represents an idealistic or innocent approach to battle. When the boy throws his toy sword on the flames, it symbolises his loss of innocence, a loss of innocence which is realised when he sees a dead woman, presumably his mother, and understands that she is actually dead, as opposed to playing in the manner he imagined with the injured Union soldiers.

Further Reading

Bierce, Ambrose, *Ambrose Bierce's Civil War*. Edited and with an introduction by William McCann. Washington: Gateway Editions, 1996. This book contains all of Bierce's stories and essays about the American Civil War, as well as offering a fascinating introduction.

Blume, Donald T., *Ambrose Bierce's 'Civilians and Soldiers' in Context: A Critical Study*. Ohio: Kent State University Press, 2004. This advanced book provides a critical evaluation of Bierce's collection of short stories and explains its history.

TESS OF THE D'URBERVILLES (1891)
by Thomas Hardy

That cold accretion called the world, which, so terrible in the mass, is so unformidable, even pitiable, in its units.

Tess of the D'Urbervilles features one of HARDY's most tragic heroines. It follows the milkmaid Tess as her life is ruined by her father, her employer, and her husband to the point where she is driven to commit murder.

Summary

The novel begins with John Durbeyfield being casually informed that his ancestral relations were actually the wealthy D'Urbervilles. Durbeyfield decides to exploit this connection by sending his daughter, Tess, to the D'Urbervilles' house to claim kinship. Tess refuses to do this at first but feels obligated when she accidentally kills the family's only other source of income, its horse. At the D'Urbervilles' house she meets Alec D'Urberville, the family son. He is immediately attracted to Tess and offers her a job as a milkmaid, which she takes for the money, even though she does not like Alec. He continues to try and seduce her over the following months until eventually he takes advantage of her tiredness one night in the woods with the result that Tess gives birth to a child nine months later. The child is called Sorrow and he dies not long after he is born.

After an unhappy year, Tess leaves her parents' house to work for another dairy. There she makes friends with some other milkmaids and is introduced to the morally steadfast Angel Clare, a parson's son who is there to learn the dairy trade. She and Angel soon fall in love with each other but Tess tries to keep

Angel at a distance because she feels unworthy of him in light of her past. Eventually, Angel proposes to her and after several attempts to tell him about her past, Tess slips a note under his door explaining everything. When Angel says nothing, she assumes it is because it does not matter to him and Tess looks forward to the wedding eagerly. However, the note actually goes unnoticed by Angel, a fact that Tess realises only just before the wedding. During their honeymoon, Tess finally confesses to her past after Angel has admitted to his less than perfect personal history. Despite this, Angel is completely unforgiving of Tess and he deserts her to go and live in Brazil and work out if he can ever forgive her.

Tess of the D'Urbervilles was condemned by many critics on its publication and had to be heavily edited to make it acceptable. It tells the story of the eponymous heroine and the tragic steps that lead to her execution.

Tess is devastated by this turn of events and doubts she will ever see Angel again. She moves to another farm where the work is much harder and there she unexpectedly meets Alec who has been converted to an ardent Christian, ironically by Angel's father. Alec makes Tess pledge never to tempt him sexually again, but he continues to visit her where she works until he gives up his vocation as a preacher and returns to his more familiar role as a seducer, trying to persuade Tess that Angel will never return. When Angel eventually does return, he finds that it is too late because Tess is now living with Alec. Tess is maddened at Alec for lying to her about Angel and in an argument she stabs him through the heart and kills him. Seeking Angel, the two run away and hide but they are soon caught and Tess is executed for her crime.

THEMES AND TECHNIQUES

Perhaps unsurprisingly given the Victorian era, Hardy's novel was roundly condemned when it was published, and even then it was heavily edited to make it acceptable. Part of the problem lies in the bias evident in the text in favour of Tess. Hardy was clearly quite attached to his heroine, speaking of her as if she were a real person and this is reflected in her characterisation. She seems to stand out in comparison to any of the other characters in the novel, even including Alec and Angel, the latter of whom Hardy barely stops short of scorning. In this regard, the subtitle is quite poignant because it refers to Tess as 'a pure woman'. This suggests that Tess is pure in the sense that her motives remain untainted even if she appears to be sexually defiled in the eyes of the conventional morality of the time. Indeed, Hardy challenges such thinking and instead proposes that both Alec and Angel are at fault, one for what he does and one for what he does not do. This sin of omission on Angel's part is also Hardy's way of questioning the absence of God. 'Where was Tess's guardian angel?' he asks when she is trapped by Alec, a man who is compared to the serpent in the garden of Eden. The answer is clearly 'not here' and at the end of the novel Hardy suggests we are left to the mercy of more pagan gods who end their sport with us only when we, like Tess, are dead.

Further Reading

Szumski, Bonnie, *Readings on 'Tess of the D'Urbervilles'*. San Diego: Greenhaven Press, 2000. This collection also includes a chronology of Hardy's life and a look at some contextual materials.

Widdowson, Peter (ed.), *New Casebook on 'Tess of the D'Urbervilles'*. London: Palgrave Macmillan, 1993. This collection of essays looks at many different aspects of Hardy's novel from a variety of theoretical angles, including the novel's famous subtitle.

TOM JONES (1749)
by Henry Fielding

In reality, the world have paid too great a compliment to critics, and have imagined them men of much greater profundity than they really are.

Tom Jones is a boisterous novel about the eponymous male hero. With a good deal of humour, it tells the tale of the impediments to Tom marrying Sophia Western and inheriting his uncle's estate.

Summary

When the novel opens, wealthy Squire Allworthy returns from a trip to discover a baby in his bed. He soon surmises that a servant, Jenny Jones, is the mother, while a local schoolteacher is the father. When they both leave, Allworthy undertakes to bring up the boy as his own, calling him Tom Jones. Meanwhile, Allworthy's sister, Bridget, marries Captain Bilfil and they bear a child, a boy called Bilfil. As they live with Allworthy, Captain Bilfil begins to resent Tom, whom he fears may inherit the estate. The Captain passes his dislike of Tom on to his son before he dies, and as Bilfil grows up he does all he can to get Tom into trouble. Nevertheless, Tom proves popular with the locals, for whom he sometimes steals food, while Bilfil is not liked at all. One such local is Molly Seagrim, the gamekeeper's daughter. When Molly falls pregnant, Tom admits that it was his doing and prepares to take responsibility.

Henry Fielding described *Tom Jones* as a 'comic epic poem in prose'. Packed with boisterous good humour, it tells the story of how the eponymous hero overcomes all the impediments to him marrying his beloved Sophia.

Tom finds this difficult because he has lately fallen in love with Sophia Western, daughter of Allworthy's wealthy neighbour, Squire Western. For her part, Sophia has long admired Tom. When Tom catches Molly in bed with one of his tutors and learns that the baby is not in fact his, Tom feels free to pursue his interest in Sophia. However, Allworthy falls ill and Tom attends to his bedside day and night. When Allworthy recovers, Tom gets drunk to celebrate, but Bilfil tells Allworthy, who is busy mourning the death of his sister, that Tom was rejoicing over the impending death of Allworthy himself. Aggrieved by this information, Allworthy banishes Tom from the estate. Tom is desperate at this news, not least because of his love for Sophia. She meanwhile has been promised by her father to Bilfil, a promise she feigns to keep but only to buy herself the time to escape.

Sophia then sets off in search of Tom, and

Western in search of his daughter. Tom, meanwhile, rescues a Mrs Waters from being robbed and commences an affair with her. Sophia finds out about this act of inconstancy on Tom's part and departs. Distraught, Tom sets off after Sophia. He then becomes involved in a duel, started by a man who thinks Tom is having an affair with his wife. When Tom stabs the man he is thrown in jail. While there he learns that Mrs Waters is, in fact, Jenny Jones, his mother. She explains to Allworthy that Tom did not initiate the duel and that she had been asked to conspire against Tom by a lawyer acting for Bilfil. Furthermore, Jenny is not Tom's mother, rather she pretended to be for the sake of Bridget Allworthy who really was his mother. Allworthy subsequently disinherits Bilfil and invites his nephew Tom back to the estate. Western is now happy for the new heir to marry Sophia, and Sophia, after she has been persuaded that Tom did not intend to marry another woman, consents to a marriage with Tom.

THEMES AND TECHNIQUES

FIELDING described *Tom Jones* as a 'comic epic poem in prose'. In saying this, Fielding draws a comparison with such classical works as Virgil's *Aeneid* or Homer's *Odyssey*. There is certainly a great deal of classical symmetry in the plot of *Tom Jones* of the kind used by poets of earlier ages. For example, both Tom and Sophia are brought up on large estates where they enjoy the presence of their birth mother in the case of Tom and birth father in the case of Sophia, while also having a surrogate other parent – Allworthy, actually his uncle, is Tom's surrogate father, and Western's sister, actually her aunt, is Sophia's surrogate mother. This balance between the two sides of the plot continues in terms of the 18 books of which the novel is comprised. In the first six books, Tom and Sophia fall in love with each other but are both prevented from continuing their relationship by their parents' actions. In the second six books, Sophia pursues Tom across the country, while in the last six books, Tom pursues her across country until they are united in marriage at the end. These are just some of the ways in which the seemingly ramshackle plot is actually held in constant equilibrium like some perfectly designed neo-classical building. However, while Fielding imitates the

classical tradition, he is also producing something quite original here in that *Tom Jones* is one of the first novels to be recognised as such. Fielding's constant references to the process of writing reveal him negotiating with the boundaries of the new, trying out different approaches to narration from the omniscient to the partial point of view, from being objective to being ironic. In this way, Fielding helped to establish many of the techniques which we now take for granted in novel writing.

Further Reading

Baker, Sheridan (ed.), *Tom Jones*. New York: W.W. Norton, 1994. This edition of the novel comes with a collection of essays, including contemporary reactions to its publication.

TURN OF THE SCREW, THE (1898)
by Henry James

The story had held us, round the fire, sufficiently breathless, but except the obvious remark that it was gruesome, as on Christmas Eve in an old house a strange tale should essentially be, I remember no comment uttered till somebody happened to note it as the only case he had met in which such a visitation had fallen on a child.

One of a number of novellas written by JAMES, *The Turn of the Screw* is now probably his most famous and popular work. It tells the tale of a tortured governess about whom we are never sure if she is mad or is actually combating evil.

Summary

The story opens with a group of people telling stories around a fire. A man named Douglas confesses to having a manuscript sent to him by his sister's governess who is now dead. He informs the gathering that when she was younger, she was hired by a rich bachelor to look after his nephew and niece. Initially reluctant to accept the job, she is paid a large sum of money and accepts it but only after the man has established one condition – that she never bother him with any news or troubles of the children. Upon arriving at the man's country residence, she is met by the friendly housekeeper Mrs Grose. Mrs Grose introduces her to the girl, Flora, whom she immediately likes.

The little boy, Miles, returns shortly from boarding school, but only after the governess learns that he has been expelled. The letter from the school does not explain the reason for this and she does not ask him why. However, in trying to piece together the background of the boy, the governess learns that the former governess, Miss Jessel, died in mysterious circumstances. Apart from this, everything seems to be going well for the governess until, one evening while she is in the garden, thinking about how her employer might be impressed with her, she looks back at the house and sees a man in one of the towers. At first she thinks it is her employer, but then sees it must be a trespasser. She thinks no more of him until she sees him again one afternoon looking in through the window. When she informs Mrs Grose and describes him, Mrs Grose replies that it is Peter Quint – the uncle's dead valet.

One of Henry James's most popular works, *The Turn of the Screw* brought a new psychological depth to the ghost story. It tells the tale of a tortured governess and leaves the reader wondering if she was mad or really fighting evil.

The governess becomes convinced that Quint is after Miles and she vows to protect him. Soon afterwards, she sees a woman by the lake when she is playing with Flora. She is certain that it is Miss Jessel and that Flora also saw her but pretended she did not. Persuaded that the two ghosts are in league with each other, as Mrs Grose affirms they were in life, and that, furthermore, they are secretly in league with the children too, the governess decides not to let Flora and Miles out of her sight. She also writes a letter to the uncle, but never posts it. After a few more incidents which show that the children resent her protectiveness, the governess is sitting one day listening to Miles play the piano when she

realises that Flora has slipped out of the room.

The governess and Mrs Grose go to the lake, where Miss Jessel was last seen, and there they find Flora. She refuses to admit that she has seen a ghost and the next day develops a fever and is terrified of seeing the governess. The governess then sends Flora and Mrs Grose to the safekeeping of the uncle, while she remains in the house with Miles, determined to get to the bottom of the whole mystery. While she questions him about what happened at school and about his relationship with Quint, the former valet appears at the window. Miles claims he is unable to see him but the governess pulls him close to protect him, fearing that Quint wants to claim his soul. Suddenly the boy groans, Quint disappears, and she realises that Miles's heart has stopped.

THEMES AND TECHNIQUES

The Turn of the Screw is a frustrating read because, after building up the tension notch by notch, as the title suggests, James then fails to relieve that tension by explaining precisely what everything means, as one might expect with a normal story. We are left, then, with a number of mutually exclusive interpretations that can boiled down to two main alternatives. On the one hand, the governess is actually battling to save the souls of the two children against Jessel and Quint, a battle in which she saves Flora, but loses Miles. On the other hand, the governess is mad. She is the only one that sees the ghosts and in her mania she crushes little Miles to death at the end of the story. One reason often suggested for this madness is that she is sexually frustrated, an interpretation that seems to be confirmed by various allusions in the text. In particular, her desire for the absent uncle leads her to see people that are not there. She imagines corrupt relationships between them and the children, children whom she really wants to save from the burden of sexuality. Either way, *The Turn of the Screw* denies a final interpretation, leaving some to propose that it is an exercise about the nature of storytelling itself. By refusing to provide a satisfactory conclusion and by using an unreliable narrator who limits us to a partial view of events, James highlights the complex art of writing fiction and makes us aware of the conventions we normally never question.

Further Reading

James, Henry, *The Turn of the Screw*. Edited by Peter G. Beidler. London: Palgrave Macmillan, 2004. This edition of the novella also contains a number of essays from varying modern critical perspectives.

Pollak, Vivian R. (ed.), *New Essays on 'Daisy Miller' and 'The Turn of the Screw'*. New York: Cambridge University Press, 1993. This collection looks at a number of aspects in James's novella, including the question of female authority.

TWELFTH NIGHT, OR WHAT YOU WILL (1601)
by William Shakespeare

If music be the food of love, play on,
Give me excess of it, that, surfeiting,
The appetite may sicken, and so die.

Often considered to be the last of Shakespeare's true comedies, *Twelfth Night* is thought by many critics to be his most perfect too. It centres upon the tangled relationships between Orsino, Olivia, Viola and Sebastian – relationships which are only resolved happily when it is revealed that Viola and Sebastian are actually sister and brother.

Summary

Set in the ancient region of Illyria (the eastern Adriatic coast), the play opens on Orsino, the Duke of Illyria, opining on his unrequited love for Lady Olivia. She is in mourning for her dead brother and refuses to acknowledge Orsino. Meanwhile, a dreadful storm has caused a ship carrying a young noble woman, Viola, to be shipwrecked off the coast of Illyria. Although she manages to escape to shore, she fears that her brother Sebastian has drowned. Learning from a sea captain of the relationship between Orsino and Olivia, Viola then resolves to make the best of her situation and work for the Duke. In order to do this, she disguises herself as a man called Cesario. Orsino is immediately impressed with Cesario and sends him with a message of love to Olivia. Unfortunately, Cesario/Viola has herself fallen in love with Orsino. Despite this, Cesario/Viola determines to do her best by Orsino and ends up pleading his case to such effect that Olivia falls in love with Viola mistakenly thinking her to be a man.

Meanwhile, we learn that there is another suitor for Olivia in the form of Sir Andrew Aguecheek. Aguecheek is a wealthy man, deceived by Sir Toby Belch, Olivia's uncle, into thinking Olivia likes him while Sir Toby spends his money on mindless revelry. They are joined in this revelry by Feste, the house clown and Maria, Olivia's lady-in-waiting. Also part of Olivia's household, but firmly opposed to their fun, is Malvolio, Olivia's steward. In order to get their own back on Malvolio, Maria forges a letter in Olivia's hand. It is addressed to an unnamed, secret love inviting the man concerned to wear yellow stockings and crossed garters while acting haughtily and smiling constantly. Maria leaves the letter where Malvolio will find it and, when he does, he immediately believes that it is addressed to him, having long held a secret affection for Olivia. When Olivia witnesses Malvolio's new behaviour, however, she thinks he has gone mad and has him locked up. For the rest of play, Malvolio is left to the mercy of the other members of the household who torment him at will.

In the meantime, Viola's brother arrives in Illyria. He looks just like Viola when she is dressed as Cesario, and, as such, is quickly accosted by Sir Andrew, who has challenged Cesario to a duel over Olivia. Of course, Sebastian beats both Sir Andrew and Sir Toby. Olivia demands that Sebastian marry her, thinking that he is really Cesario. Quickly estimating the value of Olivia, Sebastian agrees. When Orsino learns of this, he feels betrayed until Viola reveals that she is really a woman and that Sebastian is her brother. Happy at this, Orsino asks Viola to marry him. We also learn that Sir Toby has married Maria as recompense for her writing the letter to Malvolio. Finally, they remember to let Malvolio out and he departs, swearing vengeance on all.

THEMES AND TECHNIQUES

In Elizabethan England, Twelfth Night – the Feast of the Epiphany on January 6 – was the final night of the Christmas festivities. On that night the normally rigid hierarchy of society temporarily gave way to a period of misrule.

This period of misrule involved inverting the normal structure of society, allowing apprentice boys to be given mock crowns for the day, for example, and generally permitting forms of authority to be lampooned and parodied. As the alternative title of the play suggests, it was a carnivalesque atmosphere of 'what you will' in which ordinary people were given extraordinary licence.

> For many critics, *Twelfth Night* is Shakespeare's best comedy. Like the traditional feast day that it celebrates, Twelfth Night is a festive play in which all expectations are reversed and all hierarchies are inverted.

The theme of carnivalesque inversion is present right from the opening scene of *Twelfth Night* which finds the noble Duke Orsino laid low by love and surfeiting on an excess of self-pity. From that point onwards, everything is turned upside down in the play and all expectations are reversed. Olivia falls for a man who is a woman, Viola mourns a brother who is not dead, Malvolio assumes a love he does not have, Sir Andrew duels a woman who turns out to be a man, and so on. Everything is inverted, as Feste remarks when he meets Sebastian thinking he is Cesario:

> '*No, I do not know you; nor I am not sent to you by my lady, to bid you come speak with her; nor your name is not Master Cesario; nor is this not my nose either. Nothing that is so is so.*'

Of course, as with the festivities of Twelfth Night itself, the period of inversion is strictly proscribed. At the end of the play all the confusions are miraculously sorted out and, somehow, everyone ends up with someone else of the appropriate gender and social status. This point of harmony is expressed through the three marriages that finish the play.

Further Reading

Davies, Steve, *Shakespeare's 'Twelfth Night'*. London: Penguin Books, 1993. As well as offering a close analysis of the play's action, this book also offers chapters on the

tradition of folly and the comedy of sexual ambiguity.

Shakespeare, William, *Twelfth Night*. Edited by J.M. Lothian and T.W. Craik. London: The Arden Shakespeare, 1975. This is one of the standard editions of *Twelfth Night* and, as well as being scrupulously edited, it also contains detailed notes and commentaries.

White, R.S (ed.), *Twelfth Night (New Casebook Studies)*. London: Palgrave Macmillan, 1996. This book provides a number of essays looking at *Twelfth Night* from different modern perspectives.

UNCLE TOM'S CABIN (1851–52)
by Harriet Beecher Stowe

The longest day must have its close – the gloomiest night will wear on to a morning. An eternal, inexorable lapse of moments is ever hurrying the day of the evil to an eternal night, and the night of the just to an eternal day.

Outsold only by the *BIBLE*, *Uncle Tom's Cabin* was a huge popular success in the second half of the nineteenth century. It tells the stories of a number of slaves, among them Uncle Tom, who dies a martyr's death.

Summary

The novel opens with Arthur Shelby, a slave owner in Kentucky, being forced to sell some of his slaves in order to pay debts. Shelby apparently regrets having to sell Uncle Tom, a middle-aged slave who has become something of a friend to him over the years, and Harry, a young boy whose mother also works on Shelby's plantation. Shelby had promised Harry's mother, Eliza, that he would never sell Harry, so when she hears Shelby arguing with his wife about it, Eliza decides to take matters into her own hands and run away to Canada with her son. She warns Uncle Tom about what is to happen but he decides to stay. Carrying her son with her, Eliza just manages to cross the Ohio River because it is half frozen. On the other side of the river slavery is illegal and she is safe from Haley, the man who bought her from Shelby. This does not stop him from hiring a slave catcher named Coker to bring Eliza and Harry back to Kentucky. She then seeks refuge in a Quaker settlement where her husband George meets up with them.

Meanwhile, Uncle Tom is taken by Haley down the Mississippi to a slave auction. On the boat, Uncle Tom strikes up a friendship with a young white girl named Eva. When she falls in the river, Uncle Tom jumps in and saves her. She then persuades her father, Augustine St Clare, to buy Uncle Tom from Haley and they return to St Clare's plantation. Eva and Uncle Tom spend a lot of time together sharing in their deeply Christian faith, but their happiness is cut short when Eva dies. Before she does she persuades her father to set Uncle Tom free. Having agreed to do this, St Clare himself is then killed mediating in a barroom brawl. St Clare's wife then sells Uncle Tom to the brutal Simon Legree. Legree treats his slaves abominably and resolves to beat Uncle Tom's faith in God out of him. Uncle Tom is urged to fight back by Legree's slave mistress, Cassy, but he refuses because he is a pacifist.

Cassy also tells Uncle Tom that she was separated from her daughter by slavery, and that when she had another child, she killed it in order to save her the anguish of being a slave. Cassy then escapes with another slave and although she urges Uncle Tom to join her, he stays and is eventually beaten to death by Legree. Too late, Shelby's son George arrives with the money to buy back Uncle Tom. Meanwhile, Coker, having been shot by Eliza's husband, is nursed back to health by the Quakers and changes his mind about slavery. With his help, Eliza, Harry and George arrive safely in Canada. There they meet Cassy who finds that Eliza is actually her long-lost daughter. The reunited family then move to France and from there to Liberia, the country set up for freed slaves. Back at the Shelby plantation, George sets free all the slaves and urges them to remember Uncle Tom and his Christian beliefs.

THEMES AND TECHNIQUES

STOWE's novel was written just after the passage of the Fugitive Slave Act in 1850, which made it illegal for people in the Northern States to help an escaped slave from the South. Stowe wrote her novel with the intention of trying to change the minds of Northerners about the fairness of slavery in the hope that the Act would be repealed and slavery abolished. With this in mind, Stowe attempts to defeat every kind of argument made in favour of slavery. She deliberately begins the book with the milder slave regimes of Shelby and St Clair. Such supposedly enlightened regimes were often held up by supporters of slavery as places where the welfare of slaves was at the heart of the system. However, by showing how the slaves' interests are always secondary to those of their owners, Stowe demonstrates that slavery is an unmitigated evil, be it in the form practised by St Clair, or the form practised by Legree. The book contrasts the interests of slave-owning with the loving ethic of Christianity, which is always shown as opposed to slavery. In particular, Uncle Tom is depicted as a Christ-like figure in the novel, someone who would always rather turn the other cheek and who, ultimately, sacrifices his life for the benefit of others.

> Written as a furious response to the passing of the 1850 Fugitive Slave Act, *Uncle Tom's Cabin* was designed to demonstrate that slavery was an unmitigated evil. The book opposes slavery to Christianity, presenting Uncle Tom as a Christ-like figure.

Further Reading

Lowance, Mason I., Westbrook, Ellen E. and De Prospo, R.C. (eds), *The Stowe Debate: Rhetorical Strategies in 'Uncle Tom's Cabin'*. Amherst: University of Massachusetts Press, 1994. This collection of essays examines a number of issues relating to Stowe's novel, including the charge of sentimentality that is often levelled at it.

Sundquist, Eric J. (ed.), *New Essays on 'Uncle Tom's Cabin'*. New York: Cambridge University Press, 1987. This book contains a number of essays looking at Stowe's novel from various modern standpoints, including analyses of the portrayal of women in the book.

VANITY FAIR (1851–52)
by William Makepeace Thackeray

As we are to see a great deal of Amelia, there is no harm in saying, at the outset of our acquaintance, that she was a dear little creature; and a great mercy it is, both in life and in novels, which (and the latter especially) abound in villains of the most sombre sort, that we are to have for a constant companion, so guileless and good-natured a person.

Set during the Napoleonic Wars, THACKERAY's novel takes a sardonic look at morality and manners in all areas of society. It follows the mixed fortunes of the calculating but interesting Becky, and the dull but worthy Amelia as they make their way in the world.

Summary

The novel begins with Becky Sharp and Amelia Sedley leaving Miss Pinkerton's Academy for young ladies. Becky, the orphaned daughter of an artist and an opera singer, is relatively poor and set for the life of a governess. However, she indicates her dissent from the life fate has set for her by flinging her copy of DR JOHNSON's dictionary out of the carriage window. She aspires to having the kind of comfortable life destined for her friend Amelia. Amelia is the daughter of a stockbroker and she invites Becky to stay at her sumptuous house in London. Impressed by the wealth in the family, Becky does her best to try and court Amelia's hapless brother Jos. However, Jos's nervousness and embarrassment cause him to run away to Scotland once he has proposed to her, thereby ending any hopes Becky has of social advancement through him. Meanwhile, Amelia falls in love with George Osborne, a lieutenant in the army, and the man Becky blames for ruining her chances with Jos. Osborne's friend, William Dobbin, also a lieutenant, is in love with Amelia, but defers his interest in favour of his friend.

Forced to become a governess, Becky then moves into the house of Sir Pitt Crawley. She makes herself so agreeable to everybody that Sir Pitt asks her to marry him. However, Becky has already secretly married his younger son, Captain Rawdon Crawley in the hope that when his rich aunt dies, he will inherit her fortune. Amelia, in the meantime, has lost her fortune because Napoleon has restarted the war with England. In the light of this, Osborne's father denies him permission to marry Amelia. Dobbin, however, forces him to keep his promise and the two marry in secret, at which point Osborne is disowned by his father. This does not stop Becky from trying to seduce George, against whom she still hopes to revenge herself. Her plans for revenge are cut short when George is called to fight and dies in battle, leaving Amelia with their new-born child. Becky also has a child, a fact which causes Rawdon to be struck from his aunt's will.

When his aunt dies, Rawdon is helped by Becky to curry favour with his brother, Pitt Crawley, and his wife, Lady Jane. Becky uses

As the title suggests, *Vanity Fair* takes a wry look at the pretensions of Victorian society. It follows the fortunes of Becky and Amelia as their ambitions and principles are thwarted by a series of compromises.

Pitt Crawley to gain an entrée into high society and there meets Lord Steyne. He bankrolls her spending while her husband, Rawdon, falls further and further into debt, unaware of the money held by his wife. When he does find out, he is so appalled that he agrees to take up a post as Governor of Coventry Island, leaving Becky behind. Elsewhere, Amelia is so poor that she agrees to Osborne's father giving her a sum of money and taking her child and his grandson off her hands. Dobbin is appalled by this and urges a reconciliation which results in Osborne's father leaving Amelia a sum of money when he dies. Amelia then marries Dobbin when she finally gets over Osborne's death after Becky reveals to her his intended infidelity with Becky. Becky herself falls ever further from the goal of respectability she had once aimed for until Jos dies, leaving her with enough money to become a charity worker as a penance for the life she has led.

THEMES AND TECHNIQUES

Thackeray subtitled *Vanity Fair – A Novel without a Hero*. Amongst other things, this suggests that the novel lacks the romantic pretensions of previous fiction, such as SIR WALTER SCOTT's *IVANHOE*. It is not, in other words, quite so fictional as some of its predecessors, but rather more concerned with portraying its subjects realistically. The subject of *Vanity Fair*, in large part, is the middle class – the emerging sector of Victorian society that was keen to advance itself both economically and socially, the latter in accordance with the standards set down for it by the upper classes.

In no character is this aspiration more clearly evinced than in Becky Sharp. She is quite ruthless in her bid to become materially comfortable. Happy to forgo any of the more ennobling emotions, such as love, in order to achieve her goal, she becomes something of a social entrepreneur. This is in contrast to Amelia, who begins the novel with such material confidence that she can afford to indulge herself to excess in pity and love. When her material base crumbles from under her, Amelia gives up her child, leaving Thackeray to expose the shallowness of even the purest sentiments once they are shorn of the money that supports them. In this regard then, neither Becky nor Amelia is the kind of noble champion of earlier fictions, but at the same time they foreshadow the gritty heroines that will come to dominate modern novels where just surviving is of merit in itself.

Further Reading

Harden, Edgar F. *Vanity Fair*. New York: Twayne Publishers, 1995. This short book looks at a number of aspects relating to Thackeray's novel, including an extended analysis of its sophisticated narrator.

VICAR OF WAKEFIELD, THE (1766)
by Oliver Goldsmith

It is impossible to describe our good-humour. I can't say whether we had more wit among us now than usual; but I am certain we had more laughing, which answered the end as well.

The Vicar of Wakefield is a novel set amidst the declining fortunes of a clergyman's large family. It tells the story of the Reverend Primrose and his attempts to keep his family's spirits aloft when they are thrown into adversity.

Summary

The novel opens with an introduction to the Reverend Dr Charles Primrose and his family, George, Olivia, Sophia, Moses, Dick and Bill. George is due to marry the daughter of a neighbouring clergyman, Arabella, but when it is discovered that Primrose's fortune has been lost by a dishonest broker, Arabella's father breaks off the engagement. Their reduced circumstances force the family to move to another posting, one overseen by the libertine Squire Thornhill, who is funded by Sir William Thornhill, known to Primrose as a generous philanthropist. They are accompanied on part of the journey by Mr Burchell, Sir William in disguise. He manages to save Sophia from drowning at one point and a relationship develops between them. Olivia, meanwhile, is struck by the shallow charms of the Squire. The Squire, eager to get the girls away from their father, encourages two female acquaintances of his to hire them as ladies-in-waiting. However, this plan fails when a letter from Burchell seemingly recommends that the Primrose girls not be accepted for the positions.

Pledged to marry a local farmer, Olivia then elopes with a mysterious stranger instead. Believing the villain to be Burchell, Primrose sets off in pursuit. On his journey, Primrose discovers his son, George, acting in a theatre company. It so happens that Arabella is also in the audience and the couple are reunited. Later, Primrose finds Olivia who tells him that she had actually eloped with the Squire, only to find out that he cared little for her. When they return home, they find that it has burnt to the ground. Primrose's anger at the Squire causes Thornhill to exact payment of a bond owed to him. When Primrose cannot pay this, he is sent to debtor's prison where he is joined by the rest of the family. George is then sentenced to execution for attempting to attack Thornhill. At this point Burchell reveals himself to be Sir William and, being utterly persuaded of Thornhill's guilt, he exposes a series of deceptions by the Squire, deprives him of almost all his money and lands, and has the Primroses released. Primrose subsequently learns that his fortune has been restored. He then officiates at the ceremony which sees Sir William marry Sophia and Arabella marry George.

> The Vicar of Wakefield follows the fortunes of the Reverend Primrose and his family as they struggle to maintain their moral principles in the face of wealth and adversity.

THEMES AND TECHNIQUES

GOLDSMITH drew heavily on his own life for many of the elements of *The Vicar of Wakefield*. His father, uncle and brother, for example, were all clergymen, while Primrose's warm-hearted philosophy shares much with that of Goldsmith's own approach to life. In focusing the novel on Primrose, Goldsmith helped to establish the stereotype of the well-meaning clergyman which has somehow survived even into the profoundly anti-clerical consciousness of the present. The Reverend Primrose figures as a moral corrective in the novel, reminding his family and almost everyone else of the shallowness of wealth. This is not just the familiar lesson that money cannot buy happiness, rather it extends to remind the rising middle classes, of which the clergy were the spiritual vanguard, that money is no replacement for class. Sir William is a noble man whether he is playing the part of the impoverished Mr Burchell or assuming his responsibility as a lord. Equally, or perhaps not quite equally, Primrose is the same principled man whether he is in possession of his large fortune or locked up in debtor's jail. Conversely, those who follow wealth, as the rest of the family do when being charmed by the Squire, will inevitably court disappointment and very often ruin too.

Further Reading

Goldsmith, Oliver, *The Vicar of Wakefield*. Edited by Arthur Friedman. Oxford: Oxford University Press, 1999. This is an excellent edition of Goldsmith's novel, including a thoughtful introduction and numerous glosses.

> ## VINDICATION OF THE RIGHTS OF WOMAN, A (1792)
> by Mary Wollstonecraft
>
> *My own sex, I hope, will excuse me, if I treat them like rational creatures, instead of flattering their fascinating graces, and viewing them as if they were in a state of perpetual childhood, unable to stand alone.*

Written in just six weeks, *A Vindication of the Rights of Woman* is now widely regarded as the founding text of modern feminism. Drawing on other founding texts of liberalism at the time, such as THOMAS PAINE's *Rights of Man*, WOLLSTONECRAFT argues that increasing the rights of the individual must also include increasing the rights of the female individual too.

Summary

The book begins with an appeal to reason, the attribute which, with virtue and knowledge, distinguishes us from the brutes. However, Wollstonecraft finds that very often reason is employed to justify keeping existing prejudices rather than rooting them out and accepting rationally thought-out first principles. Wollstonecraft then points out that women are very often denied the means to reason and education. It is little wonder therefore, she argues, that women are said to be capricious and shallow when they have been deliberately kept this way by men. The characters of people, both men and women, she continues, are in large part determined by the contexts in which they live and are brought up. As a consequence of denying reason to women, they are forced into states of degradation appropriate to their second-class status, such as marrying men for money rather than love, and performing endless needlework.

Wollstonecraft then attacks various writers who have depicted women as objects of pity bordering on contempt, including the French philosopher Jean Jacques Rousseau. These writers propagate impressions of women that instil falsehood in the minds of those that read them, whereas a more positive set of role models would prove to have more beneficial effects. Furthermore, traditional female virtues, such as modesty, could equally be held as morally appropriate to men as to women, while other virtues, such as a good reputation, corrupt the commerce of truth between men and women and could be profitably dispensed with. Maintaining the way in which women are treated, however, will have a pernicious effect on the next generation. For if women are treated as brutes, devoid of reason, they are likely to pass this brutishness on to their children. Children, she argues, should be educated in proper day-schools so as to reap the best of both private schooling and education at home. Women, in particular, will benefit from this arrangement. Indeed, Wollstonecraft finishes with the following advice: 'Let woman share the rights and she will emulate the virtues of man.'

> *A Vindication of the Rights of Woman* is now widely recognised as one of the founding texts of feminism. Here Wollstonecraft argues that the oppression of women is detrimental to both genders.

THEMES AND TECHNIQUES

Written after she had already published *A Vindication of the Rights of Men*, *A Vindication of the Rights of Woman* was a powerful polemic in defence of the cause of women at a time when they had next to no rights. For example, women lost their property upon marriage and effectively became the property of their husbands who had, amongst other privileges, the right to beat their wives as they wished. Educated only in domestic skills and disbarred from all but the lowliest of jobs, women, Wollstonecraft argued, were forced into a position of dependence upon men. They were therefore obliged to achieve their aims by whatever underhand means were available to them, such as coquetry and flattery. This is a common theme in English literature from CHAUCER's CANTERBURY TALES onwards. Unusually for the time though, Wollstonecraft proposed that it was as inimical to men as it was to women. In this way, Wollstonecraft demonstrated her own impartiality and reasonableness and pressed her case more forcibly than she might otherwise have done.

Further Reading

Craciun, Adriana (ed.), *A Routledge Literary Sourcebook on Mary Wollstonecraft's A Vindication of the Rights of Woman*. London and New York: Routledge, 2002. This book contains a variety of contextual materials as well as annotations of key passages from Wollstonecraft's text.

VOLPONE (1606)
by Ben Jonson

Volpone, childless, rich, feigns sick, despairs,
Offers his state to hopes of several heirs,
Lies languishing; his parasite receives
Presents of all, assures, deludes: then weaves
Other cross-plots, which open themselves, are told.
New tricks for safety are sought; they thrive: when, bold,
Each tempts the other again, and all are sold.

Volpone is a play that caricatures greed. It tells the story of Volpone, a man who pretends to be dying in order to elicit gifts from people who want to be his heirs.

Summary

The play begins at the house of Volpone, a wealthy Venetian nobleman. In conversation with Mosca, his servant, it is revealed that Volpone has earned his wealth by various underhand schemes. He is currently involved in a scheme in which he has let it be known to Voltore, an advocate, Corbaccio, an old gentleman, and Corvino, a merchant, that he is dying. Believing him to be wealthy and childless, Volpone has been encouraging these men to give him gifts in the hope that they will become his sole heirs. Under the guidance of Mosca, Voltore and Corvino give Volpone some expensive gifts while Corbaccio agrees to make Volpone the beneficiary of his own will if Volpone will do the same for him. Volpone agrees, believing that he will outlive the old man. Mosca then informs Corbaccio's son, Bonario, of this arrangement and has him hide in Volpone's apartment in order that he might witness his father surrendering his inheritance and, enraged, kill Corbaccio.

Meanwhile, Corvino consents to Volpone sleeping with his wife, Celia, as a form of medicine. When Celia arrives at Volpone's apartment, Bonario is already hidden there. Upon being left alone with Celia, Volpone reveals himself to be a sprightly man and she resists his advances. Incensed by this behaviour, Bonario jumps out from the curtain and rescues Celia. They go to court to press a case against Volpone for being a fraud, but Volpone is very convincing and he wins the case instead.

Volpone was written by Ben Jonson as a humorous but moral corrective to urban greed. The play follows Volpone as he pretends to be dying in order to lure fortune hunters into giving him gifts in exchange for being written into his will.

Volpone then decides to pretend to be dead in order that he may also pretend to have left everything to Mosca and thereby humiliate the three men. This he does but the plan goes awry when Mosca declares that he will reveal that Volpone is still living if he does not give him a bigger share. Volpone eventually decides that the best course of action is to call Mosca's bluff. Mosca is then sentenced to a life of slavery, while Volpone is consigned to prison. The three dupes are also punished for their hypocrisy: Voltore is disbarred, Corbaccio is forced to sign his wealth over to Bonario, and Corvino has to wear donkey's ears around Venice.

THEMES AND TECHNIQUES

At one point in the play, Mosca declares that almost everybody is a parasite of one sort or another. This play explores this idea, showing what happens to people who are consumed only by the idea of greed. For, despite its rambunctious humour and sly ironies, *Volpone* is essentially a moral play, one which JONSON hoped would apply a small corrective to the greedy urban spirit. Despite the fact that the lead characters are written in such a way as to be almost endearing in their ingeniousness,

Jonson leaves us in no doubt as to where our sympathies should lie. For example, 'Volpone' is Italian for 'old fox', while 'Mosca' means 'fly'. Ironically, of course, both Volpone and Mosca live by their wits in the same way that Jonson, as a playwright, did. Indeed, while the two of them are still gulling the three men, it almost seems at times like they are putting on a play with their use of various theatrical devices, such as make-up and props. The proximity of the conman's profession to Jonson's own profession of playwright may thus account for not only the affection injected into Volpone and Mosca's portrait but also, ultimately, for the severity of their punishments when they are finally uncovered.

Further Reading

Barish, Jonas Alexander (ed.), *Jonson's Volpone: A Selection of Critical Essays*. London: Palgrave Macmillan, 1972. This generous selection of critical essays looks at various aspects of the play including its moral import and its theatrical connections.

WALDEN (1854)
by Henry David Thoreau
Talk of heaven! ye disgrace earth.

Walden is the record of two years that THOREAU spent living on Walden Pond. It tells of his spiritual journey during that period and the lessons he learned from living in close contact with nature.

Summary

Walden opens with Thoreau asserting that he wrote the following pages while living in a house that he had built himself on the shore of Walden Pond, in Concord, Massachusetts. The first chapter, 'Economy', outlines the philosophy behind Thoreau's project. He proposes that most people waste their lives seeking after material gain, and that because they are so busy labouring, they have little time to attend to spiritual matters. He, on the other hand, keeps to a minimal lifestyle which demands very few material goods and therefore he only has to labour on his bean fields in the morning in order to make enough money to live. The rest of the time he is able to spend in instructive reveries, enjoying his freedom. He also contends that many people waste what free time they do have by reading popular fiction instead of attending to the classics, such as Homer and Aeschylus, which he describes as 'the noblest recorded thoughts of man'.

However, Thoreau goes on to remark that during his first summer he was so overcome with the beauty of nature that he even forwent reading books in order that he might enjoy extended reveries in the silence. In this cloistered atmosphere, Thoreau admits to being attracted to his own solitude. He does not miss the casual interactions of everyday society, although he does enjoy the company of the occasional person such as the Canadian woodcutter, Alex Therien, who, while not intellectual, is nevertheless profound to Thoreau. Thoreau's dislike for society grows when he goes to town one day and is thrown into jail for refusing to pay a tax because, he argues, the government supports slavery. Returning to Walden, he attends to the local animal life, from the warring ants to the wayward loon, all of which he endows with a symbolic significance. During the winter, Thoreau takes a great interest in the depth of Walden Pond. It is reputed to be bottomless by the locals but Thoreau measures it at about 100 feet. The discrepancy between the two suggests to Thoreau that everyone has a need for infinity in their lives. Indeed, the end of the book is given over to articulating Thoreau's belief that people should develop the potential trapped within themselves.

THEMES AND TECHNIQUES

Apart from being a biography of two years in Thoreau's life, *Walden* is also a manifesto for living and one that has proved highly influential. One of the main tenets of this philosophy is the notion of self-reliance. Thoreau is keen to emphasise at every juncture quite how independent he is from local society and from the larger government generally. All the facts and figures he provides are there to prove his financial independence. In turn, this financial autonomy is both the basis of his spiritual freedom and symbolic of it too. Thoreau frees himself from the material ties that bind society and by so doing develops what he describes as a spiritual awakening. In contrast, the majority of people are merely sleepwalking their way through life, unappreciative of their natural surroundings. Walden Pond itself becomes the supreme symbol of the natural world for Thoreau, upon looking into which, he surmises, 'the beholder measures the depth of his own nature'.

> *Walden* records two years that Thoreau spent living by Walden Pond. Throughout the book, he advocates a philosophy of independence from both local society and national government.

Further Reading

Bloom, Harold (ed.), *Henry David Thoreau's 'Walden'*. New York: Chelsea House Publishing, 1987. This collection of modern critical interpretations of Thoreau's masterpiece also provides some biographical information and an introductory essay.

Thoreau, Henry David, *Walden*. Edited by William Rossi. New York: W.W. Norton, 1992. This edition of the Thoreau's book also contains a number of extracts from his journals, as well as reviews and essays.

WASHINGTON SQUARE (1881)
by Henry James

For a man whose trade was to keep people alive he had certainly done poorly in his own family; and a bright doctor who within three years loses his wife and his little boy should perhaps be prepared to see either his skill or his affection impugned.

Inspired by an anecdote about a jilted heiress, *Washington Square* is a short and brutally witty novel that seeks to demonstrate the dramatic qualities of goodness. It tells the story of how the ordinary and gentle Catherine Sloper is caught in a battle of wills between her suitor and her father.

Summary

Set in the Washington Square district of New York during the 1840s, the novel begins by recounting the family circumstances of the Slopers. Dr Sloper is a renowned physician whose wife and son have both died, leaving him to bring up his solid but unremarkable daughter, Catherine. In this enterprise he is helped by the interfering and overly dramatic Aunt Penniman.

Inspired by an anecdote about a jilted heiress, *Washington Square* is probably Henry James's wittiest novel. It recounts how the gentle but ordinary Catherine Sloper is caught between the wishes of her intractable father and the man she loves.

One day, when Catherine is about 20 years of age, she is invited to her cousin's engagement party. There she meets Morris Townsend, a distant relation of her cousin's fiancée who has recently been travelling. Quickly latching onto Aunt Penniman's flair for the dramatic, Townsend ingratiates himself with her in order to get to Catherine. Inexperienced in matters of courtship, Catherine is flattered by the attentions of Townsend. Sloper, however, sees in Townsend nothing but a bounty-hunter eager to bag Catherine for her eventual inheritance.

After several attempts, Sloper realises that he will find it difficult to persuade Catherine of Townsend's real nature while she remains under his influence. He therefore proposes to take her to Europe for six months in the hope that distance will lessen her affection. However, after six months Catherine remains stubborn in her desire. The doctor delays their return for another six months but it makes no difference to Catherine. Upon their return, Catherine is forced to reveal to Townsend that she is unable to guarantee that she will inherit her father's fortune. After a series of diffident meetings, Townsend disappears. Catherine is heartbroken, but her father suspects that it is a ruse to make him think she no longer loves Townsend. With this in mind, when Sloper is on his deathbed he asks Catherine to promise him never to marry Townsend. Catherine has no intention of marrying Townsend but she is too indignant at the request to promise this to her father. Sloper then leaves most of his money to charity. Some years later, Townsend returns to Catherine but she wishes to have nothing to do with him and remains a spinster.

THEMES AND TECHNIQUES

Sometimes dubbed the HENRY JAMES novel for people who do not like Henry James, it is ironically a novel that James himself did not like. It is hard to understand James's judgement in this regard because the novel contains four of his most memorable characters in the form of the dull but dogged Catherine, the dramatic Aunt Penniman, the bounty-hunting Townsend, and the savagely ironic Sloper. The interaction between these characters is beautifully handled by James as each of them, for their own reasons, refuses to say anything directly and they are thus left to interpret situations according to their own particular traits. This proves to be a particularly vexing approach to communication as Catherine and Aunt Penniman largely think what they feel, while Sloper and Townsend feel what they think. The character who seems to glean most enjoyment from all this confusion is the narrator. In many ways a version of the doctor, the narrator continually feigns a degree of impartiality by letting loose ironic invectives against each of the protagonists. However, the narrator's irony is ultimately a form of moral silence which, like Sloper's irony, fails to yield a commitment to anyone until it is too late and Catherine is lost.

Further Reading

Shelston, Alan (ed.), *Casebook on 'Washington Square' and 'Portrait of a Lady'*. London: Palgrave Macmillan, 1984. *Washington Square* and *Portrait of a Lady* were published at the same time and this generous collection of essays examines their contexts, as well as their style and themes.

WHITE HERON AND OTHER STORIES, A (1886)
by Sarah Orne Jewett

The tree seemed to lengthen itself out as she went up, and to reach farther and farther upward. It was like a great main-mast to the voyaging earth; it must truly have been amazed that morning through all its ponderous frame as it felt this determined spark of human spirit creeping and climbing from higher branch to branch.

JEWETT established her reputation with the publication of this collection of short stories, as well as helping to shape the character of the American short story genre for the next century. The title story tells of a girl faced with a moral dilemma over revealing the whereabouts of a rare bird.

Summary

Set in New England, 'A White Heron' opens with Sylvia, a 9-year-old girl, driving a cow home to be milked one summer evening. The cow is apt to play hide and seek with anyone who comes to fetch her so Mrs Tilley, Sylvia's grandmother and the owner of the cow, is not surprised that Sylvia is taking so long. She does, however, believe that Sylvia enjoys dallying in the countryside after having spent the first eight years of her life in a manufacturing town. Meanwhile, Sylvia is reflecting upon her first year in the countryside when she is waylaid in the woods by a young man with a shotgun. He claims to be a hunter and asks if he may stay at Sylvia's house for the night. Sylvia leads him back to her grandmother's farmstead and she happily invites him to stay.

After supper the hunter explains that he is interested in shooting two or three very rare birds in order to stuff them and complete his collection. He is particularly keen to catch a white heron he has seen in the vicinity. Sylvia, who Mrs Tilley has revealed knows the area intimately, is aware of the heron but she says nothing, even when the hunter remarks that he is willing to pay ten dollars for it. The next

day Sylvia goes hunting with the man but they do not find the heron. Sylvia, who is now half in love with the man after all the attention he has paid her, decides that night that she will be able to see the heron leave its nest in the morning if she climbs the tallest tree in the wood. This she does and is duly able to spot the heron leaving its nest. However, when she returns to the farmstead in the morning and is met by the expectant hunter and her grandmother, she does not reveal that she now knows the heron's whereabouts.

Sarah Orne Jewett cemented her reputation as a great writer with the publication of *A White Heron and Other Stories*. This collection also helped to redefine the character of the American short story.

THEMES AND TECHNIQUES

Jewett's *A White Heron* perfected the modern short story form. Paring back the earlier form of complexly plotted stories, Jewett here bases the story around a single event and the emotions that spring from it. Like many modern short stories, it does not so much follow the resolution of a conflicting action, but rather the resolution of a conflicting emotion. Here Sylvia is torn between satisfying the 'great wave of human interest which flooded for the first time this dull little life' in the form of the attention that the hunter bestows upon her, or keeping faith with the satisfactions she already enjoys 'of an existence heart to heart with nature and the dumb life of the forest'. Again, like many other modern short stories, this conflict, as it is described by Jewett, is also pregnant with a series of densely packed symbols and allusions. The tree, for example, has been a symbol of knowledge at least since the story of Adam and Eve in the *BIBLE*, and so it is appropriate that Sylvia has to climb the tree in order to gain access not only to the heron's nest, but to the larger world of knowledge of which she has dreamt. However, unlike the Biblical characters, Sylvia does not return to earth stricken with a desire she can never resolve. Rather, she turns her back on it, leaving the restless hunter plagued by the contradictory nature of a yearning which causes him to 'kill the very birds he seemed to like so much'.

Further Reading

Nagel, Gwen L. (ed.), *Critical Essays on Sarah Orne Jewett.* New York: G.K. Hall and Co., 1985. A generous collection of essays that looks at all aspects of Jewett's work including her status as a regionalist and a feminist writer.

WUTHERING HEIGHTS (1847)
by Emily Brontë

My love for Heathcliff resembles the eternal rocks beneath – a source of little visible delight, but necessary. Nelly, I am Heathcliff – he's always, always in my mind – not as a pleasure, any more than I am always a pleasure to myself – but as my own being.

One of the most famous loves stories of all time, *Wuthering Heights* describes the intense love between Catherine and Heathcliff. Set on the bleak Yorkshire moors, BRONTË's novel gives life to a passion so profound that not even death can tame it.

Summary

The novel begins in 1801 when Mr Lockwood becomes the tenant of Thrushcross Grange situated on the bleak and isolated terrain of the Yorkshire moors. He is immediately fascinated by his brooding and surly landlord, Mr Heathcliff, who lives a few miles away in the manor house, Wuthering Heights. When he asks his housekeeper, Nelly Dean, about him, she relates the story of Heathcliff which Lockwood then writes down.

One of the most famous love stories of all time, *Wuthering Heights* tells the tale of the passion between Catherine and Heathcliff and how it threatens to ruin not only themselves but also their descendants.

The young Nelly is a servant in Wuthering Heights, working for Mr Earnshaw. One day he returns from a business trip to Liverpool with an orphaned boy, named Heathcliff.

Earnshaw insists on bringing up Heathcliff as one of his own, even though his son, Hindley, and his daughter, Catherine, initially reject the wild-looking youth. Hindley, in particular, torments Heathcliff. However, Catherine soon finds herself devoted to Heathcliff. When their mother dies, Heathcliff becomes Earnshaw's favourite child, causing Hindley to resent Heathcliff even more. He soon finds expression for this resentment when Earnshaw dies and Hindley becomes master of Wuthering Heights. Heathcliff is immediately banished to the servants' quarters and treated as a common labourer by Hindley. Catherine's passion for Heathcliff only grows and they roam the moors together. One night they venture to Thrushcross Grange, the home of Edgar and Isabella Linton. When Catherine is bitten, she is forced to stay there and recuperate for five weeks, during which time she becomes attracted to Linton and to the idea of being a lady.

Upon her return to Wuthering Heights, Hindley's wife dies giving birth to his son, Hareton. Hindley descends into alcoholism and treats Heathcliff even more cruelly. When Catherine becomes engaged to Edgar, despite her passion for Heathcliff, Heathcliff can take no more and leaves the house. He returns three years later a wealthy man but full of bitterness towards Hindley and Edgar now that Edgar has married Catherine. Heathcliff sets about exacting his revenge by luring Hindley into massive debts that eventually result in Hindley dying and Wuthering Heights becoming Heathcliff's. He also treats Hareton, Hindley's son, as he was once treated by Hindley. Partly to spite Catherine, Heathcliff also marries Isabella, whom he treats abominably because he still loves Catherine. Heathcliff and Isabella have a son called Linton. Catherine herself dies shortly afterwards giving birth to a girl, also called Catherine.

Some years later, Isabella dies and Linton, now very sickly, is manipulated by Heathcliff into courting the young Catherine. As Edgar grows closer to death, Heathcliff all but kidnaps the young Catherine and forces her to marry Linton. Edgar dies shortly afterwards and Catherine inherits Thrushcross Grange. When Linton dies, Heathcliff controls both Thrushcross and Wuthering Heights. He forces Catherine to work as a maid at

Wuthering Heights while he rents the Grange to Lockwood. Lockwood is horrified to hear this and so ends his tenancy. However, some moths later he returns to visit Nelly and hears that Heathcliff has died after becoming obsessed with the ghost of Catherine. Meanwhile, the younger Catherine and Hareton have fallen in love, married and inherited both properties to which they now bring a reign of comparative happiness.

THEMES AND TECHNIQUES

At the centre of *Wuthering Heights* is the tremendous passion of Heathcliff and Catherine. It is a disturbing love which hounds both of them out of their senses, but is so profound in its make-up that Catherine is forced to declare that 'I am Heathcliff' and that Heathcliff, for his part, avows that Catherine is his soul. With such a grand vision of love, there could well be a danger of the book toppling over either into farce or into the realms of the unbelievable. What saves the novel is its narrative structure. For the story of Catherine and Heathcliff is told primarily by Nelly. Although she is part of the story, she is not one of the protagonists, so she lends the tale a degree of objectivity and some distance. This objectivity is compounded by the fact that Nelly's tale is told within the compass of Lockwood's narration. He is an outsider to the drama of Wuthering Heights and so he offers the reader an even greater distance to its sublime passions. By thus doubling our detachment from the two principal characters, we can be more critical of their difficulties, but we are also made more susceptible to accepting the strange and monstrous story in the first place. It is as if Lockwood and Nelly between them manage to domesticate what Charlotte Brontë described as its 'storm-heated and electrical atmosphere' just enough to filter out what is unreal, but not enough to smooth away its wild edges.

Further Reading

Allott, Miriam, *'Wuthering Heights': A Selection of Critical Essays*. London: Palgrave Macmillan, 1992. A splendid collection of essays, this volume tracks critical reception to Brontë's novel from the date of its publication through to more recent analyses.

Brontë, Emily, *Wuthering Heights*. Edited by Heather Glen. London and New York: Routledge, 1988. This version of the text offers a guide to the historical context of the novel, as well as taking a look at modern interpretations of Brontë's novel.

Glossary of terms

(Cross-references within this Glossary are denoted by the use of ***bold italic***.)

Allegory

An allegorical work is one that has two separate meanings. In EDMUND SPENSER's *THE FAERIE QUEENE*, for example, the Faerie Queene is, on one level, a character in the story, but on another level she is also Queen Elizabeth I.

Alliterative verse

The predominant form of Old English poetry, alliterative verse is built around a pattern of words made from similar sounds. In the phrase 'strong and strident strode the giant', the *str* sound connects the line together in a series of rhythmic stresses. Alliterative verse experienced a revival in Middle English literature, such as *SIR GAWAIN AND THE GREEN KNIGHT*.

Augustan

Augustan literature refers to those works written in the eighteenth century which are inspired by the qualities of proportion, wit and elegance said to be evident in the works of the Roman writers, such as Virgil, Horace, and Ovid, who lived during the reign of Emperor Augustus. ALEXANDER POPE is the archetypal Augustan writer.

Blank verse

Probably the most common verse form in the English language, blank verse is unrhymed and consists of five stressed and five unstressed syllables, such as in JOHN MILTON's *PARADISE LOST*:

Of man's First disobedience, and the Fruit
Of that Forbidden Tree, whose mortal taste
Brought death into the World, and all our woe,
With loss of Eden, till one greater Man
Restore us, and regain the blissful Seat.

Comedy

Usually associated with drama and used in distinction to tragedy (see **Tragedy**), a comedy is not only a funny play, but also one that ends optimistically, such as with a wedding. An obvious example in this regard is WILLIAM SHAKESPEARE's *A MIDSUMMER NIGHT'S DREAM* which, despite the threats of banishment and execution and the vicious jealousies, is actually a comedy if only because it ends with a triple wedding. More generally, if tragedy is about the downfall of an individual, it is often said that comedy is about the downfall of society as a whole. This is because the predominant theme in comic drama is the social bond. Comedies tend to be about the way in which a society is organised, the rules and ethos that hold society together, and, in particular, the way in which the ideal embodiment of a society is never matched by a real society.

Comedy of humours

A play that draws for its characters upon stock types who are based around dominant characteristics or humours. This type of comedy was perfected by BEN JONSON in such works as *Every Man in his Humour*.

Courtly love

A form of ritualised adoration which became popular in the twelfth century. It usually featured a young man idolising an unattainable and virtuous young woman. This stylised love very quickly became a subject for satire, perhaps most famously in the love of Romeo for Rosaline in WILLIAM SHAKESPEARE's *ROMEO AND JULIET*.

Drama

Designed to be performed by a group of people in front of another group of people, the early forms of drama were associated with public occasions. The earliest recorded plays, such as *Antigone* and *Oedipus the King*, were performed during state-sponsored festivals, most notably the *Lenaea* and the *Dionysia*. These plays upheld the transcendental authority of the Greek gods, upon which also rested the authority of the state.

With the advent of Christianity in the Roman Empire, acting was outlawed and drama almost disappeared from Europe altogether. Gradually, during the Middle Ages, drama was resurrected by and within the Church. This resurrection initially took the form of Mystery Plays which were short dramatisations of scenes from the *BIBLE* performed by priests and their attendants in Latin. Over time, the Mystery Plays were translated into the vernacular and performed by the various trade guilds as part of town festivals. In addition, Miracle and Morality Plays were developed which, despite being religious in theme, were more secular in that they dealt with non-biblical stories.

The process of secularisation continued with the Reformation, which was a movement to reform the Catholic Church, partly involving the removal of theatrical elements from it. This created the conditions for the building of the first fully secular theatre in Britain in the late sixteenth century. It did not, however, allow dramatists *carte blanche* to write about whatever they liked, as there was still strict political censorship. So if playwrights like WILLIAM SHAKESPEARE no longer had to pay direct homage to the Church, they still were obliged to pay homage to the monarch of the day who was then next in line to God. Plays such as *RICHARD III* or *Henry IV* were concerned with themes like reinforcing the divine rights of kings to rule and establishing the rights of succession.

The problems of who should succeed Elizabeth I and which church (Catholic or Protestant) was the true one became manifest in the bloody intrigues of Jacobean drama in which all hierarchies seemed to collapse. Following this, most theatre was again banned in Britain until these sensitive political and religious issues were finally settled. The type of drama that emerged following the Restoration was rarely concerned with gods or kings. Instead the new focus became the competing claims of the aristocracy and the rising merchant classes of the time – a conflict that was often dramatised as a battle over matters of taste, manners and decorum, or money versus class. The theatre itself, although still subject to state censorship, no longer formed part of the state and was gradually becoming a diversion for the middle classes.

Following this period until the end of the nineteenth century, very little noteworthy drama was produced in the English-speaking world. The impetus for the revival of the theatre came from other, less individualistic cultures. In particular, GEORGE BERNARD SHAW took his cue from the work of Norwegian playwright Henrik Ibsen, who produced a new type of realistic drama which examined social problems. Shaw's plays, such as *MAJOR BARBARA*, were no longer just there to entertain people, but, like the Mystery Plays, attempted to provide people with a degree of moral instruction too.

Dramatic monologue

A poetic form in which the voice of the poem is given over to a character rather than the poet. The technique was developed by ROBERT BROWNING in works such as 'Fra Lippo Lippi' in which a monk gives vent to his frustrations after being arrested for drunkenness.

Epic

A lengthy work about a great subject often involving supernatural beings. The most famous and influential epics, such as Homer's *Iliad* and Virgil's *Aeneid*, date back to classical Greece and Rome respectively. While later poets would turn to these for inspiration, *BEOWULF* is the oldest surviving epic in the English language. Like the *Iliad* and the *Aeneid*, *Beowulf* takes as its theme and its aim the forging of a national identity.

Free verse

Poetry based on the irregular rhythmic cadence rather than the conventional use of metre. Rhyme may or may not be present in free verse, but when it is used, it is with great freedom. During the course of the nineteenth century, some poets began to reject the regular metre, in much the same spirit as MILTON had rejected rhyme, preferring irregular metres that could give free rein to the expression of their individual voices. However, the use of cadence as a basis for poetry dates back much further. The poetry of the BIBLE, particularly the *King James Authorised Version*, rests on cadence and parallelism. The Psalms and The Song of Solomon are noted examples of free verse.

The most famous early exponent of free verse was WALT WHITMAN in his collection of poetry *LEAVES OF GRASS*. MATTHEW ARNOLD also sometimes used free verse, notably in 'Dover Beach'. The words of HENRY DAVID THOREAU perhaps best explain the attraction of this form of verse for later poets: '. . . perhaps it is because he hears a different drummer. Let him step to the music which he hears, however measured or far away.'

Gothic

Describes those parts of our culture which culture has to exclude in order to make sense of itself, such as madness, terror and even nature. In this regard, the Gothic is the natural inheritor of the legacy of Romances and has come to be associated with anything fantastic. Although it exists as a genre in its own right, HORACE WALPOLE's *THE CASTLE OF OTRANTO* being widely recognised as the first Gothic novel, 'the Gothic' is now increasingly understood as a constituent element in various other art forms, including the novel and the cinema.

Heroic couplet

Two lines of rhyming verse, usually with ten syllables in each line. The rhyme and length of an heroic couplet provides a natural pause, making each couplet a self-contained unit. It is an *heroic* couplet because heroic or epic poems, such as JOHN DRYDEN's translation of Virgil's *Aeneid*, were written using this verse form.

Metaphysical poetry

Originally used as a term of abuse by JOHN DRYDEN, Metaphysical poetry refers to verse that employs elaborate images composed of far-fetched comparisons, such as JOHN DONNE's pair of compasses in 'A Valediction Forbidding Mourning'. The Metaphysical poets include John Donne and ANDREW MARVELL.

Metre

The pattern of syllabic stresses in a line of poetry. In standard notation, a heavily stressed syllable is marked / and a weakly stressed syllable is marked *x*. In ANDREW MARVELL's 'To His Coy Mistress', for example, the metre of the poem is four alternate weak and strong syllables per line.

```
  /    x    x    /    x    /    x    /
Had we/ but world/ enough/ and time,
  x    /    x    /   x    /    x    /
This coy/ ness, la/ dy, were/ no crime.
  /    x    x    /    x    /    x    /
We would/ sit down/ and think/ which way
  x    /    x    /    x    /    x    /
To walk/ and pass/ our long/ love's day.
```

As can be seen here, the poem does not always respect the metre, but sometimes alters it, beginning the first and third line, for example, with stressed syllables. This variation of the metre is called the rhythm of the poem. In this regard, the metre of a poem is the raw state of it, while the rhythm is the cooked version of it.

Middle English

The form of the English language used in England approximately from the invasion of the Normans in 1066 to about 1500. This is the English used by GEOFFREY CHAUCER in THE CANTERBURY TALES.

Mock epic

A work that uses the conventions of the epic, such as majestic language, to describe and so satirise an insignificant subject. ALEXANDER POPE's THE RAPE OF THE LOCK is a poem written in lofty terms about someone cutting off a lock of hair.

Modern English

The form of the English language used in England and later the varieties of it used in the rest of the world from approximately 1500. This is the English used by WILLIAM SHAKESPEARE in HAMLET.

Novel

Usually defined as an extended fictional prose narrative which focuses on the development of a plot and/or a character. Such a broad definition reveals the flexible qualities of the novel which, of all the genres, is able to assimilate other forms of literature and still remain true to its generic expectations. Partly this is a development of the novel's origins, for the novel began life as a form of anti-romance. While the romance focused on the chivalric adventures of knights, damsels, magic and monsters, the novel explored less fantastic subjects. In this regard, many critics consider that Miguel de Cervantes' *Don Quixote*, published in 1604, was the first proper novel. This book was an explicit parody of the chivalry and derring-do featured in romances. However, like many prose narratives that followed, *Don Quixote* was more episodic than plot-driven and, as such, was not quite what we think of as a novel today.

The development of plot-driven narratives, that is narratives with an overall pattern, probably began with the most familiar pattern of all – a person's life. This template, with its familiar beginning at birth and equally familiar end at death, became popular in English language fiction around the beginning of the eighteenth century. It took its popularity from the many biographies of notorious figures, particularly executed criminals, which excited the public imagination at the time. Rather than publishing histories of actual people, which were anyway altered to make them more interesting, authors, such as DANIEL DEFOE began to produce fictional lives, one of the most famous being *MOLL FLANDERS*. In another difference from romances and earlier forms of prose narrative, these early novels offered readers a chance to get to know a character with some degree of psychological depth. These were no longer just fantastic figures defined by their actions, but realistic individuals with unique styles of thought which the reader was allowed to observe at first hand.

Very quickly, the realistic pattern of the biography gave way to more plot-based fiction in which the randomness of life was subordinated to a grand design, such as in HENRY FIELDING's *TOM JONES*. Indeed, the realistic qualities of the novel which had initially defined it as a separate genre came to be restricted more and more to the psychological responses of characters as opposed to the action of the novel. In Gothic fiction, for example, the strange events in HORACE WALPOLE's *THE CASTLE OF OTRANTO* or the return of the ghost in EMILY BRONTË's *WUTHERING HEIGHTS* are incompatible with a strict correspondence to reality, even though the responses of the characters themselves are realistic.

This pattern continued throughout much of the early part of the nineteenth century, the so-called golden age of the novel. However, people once again wanted to distinguish the fantastic narrative from the realistic one, as, for example, NATHANIEL HAWTHORNE does in the preface to *THE SCARLET LETTER*. While Hawthorne returned to using the description 'romance' as distinct from the 'novel', other critics began to categorise the novel into the genres we know today, such as gothic, science-fiction and realist. In regard to this latter category, American writers, such as THEODORE DREISER and STEPHEN CRANE, began to practise a new, unflinching form of realism which removed as much of the design and authorial interference from the novel's narrative as possible and left instead the closest approximation to reality they could manage. At the beginning of the twentieth century, then, the novel had returned to its roots, situating itself in direct opposition to the fantastic form of the romance.

Old English

The form of English language used in England until the invasion of the Normans in 1066. This is the English of *BEOWULF*.

Picaresque

Picaresque designates a narrative that recounts a string of adventures experienced by a likeable rogue. DANIEL DEFOE's *MOLL FLANDERS* is a typical example. A picaresque novel is largely episodic, lacking the overall design of a fully plotted narrative.

Plot

A plot is the arrangement of a story (see **Story**). In EMILY BRONTË's *Wuthering Heights*, for example, the *story* is that Catherine and Heathcliff fall in love, Catherine dies and Heathcliff is grief-stricken. The *plot* of Wuthering Heights is arranged so that we encounter the grief-stricken Heathcliff and then hear about Catherine and Heathcliff falling in love and Catherine dying.

Poetry

Poetry distinguishes itself from prose by virtue of the relative regularity of the pattern of the words. In the Old English of epic poems such as *BEOWULF*, or in the Middle English of poems such as *SIR GAWAIN AND THE GREEN KNIGHT*, this pattern was produced by the alliteration of the initial syllables of each word, usually in groups of four heavily stressed syllables. The importance of ***alliterative verse***, however, eventually gave way to patterns based more exclusively on different ***metres***, or the arrangement of regular stresses in a line of verse. Very often, this arrangement of stresses was complemented by rhymes, where pairs of sounds were used at the end of each line. GEOFFREY CHAUCER used this technique in creating the heroic couplet for such works as *THE CANTERBURY TALES*. Well suited to comedic verse and satire because of its epigram-like qualities, the ***heroic couplet*** also found favour as the standard pattern of the epic, such as JOHN DRYDEN's translation of Virgil's *Aeneid*.

Despite its popularity, which lasted largely until the middle of the eighteenth century (LORD BYRON's *Don Juan* being the most notable exception), the heroic couplet was unsuited to conveying dramatic dialogue. In its stead, the verse form that eventually came to dominate English language poetry was ***blank verse***. Blank verse is unrhymed and consists of five stressed and five unstressed syllables. It is the verse form most closely matching the pattern of ordinary speech and was thus the form adopted by the Elizabethan playwrights, CHRISTOPHER MARLOWE and WILLIAM SHAKESPEARE. Its versatility ensured that it was also the form adopted by JOHN MILTON and WILLIAM WORDSWORTH for their very different epic poems – *PARADISE LOST* and *THE PRELUDE* respectively.

As the themes of poetry became more and more personal over the years, in tandem with the development of a more individualistic focus in the novel and the waning of drama as a major genre, so the verse forms themselves became more individual and less regulated. In this regard, and despite its relative flexibility, the nineteenth century saw blank verse begin to lose ground to different forms of ***free verse***. Free verse is still verse rather than rearranged prose in so far as the words are arranged rhythmically, but it is far less restrictive than blank verse. The most popular exponent of this type of verse was WALT WHITMAN in such poems as 'I Sing the Body Electric' from *LEAVES OF GRASS*. His work inspired such diverse poets of the twentieth century as D.H. Lawrence and Allen Ginsberg.

Realism

A movement in fiction begun in the nineteenth century which bases its subject matter in reality. The implicit contrast is always with the romance which takes the fantastic for its subject matter. The grittier and more prosaic a work is, the more it is held to be realistic. However, as reality is different for each of us, this is rather a subjective term. THEODORE DREISER's *SISTER CARRIE* is a realist novel.

Reformation

A religious movement begun in the sixteenth century which aimed to reform the Roman Catholic Church. It led to the formation of Protestantism, a form of worship which aimed to invoke a direct relationship between each individual and God, thus bypassing the Church. Consequently it placed a great emphasis on vernacular translations of the *BIBLE* in order that everyone could read it.

Regionalism

A literary movement in the United States of America in the second half of the nineteenth century. Regionalists set their work in local settings, described local customs and used regional dialects. The work of KATE CHOPIN is regionalist in its descriptions of Louisiana life.

Renaissance

The flowering of the arts and sciences which began in southern Europe in the fifteenth century and reached a peak in Britain during the reign of Elizabeth I. Literally meaning 're-birth', the Renaissance encouraged a return to the principles of classical Greece and Rome.

Restoration

The period immediately following the return to the throne of Charles II in 1660. His predecessor, Charles I, had been beheaded at the end of the English Civil War in 1649. The Restoration is associated with bawdy comedies such as APHRA BEHN's *THE ROVER*.

Rhythm

See **Metre**.

Romance

Originally used to describe any work written in French, by the end of the twelfth century it had come to refer more specifically to any work, in poetry or prose, which dealt with chivalric adventures involving knights, damsels, magic and monsters. The term also came to refer to any narrative dealing with the fantastic, as opposed to the realistic. *SIR GAWAIN AND THE GREEN KNIGHT* is typical of the romance genre.

Romantic

Romanticism (written with an upper case *R*) refers in Britain to literature that celebrates the imagination and the individual. It is also usually used to define the period beginning approximately with the French Revolution in 1789 to the accession of Queen Victoria in 1837. Romanticism is commonly associated with the poetry of such writers as WILLIAM WORDSWORTH and SAMUEL TAYLOR COLERIDGE.

Satire

A work which holds up a person or subject to ridicule. JOHN DRYDEN's *MAC FLECKNOE* is a satire about a rival writer.

Short story

The short story started out as just that – a story that was short. Not long enough to be short novels (which are called novellas), the early short story was simply a fictional sketch or tale of limited length. Pioneering in this regard was the work of WASHINGTON IRVING whose tales such as 'Rip Van Winkle' and 'The Legend of Sleepy Hollow' in *THE SKETCH BOOK* helped to popularise the form. Newspapers and periodicals were great subscribers to this type and length of tale and many authors, such as EDGAR ALLAN POE and NATHANIEL HAWTHORNE, started out submitting short stories to such publications.

As the genre developed, the short story, like the novel, began to be dominated more by its plot. In particular, short stories, such as MARK TWAIN's 'The Man Who Corrupted Hadleyburg' or EDGAR ALLAN POE's 'The Murders in the Rue Morgue', became ends-orientated, basing the whole story on a revelation or twist at the end. Initially, such revelations were the results of the development of an action or the logical end point of the plot, such as when we discover who has been committing the murders in the Rue Morgue. However, drawing on the work of other non-English language short story writers, such as the Russian Anton Chekov and the Frenchman Guy de Maupassant, the English language short story changed from being predominantly a plot-driven tale to a character-driven one. These new stories, such as SARAH ORNE JEWETT's *A WHITE HERON* were based around the resolution of an emotion rather than an action. By the beginning of the twentieth century, then, the short story was no longer just a short story; rather it was a genre in its own right which concentrated upon limited characters undergoing a singular experience or emotion using an economy of expression that is not normally found in lengthier prose works.

Story

The chronological sequence of events in a novel. See **Plot**.

Theme

A theme is an idea or topic. In literature a theme is the abstract subject of a text; for example, love is a theme of *ROMEO AND JULIET* while revenge is a theme of *HAMLET*.

Tragedy

Usually associated with drama and used in distinction to comedy (see **Comedy**), a tragedy tends to be defined by a story that involves an individual's descent into calamity, and by the production of an overwhelming or shocking emotion as a result. This definition relies on that first put forward by the Greek thinker Aristotle in his *Poetics*. He argued that a good tragedy purged people of bad emotions in a purification process called catharsis. In English literature, the golden era of tragedy was the time of WILLIAM SHAKESPEARE and CHRISTOPHER MARLOWE, both of whom wrote remarkable tragedies, such as *HAMLET* and *DOCTOR FAUSTUS*. Tragedy is also used more generally to refer to any work of literature that has an unhappy ending, such as one ending in death.

A–Z of featured writers

Index